A TREATISE

ON

THE MORAL IDEALS.

Cambridge:
PRINTED BY C. J. CLAY, M.A.
AT THE UNIVERSITY PRESS.

A TREATISE

ON

THE MORAL IDEALS

BY THE LATE

JOHN GROTE, B.D.

FELLOW OF TRINITY COLLEGE, AND PROFESSOR OF MORAL PHILOSOPHY
IN THE UNIVERSITY OF CAMBRIDGE.

EDITED BY

JOSEPH BICKERSTETH MAYOR, M.A.

PROFESSOR OF CLASSICAL LITERATURE AT KING'S COLLEGE, LONDON;
LATE FELLOW OF ST JOHN'S COLLEGE, CAMBRIDGE.

CAMBRIDGE:
DEIGHTON, BELL AND CO.
LONDON: GEORGE BELL AND SONS.
1876.

PREFACE BY THE EDITOR.

In the Author's Introduction to the *Exploratio Philosophica*, the present treatise is alluded to in words to which I have already called attention in my Preface to his *Examination of the Utilitarian Philosophy*. After mentioning that he had contemplated publishing an answer to Mr J. S. Mill's *Utilitarianism* in the year 1863, he continues, 'I altered my mind as to this, and determined rather to put together in an uncontroversial form what seemed to me the truth, in opposition to what I thought error. This, if it please God, is in the way of being accomplished, subject to all the delays which interest in other employments, uncertain health, and some not, I think, uncalled for scrupulousness and anxiety as to what one writes on a subject so important, may throw in the way of it.'

The *Exploratio* itself was published in 1865, and the Author died in the summer of the following year. On examining his MSS., I found, amongst the latest written, a series of chapters, each with its own heading, but not arranged in order, and often incomplete, which appeared to answer to the description given above. I subjoin the headings in the order in which the chapters were apparently written.

1. Aretaics and Eudæmonics, 17 pp.
2. Moral philosophy as an art referring to an ideal, 21 pp.
3. Moral philosophy not mere imagination, 21 pp.
4. Consistency of moral ideals, 28 pp.
5. Moral ideals, their relation to positive science, 12 pp.
6. On moral value, 22 pp.
7. Duty, 35 pp.
8. On moral judgments and sentiments, 69 pp.
9. Distribution of action, law, justice, &c., 57 pp.
10. Relation of moral ideals to fact and imagination, 57 pp.
11. Anatomy of wrong-doing, 40 pp.
12. Pleasure, pain and happiness, 84 pp.
13. Moral elevation, 33 pp.
14. Application of moral philosophy, 50 pp.
15. Character, will and education, 43 pp.
16.[1] (Diversity of ethical systems), 20 pp.
17. Discussion, controversy, war, 35 pp.
18. (Importance of right belief), 18 pp.

Along with these chapters I found three Appendices, one of nearly a hundred pages entitled *Idealism and Positivism*, the others much shorter, without any title. There can be little doubt that it is to

[1] The 16th and 18th chapters are without a heading in the MS. The former I have not printed, as it is mainly a repetition of what had been said elsewhere.

them the Author alludes in the Introduction to the *Exploratio*, where he says that, in connexion with his intended answer to Mr Mill, he 'was led to put together the intellectual views on which the moral view rested, and had meant, if they should come within reasonable limits, to publish them in an Appendix.' Instead of doing this he finally resolved to bring out the *Exploratio* as a sort of general Prolegomena to his ethical writings. My first intention, as may be seen from the references in pp. 13, 60 and 380, was to have printed a portion at least of the Appendices at the end of this volume with the new title *Relativism and Regulativism*, but for various reasons I have now thought it better to reserve it for the second part of the *Exploratio*, which I hope shortly to prepare for the press.

It will be seen, from a comparison of the printed chapters with the headings of the MS. chapters, that I have used the same liberty in breaking up, rearranging, and omitting in this volume as in the one previously edited by me. I have also made large additions from other MSS. wherever the Author's views seemed to be imperfectly stated in the treatise itself. Such additions, where they do not extend beyond a few lines, are silently inserted in the text: otherwise they appear as Appendices following the chapter to which they refer. I am further responsible for the Table of Contents, Marginal Summaries, and all Notes signed Ed.

To prevent mistakes it may be well to mention

here that a change has been made in the general title of the volume. As originally advertised it bore the name *Aretaics and Eudæmonics*, the Author's heading for the first chapter, accompanied by the editorial interpretation, *A treatise on the Moral Ideals.* In deference to the opinion of friends this addition, as less startling and more easily understood, is now left to stand by itself in place of the original title. The form *aretaic* from ἀρετή, analogous to *spondaic*, *mosaic*, *prosaic*, *algebraic*, &c., is only one out of many instances to be found in this volume, of Prof. Grote's fearlessness in the use of neologisms. Such are *egence*, *hedonometry*, *equalitarianism*, *felicificable* and *felicificativeness*, *bewilled* and *unbewilled*, *outgoingness*, *acturience*, and even the Greek νουπρακτής. For an account of this and other peculiarities of his style the reader is referred to my preface to the former volume.

This may be a fitting place to say a few words on Prof. Grote's dislike to a systematic treatment of ethical questions, which was, I venture to think, a little exaggerated in some of the reviews of his *Examination of the Utilitarian Philosophy*. It is not in a controversial work that we expect to find a full statement of a writer's views in their natural arrangement and with a due subordination of parts: those who will take the trouble to read carefully the chapters on Duty and Virtue in the present volume, and to notice the criticisms passed upon Bp Butler for failing to make his system hang together (see pp.

118, 141, 163, 181, 284, 344, 443), will at any rate not charge the Author with being indifferent to exactness and coherence of thought. No doubt his mode of exposition is generally unsystematic. Writing, as he did, without any view of immediate publication, he thought more of putting his matter into the form which was most natural and expressive to himself than of putting it into the form which was most intelligible to his readers. Thus he suddenly diverges in the midst of an argument, returns again, repeats what has been said before, and not unfrequently passes over some point which had been previously left for further consideration. Again, in his fear lest the scaffolding and machinery should be mistaken for the actual building, lest phrases and formulas and logical divisions should be mistaken for the truth itself, he is perhaps too ready to change his form of expression, or at any rate to represent it as a matter of indifference whether one form or one analysis is preferred to another. Besides these peculiarities in his mode of exposition, there is a peculiarity in his general view of ethics which may tend to make it appear both complicated and disconnected as compared with other systems. While some philosophers start from a single principle, such as man's natural love of pleasure, and profess to deduce a whole system of morality by rigid inference from this, he tells us on the contrary that we cannot have a single science of ethics, but that we may have what he loosely expresses as 'a manner of thinking (not even a philosophy) attended by several subordinate sciences or philosophies.' What he means by this is, that there are several starting points for determining the rule of human action, each of which, if followed out, will lead to interesting and valuable results; that for a perfect rule of action we cannot afford to disregard any, but that these results, as far as we are able to trace them, are not always consistent; that this apparent inconsistency would lead to a stultification of human action if it were not for an underlying faith in the moral order of the universe, which faith or 'manner of thinking' he holds to be the essential part or foundation of ethics. As he says in an unpublished essay on the relation between ethics and religion, 'the one fountain-head of both, the primary principle of man and his actions as they should be, is the idea, or proposition, God is good.'

To illustrate the manner in which Prof. Grote harmonized opposing views on this principle, I will here quote from a MS. marked V which may be considered in some respects a rough draught of the present treatise. A comparison of the quotation with the first three chapters as well as with the 12th (on Pleasure) will also throw light upon a point which is not quite cleared up here, the relation between Activity and Sentience on the one hand, and Want on the other.

The object of Ethics, as a practical science, being to determine future action, what it looks to in the first instance is not what *is*, but what *is needed*, what it is right or desirable should be. And for a creature such as man, there is, we may say, a double need; need of satisfaction for his desires, and need of direction for his action.

It is not always sufficiently remembered that man is as essentially an active being as a being capable of happiness. Of course, the term happiness, or the supreme good, may be taken in a perfectly wide sense, and consciously well directed action may be taken as a part of it as well as enjoyment or gratification. But so far as this is so, we must mean by happiness something too general for us to be able to speak of the *attainment* of it, or even for us to speak of it as an *end* to be striven after. The will craving action, the counterpart in the moral being to that spring of irritability and uneasiness in the physical being, which is the source of all physical movement, demands to be considered, and calls for *its* happiness, as much as the capacities for enjoyment, and the desires corresponding to them, call for theirs. Supposing our impulse to action to continue, we should be more unhappy beings without wants to satisfy, or purposes to gain, than we can be with them. We may imagine a state of simply quiescent enjoyment, but it would not at all correspond to man's moral being as we have experience of it.

Theories formed with reference to a supposed supreme good or end of human action, all rest upon the unconscious axiom that the entire object of life is to gain or attain something. This axiom supposes the one great fact of life to be ungratified desire, unsatisfied need. This is plainly an insufficient account of life. By the side of this fact there is another as great, namely, the fact of power. And as the former fact suggests to us, as the great aim of philosophic research, the supreme good to be gained, so the latter fact suggests to us as something of equal importance, the knowledge of the right or best thing to be done. If by *want* we understand that which conditions and circumstances call for, (what the Latins expressed by the term *egeo*), the want of direction for action is as primary and native a want of the human being as the want of satisfaction to desire: in other words, the *right*, or good in action, is as intimate a need of our nature as the *desirable*, or good in enjoyment. The former indeed is not necessarily wanted, in the sense of 'wished for,' as the latter most commonly is. More properly, perhaps, the want in this view is confused and half-unconscious. In accordance with the feeling or principle before spoken of, which I have called a kind of faith, and which we must, it seems to me, take with us in all our thoughts on these subjects, we have reason to expect that these different lines of thought will not lead us to contradictory conclusions.

On the whole, if we knew the supreme good, we might be sure that the right action would be that which would lead us to it; not more, however, than conversely, if we knew the right action, we might be confident that what it led us towards would be our supreme good. As we cannot hope to know either of the two things more than τύπῳ, most vaguely and generally, it is a question whether ethical science is not properly to be pursued along both roads. Have we any reason to assume, that the end to which our action is directed, or which it subserves, is the only quarter towards which we are to look for guidance? Shall we not know our proper action in proportion as we become acquainted with our nature and with the moral circumstances in which man is placed, one part of this knowledge being the knowledge of what makes our happiness, but *one part* only?

The view which I have been taking depends upon the supposition, that constituted as we are, action is with us a necessity in the same sense, and to the same degree, in which satisfaction of desire is. This is a supposition of a fixed order of things of which we with our definite constitution form a portion, a supposition therefore to a certain extent of an absence of freedom on our part implied in the want of direction of our action, in the same manner as in the want of satisfaction is implied a degree of imperfection. Possibly, if we could place ourselves in imagination before the constitution of anything, when there existed nothing but the Creator with His knowledge, and with those moral attributes which must have been the incitements in Him to give to things their being, we might be right in assuming the prime mover of all to be the anticipated enjoyment of future sentient beings, animating and setting in action the primæval love. But with constitution of anything, begins a more complicated consideration of direction of action than that of its being simply to produce happiness. With constitution of anything, begins rightness or duty; that is, the notion, not only of what may be done with resulting increase of happiness to some one, but what should be done by the agent under such and such circumstances. Even the Creator must be considered to have brought Himself into a position of self-imposed and self-maintained duty towards that part of what He had made, to which good and happiness are possible. Pure beneficence we may imagine as the beginning of all things, but it must soon have generated much besides.

It will be seen that the earlier view given in this quotation is not in all respects the same as the later and more developed view which we find in the present treatise. In the former a foundation for ethics is sought in the double want of human nature, the want of satisfaction for desire, of direction for action :

in the latter the analysis is carried further back; the primary axiom of eudæmonics is declared to be the existence of pain as a thing undesirable to suffer, suggesting the ideal 'happiness;' the primary axiom of aretaics is the existence of pain as a thing undesirable to inflict, suggesting the ideal 'right' (p. 3); and it is not till the end of the 2nd chapter (p. 22) that we are introduced to want as a fact of man's sentient, not his active, nature. The difference is partly explained if we remember the distinction, already marked in the quotation, between the felt want of satisfaction and the confused and half-unconscious want of direction, and on the other hand by the subordination, in the present treatise, of the ideal 'happiness' to the ideal 'good' suggested by the fact of want. In p. 145 the relation between the two former ideals receives yet a further explanation: 'Our *active* nature,' it is said, 'adds this to our simply sentient nature, that pain is instinctively felt by us, not only as unpleasant, but as to be avoided: our *social* nature superadded widens this into the more general feeling that pain is to be prevented, *a fortiori* not to be inflicted. We find thus, from the very first, a determinant of our action beyond ourselves, a restraint, as it were, laid upon it.' Again, in the twelfth chapter we have a broad distinction between the two kinds of pleasure, the pleasure of enjoyment which is a passive affection of the sentient nature, and the pleasure of gratification which is preceded by a sense of want, and accompanied by the exercise of the active powers. The distinction here laid down between the facts suggestive of the ideals of good and happiness is extended to the ideals themselves in the present treatise, while in the earlier summary the less important ideal is merged in the more important.

As the Author thus recognizes the principles assumed by Epicurean and Utilitarian moralists as being equally valid with those of their antagonists, so is it with other principles which have been turned into party watch-words by one-sided thinkers. Reason and sentiment, honour and conscience, fact and ideal, all find their place within the limits of moral philosophy as he viewed it: each serves as a corner-stone to build up the practical science of which the object is to determine how man should live. What appears to be breadth of view is sometimes nothing more than hastiness and looseness of thought, which brings together a number of opposing principles, and adopts the language now of one, now of another, without being conscious of any inconsistency. From this, which I should almost venture to call the besetting sin of modern writers, Prof. Grote was remarkably free. Consistency was no less conspicuous a feature in his mental character than breadth of view. If he is tracing out some special line of thought, he never allows it to blind him to the fact that there are other lines of thought which may be equally important for the attainment of the truth; and he is careful to warn us beforehand that he is about to make what he calls an 'abstraction', taking for a while a partial and limited view. It was impossible for him with his far-ranging vision to uphold in one department the contradictory of a proposition which he asserted in another, to maintain for instance that what was false in philosophy might be true in theology. For the same reason he was disposed to be impatient of the splitting up of philosophy into parts, considering that confusion lurked in the separation of logic and ethics from psychology, and in the consequent duplication of names for the same thing.

Three other characteristics I will mention which seem to me to give a special value to all that Prof. Grote has written. He had, in the first place, a singular *εὐφυία*, a moral sensitiveness quick and delicate to a most unusual degree. Few could be even slightly acquainted with him without being struck with this nobility of nature: *ὁ δὲ τοιοῦτος*, as Aristotle says, *ἢ ἔχει ἢ λάβοι ἂν ἀρχὰς ῥαδίως*. It was the union of this fine sense of rectitude with sobriety of judgment and large-mindedness, a union rare in itself and still more rarely found in conjunction with speculative and analytical capacity, which led to his being much consulted in cases where it was difficult to discern the right line of conduct. The second characteristic which I will notice is one which is closely connected with the first, I mean his freshness of view: *οὗτος μὲν πανάριστος*, as Aristotle goes on, *ὃς αὐτὸς πάντα νοήσει*. While most of us in the course of years get embedded in an accumulation of other people's ideas and vainly strive to penetrate to the native sentiment beneath, his mind remained a clear mirror reflecting back the forms of nature in their original purity. Whatever he says has at least the merit of being genuine thought at first hand, not a mere repetition of what others have said or the imagination of what might be the right thing to say. This again is a part of his simplicity of nature, the naturalness which endeared him so much to friends, and which shines through all his writings. There is much in the chapter on Happiness, especially where it speaks of the enjoyment of simple pleasures, which will recall him to the memory of those who knew him. The homely scenery of Cambridge and Ely, the sight of the common wayside flowers, were to him the sources of as keen delight as Italy or the Alps are to others. His pocket-books contain a curious medley of philosophical jottings mixed up with notes on the songs and habits of birds and memoranda as to the wild plants seen in his walks.

The third characteristic I have to mention is almost implied in what has been said already as to his large-mindedness: I refer to the fairness and freedom from prejudice which have been generally recognized by the reviewers of his former treatises. Like his brother, the historian, he had an almost fanatical love of freedom of thought, even when it took a form with which he could not himself sympathize. His bias, if he had one, was always in favour of the unpopular side, *i. e.* of the side, whichever it might be, which seemed to be in danger of being unfairly treated.

These then are the merits I should especially claim for the Author whose speculations it is not less my privilege than my duty to bring before the public; fairness, freshness of thought, moral sensitiveness, consistency and yet breadth of view: and these I think must make his writings of importance even to those who may be most inclined to dissent from the conclusions at which he arrives.

It only remains for me to return my thanks to the Syndics of the Cambridge University Press for the liberal grant which they have made towards defraying the expenses of the present volume.

CONTENTS.

CHAPTER I.

Two sciences included in moral philosophy.

CHAPTER II.

Moral philosophy as an art referring to an ideal.

APPENDIX.

On Want.

CHAPTER III.

General view of the moral ideals and of the relation between them.

CHAPTER VII.

Duty.

CHAPTER VIII.

On the genesis of virtue: its emotional elements, benevolence.

APPENDIX.

On benevolent impulse in its relation to virtue.

CHAPTER IX.

Genesis of virtue: its intellectual elements, principle.

APPENDIX.

On conscience and honour.

CHAPTER X.

Distribution of action considered from the ideal point of view.

APPENDIX.

On distribution of action in reference to existing law.

CHAPTER XI.

The anatomy of wrong-doing.

APPENDIX.

On Malevolence.

On justice and truthfulness.

CHAPTER XII.

On pleasure and pain.

CHAPTER XIII.

On happiness.

APPENDIX.

On the unhappiness of human nature.

On the promotion of the happiness of others.

CHAPTER XIV.

On moral elevation.

CHAPTER XV.

On the relation of the ideals to higher and lower fact.

CHAPTER XVI.

Actual and ideal human nature.

CHAPTER XVII.

On the goodness of custom.

CHAPTER XVIII.

Relation of individual to custom.

PAGE

CHAPTER XIX.

On character, will, and education.

APPENDIX.

A.

B.

ERRATA.

p. 3, l. 21, *for* : *read* , .
,, ,, 22, *for* , *read* : .
p. 31, l. 9, *for* is *read* in.
p. 47, l. 21, *for* they *read* we.
p. 106, l. 14, *for* other's happiness *read* happiness of others.
p. 179, l. 25, *for* αἴδως *read* αἰδώς.
p. 202, l. 5, *for* yourselves *read* yourself.
p. 207, l. 21, *for* fortitude *read* fortitudo.
p. 380, l. 21, *for* different *read* difficult.
p. 381, l. 22, *after* be *insert* known.
p. 434, l. 19, *omit comma after* call.

CHAPTER I.

TWO SCIENCES INCLUDED IN MORAL PHILOSOPHY.

Eudæmonics cannot cover the whole ground of moral philosophy.

THE following treatise is constructed upon this principle: that in what is commonly known by the name of Moral Philosophy, there are two sciences; one the science of virtue, Aretaics; the other the science of happiness, Eudæmonics. The two sciences need each other, and affect each other; but they start from different points. That of these two sciences the latter exists, cannot be seriously doubted: the question is, whether the former exists also. Again, that this former science (i.e. a moral philosophy which is not eudæmonics) exists as a matter of fact, in so far that there is a literature purporting to be the literature of such a science, cannot be doubted; the question is, whether this so-called science is chimerical and unreal. The reason for conceiving it not to be so, is this: that however we expand and manipulate the science of eudæmonics, it cannot, while it continues anything which that term can at all represent, fill nearly the whole ground which moral philosophy is required to fill, or give a reasonable account of all that is to be accounted for.

Shewn in regard to the infliction of pain.

When, for instance, a man, without cause, inflicts pain upon another, the misdeed on the part of the agent is a fact as well as the pain suffered by the sufferer, and it is a fact with a character about it different from any which it can derive from the pain. It is not a sufficient account of the misdeed to say that it is something which gives pain to another, and which therefore perhaps may be expected, if not now, at some future time, to give pain of remorse to the doer, and which moreover, since he has been educated to think badly of actions which give pain to others, and to call them wrong, he himself perhaps thinks wrong, disapproves, and dislikes, even while he does it. I do not think that such a doctrine will ever maintain itself against that which is called intuitivism, but which seems to me to be the necessary voice of human reason, viz. that the doer and men in general think the action wrong, not merely because they have been trained to do so by education, but because it is in reality wrong. Its being wrong is a fact; the judgment of the doer and of men follows this fact, as it follows other facts. 'Wrong' is not merely a name by which it is called, but there is considered to be something attaching to it which we know by the name of 'wrong.' And this which attaches to it is not simply that it causes pain, for it might cause pain without being wrong: it is that it causes pain under particular circumstances, pain which it *ought* not to cause. What is the nature of these circumstances, the meaning and results of this *ought*, it is the business of *aretaics* to investigate.

The evil of suffering pain the subject of eudæmonics, the evil of inflicting it the subject of aretaics.

Supposing then it is said that we use the term 'wrong' of anything which causes pain without causing, in some way, greater pleasure or happiness on the whole to overbalance the pain: if we grant that this, so far as it goes, is a true description of what 'wrong' means, and that wrong actions *have* this character about them; we have then, as a fact of the universe,—as much a fact of the universe as pain, or as happiness itself,—that actions bearing the above character are marked off from others, and marked off as what ought not to be done, what are undesirable, improper, or however we may express it. We may put the fact in this way, that pain has two characters, according to the side from which we look at it: that it is not only something unpleasant to, and dreaded by, the sufferer, but also that it is something which another ought not causelessly to inflict upon him. This second fact about pain is one entirely different from the former: it is one, no doubt, which in our judgment or feeling instantly follows from the former, but its so following is not from anything in experience, not from anything involved in the nature of pain *as we feel it:* the conclusion is essentially necessary and intuitive; and it is just the drawing this conclusion thus which constitutes us moral beings.

Pain, thus, is a bad thing in the universe: with *its* badness, and the study of this badness (so for the present to describe it), with a view to its avoidance, is the business of eudæmonics: the inflicting causeless pain is a bad thing in the universe with a different badness, and the study of this latter badness, with a view to avoiding that, is the business of aretaics.

The fundamental axiom of eudæmonics is the existence of pain as a thing undesirable for the sufferer to suffer.

In both the above views of pain, the science, whether it be eudæmonics or aretaics, rests upon a natural fact, not upon an observation of what men do or feel. The fundamental fact of eudæmonics is, not that men do avoid pain, supposing this a matter of experience or observation, or in other words, supposing it conceivable that they might do otherwise, but that pain is something which has in it that which makes it avoided. Let it be said, it is only by experience that we know this, or in fact know pain at all: the saying this seems to me only applying the term experience to our perception and knowledge altogether, and I feel no objection to its being so applied. But the real point of consequence is, that our knowledge that pain is a thing undesirable, or to be avoided, is not something which we can be supposed possibly to doubt about, in regard of which we settle our doubt by observation of what men do: the natural fact, the prime assumption of eudæmonics, is not that men do dislike and avoid pain, but that there exists in the universe something which we call pain, and that, in the very notion of it, it is something undesirable and to be avoided.

Fundamental axiom of aretaics the existence of pain as a thing undesirable for the giver to give.

In the same manner the fundamental fact of aretaics, or what for the present we will suppose the fundamental fact of it, is not what might be a matter of observation, whether of our consciousness or of men's action, viz. that men do avoid giving pain to others, or have a feeling in them telling them they ought to avoid it, but is the natural fact that pain is something, the giving of which on the one side is as undesirable for the giver and as much to be avoided by him, as the suffering of it is on the other side for the sufferer. So far as we can look at the thing in itself, no man wants to give pain any more than to suffer it; and, in any case, what he wants, or does not want, is not the ultimate fact. Men's avoidance of giving pain is a result of, and a testimony of, its being wrong to give it, in the same way as their avoidance of suffering it is a result of, and a testimony of, its being unpleasant to suffer it. Let it be granted, that unless a man knew pain as suffering himself first, he would have no feeling of repugnance to the giving it: the existence of pain as suffering (or, which is the same thing, of possibility of increase and diminution of happiness), may be necessary as a condition to the existence of moral virtue; but the feeling of repugnance to the giving pain does not follow from the feeling of dislike to the suffering it, except through the addition of some new element, of a something fresh which does not belong to eudæmonics, and which is the foundation of aretaics.

We need a science which investigates the various circumstances under which pain is inflicted, as well as a science which investigates the varieties of pain.

But, it will be said, is there any occasion for more than one science, when after all it is confessed that pain (so we will speak at present) is the leading idea; when what is *morally* to be avoided, for whatever reason, is after all only the causing pain, as what is *physically* (so to speak) to be avoided is the suffering it? For the one as the other, have we anything else to do than to investigate what causes pain, that we may in *both* ways avoid it?

What I have hitherto said has been said for the sake of illustration, rather more simply than the case will properly bear, and we shall see, as we go on, with how many other considerations it has to be complicated. Let us take the science of eudæmonics first, which I fully admit to exist, and to be a most important science; the only question being, whether it represents what people really mean and want by moral philosophy, and covers the ground which that must cover. We have then, in eudæmonics, to study what is meant by suffering pain (enjoying happiness we may say, if we like, proceeding the reverse way), to compare different kinds of it, to say how it arises, how it is to be avoided. But just as, on the one side, there is an endless variety of pains which may be suffered or given, and it is the fact of this variety which renders necessary the study of eudæmonics, so, on the other side, there is an endless variety of circumstances under which one pain, or one pleasure, may be given, and it is this latter variety which causes the science of aretaics. Were there but one kind and one degree of pain (or on the other hand of pleasure) possible in the world; were there no other harm, for instance, possible to be done to a man, except that of killing him; there would then be no scope for a science of eudæmonics; but, as there is a vast variety of circumstances which might lead one man to kill another, there would still be room for a large science about these, which, on this supposition, would be the science of aretaics. And by multiplying, in supposition, the ways in which we may do people harm, i.e. supposing things, in that respect, as they are now, we by no means lessen the necessity for the aretaics, however we may introduce another science besides: we really enrich the aretaics as well.

The former, the science of aretaics, is not based upon the latter, though it presupposes the eudæmonic notion of pain.

As there are some, on the one hand, who assert that there is but one science contained in moral philosophy, the science, namely, which I have called 'eudæmonics;' so, on the other hand, some will say that there is but one science, and it is what I have called 'aretaics.' The controversy, in fact, which of these two sciences is to be considered moral philosophy, is what has constituted the history of moral philosophy from the beginning. The subject, they will say, of moral philosophy, is *virtue*, not pain or pleasure, however these may, in one way or another, enter into it.

Nor can it be denied that there is at least as much reason for saying that it is aretaics which constitute moral philosophy as for saying that it is the other. Pain is indeed a reality in a sense in which no feeling of right or wrong can be: what we say about pain or pleasure can be brought to the test of a particular kind of experience, and comparison can be made of individual experiences, in a manner which cannot be done with regard to our sense of wrong-doing. But it is quite clear that the fact, that the inflicting causeless pain is a misdeed, an evil in the universe of a different kind from, but as real as, the suffering of pain, a something in the universe which we think ought not to be, which is a defect in it, a something undesirable;—it is clear that this is a fact which need not wait for any observations upon the nature &c. of pain, that is, for eudæmonics, for its establishment: if we do not have it from the first, we can never get it from experience. In entering upon eudæmonics, or the science of happiness, as a science of experience, let us suppose our minds, as they should be, free from previous opinion, prepared to receive what experience gives us. Experience about pain and pleasure will doubtless shew us many things: there may be a regular inductive science on the subject: but just as no one dreams that any amount of experience can alter our opinion as to pain being a thing in itself undesirable to suffer; so no experience, everyone sees, can alter our opinion as to pain being a thing in itself wrong to inflict. The eudæmonical induction, if well carried out, may lead us to conclusions about happiness or about pain, as general and as vast as the Copernican or Newtonian conclusions: but these conclusions, whatever they may be, can have no effect one way or the other on the fact, or on our feeling of the fact, that pain in itself is an evil, in one way to suffer, in another to inflict. The axiom then of aretaics, that it is evil or a misdeed to inflict pain, as pain and causelessly, needs, and waits for, no experience to suggest or prove it: no one would think for an instant that it could be doubted, and its truth made to depend on a trial by experience: its truth is the same whatever the pain or happiness, in our observation of them, turn out in their particulars to be. It is true for all possible pain, or for all possible happiness, so long as what we call such answers to the definition. The inhabitants of the planets, if there are such, may have very different sorts of happiness from us, but it has the same truth for them as for us.

Aretaics is the essential part of Moral Philosophy, though it requires to be supplemented by eudæmonics.

While therefore we may admit that the fact, which, if it is wished, we may call a fact of eudæmonics, the fact of the existence or possibility of pain, is the first, and is necessary as a previous condition for the existence of aretaics, yet, on the other hand, it is with aretaics, or with the above axiom, that anything which can be called moral philosophy begins, and all moral philosophy is no more than a deduction from that axiom. It is indeed exceedingly possible that the axiom might be very sterile in results without eudæmonical observation to give us particulars about the pain, the infliction of which is thus to be avoided; this we shall see as we go on. So far as this is the case, aretaics, to be fruitful and useful, needs (besides its presupposition of the eudæmonical notion of pain or happiness) to be largely supplemented by eudæmonics: and this is the case with all possible aretaics.

Similarly *human* eudæmonics requires to be supplemented by aretaics.

Eudæmonics, conceived quite generally, need not require to be supplemented by aretaics: but (and I refer to what follows for more full illustration), *human* eudæmonics do require to be largely so supplemented. This is because man is what we commonly describe as a moral being, that is, his feeling and reflection about what he does, together with his sympathies with others and many other feelings of a like nature, enter very largely as an element into his happiness and his pain. The eudæmonical analysis of pleasure and pain has, therefore, with other things, to be an analysis of man's moral nature ; and it is impossible to analyse feelings and thoughts without a reference to what the feelings and thoughts are about : and this, when the feelings or thoughts are what we call *moral*, is aretaics. We have thus, it would appear, in reference to man, the two sciences interlocked in an exceedingly complicated manner.

If this is the case, it will be said again, What is the use of calling them two? Why cannot they be treated as one subject?

Five reasons for treating them as distinct sciences.

As one *subject* I do treat them, but as two *sciences*. The reasons are various.

The first is, that I wish to leave no part of the ground belonging to moral philosophy unexplored (to the small extent to which I can speak about it), and I believe this is the only way.

The second is, that I wish to give its full force to all that has been said, and often most truly said, on each side in the great and noble, but often most blind and confused, moral controversy of ages.

The third is, that I wish that the student should learn to value and respect (if he cannot of himself perhaps know much about) the various methods which moral controversy has followed and the literature with which it has been associated. I should like the study to take with him a character different from that which it has sometimes done, and to teach him to think liberally, without depreciating and caricaturing what he is ignorant of.

The fourth is, that I think in this way it may be more easy to grasp the exceedingly difficult relation of different parts of the subject together, as intuitive and inductive (to use for a moment terms which I disapprove). I am as anxious as any Utilitarian to have, as far as possible, a good and real inductive science of eudæmonics. And I think that the taking of eudæmonics for the whole of moral philosophy, instead of a portion of or adjunct to it, has been a hindrance to this in every way. One side in the traditionary moral controversy have despised eudæmonics, while those who have admired and cultivated them have always had something to prove by them: they have been *users* of them, not bonâ fide inquirers into them. They have, for instance, wanted to establish, as a result of their investigation, that eudæmonics would really bear upon them the whole weight of morality. Whether they were right or wrong in this, it is at least not the right temper for an inductive inquirer. Or, if they were more practical and less philosophical than this, they have had a prejudice either for, or against, things established: and their inductive inquiries have correspondingly had a strong tendency to turn into a justification, or an inculpation, of these. I have hoped, by relieving eudæmonics from part at least of this weight of consequence, to be able to look at them more with the eye of a simple investigator.

Fifth and last, a reason which might have superseded any others, I have treated these two portions of moral philosophy as two sciences, because, however complicated together, I think they *are* so.

This distinction arises from man's double nature, *sentient* and *active*, corresponding to *want* and *power* in the universe.

Man craves

Their being so seems to me to depend in the main upon this fact,—and I think that the bringing out of the full force of this fact is the most important business of moral philosophy at the present day—that man is an active being in the same manner in which he is a sentient (or pain-feeling and pleasure-feeling) being: that his activity and his sentience are two independent portions or features of his nature, each as early, as native, and as important, as the other[1]. Man's nature, in fact the universe in general, has two portions or characters counter-fitting (if I may use the word) the one to the other, want and power in the universe, or, as I have called them in man, sentience and activity. I take as my principle, that man as early and as naturally asks for an employment of his activity as for a relief from his pain; and that the fitting of these together, going beyond the individual, is the business of moral philosophy, as the fitting them together with reference to the individual is the business of simple prudence. On this however I will not dwell now; except to say, that the inquiry which proceeds from the assumption of activity is that which I call aretaics, that which proceeds from the assumption of sentience is eudæmonics; that in many particulars they treat, from opposite directions, the same subjects; and that the method which I hope to take will not be that of a rigid separation of them, but a treating of the subject in the way in general most convenient, with an indication to which of the sciences the manner of treatment belongs.

employment for activity just as naturally as relief from pain.

[1] With this agrees the division of the nerves into *sentient* and *motor* nerves. Compare *Exploratio Philosophica*, ch. 3, and Prof. Bain's language (*Senses and Intellect*, Book I. ch. i.), "Movement precedes sensation, and is at the outset independent of any stimulus from without: action is a more intimate and inseparable property of our constitution than any of our sensations, and in fact enters as a component part into every one of the senses, giving them the character of compounds while itself is a simple and elementary property." ED.

CHAPTER II.

MORAL PHILOSOPHY AS AN ART REFERRING TO AN IDEAL.

Moral Philosophy is the Art of Life.

MORAL Philosophy is the Art of Life in its highest sense. If we understand by *life* what the Greeks meant by *βίος* as different from *ζωή*, and by *living* the putting forth the powers and faculties for use and for enjoyment, moral philosophy is the general and summary, or architectonic, art of this. That is, it deals with the relation to each other of the powers, faculties, and other portions of man which are concerned with his activity, and with their harmony as a whole.

By describing moral philosophy as an art I mean pretty much the same as that which Aristotle meant by describing it as a practical science, though I would not in all respects apply the view as he did.

It sets before itself an ideal.

Moral philosophy however is more than simply thus an art or practical science: it is an art which sets before it an *ideal*.

Sense in which this word is used.

In the difficulty as to the use of language on these matters, I shall use the word ideal doubly, i.e. both as an adjective and a substantive: I shall speak of *an ideal* as what moral philosophy sets before itself, and I shall speak of moral philosophy as ideal in so far as it does set this before itself: and for contrast to *ideal* in its adjective sense, I shall sometimes use the word *positival*. For a discussion of this latter term I refer to the Appendix.

Eudæmonics *might be* unideal. That is, in thinking how we should live, and thinking about pleasure and pain in this view, we might stop short of forming in our thought any idea of *happiness* as something to be gained: we might form our scheme of life on the plan of avoiding pains and laying hold of pleasures as they pass, with little imagination about the future, and no mental combination of pleasures into an ideal happiness.

Eudæmonics may be unideal.

Eudæmonics however has generally been, and is likely to be, exceedingly ideal. Man is an imaginative being, and is both inclined to look forward to the future and inclined to set himself an end to work for. Though activity and sentience both exist in man independently of each other in the manner which I have described, yet man's nature is *one*, and the treatment of eudæmonics, or the science of man's sentient nature, inevitably takes a colour from his active nature. In meditating how we may enjoy ourselves, we cannot help the notion forcing itself upon us, that happiness is something to be worked for. We in vain try to make ourselves recognize (what reason, misapplied, tells us) that for enjoyment we ought to have no ideal; that to set ourselves a happiness to work for is after all to enslave ourselves, and to leave the notion of enjoyment; that life, on this view of it, is not happiness but toil after happiness, and that toil after one thing is no better than toil after another. Eudæmonists have at various times laboured hard to produce an unideal eudæmonics, a real science of pleasure as distinct from a science of happiness. There is in the actual life of man a great abundance of such unideal eudæmonics: but, even in the actual life

but it is more commonly ideal, owing to the influence of man's active nature on his sentient nature.

of man, it is the ideal portion, the imagination, hope, and enterprise, which gives it its vigour and interest; and the difficulty of escaping idealism becomes greater as soon as life is made a matter of thought and reflection. A life of passing pleasure is natural enough in itself: but not a thoughtful, deliberate, reflective, life of passing pleasure.

And thus the idea of duty may attach itself to eudæmonic systems.

It should be observed, that as it is difficult to prevent the *active* side of human nature from coming in, and making eudæmonics ideal, so it is difficult to prevent the moral notions which belong to this active side of human nature from following and giving to this pursuit of an ideal happiness a character of *duty*, which, from the point of view of eudæmonics, can never belong to it. So far as our activity or our powers are of any importance beyond ourselves, what we do in regard of our own happiness is eminently a matter of moral consideration, or for the notion of duty, for it may very greatly affect this. But in this we leave eudæmonics. And in reality, whenever, in eudæmonic investigation, the notion comes in, as it must do, that it is a matter of duty with us to live not for passing pleasures, but for an ideal happiness, so far as pleasure and happiness enter into our consideration at all, we are bearing witness to ourselves, so to speak, of our own importance and value, and of there being something to be considered about us beyond our happiness.

Happiness is essentially an ideal.

The term 'happiness,' *εὐδαιμονία*, itself represents an ideal, and in fact represents little more. All that is positive, or known to us as in this way, is pleasure or freedom from pain; and the unideal form of eudæmonics of which I have spoken is *hedonics*, or a science of *indolentia*. Whatever it is that people are aiming at, if they look at it as it is in relation to themselves, they will call it their happiness: this ideal character in happiness is more intimate and more universal than any particular character attaching to it.

All aretaic systems are more or less ideal.

Aretaics however is more essentially ideal than eudæmonics. The words *virtue, duty, ought, should,* &c., express an ideal, whatever else they may express: and however we may define them or whatever line of conduct we may consider to answer to them, they must keep *this* character, or they are no longer themselves.

'Ought,' 'should,' &c. are terms of *art* expressing the 'faciendum.'

The words 'ought,' 'should,' and the other similar ones, are what may be called terms of *art* in this sense, that they express something to be done, a line of conduct to be pursued, ordinarily in view of the attainment of a particular purpose. There is understood with them, as terms of art, the expression of the purpose which is aimed at: they express a condition (at least a probable condition) of the attainment of this: if you would attain this or that end, if you want this thing or that, you must, you ought to, you should, do this other thing, whatever it is: 'must,' 'ought,' 'should,' are only different degrees of intensity of the expression of the same thing; and it may be expressed still otherwise by saying, this thing is *to be done,* if you wish to gain that: the Latin expresses this simply in the form 'faciendum.'

In the absolute 'faciendum' means and end are involved together.

Now moral philosophy being, in the manner which I described, the art of life or living, suppose we say to ourselves, we wish, so far as what we are now dealing with is concerned, to attain no purpose, but simply to live, to consider life, according to the Aristotelian notion, its own end and purpose, with this important addition to his notion, 'except so far as the consideration of our life itself may reveal to us a purpose for it beyond itself.' The question then of aretaics will be simply what we must, should, ought to do : the addition expressing the purpose we want to gain disappears, for we want to gain no purpose ; or it becomes a mere identical repetition, for all that we want is to live, is to do what we ought to do or should do : we want, it will be said, to live *well*, but 'well' here is nothing more than the same identical repetition, it expresses no more than *as we should* expresses, that is, simply an ideal : to live, as something which by supposition we want, and to live well, are the same ; we are left simply with the notion of a *faciendum*, of a something which we should do, without any purpose beyond it.

To some this will appear a playing with words, to others it will appear the saying of something too plain to be worth saying. Trifling and plain as it may be, this notion is that from which the whole of moral philosophy is a deduction, and the clear view of which would save infinite mistake and controversy.

The *faciendum*, or thing which is supposed as that which is to be done, is what is called in philosophical language 'absolute,' which means this : that it is disengaged from the addition, or expression of purpose, which determined it and made it conditional or dependent in the former uses of it which I instanced : what is to be done is not means only, but means and end both : and the art which treats of what is thus to be done is an unique and special art, in which means and end are involved together.

Different forms under which the 'faciendum' may be represented.

The question whether there is such a thing as an independent or intuitive morality, or however else we may express it, is really no other than this : whether the notion that there is for us an absolute faciendum (i.e. a thing or things which for reasons contained in themselves, we ought to do, or should do, rather than other things) is a notion which naturally (so I will speak at present) suggests itself. The form in which this is put may be varied infinitely: it may be put in a markedly ethical form by some philosophers, by some in a form very non-ethical or untechnical; but the substance is the same. We may put it in this form: that the choice which we make as to what we do is a matter of importance or of consequence; or in this, that, in the infinite variety of possible action, there exists reason why we should choose one part rather than another part: or we may put it in the ideal form of imagining the life which we ought to lead, which we feel it is well we should lead, and perhaps give to this ideal a religious character by considering that we were intended to lead such a life, created for it; or perhaps give it rather an æsthetic character by considering it something to be admired and delighted in. However we may think of it, the substance is the same: it is that, when we think of ourselves as beings with faculties and powers, the notion inevitably suggests itself of there being some things which we should do, ought to do, (morally) must do, and others which we ought not to do.

Granting the existence of an absolute 'faciendum,' moral philosophy cannot be a mere inductive or positival science.

What is commonly called the morality of *consequences*, i.e. the assumption that the reason of this choice of action must lie in consequences to flow from the action, I will speak of presently[1]. The importance of what I have said above lies in this: that a due consideration of it will effectually prevent us from thinking that moral philosophy can be, as regards its starting-point and main principles, a science of the

[1] See Ch. VI.

kind now called inductive, and which I will call positival, and that it can take its rank, as regards these main principles, with sciences of experience and of observation. The idea of 'what should be,' the expulsion of which from physical science in favour of the observation of 'what is,' has led to vast progress in such science, lies at the heart of moral philosophy, and can never be eradicated from it.

Its principles must be intuitive, though observation may be of great service in regard to their application.

It will be my endeavour, as we proceed, to consider very carefully the importance of observation, both in eudæmonics, as a subsidiary part of moral philosophy, and in some portions of aretaics, where we are concerned with the particulars of human feeling. But the problem of moral philosophy has been from the first: What *should* I do? and the *principle* upon which this question is to be answered is what no observation can possibly give us. No observation, however long continued, can tell us whether it is our own happiness or that of others which we ought to prefer. It is indeed exceedingly possible to suppose (I will not say whether it is the fact) that the *intuitive* principles (so to call them) which lie at the base of the sciences may be very simple and evident, and that the importance of the philosophy may lie in the observation which is to regulate the application of them. But this, if it is so, is quite a different thing from the supposition that the observation can come in the place of the first principles, and that it is a great advance thus to reform the philosophy, and change it into a so-called inductive science.

Illustration from Bentham's 'greatest happiness' principle.

When I see a philosopher like Bentham captivated with his new phrase as to 'the greatest happiness of the greatest number,' and considering it a discovery which would reform all moral philosophy, and then proceeding, with the noble enthusiasm with which he did proceed, to construct, in his way, a methodical cience of eudæmonics in order to the application of is principle, and devoting his life to this unselfish abour,—I seem to see, in his mind and feeling, a egion for moral philosophy which his system obtinately refuses to recognize. He says, in fact, 'I ake as my ideal to be pursued, nothing selfish, but he greatest happiness of the greatest number, and choose as the work of my life the study of the articulars of happiness in order that my ideal may e carried out.' I feel inclined to say to him, A oble work indeed, and you are nobly aiding moral hilosophy by it, but I seem to see another work not ess important for moral philosophy in the study of *ou,* and in the consideration how it is that you ave come to take this as your ideal, instead of trying or instance to make yourself rich and powerful. How is it that the promoting other men's happiness resents itself to you, out of all the possible things which you might do, as the particular thing which ou should do or which it is well for you to do? And if you say (I have not used the word which you lo not like, 'ought') that you do not recognize even should,' but that you only *choose* to do it[1]; I ask gain, There is then something in it to fix your choice: t is conduct *in itself,* in your view, preferable to ny other: how is it you came to choose it? I would ather know that than all your eudæmonics: for in act, for what you want, it is more necessary that nen should have your mind and feeling on the matter, han that they should study your system. You ersist in claiming the name of complete moral philoophy for that which seems to me only a subsidiary,

[1] Cf. Bentham's words quoted in the *Examination of the Utilitaian Philosophy,* p. 137, "I am a selfish man, as selfish as any man can e. But in me, somehow or other, selfishness has taken the shape of enevolence."—Ed.

though an important part of it, and you call by the name of sentimentalism, intuitivism[1] (though this I think is not your word), or I know not what, that without which all your eudæmonics will be valueless. You say you cannot conceive it possible that any one can think differently from you, as to 'the greatest happiness of the greatest number' being the all-important ideal. I answer, You seem in that to be placing the foundation of moral philosophy where I think it ought to be placed, on what some of your disciples will call intuitivism: only, doing this, you might have spared some things which you have said yourself.

On the terms 'virtue,' 'excellence,' as expressive of an ideal.

Aretaics is thus ideal in its very essence. The ἀρετή or virtue which suggests the science is an ideal, and in itself is little more. The existence of the word only proves the existence of degrees of estimation of different feelings and different courses of conduct, together with (and this is the main point of consideration) a belief in the existence of a reason for this preference, in the real preferability of one feeling or one action, as feeling and action, to others: a belief in certain feelings as what we *should* have, and certain actions as what we *should* do: a notion of the valuableness or admirableness of such feelings and actions in themselves, independent of whatever valuableness they may have on account of consequences they may produce. The word 'virtue,' if we disengage it from the application which, in moral use, it has had to particular courses of conduct, and from the associations which have clung about it, means primarily *excellence;* and this in itself means no more than *what should be,* i.e. expresses an ideal. The word 'excellence' itself has got an extraneous association clinging to it, that, namely, of comparison or

[1] Cf. Mill, *Utilitarianism*, p. 3.

superiority of one to another, which comparison is only a way of ascertaining how far the ideal has been attained: the excellence might exist without the existence of beings less excellent, because the superiority implied in the word is only an accident of the thing. It is the same with the words valuableness, admirableness; virtue is a thing which people esteem and admire, but it is not their esteeming and admiring it which makes it virtue; they esteem and admire it because (rightly or wrongly) they consider there is a reason why they should esteem and admire it, and the person who has it himself esteems and admires it as they do; it is not *constituted* to him, by the esteem and admiration which it meets with, though it may be described and named by them. What *constitutes* it is its character of an ideal, of that which *should be.*

On the terms καλός, *honestus.*

The Greeks and Romans did not form, as we have done, an adjective from their ordinary words for virtue, but used words suggested by the *admirableness* which I have spoken of, the words καλός and 'honestus.' No doubt these words would not have been the words chosen, unless they had been considered, by those who chose them, better words than others to express the ideal which was intended: and this they could only be, in consequence of the character of beauty (so we will call it) in the one case, of meeting with the approbation of men in the other, being characters which attached themselves very closely to the ideal. Some philosophers taught that the words not only aptly expressed what was meant, but gave the essence of it; that virtue consisted in moral beauty, or in deservingness of human approbation. But this was in neither case the view of those who used the words with most earnestness, and most, so to speak, believed in them. Cicero, following the Stoics, disclaimed in the strongest terms, in reference to the word 'honestus,' the notion, that the use of it in any way suggested that it was its meeting with human approbation which constituted virtue[1]. With him, and others like him, the words simply expressed the ideal, what should be.

On the term 'duty.'

Virtue expresses the ideal subjectively, expresses, that is, an ideal disposition: καλός and 'honestus' ordinarily express it objectively; that is, express an ideal course of action. Another famous term for expressing the ideal objectively is 'duty.'

Duty is in reality the word which expresses the ideal character of what is meant with the most clearness, but it is not a word of such ancient use in this application as the others: it is a word also which has been a good deal used in that which I alluded to as being the less ideal portion of aretaics, that namely, where the particular relations of individuals to each other are dealt with. It is not my purpose however, just now, to say anything upon this portion of aretaics, or upon the words expressing the moral ideal in this view of it: both these subjects I will for the present reserve.

But there is another view of the moral ideal, as important as that which we have just been speaking of, to which we must now turn.

I described man as possessing activity or power, and sentience or feeling. Let us examine a little the relation of these the one to the other.

Man's sentient nature is suggestive of 'want.'

It is perfectly possible to conceive man possessing a sentience which had no relation to his activity. He might be (i.e. we can conceive him) always

[1] "Honestum, quod, etiam si nobilitatum non sit, tamen honestum est, quodque vere dicimus, etiamsi a nullo laudetur, natura esse laudabile." *De Off.* I. 4. Cf. *Tusc.* III. 2.—Ed.

happy, always enjoying himself: or he might suffer pain which he perfectly well knew he was powerless to prevent or diminish: and there are various other suppositions which we might make. But, as it is, the great mass of his feeling is indicative of a fact which concerns him greatly, a fact which might exist in regard of him, and does to a considerable extent, without his feeling it: a fact which I will call *want*. And on this *want* I will dwell for a few moments with a somewhat wider view.

The term 'want' here used to express the fact, not the feeling of the fact.

I propose to use the word 'want' strictly for a *fact* (or supposed or possible fact), as distinct from our *feeling* of the fact, if we have such a feeling. Facts which we feel, and our feeling of them, are in language constantly confused, and this is the case in respect of the term 'want.' But the fact, for instance, that our stomach is empty and that there is going on in our system none of that nutrition which we will suppose ought constantly to be going on in it, is a very different thing from our feeling, if we do feel, that such is the case, in consequence of some pain, of hunger or otherwise, resulting from it: the former might perfectly exist without the other. We use the word 'want' for both: if we say 'our system wants food,' we mean the former: if we say 'we want food,' we might mean either, but most likely should mean the latter; as if we said, 'the baby wants a coral,' or 'I want the newspaper.' Now the word 'want,' whenever I use it, will be meant to express the former of them, the *fact*.

Activity and want in man and in the universe.

We are thus something besides active and sentient beings, we are active and wanting beings: and, extending our view beyond ourselves, the universe is an active and a wanting universe. Not, indeed, exactly in the sense in which we are active and wanting, but in this sense, that there is a great deal of power in the universe, and also a great deal of want. I use the word universe with intentional vagueness: what I say will apply equally whether we make the widest possible supposition of the universe, taking in God as the Creator of it, or whether we consider it to be merely a physical *compages* of matter and force. What I mean is simply this; that the universe, so far as the action in it is concerned, is made up of two elements; of beings (so we will speak at present) possessing powers, and of opportunity or call for the exercise of their powers, which is what I have called 'want.'

Man's sentient nature suggests the ideal of *happiness*, his activity suggests that of *duty*, his want suggests the third and highest ideal, that of *good*.

It is man's sentient nature, as we have seen, which leads to the formation of that ideal which I have called happiness: it is man's active nature which leads to the formation of the ideal which I have last described, in speaking of virtue and the corresponding terms: it is man's nature as *wanting* which leads to the formation of a third ideal more important than the first of them, and equally important with the second—the notion of 'good.' In one point of view this ideal is more important than the second: that the character of individual appropriation which belonged to the two former does not belong to this. Man can only feel his own feelings, and act with his own powers: but the *wantingness* which is the call to action he can be informed of by his intellect as much *beyond* himself as *in* himself, and the ideal 'good' is *in this point of view* the noblest and grandest of all.

Want is wider than sentience, and good than happiness.

The notion which I have here given of 'want' or 'wantingness' may be objected to as really conveying nothing, and not making at all more clear the notion of good, as the ideally desirable. I am indifferent what words are used, and what I wish to draw attention to is the ambiguity and difficulty attending even such words as 'desirable'; the same which I have noticed in respect of 'want'. The universe is, on any hypothesis of it, an orderly constitution of things, containing in it a number of beings who can feel happiness, but who, so far as they do feel happiness, must feel it in virtue of, and by means of, their particular constitution, which is a part of this order. So far as they do not feel happiness, it arises from their state not being what *it should be*, by which I mean no more than that they are not in their *ideal* state, and the degree to which they fall short of it is the measure of what I call their want; and this falling short of an ideal state may exist in that which is *not* capable of happiness: to that *itself* which is not capable of happiness this falling short may not be important, but it may be important on account of the relation of things together, and the orderly constitution of the whole.

Good, of all the ideals, is that which has played the most important part, and speculations as to the nature of the summum bonum have been the most important of moral speculations. I hope hereafter more fully to dwell upon it.

This last ideal involves both aretaics and eudæmonics.

This last ideal involves together both aretaics and eudæmonics: that is, it deals with a kind of eudæmonics which I shall have a good deal to speak of, in which the idea of 'should be' enters into combination with that of pleasure or happiness, and one kind of happiness is considered as superior in kind to another. But for the present enough.

APPENDIX ON WANT[1].

Aug. 20, 1864. Byron's Pool, 8 A.M.

Action characterised from its starting point, want, as well as from its end, happiness.

INSTEAD of taking the *epitelic* view of action, what we might do would be to take the *aparchic*. With Aristotle (is it not so?) the ἀρχή of action is really only another word for the τέλος, purpose, or aim: but we might consider in regard of action its origin, or that which it starts from, as well as its τέλος, or that which it tends to.

As its τέλος, or what it tends to, may be called good or happiness, and what we wish to find out the *summum bonum;* so its ἀρχή, or what it starts from, may be called *want,* and what we wish to know the *prima egestas.* This and the *summum bonum* would probably from different ends coincide. As we call the first *good* (or happiness), so we might call the second *want* (or uneasiness). In reality, both these additions are doubtful. Good and want are states, and are not necessarily conceived or *felt:* happiness and uneasiness are the feeling of each of them.

What, in addition to intelligence and fact, has to be taken account of when we think of action, is *want.* And what in addition to this again, has to be taken account of when we think of *moral* action, is the existence of a *plurality* of *sentient,* some or all also *active,* beings.

Want exhibited in a scale passing

Want or egence is the great fact conditioning, and stimulating real action (by which I mean action as different from conceivable chaotic movement). Satisfaction is the fact cor-

[1] The pages which follow seem to contain the germ of the treatise on Aretaics and Eudæmonics. They are taken from a note-book with the accompanying notices of the time and place of their writing. Professor Grote was literally a peripatetic philosopher, and the places mentioned were among his favourite haunts for philosophic meditation. What was thus thought out was written down afterwards, generally with great rapidity and with scarcely any correction or erasure.—ED.

responding to it: good is the idea, i. e. this latter fact, extended, heightened and developed, by the intelligence.

from the objective to the subjective.

The degrees of *withoutness* are (1) simple *non-habence*; (2) *carence, i. e.* the being without a thing when there is at least some conceivable reason why it should be present (we say a pronoun or a particular noun *caret vocativo,* we should with less reason say it *caret modo indicativo,* and with no reason at all it *caret foliis*); (3) *egence,* where the want is of some particular thing according to the nature of that which wants, and where there exists in nature a possibility of the satisfaction of the want, such satisfaction being probably striven after or provided for in some way; (4) *desiderium,* or craving and yearning, which is the last subjectively felt, and possibly amplified by imagination, &c.; (5) *cupido,* or general imaginative desire, which may be without any egence as fact.

Want in plants: is it accompanied by feeling?

Is egence always in some measure felt or subjective? If it is, there is personality or consciousness in plants; and who shall say there is not, or that rudimentary (of course unreflective) personality or consciousness does not begin as early and as low down as real organic unity?

It is the nature of the leaf or root of a plant, say, to imbibe water or air: there is egence in the plant, and there are movements in the parts of it by which the water or air is imbibed; the egence leads to the activity; must there not be something like sentience and will in the passage from the one to the other? Is not the plant in an uncomfortable or uneasy state without what it wants; must it not have, that is, a sort of feeling to the extent of its unitariness of organization?

So far as we start from fact, want is the reality, not good. Good is the ideal, the absent which *should be* present. *Ideal* and *should be* express the same. Good, absent, is felt, so far as there is feeling, as want. Good, particular, depends upon particularity of want.

Want or egence, and *want-feel* or craving, are not exactly the same thing: there may be real want unfelt, and there may be mistaken want-feel.

Sept. 1, 1864. Great Meadows, 8 A.M.

Want is to action as sensation to intelligence. Want is source of action, as sensation of intelligence.

The simplest want is the absence of physical communication between two things, where such communication would be to the advantage of one of them.

Advantage or disadvantage in this case is rather a vague term, the same as perfection or imperfection, &c.: all imply a fixed or regular nature.

Mutual want in chemical elements.

In the case of chemical elective affinities, there may be said to be mutual want when two elements are in a position which, when other bodies are presented to them, they would change, or in a so far unnatural position. There is not in the elements any thing which we should describe as sentience, disposition, impulse, or tendency; but as a fact, they change their circumstances when the opportunity is presented to them, and this may be described as want of such change.

When a plant is said to imbibe air or water, what takes place is a certain mechanical movement of the parts of the plant to which the air or water lends itself according to *its* nature. In this case such advantage as occurs is one-sided, and we say that there is in the *plant* want of the air or water.

Recurrence of want and satisfaction constitutes life.

When such want is continuous, recurring after satisfaction, as in the plant, there is what we call *life* in the sense of growth or vegetance.

The word 'unity' is too general, and the word 'personality' too restricted, to express something which we want a word to express, viz. life as containing or involving the conditions of possible consciousness, though we may not know whether the consciousness exists or not, and may rather consider that it does not. We only use the word 'personality' where there is distinct consciousness or power of reflection. The word unity, though likely enough suggested in the first instance only by our felt consciousness and then by the perceived unity of life, yet is widely extended to any form of *thinghood* or reality.

Has the plant *appetite* after water, air, the immixture of the pollen with the stigma, &c.? There is the same fact, independent of any feeling on the part of the plant, that there is in the case of appetite of animals: whether there is appetite or not depends on whether we consider that there is, or is not, feeling or sentience.

Localization of

The words appetite, desire, &c. denote generally the

fact of want or *desence*, felt in some manner, and thus stimulating the will to act through the intelligence for the supply of it. That the feeling corresponds to the fact of want is what we can hardly tell: in fact we can hardly attach distinct meaning to the words. The absence of food in the stomach we might perhaps feel in the head—perhaps indeed do. The *feeling* of hunger is one particular result, among many others, of the *fact* of the body's wanting food: the two are conceivably quite separable. And similarly, the gratification of the feeling of hunger and the supply, as a fact, of the want of the body, are two things quite distinct, though they may be concomitant.

want in an organized being.

All proper want (as distinguished from the case of chemical affinities above, and similar cases) implies a more or less complete unity, and therefore possibility of sentience, in the wanting being. All want is thus want of the *whole* being. But the want may be of different kinds, and the different kinds may be arranged along a scale similar to that of sensation. The fact of the want may be the absence of a corporeal or material communication which, according to the nature of things, and of the particular being, ought at the time to exist. Of this kind is the stomachic want of food. This is *felt* as hunger, which is a feeling, not of the stomach, but of the man, and of man not in the stomach more than elsewhere in the body. Still, the material communication wanted is between the stomach and certain nutritious materials.

The feeling of want is not local.

The want and, either self-supplying or suggestive and stimulating, absence of communication between the stomach and such materials in this case is analogous to the fact of communication between members of the body, limbs or senses, and natural material agents, which aliments the intelligence.

The good, benefit, advantage of the man consists thus, as to one part of it at least, in the fact of the former of these communications, or the supply of physical wants: and the fact of the supply of the wants is accompanied, ordinarily, by another fact, viz. the gratification of some particular feeling (in the above case hunger) by which the want is accompanied. The enjoyment is two-fold: the concentrated and momentary enjoyment of the gratification: and the diffused

Two distinct kinds of enjoyment resulting from satisfaction of want.

and continuous enjoyment arising from the better state of the body, and the supply of its want.

For action, in an intelligent being, both of them must be taken into account, and to take the last into account requires much of intelligence.

Enjoyment suggests to us the ideal good to the same extent as sensation suggests an external universe.

If we conceive the ideal good or desirable, the *summum bonum*, we must conceive it as a complicated whole as we conceive the material universe. The ideal good is given to us by the gratification of appetite or simple desire just to the same extent as the material world is given to us by chemical sensation. The mere gratification and chemical (or pleasure-pain) sensation, suggest to us, in virtue of our intelligence, in the one case good (advantage, benefit, &c.) as a fact, in the other case independent reality as a fact.

Enjoyment or happiness is in the same sense the *summum bonum* as *sentition* or bare sensation is the *summum reale* or *summum verum*: enjoyment is an incident or result of good, as sensation is of reality.

Happiness may indeed be the ultimate good, as being *known to be* may be the ultimate reality: but this is far off and in *the whole* of things, and human action must be for good conceived by the intelligence; to the notion of which felt gratification or enjoyment contributes a most important part indeed, but only a part, in the same way as human understanding is of an orderly universe to which bare sensation contributes only a portion.

The analogy between the scale of ethics and the scale of sensation.

That our action should be regulated by the intelligence, is, in a manner, a higher appetite or desire, leading to regularity, orderliness, conduct on principle, and, at a later stage, when the presence of other moral beings with us is taken into account, to fairness and justice: such desire is analogous to the *middle* part of the scale of sensation[1].

That our conduct should be worthy and excellent, is, as it were, a higher appetite or desire still, and corresponds to the *highest* portion of that scale.

Sept. 3, 1864. Byron's Pool, 8 A.M.

Egence, and difference of egence, are the great facts of the universe.

[1] Cf. *Exploratio*, ch. VI.

We want, first expresses a fact: and what we want in this view is some particular thing, which may be called our happiness, but all this possibly, irrespectively of our feeling.

Want and the feeling of want.

We want, next expresses our feeling, so far as it goes, of the above fact: what we want in this case again is some particular thing, more or less correspondent with the above: our happiness in this case is in the presence of the particular thing, and besides this, is the two satisfactions, the complete satisfaction of our *want-feel,* the partial satisfaction, so far as it goes, of the actual fact of our want.

The subjective feeling of want might be divided into craving and wish: craving, which is blind, wish, which is imaginative and more or less intelligent. *Mis-craving* is physical disease, *mis-wish* is mental.

Imaginative wish is, as it were, double: there is uneasiness with the desire of *something* to satisfy it, of whatever therefore will satisfy it: there is imagination of *what* will satisfy it, and the consequent wish for this. A great deal of moral puzzle, intended or involuntary, arises from this doubleness. People say, 'That is not the thing you really wish for:' meaning, when it is present, it will not satisfy you; you will not find it what you expected.

Egence is the life of the universe: the highest forms of egence are variously called 'love': the lowest are simple appetence, perhaps merely physical.

Want or egence in God.

When we speak of moral attributes in God, we ascribe to Him an egence of the highest, but of the most imperious kind: for what are such attributes without other sentient and moral beings on which they may be exercised? Love with nothing to fix on—can we imagine a state of greater defect, imperfection, unhappiness?

Suppose sentient beings created, there is a transfer of part of this original egence: they want *Him,* as He wants them.

As it is, they are created with rich and varied nature, and with them is a rich unsentient nature as framework to them: they want each other, and variously want *it.*

All this egence still again inactionates itself, and keeps reality alive, and ever still freshly varying.

There is a principle of conservation of egence like the mechanical principle of the conservation of force.

Philosophically viewed, all that has been, or will be, is now.

The egence which there is there has always been, the great original repository of it being God.

In this same sort of view we might philosophically abolish tenses, and say that everything which has been, is.

Absence in time is like absence in space: the absent is separated from us, and we can only mediately and by effort be aware of it.

The susceptibility of a thing to be acted upon is as much *δύναμις* as the power to act upon it, and both point to a *δύναμις* previous to and higher than both.

If we consider time as we do space, and look with an equal eye along its two directions, we see that what we call the end is in one view the beginning, and vice versa. Action proceeding from intelligence has a double beginning or source; the end or purpose as viewed by the intelligence, and the force in the agent.

The past and the future both *are:* the past is the experienced and already *bewilled*, which has had will expended upon it: the future is the unexperienced and *unbewilled*, but (independent of the manner in which will, which has to be spent on it, may effect it) it is continuous like the past, real and certain like it, and only not knowable by us because there is no experience to connect our intelligence and it.

The future, looked upon as real with a quasi-reality modifiable by will, is real again in a higher view, inasmuch as even all that this *will* will do is contained in the existing egence, most widely taken.

The two primæval facts.

The two great primæval facts are the possibility of good, which is in fact egence, and the fact that God has chosen (or has been such a being as to choose) to act *for* this possibility, to act, that is, morally and rightly, when He might (or the being in his place might) have acted otherwise.

There has not been temptation in God to act wrong, but there has been the presentation of wrong to Him with the attendant reasons for it; and it is in the acting nevertheless right that has consisted His moral choice: and the same intellectually, among various courses He has chosen the best, and therefore has not mistaken or failed.

The original egence of God, which is the source of all things, is in another word *felicificativeness,* and this produces by creation *felicificability* or the capacity for happiness in the creature.

CHAPTER III.

GENERAL VIEW OF THE MORAL IDEALS AND OF THE RELATION BETWEEN THEM.

The 'summum faciendum' is the first moral ideal in order of time (chronologically).

THOUGH I have spoken of the ideal *good* as in one point of view the noblest of all the ideals, yet from another, the summum faciendum, that which should be done, is more important still. The forming it in the mind implies the following things: that the question, in regard of the conduct of our life, which most naturally suggests itself, is not so much, what *shall* I do, simply, as what *should* I do, involving a presumption, or, if we like to call it so, an *à priori* belief, on our part, which we may variously express; as by saying, that there exists, in such a manner as matter of abstract thought can exist, a course of life which is adapted to us, which belongs to us, which there is reason we should choose: these various ways of expression seem to me to mean *one* thing, viz. the presumption or belief on our part that there is a proper course of conduct for us. This ideal course of conduct is that to which I shall give the name of 'rightness.'

Action however is in the nature of it for a purpose, and, with certain qualifications, actions which serve no purpose are wasted. The main feature of the reasonableness of action is its subserviency to some purpose: we apply reason to action mainly in order to make action *useful*, if I may use the word in a wide sense, without danger of its being wrested to a technical or sectarian meaning. 'Rightness' may be called the first moral ideal, because the question, 'what should I do?' comes before the question, 'what shall I aim at?' but this latter very speedily suggests itself, possibly without the former, very likely as a result or kind of interpretation of it. Perhaps the best word in English to express the ideal *purpose* or *aim* of action is the *desirable*, though here we must guard against ambiguity, because the summum faciendum may be described as that which is desirable to be done, in a different sense from that in which 'the desirable' stands for something to be won, gained, succeeded in. The ideally desirable is the *τὸ ἀγαθόν*, the *bonum* or *summum bonum* of the old philosophy.

The two ideals played an equally prominent part in ancient morals, though the second was the more treated of in philosophical systems, the former ideal appearing rather in religion and in practical views as to society and law.

There is another reason why the former of these ideals should be put first. It not only suggests itself first, but it is the simpler. The desirable, or the to be desired, is a much more complicated notion. Has it, or has it not, the former ideal mixed with it? Is the 'to be desired' in any way that which 'ought' to be desired? or is it 'the desired,' with appeal to human feeling and human history? or is it 'the reasonably desired' pointing to some other ideal still for its interpretation?

It is also the simplest moral ideal.

Of course, as this latter ideal is more complicated than the former, so, through being the more concrete and nearer to life, it may be the more valuable of the two. But it leads on, in the minds of many, to another and different ideal.

The summum bonum, the 2nd moral ideal, is complicated with the 3rd, happiness suggested by pleasure.

This is the ideal 'happiness as suggested by pleasure.' I use these words, because the more vague or general ideal 'good' might also be called by the name of happiness. This third ideal is nearer to fact than the other two, because pleasure, or at least that of which it is intended to express the opposite—pain, is an undoubted fact of actual nature.

The important character of this ideal, that which has made it enter so largely into all conduct of human life and all moral philosophy, is this: that while on the one side it touches the earth by our actual sensation of pleasure and pain, so on the other it seems to go further back than any other and to mount higher, and to be the only one of all which offers us any answer to the question, why should anything have existed at all? or why should there ever have been any action? It is an ideal which, while associated with Epicureanism on the one side, is much associated with un-Epicurean notions, as of final causes, on the other.

As the 3rd ideal arises from the union of 2nd ideal with observation of sensible fact, so a 4th, 'the natural,' arises from union of 1st ideal with observation of fact.

This last ideal arises from the coupling of the sensible fact of pleasure and pain with the previous ideal of 'the desirable.' The next ideal which I will mention, arises rather from the coupling more general observation as to actual fact with the first ideal, or 'that which should be done.'

I will call this ideal 'the natural.' Perhaps it may be said to take its origin from the union of a belief in an universal constitution of things, all belonging to all (a belief which I hold to be connected with all our ideals, especially the first, and of which I shall speak at more length hereafter), and of observation of the particular constitution of things, especially of man and physical nature. Hence arises the notion of there being something which man ought to do, in virtue of his being man, and not something lifferent from man : and human nature is estimated in rarious manners, with the view of determining this.

Other ideals.

The number of ideals which people may form as to he conduct of their life is of course endless. Among others, which are scarcely less important than those which have already been noticed, may be mentioned he following :

The fair.

The fair, or just, is an ideal formed by mixing the irst, or what ought to be done, with an observational view of the conflicting interests, and various inter-relations of men.

The conscientious.

The conscientious, or, in other words, the ideal of a life in which there shall be no self-condemnation, is a mixture of the first ideal with the felt tendency to self-judgment and to reflection.

I will not however dwell on any more of them : but will call attention to one thing about them which is of importance.

How these ideals are affected by the consideration that man is not solitary but exists in society.

Whether such a thing as morality would be conceivable, if we were any one of us the solitary sentient being in creation, is a speculation on which we can hardly enter. We can hardly affirm the contrary; for we suppose an existence of the Deity, good and moral, previous to everything; but I conclude that we should not consider the affixing moral epithets to Him in such a position to have any meaning, unless we supposed in Him the power of terminating this solitude, and correspondingly, of imagining beings in regard of whom His moral attributes might be exercised.

As it is however with us, and so far as *we* need conceive it, morality begins to be possible when two sentient beings, one of whom at least is active, come into any sort of contact or relation with each other.

Especial import-ance of

The ideals, as we have hitherto noticed them, take no account of this consideration, which is quite as im-

this consideration in regard to the 2nd and 3rd ideals.

portant in morality as any of them, whether the action (say the will and choice determining the action) and the good or purpose of the action, are in the *same* being, or in different ones.

This consideration is so important, that, in respect of the ideals which have any relation to good or purpose, it splits each into two, the good of ourselves, and good that is not ours, and similarly as regards happiness and utility.

On the interpretation of one ideal by another.

I proceed now, in reference to these ideals, to consider how far it is possible to find the line of conduct (or any line of conduct) to which they point: and first, how far there is any advantage in explaining or interpreting any one of them by another.

(1) No advance is made by mere exchange of terms: (2) where there is advance by approaching nearer to fact, there is corresponding loss of ideality.

On these subjects it seems to me that there are two maxims which we may take: which I will state at first generally, subject to some qualification: the one, that by converting one ideal into another, or interpreting one by another, we make no step, and get no forwarder in knowledge: the other, that where we do advance in knowledge by *fixing* an ideal, or converting it into something partaking of fact, observation and experience, we must bear in mind that it loses its ideal character, more or less, and that it becomes subject to a variety of difficulties, which attach to everything belonging thus to fact and experience.

These maxims illustrated by the passage from summum bonum to utility or happiness.

Both these maxims may be illustrated by the passage from the second ideal to the third, i.e. from the 'summum bonum' to the principle of (so called) utility or happiness.

This latter involves, as we have seen, a mixture of the ideal with matter-of-fact or observation: so far as this is so, we make a step of thought, true or false, in the forming it. What I wish to remark is, that so far as we keep to an ideal character in respect of it, we gain nothing by changing the second ideal into it: and so far as we do gain by getting hold of tangible or actual matter to go on, we come into difficulties which previously we were free from.

I am not meaning by this to make a charge against this ideal, or semi-ideal: for what I am saying, by way of illustration of it, is true of any change from a higher region of ideality to a lower.

Happiness, in the ideal region, is an exceedingly vague term, as was the Greek *εὐδαιμονία*, of which it may be called a translation, and when we say that happiness is what all creatures desire, or that the general happiness is what all ought to aim at, no one will dispute with us. By saying here happiness, instead of the desirable or the summum bonum, we have made no way.

But if we want, in these two propositions, for instance, to mean more than this, or to *fix* the term happiness, and understand what it *contains* or applies to, we do indeed begin to make way in thought, but we begin also to experience the friction or resistance which, as soon as we move, actuality opposes to us.

Pleasure and pain, as we feel them, and happiness (if by this term we mean, not the ideal above mentioned, but agreeable feeling in life, if we can conceive this as a sort of whole in the life of each, very variable of course in degree in the life of one and of another), are matters of exceedingly difficult observation. The above propositions, as soon as we pass from ideal to fact, no longer even approximate to self-evident truth. Let us try, for instance, to deal with pleasures as we deal with plants, to dissect them first, and then to classify, define and describe them, as thus examined. We shall find that it is a very small minority of our actions which are done in order to

pleasure as thus describable: they are done for an infinity of motives into which pleasure only enters as one. Take then the proposition, All creatures act for happiness. As soon as we begin to mean anything by happiness beyond the meaning which the proposition itself gives the term (beyond, that is, the notion that it is that for which all creatures act), the proposition begins to mean something definite indeed, which is an advance, but at the same time to lose all its self-evidence and generality: it becomes a question to be examined and tested, a question which probably we shall only be able to answer affirmatively in a very qualified acceptation of its various terms.

by Aristotle's "life according to virtue" and the Stoical "life according to nature."

In the long line of controversy which makes up the history of moral philosophy, it appears to me that there are two things of prime importance to be observed: the one how far, in any portion of it, there is *advance* of thought, or only the changing, in our conception, of one ideal for another. This latter is not entirely useless or unmeaning, as we shall see: still the ideals are of value in regard to *conduct*, and advance in moral philosophy is in applying them to life, and finding the actual line of conduct which they indicate. For instance: was it any advance in thought for the Stoics to say that the summum bonum was a life according to nature, or is the one of these ideals as difficult to fix and apply as the other? Or was it any advance in thought for Aristotle to say that happiness was a life according to virtue, or do we find that we have no clearer notion of happiness through knowing this about it? I only give these questions as instances, without prejudging the answers.

The next thing to be watched in moral controversy is, whether, when it does make an effort to advance, it keeps itself clear of confusion between the fact and the ideal. For example: a happy life is the name which we give to the sort of life which we should any of us wish to live. And, again, we observe in fact, that riches make some men what we call happy, fame others, and so on. Here we have happiness as conceived and as experienced. But the passage in thought between the two is through a region somewhat similar to Satan's way between Pandemonium and earth, a region in which fact and imagination blend into something without value in either direction. We are trying, we will say, to demonstrate as a proposition of experience, that people act for pleasure, and if there seems to be any doubt about it, we are at once disconcerted with the response : O, but you see it must be pleasure, or else people would not act upon it.

CHAPTER IV.

THE IDEALS ARE NOT MERE IMAGINATION.

Is this forming of ideals more than dreaming?

It would appear from what has been stated in a previous chapter that Moral Philosophy cannot possibly, as regards the higher and more important portions of it, be considered an inductive science. But, it may be said, in regard to this portion of it which is not thus positive or inductive, is it anything other than a mere imagination? Of course, in our imagination, we may form any ideals we please: but is this anything other than a sort of poetry or dreaming? is it even philosophy, not to say science? It is difficult to know on which side one should take hold of a question like this. Some writers have considered moral sentiments to be much akin to æsthetic sentiments, a fact which I have before alluded to in speaking of the term καλός. Those who take this view would not disclaim their partaking largely of an imaginative character, and would not think them on that account the less subjects for a real philosophy. The general question, to which this question of the nature of the moral ideals is closely subordinate, of the relation of imagination or poetry to matter of fact, conception or judgment, is of itself a large and difficult one. Without entering upon it here more than can be helped, I may just express my opinion, that the distinction ordinarily made between reason and imagination is entirely fallacious. So far as they represent different things, they are not, in my view, contrasted with each other,

The imaginative character of ideals is not denied, but the value of the imagination is upheld as being the very life of our intelligence.

but are intimately connected, and mutually helpful. I look upon imagination as the active portion of the intelligence, that in which the life of the intelligence consists, and from which, as the intelligence advances, new deposits are ever made of actual knowledge, which thenceforward loses a portion of its interest, and becomes for some purposes dead. Certain portions however of what the imagination presents to us will never crystallize into this actual knowledge; while yet, it seems to me, they are not merely worthless or chimerical. It is the main purpose of poetry, taken in the widest sense of the word, to express such imagination, which possesses a truth no less real,—it may be more real,—than actual knowledge; the difference simply being that this truth is not put together into a whole, and looked at from all sides, so to speak, as truth is in knowledge. In poetry we see a number of partial views, which we cannot harmonize and *totalize* or bring into a whole: this leaves such truth as there is, better in one way than the truth which is embodied in knowledge, because less handled about by the human intellect—more fresh, as it were: still the effort of the intellect is ever after the gaining of definite knowledge, and imagination is the way to the gaining it, while such portion of the matter of imagination as is not or cannot be thus definitized remains as poetry.

Comparison of these ideals with imaginary schemes.

Let us suppose then, to begin with, that the moral ideals are pure matters of imagination—something which people take into their heads, with nothing at all about them of the nature of science. Men set before themselves schemes of all kinds: one man dreams of the building of a church, another of making a fortune, Alexander of conquering the world, Columbus of sailing across the ocean to

Cathay: so one person forms in his mind, as the ideal purpose or rule of his action, the notion of promoting the greatest happiness of the greatest possible number; another that of acting in such a way that he shall never feel self-condemnation or remorse, and so for other ideals. The more general ideals may be formed either by themselves, or in companionship with the less general and nearer ones. Thus, a man may either simply dream in general that there is an ideal 'what he should do,' or duty, which is nearly the same thing as having the notion of his action being of importance; or, (in respect, for instance, of the ideal greatest happiness,) he may add, to his imagination of acting in order to this, the further imagination of its being *well* that he should do this, of its being the proper thing for him to do, &c.

The ideals are not arbitrary or individual.

It will probably readily suggest itself that (on this view) the point at which imagination has to pass into moral philosophy is where a man begins to talk about his ideal to others as something which belongs to them as well as to himself. In respect of Bentham, I have said, that, in his feeling so strongly, as apparently he did, that the promoting the greatest happiness was what he and others should do, he seemed to confess the intuitivism, or whatever he would call it, which he so strongly disclaimed. When pressed, he might say that he had no feeling that this was what he *should* do, in the sense of its being fit, proper, incumbent on him, but only that this was what he chose to make his ideal of the work of life, as Alexander made *his* conquering the world, and that he constructed his system of eudæmonics with a view of aiding those who might form the same ideal. No one however can really think that when ideals as to what is to be done are formed in this manner, it is as simple individual imaginations that they are formed. Neither Bentham, nor any man in earnest about life ever said, Well, this is *my* way of thinking: you take yours. The same force which makes a man form, with any earnestness, an ideal like this for himself, makes him also feel, that it is what ought to be the ideal of all, and makes him teach and preach it as such. The first ideal, that of the faciendum, or what should be done, is thus present in its full force: and it is *this* special circumstance about it, that he not only has the ideal himself, but that he feels himself entitled to urge it upon others, which makes it evidently present to him not as a mere individual imagination, but as— I will not say what, but evidently something which is neither mere imagination nor mere matter of experience[1].

They necessarily involve the notion of the absolute 'should be.'

However much then we may *suppose* these moral ideals, as men form them, to be simple imaginations or dreams, we cannot, in our supposition, keep them so. Men *will* not only form ideals for themselves, but judge about those of others, and try to urge their own upon others; that is, the notion of the absolute 'should be' will come in. And this 'should be' really means that there exists reason why one (whatever it may be) of these ideals is better than another: otherwise comparing them, or urging our own upon others, is unmeaning. Actually, moral philosophy may be said to have existed from

[1] I am not sure that this is quite satisfactory. The difference spoken of seems to me not to lie in the actions recommended, but in the persons who recommend them. An enthusiastic person urges his hobbies on every one else, whether it be to buy his favourite wines, or read his favourite books, not with an idea of their being morally incumbent, but because he is social, and fond of sympathy, perhaps fond of power. On the other hand, a man may have strong convictions as to what is right or wrong for himself, but be very little of a proselytizer, and shrink from urging *any* course upon others.—ED.

the earliest dawn of human reflection, and to have existed in virtue of man's recognition, by reflection, that he does form in himself an ideal of something, as what he should do: moral philosophy is his process of discovering this. But when, in later times, any-one chooses to say that we do not form such an ideal, but that this is merely one particular imagination among others; still, moral philosophy, kept out for a time, comes in afterwards in the way above mentioned: we cannot, more than for a momentary hypothesis or by a mental force upon ourselves, look on these moral ideals as dreams.

The ideals have their rise in our sense of *want* informing us of something non-existent or absent which may be made existent or present.

The moral ideals then are certain dreams or imaginations of the human race, which we cannot look at without recognizing them as something more than dreams, though what more, moral philosophy finds it hard to tell us. They lie in the middle ground between imagination and knowledge of fact: but they are best approached from the side of imagination, for this reason—that, though they unite themselves with fact, and lead to fact, and spring indeed indirectly from fact themselves, yet their *immediate* rise is *not* from fact, but, if I may so speak, from *absence* of fact. We have them in virtue of our active nature:—I do not mean this as an explanation of these, for we might say in the same way that our active nature means little more than that we have ideals, these and others—but I mean this: our active nature is turned towards the non-existent, to bring it (if we may say *it*, that is, *something*) into existence; and these ideals are, as it were, the shadows of various existences in this non-existent. This seems abstract; but the thing itself is simple enough: experience, and all its sciences are concerned with what we *have*, with what is in some way present: moral philosophy is concerned with what we *want*, with the absent.

Experience is all a growth from our sensations of something as present to us: moral philosophy is a growth from our sensation—such sensation as we can have—of something as absent from us. This sensation of something as absent from us is, in fact, the imagination of an ideally desirable. Without this quasi-sensation of the absent, no sensation of the present would lead to action. This quasi-sensation *might* be sensation and nothing more: might point to nothing, and indicate no objective reality: then the moral ideals would be, as we have just been supposing, simple imaginations: in this respect this sensation is on a par with all sensation: it is quite conceivable that our sensation of the present might have no objective ground, and might be all imagination. In any case, this quasi-sensation of the absent, whatever objective validity it may have, has probably its own conditions, laws, meaning (however we may express it), like the sensations which we call experiences: if things were otherwise constituted than they are, if we were otherwise constituted than they are, we should idealize otherwise than we do. As I understand intuitive morality, it means (in this view) simply the taking account of, or attributing importance to, these *wants*, these action-stirring ideals, of our spiritual (i. e. our thinking and feeling) nature. There are, I suppose, different forms of this intuitivism: though what those who use the word mean by it, is rather their business than mine. But, in any case, the want as sensation (the reader will remember what I have said before about *want*) may be regarded as the farthest point to which we can go in recognizing fact: then the disposition to form these ideals will be considered a part of our nature, in the same way in which ordinary sensation is. *Or*, we may go beyond the sensation, and consider that want, as sensation argues want as fact in the same way as the sensation of hunger is a sign of an emptiness of the stomach: so far as we do this, we come upon a set of facts which depend upon our quasi-sensation of the absent, or upon our non-experience. Nor is there anything unreasonable in this. If we were removed into a world where there was no atmosphere, we should have a sensive *absentation* (the converse of presentation) which would speedily kill us. We should have an imaginational knowledge, or a quasi-sensation, of atmosphere, by its necessity to us. Of all possible things, there is a triple division, so far as we are concerned: into the things which we have, or which are present; the things which we want (quibus egemus), but which in whatever way we require or should be the better for; and into the things which we have not (quibus caremus) without its being of importance to us whether we have them or not. It is evident, that with regard to all the second class, there is a link between us and them which might be converted into a knowledge of them, without our having them: they are in a relation with us to which at any time our consciousness might be directed, and then there would be sensation of them as absent.

The active side of our nature informs us of these ideals, as the sensive side informs us of an external universe.

The moral ideals thus represent the great and higher wants of our nature, which wants, as I have said, may either be simple imaginations, or may indicate want as fact, i. e. make us acquainted with fact beyond experience. Wants, corresponding to something to be done or gained, are the necessary furniture of our active nature, as sensive capacities, corresponding to something perceivable, are of our intellectual nature. We should be as badly off without a work to do as without a world to live in. And we may fairly consider, that when in virtue of our nature to which it bears a relation, we conceive our, as yet unperformed but ideal, work; there is as much reason, though it is of a different kind, for *this* conception, as there is for our conception, in virtue of the same nature, of the world in which we are.

Moral philosophy is thus concerned with that which *is not* as well as with that which *is*, and more immediately. How to observe the actual so as to learn from it what is that complement of the actual which our action may produce, and which will be something gained to the actual and make it better, *this* is the main problem of ethics.

On the importance of the relation between the existent and the non-existent.

Our nature is one, and of course feeling and action are concerned together: and in the same way, the things which *are* not (if again I may say so) are of no importance to us, except as related to the things that *are*; but then, in the same way still, the things which *are* are of comparatively little importance to us, except in relation to the things that *are* not. It is as a pre-condition or aid to action that knowledge has its prime value: and action, as we have seen, is determined by *wants;* not by presence of anything, but by absence of it.

The ideals have a practical reality influencing the conduct even of those who do not acknowledge them in theory.

But besides being thus based on the fact of our wants, the moral ideals are distinguished from mere imagination from the fact that they are eminently practical, and guide more or less the conduct of all, even of those who do not intellectually value them. Take for instance an 'esprit positif,' one who professes to be guided by *experience* alone; meaning by experience, all that constitutes what is called positive knowledge. Such experience is only an extension of our own individual sensations, as the perception of gravitation is only a more complicated case of the same thing as our sensation of distance. It might be difficult, if we looked closely, to understand how sensation of itself can lead to action at all; even the impulse to relieve ourselves of any pain which we feel, presents something beyond sensation, viz. the rudiments of our active nature. But this is not what I want to speak of. In any case, sensation can suggest no action which goes beyond our *own* relief. Practical conclusions from sensations can go no further, legitimately, than sensation itself, and can never make us leave *ourselves*. It is quite possible indeed, that we may feel by sympathy the troubles of others, and for self-relief may relieve them; in fact, that we may carry out this relief of others, in order to self-relief, into a system: but we have still not got beyond self, and cannot do so. To the man of matter-of-fact or of sense, so far as he is true to himself in being so, disinterestedness is thus a practical chimera exactly in the same manner, and to the same extent, as moral ideals are an intellectual one. And to the extent to which he is disinterested or public-spirited, which in practice he is likely enough to be, he is admitting as a ground of action something exactly of the same nature as that which, intellectually, he will not admit as a reality. The moral ideals of which I have spoken, are what the man of matter-of-fact acts upon, and must act upon: they have therefore the same reality as human life, the reality of applicability, and even necessary application, to action: and if we call that which has this character visionary, I do not know what we are to call real. If this is visionary there has been no greater visionary in modern times than Bentham, with his ideal which we have spoken of. I think, then, that the positivist, in dealing with morals, is intellectually wrong because he is practically right; that what he admits for practice he ought intellectually to admit as real; that it is foolish to pride himself upon keeping to matter-of-fact against others as visionaries, when what he is really doing is only applying his matter-of-fact principles to the details of that which, in the substance or main character of it, is more thoroughly visionary in *him* than it is in others: it is the business of moral philosophy to see if it cannot harmonize practical and intellectual views at least a little more than this.

Allowing their practical reality, Kant disputed their intellectual validity.

This *practical* reality is by some philosophers considered to be the kind of reality specially belonging to what I have called the moral ideals; and if it is inferior in kind, or as reality, to speculative or intellectual reality, it is so far superior to it, that it is a kind of reality actually attainable or appreciable by us, which the true speculative or intellectual reality is only in a very small degree, according to the philosophers I have referred to.

Other grounds for holding the reality of the ideals.

But, further than this, I shall endeavour to shew that moral philosophy, in this its ideal or intuitivist character, is not merely visionary, by remarking a little on the degree to which it is fruitful, on the degree to which it is self-consistent, and on the degree to which the manner in which the mind proceeds in it bears an analogy to the way in which it proceeds intellectually.

They lead on to further truth and attach to themselves subordinate inductive sciences,

Moral philosophy in its ideal character, or the higher portion of aretaics, is not a science, but is an art in the manner which we have seen, or a true philosophy, not in itself inductive, but setting in action, and giving interest to, various sciences which are inductive, and which are therefore capable of all the progress of which physical science is capable. The only progress possible in this higher portion of moral philosophy is greater clearness of view, firmer hold in the mind of the principles it deals with, and happier expression of them. It is idle to suppose that any increase of experience can shew men, more certainly than they have known it from the first[1], that they ought to be public-spirited rather than selfish, just rather than unjust, kind rather than cruel. Yet there is room for consideration in respect of these things which men ought to be: room for a philosophy about them, though not for an inductive science. And there is abundant room for observation and for various methodical lines of consideration, which we may call inductive sciences, in carrying out the particulars of that which moral thought only vaguely suggests in the imperfect outline. If moral philosophy is the art of living as we should, as is best for us, as we were intended to live, as our nature indicates to us, happy with a rightly conceived happiness, or in whatever other way we may express the ideal; and of doing what we can, according to our circumstances, to help others to do the same; then it is clear that to carry out this well may absorb any amount of observation, methodized and generalized, as to what we are, and what we feel, and what we take pleasure in, and what others feel, and much besides: nobody can doubt that with the advance of experience, moral philosophy may progress infinitely in these respects; but its ideals are what they were in the time of Plato, and never can be different.

both eudæmonic and aretaic.

There is an aretaics of observation, to which belongs the observation of dispositions and of character, as to eudæmonics belongs the study of pleasures and of pains. And there are other subsidiary sciences, or inductive branches, of moral philosophy, of which I shall have to speak: but I think that for the present

[1] 'From the first' is rather ambiguous. Lower down the time of Plato is specified as a time in which the moral ideals were the same as at present. This of course is only true of the most general ideals; the author would not have denied the influence of Christianity in modifying the subordinate ideals. See *Exam. of Util. Phil.* p. 293.—Ed.

enough has been said as to the existence, in the ideals of moral philosophy, of such reality as is indicated by fruitfulness.

But do the ideals of moral philosophy point to any *one* course of conduct? and when I say that it is the parent, or mistress, of various subsidiary sciences, are these sciences in harmony with each other?

When the so-called intuitivism of moral philosophy is disliked, it is perhaps with the notion that, however we may form the ideals, and talk of a summum bonum, a summum faciendum, virtue, duty, or any such ideal, we shall be unable, with any satisfactoriness, to *fix* these ideals anywhere, or find any *particular* course of conduct to which they point. We may understand the *notion* of a summum bonum, or of there being a right thing to do, perfectly, and allow that the notion suggests itself to us, perhaps most vividly: but what is the good, we may say, of its doing so, if we cannot find what the summum bonum or the right conduct is; or if we find that our different ideals seem to point to *different* sorts of conduct? We want, we may say, to promote both our own good, and the good of others: but, upon the best consideration we can give, it does not seem to be the same course of conduct which will promote both: are these ideals other than a hopeless puzzle?

They point to one course of conduct.

On these points something has been said already and more will be said hereafter, but for the present I shall stop here, going on in the next chapter with the subject of the analogy between the mental procedure in the case of these ideals and of intellectual perception.

CHAPTER V.[1]

ON THE ANALOGY BETWEEN THE INTELLECTUAL AND THE MORAL IDEALS.

On the dualism of perception. Confusion of the ordinary view which recognizes properties in the subject and in the object apart from each other.

THERE are two views of knowledge, either of which, as it appears to me, we may take, but which we cannot, by any means that I can see, bring together. That there is a dualism in knowledge, a bringing together of two members, subject and object, is commonly understood; but the point in which I differ from most philosophers, is that I do not imagine it possible for us, in one view of knowledge, to conceive *both* of the two members possessing qualities of any kind. This looks abstract, but the thing that I mean is exceedingly simple: suppose we are looking at a prospect: there are undeniably two members of what is going on, ourselves and the prospect. This dualism we cannot get over; we are certain that there is a subject, our perceiving selves (or the perceiving something), and the perceived something, the universe we will call it. But to which side of the dualism belongs all that is intermediate between the perceiving subject and the perceived object, this is to me an insoluble problem. We are composed of bodies, which, as I may roughly but intelligibly express it, are half subjective and half objective, half ourselves and half not ourselves:

[1] On the view of Perception here given compare *Exploratio Philosophica* and Mr Shadworth Hodgson's *Space and Time*, and *Theory of Practice*.—ED.

and philosophers, extending in an unauthorized manner this supposition which is good in its place, have endeavoured to embrace, in a single view of knowledge, properties of the subject and properties of the object—a thing which seems to me not possible. They have spoken of powers (we will say) of the subject meeting or appreciating qualities of the object; but we can never, on any satisfactory grounds, make this distinction. If the subject has powers, possibly all that takes place is in virtue of powers of the subject; the subject, by its powers, converts into an object of knowledge something which, independent of the exercise of these powers upon it, is—we know not what, a mere rude material of knowledge: if on the other hand, the object has qualities, there is no need to suppose powers in the subject; powers in the subject would then, so far as they were exercised, be making the object something different from what it really is. Knowledge is *either* a standing by and gazing, on our part, on a universe with qualities, (in which case we exercise no powers upon it; *it* is the same whether we are gazing upon it or whether we do not exist:) *or* it is a thinking, on our part, in a particular way, which we call our understanding or intellectual nature, about something which has *to us* no other nature or existence except what we thus think about it: in this case the universe exercises no influence upon us except to give occasion to our thought.

Knowledge is either a passive impression by the universe upon us, or it is our active thought constituting the universe to us.

Of the above views both are incomplete: both what we may call 'abstractions[1].' They are each of them a portion of the whole fact as *surd* or insoluble. In the former, in which difference, character, quality, nature, of things is supposed to be in the *object*, truth of knowledge consists in this, that, what impresses itself upon us as this difference, character, &c.

In the one case truth is things impressing themselves according to their proper being, in the other truth is right thinking.

[1] *Exploratio*, p. 2, 83.

is really such, and not a something different from this. The question, How is it that this, or anything, impresses itself upon us at all? is one which in this point of view must not be touched on: we are bystanders, looking on at the drama or phantasmagoria of nature, and must direct our view to that, not to ourselves: if we direct our view to ourselves, there only arises an inextricable confusion; but of course, in the other case, our own nature, that which enables us to be bystanders of this kind, remains a surd or insoluble.

In the latter view, difference, character, quality, nature, of *things* (as we are compelled to say in language, for language in general goes upon the former view), is not in the things, but is difference of our thought about—the things, again we must say, with the same caution as to language as before, for the things, on this view, are not *things* except in virtue of our thinking of them: and perhaps here we have a witness to the occasional Berkeleyanism of language in the derivation of *thing* from *think*. The difference on this view is *suggested*, we are not considered to know how: whether by something in the rude matter, or by some agency entirely different from it: which agency may even supersede the necessity of supposing *any* rude matter.

Truth in this latter view is in the thinking rightly about things: and that which in this view is left surd and insoluble is on the side of the *thing*: it is the *inform* matter, the logical subject of our thought, of which, or perhaps of some unknown agency which we mentally substitute for it or combine with it, we predicate all that makes the difference or quality of things.

The opposition of inductive

Very constantly, however, efforts have been made to analyse our knowledge into two portions, a portion contributed by our mind, and a portion by the object or universe: and when it has been said of anything, that it is intuitive or intuitivist, what has been meant is, that it is something not given us by experience, but something coming in this manner from our mind. It will be seen from what I have said, that *this* kind of distinction between experience and what we will call mental creation or mental addition to experience, is one which I do not recognize.

to intuitive knowledge is a mistake founded on the wrong view of perception.

I do however recognize a very great difference between different kinds of what, according to the view taken, I should call the impressions of the universe upon us or our thoughts about the universe, and it is of this nature.

Every operation of mind appears to me to be, if we look at it from the side of the intellect, intellectual, if we look at it from the side of the universe, sensile. Colours, smells, and tastes, make an impression upon us by means of the passive nerves of feeling through which we communicate with the chemical constitution of bodies: relations of space and force, i.e. figures and distances and different degrees of hardness of bodies, make an impression upon us by means of the active nerves of locomotion and pressure; an impression in fact upon our will: and there is something in bodies besides, which it seems may similarly be described as making an impression upon us, though not by means of any nerves—a simply intellectual impression,—and that is, their unity, reality, *thinghood*, existence. The nature of this, and of other notions connected with it, I cannot here inquire into: but it will be understood that a thing is made a thing, is made what it is, by something more than the fact of its having a particular figure and colour: in our noticing, recognizing, individualizing it, we understand in it something beyond

The varied communication between subject and object may be exhibited, as passive, in a scale of sensation, or, as active, in a scale of intelligence.

anything which we can taste or handle, a λόγος, raison d'être, or however we may describe it. It is in virtue of *this* that we ordinarily notice it: in other words, *this* is what in the highest degree impresses itself upon us.

All that I have described here as sensation or impression might have been described from the opposite point of view as *thought*. Certain feelings of our own, more or less of pleasure and pain, suggest to us something beyond ourselves: we, by our understanding, interpret this something which they suggest into what we then call a coloured body, with a particular form or figure and with a unity, reality, reason, of its own.

The mistaken view of perception shows itself in attributing the higher part of the scale to the subject, and the lower to the object.

It will be seen that in all this I recognize a gradation, what I should call a regular scale of sensation or of intelligence[1]. What I differ from is, the saying that what is in the higher part of this scale is given by the mind, while what is in the lower is given by the object or universe. If colour and figure are in the object, then all the properties of the object, of every kind, abstract as they may be, are in itself, and are not mere thoughts of ours about it: it makes its impression upon us, or makes itself felt by us, with and by means of all its properties alike, abstract and concrete, ideal and material. If the more abstract properties of the object are given to it by us, or are something we think about it, then colour and space also are something which we think about it, except that in using the word *it* our language slips under our feet; for we make it what it is by thus thinking about it: *what* we think about it is something which becomes *it* in virtue of our thinking about it.

I feel no objection to the calling what is in the

[1] See *Exploratio*, ch. vi.

higher part of the scale of sensation or thought *ideas*, in contradistinction to what is in the lower as mere sensations, if only it is understood that *both together* belong either to the mind, *or* to the object: it is probably past our power to determine which.

Corresponding to this perceptional scale there is a moral scale, the higher portion of which is no less real than the lower.

And the moral ideals, in my view, stand to the sensation of pleasure and pain, considered simply and in itself, in the same relation in which perceptions belonging to the higher part of the perceptional scale, or what I have just called ideas, stand to perceptions of the lower part, or what I have just called mere sensations: which are sensations *also* of pleasure and pain, but in which the pleasure or pain is not the thing noticed, but serves only to set the perceptive or interpretative intellect in motion. The moral ideals, as formed or grasped by the mind, are not less real, or more subjective, than the bare sensations of pain or of pleasure.

Illustration from the two views of pain.

Recurring to the instance or example which I took some time since: it appears to me, that the feeling about pain, that it is what should not be inflicted on others (in which feeling the ideal 'should be,' or rightness, comes in with all its force), is one that suggests itself as naturally and necessarily, as that it is a thing to be shrunk from or avoided by ourselves. No doubt, the latter is what is called an instinctive sensation, the former is a highly refined idea, and they belong in this way to different points of a scale: but I see no reason for calling the one imagination, and the other reality. The first again requires a development of thought, it would appear, for its possibility: there is the notion of 'others'; there is the notion, how pain *could* be inflicted upon them, which how could the infant, who nevertheless instinctively shrinks himself from pain, possibly have? I say nothing here about the time at which ideas first come into distinction. Quite independently of this, pain seems to me to be thought of by us, or to impress itself upon us (whichever manner of expression we like to use), in two distinct manners: as what is unpleasant to be borne, and as what should not be inflicted. I look upon *both* of these characters, not *one* only, as constituting what we may call the natural or instinctive *definition* of pain. And as the one is the fruitful axiom from which flows eudæmonics, so is the other one main axiom from which flows aretaics.

I see no reason, then, why we should consider this notion, that we should not inflict pain, a mere imagination, while we consider the unpleasantness of pain a fact.

Truth, the intellectual ideal, takes two forms corresponding to the two views of perception. It is either the 'cogitandum' or the ὄντως ὄν.

To go back now to what was said above as to the double view of knowledge: the intellectual ideal, viz. truth, has correspondingly one or other of two characters: it is either rightness of thought, thinking as we should about what we think of, which is plainly an ideal: or it is, on the other view, things making an impression on us as they are, according to their reality or proper being. This ideal of reality or being, τὸ ὄντως ὄν, as the first to which the term 'idea' was attached, has been written about till one might suppose nothing fresh could be said about it, but with an ever-recurring growth of new terminology it revives and revives again. On the absolute, the relative, and the positive, the principal terms which *now* enter into the discussion, I hope to speak another time[1].

To these ideals are related the sub-ideals, that which is commonly

The two high intellectual ideals thus, or the two notions of truth, are these, the *cogitandum* and the contemplation of *real being:* but truth, so far as it comes actually within our grasp, does so in virtue of

[1] See Appendix at the end of the Volume.

leals, if they may be called such, much lower and earer to us.

believed, that which is practical.

Truth, as we come actually to grasp it, has two haracters, which with slight exaggeration we might escribe thus; that it is that which is generally conidered; that it is that which is practical, or will nswer in practice.

The former sub-ideal flows from the fact that man is by nature social.

What sort of notion of truth we should have, if we vere, any one of us, the solitary being in creation, is ot quite easy to tell. As I have already made this upposition once, and may possibly do the like gain, it may be expedient here to say a word on he nature of such suppositions.

Illustration from imagined case of man in absolute solitude. Use and danger of such imaginations.

The practice of supposing things other than they re, or events to have happened otherwise than s they have happened, is much derided by some, nd condemned by others. The general reason why t has been derided and condemned is from a notion, nore belonging to the last century than this, that magination is a 'forward delusive faculty'[1] which as nothing to do with religion, philosophy, or cience. I hold an opinion exactly the reverse of his, and consider that we can only so far be taken o have intellectual grasp of a thing, a fact, or a equence of facts, as we are able to compare it vith other (imagined) things, facts, or sequences, vhich, consistently with many of its conditions, night have been instead of it. There is, however, ne real impropriety in suppositions of this kind, vhich makes necessary much care in the using them. t is this. We have no business to isolate any one hing in the universe from other things which have elation to it, and to suppose *it* other than it is,

[1] Butler's *Analogy*, I. 1. "As we are accustomed from our youth up o indulge that forward delusive faculty (imagination), ever obtruding eyond its sphere, of some assistance indeed to apprehension, but the uthor of all error," &c.

without making corresponding suppositions (and where shall we stop?) as to *them*. If we do so, we are not simply making a *different* state of things from that which is, but we are making an *incongruous* state of things. Still, if we keep this fact in mind, and correct in our imagination accordingly, the making the suppositions is not likely to deceive us, and is often very useful.

Man cannot help thinking socially.

What I have meant here to convey will, I think, be at once seen in reference to this particular supposition, that we were, any one of us, the solitary being in creation. That each one of us is a social being means a great deal more than that he is an individual of the genus man, living with other individuals of the same genus, talking with them, and pursuing common purposes with them. He is social to the bottom of his mind, and each one of his faculties is different from that which it would be, if it was not part of his nature to associate himself. He *thinks* socially, and cannot think otherwise: and so far as, by a solitude inappropriate to his nature, he is thrown out of actual companionship, he is like a man deprived of his legs or anything which *ought* to be his: there is feeling of want, painful effort, and more or less supply of what is wanted from some other source in the system.

And ideal truth becomes fixed for each, from its being the way of thinking in which all men unite (1st sub-ideal).

One part of our intellectual sociality is, that so far as we think what we think, in our own view, truly, we think it what I will call *generally*: I mean, we think it not as for our own intelligence only, but as for a supposed *general* intelligence: we consider that we are in sympathy or communion of thought with all who think on the same subject, so far as we and they come up to the ideal truth. And we verify our thought accordingly. That is, the ideal truth becomes fixed or actualized to us, in one way, by its being the way of thinking in which we and others unite. Or, to use other words, we form a lower and nearer ideal of truth, in considering it the communion of intelligences.

The 2nd sub-ideal applicability to action. A false sub-ideal the latest belief.

The other sub-ideal of truth which I mentioned is its applicability to action, its holding good for every variety of our sensive capacity. Of this, and of the connexion of our active and intellectual natures, I hope to speak again, and also of another falsely assigned sub-ideal, test, or character of truth, viz. that, viewing the course of the thought of collective man, his latest judgments are, at any given moment, to be considered as truer than his earlier ones.

I shall now try to observe what is the state of our mind in regard to these ideals of truth, and shall compare this with our state of mind in reference to the *moral* ideals.

The sub-ideals practically guide our thought, but they would lose their power and interest if it were not for our belief in the higher ideals.

All advance, or attempt at advance, in knowledge is a search after the *true*, and a search in which we are very imperfectly successful. With regard to what we come to know, we can give but a very imperfect account of what we mean by saying that it is true, and why we are certain of it. If some Berkeley asks us how we know that any external thing at all exists, we can only answer in fact, that everybody says so, and that we are able to act in it: it *meets*, so to speak, fits or resists, all our senses and our will, and against any individual delusion on our part we appeal to the experience of all. But all this is much below that ideal of truth which we feel within us, or conceive, and cannot help seeking for and trying to realize. The common agreement only means that we are organized alike, and if one is deceived, it is natural enough that all should be: the answering to action is nothing more than the fact, that our organization, one part of the universe, fits what we call external things, which is another part. All this is very different from seeing things as they are, from thinking as we should.

And yet it is the fact, that unless we had and still kept in our mind the notion that these latter things were possible, we should not strive after knowledge at all. At every step of the process, we seem to see something more than we did, to think more properly. If any person could really persuade us that knowledge was nothing more than a thinking as other people did, and a relation of what we call external things to our senses and our faculties, curiosity, the spring of all our intelligence, would vanish, and knowledge itself would soon disappear. If the notion that there is such a thing as truth is a delusion, it is a delusion to which one of the most important parts of our nature owes its importance.

Meaning and importance of such belief.

I shall call the manner in which we have a notion of truth and refuse to let it go *believing* in truth: it might be called, if we liked to call it so, a believing in the universe: it is that belief that there is something to be known, which must accompany, more or less, every act of knowledge, or else I do not see how we could *try* to know anything: it is the thing which seems to me to difference us, intellectually, from the lower animals, who learn things habitually as we do, who notice things connected with their wants and pleasures as we do, who perceive things as we do, and must so far be said to reason as we do, that there can be no perception without some sort of reasoning; but who have no impulse to knowledge as knowledge, or in other words, no notion in them of there being a truth of things, attainable (apparently) and worth attaining. Not to dwell too long on this, which, as it is to me a matter of prime importance, will at various times present itself, the ideal of truth appears to us, as I have said, in a double form: as thinking rightly or as we should: and as seeing things as they are. And one part of our belief in truth consists in this, in the belief that these two aspects of the ideal represent but one thing: though most philosophers have looked chiefly at the one or the other of them.

Those philosophers who have looked at the ideal of truth most in the former aspect have generally expressed their view of it more or less in religious language. So far as we suppose the existence of One Allknowing Intelligence, there is no doubt that one character of ideal truth must be conformity to Its thoughts: but still even this, in one sense, cannot exhaust the ideal. Not even such an intelligence can *make* truth truth: its being an intelligence implies that it *perceives* truth, and there must be truth for it to perceive coæval with it.

This first ideal of truth however does not necessarily imply more than that there is a course before our minds, which, for whatever reason, is the correct and proper one: it implies, we may say, that truth is what the mind, as a mind, exists for.

The second aspect of the ideal truth, that it is the sight of what is, is the source of the ancient idealist philosophy: I shall say no more of it, but shall speak of the comparison of the *moral* ideals with these intellectual ones.

The moral ideal of rightness corresponds to and includes the intellectual ideal of the cogitandum.

The two great moral ideals, that of rightness and that of good, are analogous to these two aspects of the highest ideal of truth. The relation however is more and closer than that of analogy: the moral ideal in each case is the higher, and, more or less, includes in it the intellectual.

The first moral ideal, that of rightness, is the most genuine, and therefore, in a sense, the most vague, ideal, which can suggest itself to us. In the doing as we should, or living as we should, thinking as we should comes in of course as a part. And therefore in the ancient ethics or aretaics, the right action of the intellectual portion of our nature took its place as a portion of virtue or excellence.

It is also suggested by it.

But as the moral ideal thus includes the intellectual, so, on the other hand, the intellectual suggests the moral: the rightness which governs action is an extension or wider application of the truth which governs thought. Many philosophers, whom we may call the Intellectual Moralists, have followed out this view very extensively.

The moral ideal of Good corresponds to and includes the intellectual ideal of Real Being.

The relation of the second moral ideal, that of good, to the intellectual ideal of real being, was a matter for very early, and very beautiful, philosophic speculation. That good is the *reason* of being, that which, in the contemplation of being, we look for, that to which we look *through* being, that which being suggests to us, and by the sight of which only, so far as we can attain to see it, we can in any way understand or explain being—all this, in this high region, is of course abstruse, and requires a Plato to exhibit it to us. But it is a principle which does not belong to this high region alone, but in a certain degree to all speculation. It is a principle which has generated much truth, and the misappreciation of which has generated much error, in the treatment of Natural Theology and of Final Causes.

Similarly the moral sub-ideals correspond to the intellectual sub-ideals.

The sub-ideals of morality which I described are more or less analogous to the sub-ideals of truth. The former are *what we can find out* about right or good action, in the same way as the others are what we can find out about truth. If we consider rightness, or good, and truth to be the main ideals, the others, the subordinate notions which I have menoned, may be considered conditions or characters of ıese.

And the having the moral ideal of rightness or ›od is a belief in rightness or good in the same way the having the ideal of truth is a belief in truth. is a belief, in other words, that there is a kind of tion which is proper for us and that good is possible r us, and a belief also that both these aspects of the eal point to the same kind of action. Without this oral belief, I see no more how we could act, than I e how, without the intellectual belief, we could ink.

And the relation between the moral ideals and sub-ideals corresponds to that between the intellectual ideals and sub-ideals.

What I said as to the relation of the higher eals to the lower, appears to me to apply in the me manner to the moral, as to the intellectual eals. The attempt to engage men the better in *licific* action (so I will call it) by trying to persade them that there was nothing *right* for them, ıd that the supposition of there being such a ing as rightness was only a mental delusion, a istake for, and a call to, *this*, seems to me closely to semble the trying to stimulate their curiosity or ve of truth by telling them that all that truth eant was, generally received opinion among men.

CHAPTER VI.

ON MORAL VALUE.

Recapitulation.

IT will be remembered that I described[1] moral philosophy as a kind of thought, not exactly of the nature of science itself, but setting in action, or overseeing, various kinds of thought, each of which might be styled a science, and be treated in a systematic inductive manner.

It is not precisely the same view, but one not inconsistent with the above, and in some respects simpler, to consider moral philosophy as made up, in the main, of two sciences, one of which, the more important, is only in a very subordinate degree a positive science, partaking largely of an ideal character. This is another view which I gave, and I called the two sciences Aretaics and Eudæmonics. There is a certain degree of looseness in the use which I am making of both these terms: but I hope to go into the meaning of them, especially that of the last, more accurately.

Utility is a sub-ideal related to the summum bonum.

I have also already, to a certain degree, spoken of the meaning of *usefulness* as applied to action, or of 'the useful' as an ideal[2]. The useful, as I said, has its reference, not to pleasure, but to *good*, *bonum*, the *desirable*: the ideal of 'the useful' is a subordinate ideal to that of the good or desirable, and the action which the term designates is action which serves as a means to this latter. For any

[1] p. 51. [2] p. 34.

thing with which we are just now concerned, this ideal of the good or desirable might resolve itself into that of the pleasurable: that we will see at a future time: for the present the word 'eudæmonics,' as I said just now, is vague to us, and may, or may not, mean more than an experiential science of pleasure. The same in regard to the word 'happiness:' at present it might mean to us either a state, i. e. a fact, accompanied or not by the feeling of the fact; or it might mean a feeling, pleasure, without any account being taken of states, or of facts beyond the feeling. But whatever the ideally good or desirable may be further resolved into, it is to that ideal unresolved that all the significance of the term 'useful' applies: I must beg that this may be for the present kept in mind.

Difficulty introduced in regard to this and the cognate ideal by the distinction between *own* good and *others'* good.

In speaking also of the moral ideals, I mentioned the result produced, in regard of them, by the introduction of the consideration whether the agent were himself the sentient object of his own action, or whether there were other sentient objects of it beyond himself. This divides the second great ideal together with its subordinate ideals into two parts; and also introduces doubt, as to one of the parts in each case, what is its nature, how far it is a moral ideal at all.

According to utilitarianism actions possess value only when they effect some independent good result.

The question which I propose to consider in this chapter is the value of actions in the abstract, that which determines in regard of them, in the last resort, whether they are worth doing or not. This value of them is the ultimate reason for them. Taking the word 'utilitarianism' not in a technical and sectarian sense, but to represent what its derivation would suggest, the utilitarian view of morals may be said to be that which considers actions to be of value in the universe, in the last resort, solely in respect of their usefulness, i.e. productiveness of good, however the meaning of the word 'good' may be afterwards determined. Unless there is produced by them something which independently of them may be described as good or desirable, the universe, it is said, is no better for them; they might as well not have being; they are wasted. When I say 'is produced,' I speak broadly for greater intelligibility, but I mean to include in the view any variety of modification or qualification of it: if the actions which produce the above are valuable in the *first* instance, then a great variety of actions beyond these will be valuable in the *second* instance, as tending to produce it, or being of a kind which generally produce it, or for many other reasons.

This notion in its general form implies exclusive attention to the second ideal without regard to the first.

Utilitarianism, in this broad sense, will commend itself to many, and to many will seem even self-evident. It may almost seem to be involved in the views of all those philosophers who sought for a 'summum bonum' as the chief thing in morals, implying that all actions would be good in consideration of their tendency to that, i.e. of their usefulness.

> 'What's the worth of any thing,
> But just so much as it will bring?'

An action, it is said, is for results; it is reasonable so far as the results of it are looked to: by its results we must ultimately try it.

There is truth in this notion, not only in its most general form, which is simply treating what I called the second ideal as the first and most important; but also in its less general and nearer forms, as when we speak of happiness more or less determined by pleasure; still the truth contained in it is not the whole truth.

Consideration of the question

Let us imagine what would be our state of feeling as to this value if it were not possible, in the universe, for any one being to promote the happiness of others. It is evident that, on this supposition, the value of actions, so far as it depends on the good produced or likely to be produced by them, is the same as before: there may be as much good produced, each producing it for himself; and then it may be that the valuableness of actions varies as their usefulness. But we surely must feel that the view which, as it is, we take of the ultimate valuableness of actions, is something more complicated than this: we need something beyond simple productiveness of happiness when, going back as far as we can in thought, we reflect upon the reason which there exists for doing any action.

on the supposition (1) that each individual could promote his own happiness but not that of others:

Let us now change the supposition.

The most important point for our consideration in respect of happiness is that it is a thing which may be foregone as well as a thing which may be promoted; and it is in the mutual play of these four considerations, viz. the promotion of happiness, the foregoing of happiness, thought of ourselves, thought of others, that the circumstances of moral action lie.

[Elements of the question stated.]

If we supposed that the foregoing of happiness was possible but that its promotion was impossible, what would have to be said in regard to such foregoing of happiness? would it have value? would there be reason for it in the universe?

(2) that the promotion of happiness was impossible, but that each might, if he pleased, forego his own happiness.

As we found that, in the case of action merely promotive of happiness, there might be value (if we choose to call it so), but there would not be what we consider *moral* value, so I think we shall consider that action involving readiness to forego happiness would have, in the absence of purpose for it, only an imperfect moral value; but that it has a character which, on supposition of a useful purpose, *becomes* moral value, and that this character is the same as that which is *wanting* in order to give moral value to actions simply promotive of happiness.

We may either say that there are two kinds of value of actions—aretaic and eudæmonic—or that two elements are needed for an action to possess true moral value.

It is not quite easy to conceive this, nor quite easy to express it: but I think it may best, perhaps, be put thus; We may either consider that the moral value of action in the universe, the full reason why one is better, worth more, in the universe than another, must be sought in both the two first ideals combined;—in other words, that a good action is one promotive of happiness with cost or effort on the part of the doer:—or we may consider that there are two kinds of value, one corresponding to each of those two ideals; the value of usefulness or result, and the value of worthiness of feeling (so we will at present call it) which has gone towards the result or been expended for it. This latter is the manner of speaking which I shall the more commonly use.

The former of these is the eudæmonic worth of actions; the latter their aretaic worth, their merit, as we commonly call it.

There are various ways in which these two kinds of worth may be considered.

The idea of good applies to our active as well as to our sentient nature.

The attribution of worth or value of the latter kind to actions, i.e. of value independent of result, is connected in my mind with what I have said before, of the independent importance of the active part of our nature. I do not look upon action in the universe as a necessary evil, arising only from the existence of want or from the imperfection of the enjoyed happiness: the power and the want in the universe fit each other, and the one is employed for the relief of the other; but the action, i.e. the employment of the power, is good in itself, as well as in its result for the supply of the want which makes its usefulness: thus there exists a value besides the value of usefulness, the value, namely, which I have described.

Action for our ideal work implies the subordination of our individual happiness.

The first ideal, the *faciendum*, belongs to the ctive part of our nature, and so, as we see, does this alue. And the connection of this value with the ctive part of our nature is concerned with its relaion to self, in the following way. We are agents in he universe of what is to be done there, each with ur amount of power, and of course if this power has o be absorbed in ourselves, and to go all to our wn happiness, there is none left for the independent aciendum, our work or duty, whatever it may be. This is spoken, no doubt, very generally, and in pplication there will come many things to be conidered; but still, really, though very generally, ction for our ideal work or duty is the foregoing of appiness, however it may be accompanied with, or roduce, other happiness: there is no free action, I vill call it, or real action, without the readiness to orego happiness and the disposition to transcend elf. We are each a machine of which a certain porion must go to internal work and sustentation, but ur value depends upon what there is disposable beond this.

Self-sacrifice must be added to usefulness to make true moral value.

We might, conceivably, devote all our time and ll our power to the promoting our own happiness nd good: in this point of view, whatever is not deoted to it (being applied to our neighbour's happiess) is so much taken from it, i.e. is self-sacrifice. But it is exactly *this* action, the action which is, in a mall or a great degree, a withdrawing of our power rom effort after our own happiness to effort after loing 'what we should,' which, as we have seen, has retaic value, or merit. It *should* be useful: we form, nd with reason, the second ideal for our action as vell as the first: if it is useful, it has the double alue: if it fails of being useful, or, through error of iew, goes wrong in this particular, it may have its own value, and the question whether it has depends on other considerations than those of usefulness.

Such, then, is the nature of aretaic value, or merit, in reference to our active nature: I will now put it in another view.

True moral value only exists where there are conflicting interests.

When we introduced, in speaking of the ideals, the consideration of the agent and the object of the action being possibly different, we introduced the subject of what I may call the different interests of men. And, in reality, morality does not begin to exist till this is introduced. Usefulness of action, without this, would have, as we have seen, a value, but a value which we could not call *moral*, and the faciendum or ideal work would correspondingly be altered. The subject of moral philosophy is the conflicting interests of different sentient beings: I use the word *interests* with intentional vagueness: their conflicting *happiness* would do as well.

Sectarian utilitarianism underrates the importance of the conflict of interests.

Utilitarianism, when it claims to be the whole of moral philosophy, takes the value of actions in their *results* as the one thing of importance, on which everything else depends, and from which everything else flows. Considering then moral philosophy fully begun and all its outline drawn, it proceeds onward, taking quietly into itself various other considerations, such as this of the conflicting interests of men, as if they were matters comparatively unimportant: it treats, perhaps, fully of them, but considers them, in reference to the whole, comparatively subordinate.

Anti-utilitarian systems treat that which utilitarianism makes its basis (say, the value of happiness) as something in a manner pre-moral, something with the consideration of which morality is not as yet properly begun. It is only with the introduction of the possible conflict of interests or happiness that the real difficulties and the real importance of moral philosophy commence: utilitarianism expatiates in an easier field, and is not sufficiently ready to face these.

The interest of human action does not arise from its being, as the utilitarian would persuade us, simply action for happiness, but in its being what I may call a mutual action of moral beings for each other's happiness, and that under strong temptation for them to act each one for his own. It is, in a manner, an interchange of happiness: only an interchange not, like commercial interchanges, with a desire of getting as much as possible for oneself.

True moral value implies high estimate of others' happiness combined with low estimate of our own.

And here it is that there comes in that double character of value in action which I have mentioned. It is evident that this mutual action, this interchange, could not go on under the influence of the utilitarian motive, simple value for happiness as happiness. What is wanted, and what exists, is the concurrence, each coming in its proper place, of value for happiness, or high estimation of it, and non-value for happiness, or low estimation of it. The man who risks his own life to save that of another would never be induced to do this by any increase of his care for, or high valuation of, happiness or life, if his thought for his own life increased *pari passu* with his thought for the life of the other. But there concur in him the two feelings of quite different natures: the rising above the love of life, so far as he himself is concerned, and a very high estimation of the value of life, so far as the other is concerned.

Hence to the utilitarian principle of value for happiness has to be added the counter-principle of non-value for happiness, and each is to have its place.

Such then is the nature of aretaic value or merit, in relation to the conflict of interests: I will now speak of it again in another view.

Meaning of the phrase 'elevation of character' as descriptive of aretaic value.

The character of actions which gives them their aretaic value or merit is one which is known by a variety of terms all more or less metaphorical, as moral terms must be, and also more or less misleading. We form, in respect of action of this kind, an ideal very similar to the first ideal or the faciendum (rightness), and in many respects as vague, but not quite the same.

The constant metaphor used in reference to action of this kind is 'high,' with its opposite 'low.' Many particulars of the notion of height seem to have pertinence in this comparison, though it is not quite easy to tell which suggested it in the first instance. Action of this kind is action very frequently with effort, such as to rise up involves: it is action looked up to by men, and giving to the agent a feeling of self-approbation possibly approaching to pride, raising him, as we describe it, in his own and others' estimation: it is action belonging to a high place in any supposed scale of being or character: and much beside which might be said. Anyhow, high-mindedness, elevation of character, and other such expressions, seem generally accepted as good descriptions of it.

I have spoken of it as a disposition to rise above the thought of self, a readiness to forego happiness. But it is much more various than this would imply. And it enters very largely, as we shall find, into the notion of happiness itself. It enters also into all the notion of morality as ideal. In another chapter I hope to treat of it as itself a distinct moral ideal, though approaching to the first, the faciendum.

Recapitulation. Generosity and usefulness

What this chapter has been to establish is simply this: were there no use possibly to be made of it, no happiness which could possibly be promoted, generous and self-forgetting action would be worth having in the universe, and the universe would be the richer and better for it.

are independent qualities of action which must co-exist if an action is to have complete moral value.

In other words: there are two separate and independent good qualities in regard of action, its generosity (so to call it) and its usefulness: these *ought* to go together, for generous action which subserves no purpose is so far thrown away: on the other hand useful action, which is useful to ourselves alone, is not thrown away indeed in the universe, but is not matter for moral notice.

Man's reason enables him to transcend self. If he confines his action to self he does not act up to his nature.

This latter point will perhaps be best understood thus. Man, so long as he confines the usefulness of his action to himself alone, while passing beyond the range, or above the level, of the inferior animals in respect of his manner of action and of the powers which, in virtue of his intellect, he brings to bear on it, does not pass beyond their range, or above their level, in respect of the object and purpose of action, confining himself deliberately to that which *they* are prevented by their nature from transcending, namely self and particular pleasure. But actions of this kind do not really come into consideration when we use the word 'action' in a moral point of view. There is among the inferior animals much of affection towards each other and sometimes towards men, and various things of the same nature as those which morally concern us in man: but we do not write about the morality of the animals, or, if we did so, it would be with quite a different view from that which we take of human morality, for this reason: that they cannot rise above self. Their apparent want of reflective and generalizing power prevents them from forming the general notion of usefulness, and they act, under the impulse of nature, each for his own utility only. There are qualifications to this, which I shall notice: but it represents the general fact. Man rises above them through the wide range and great force of his intelligence, and through the power which he possesses of extending as widely the purposes and objects of his action: in other words, of transcending self. If he does not do this, he is false, in a manner, to his moral nature: he employs powers indefinitely higher than those of the animals for purposes no higher: this is a sort of monstrosity.

The whole of aretaics belongs to Moral Philosophy, but only that part of eudæmonics which regards our relations towards others.

To put this in another light. The principal of the two sciences which I have described as making up moral philosophy is 'aretaics.' The whole science of aretaics belongs to moral philosophy, whereas only a *portion* of eudæmonics does: the remaining portion of this latter, so far as it exists or has been thought of, being economics, prudentials, or to be designated in various other ways. This might be otherwise expressed by saying that 'aretaics' is moral philosophy, and eudæmonics a distinct science, partly coming into consideration in it. Which way we express this does not much matter. Usefulness therefore, the matter of eudæmonics, only comes into moral consideration as regards a *portion* of it: the doing a thing because we should do it, the matter of aretaics, comes under moral consideration *universally*, even though it should happen that the thing thus done was not useful to anybody.

'The morality of consequences' is an ambiguous expression. It may be either public-spirited or selfish.

Considering all this complication of view, it is not wonderful that there has been much difficult controversy about what is called 'the morality of consequences.'

Speaking shortly, action is virtuous or ideally right which is done for the happiness of others or the public good, and done because we conceive such action to be the action which we should do, not because we conceive it to be the action which will be most for our own happiness, though constantly with the concomitant feeling (or as I have expressed it, faith and trust) that it will be so.

'The morality of consequences' is therefore a misleading expression, tending to the confusion together, in our view, of different sorts of wrong morality. It is true indeed that the supporters of these wrong views have as great a disposition to make this confusion for themselves, as their opponents have to make it for them. What I will call true or simple utilitarianism, or the morality of general benevolence, has been confused with Epicureanism (or other forms of selfish morality) by the opponents of both, in order to involve the former in the odium supposed to attach to the latter, and by the supporters of both, in order to claim for the former the character of a matter of positive science, experience, observation, which attaches in their view to the latter[1].

If the former, it is perfectly consistent with Independent or intuitive morality.

It is an erroneous view of morals to consider that because we do an action for the happiness of others, or, which is the same thing, conceive that its usefulness is a proper and sufficient reason for our doing it, therefore, we can have no feeling that we do it because this is the sort of action which we *ought* to do, or, which is the same thing, that there is *reason* why one sort of action (in this case it is useful action) should be preferred to other sorts, so that not only, in doing this useful action, we are right, but if we did other action instead, we should be wrong. There is no kind of *necessary* contradiction between the morality of consequences (if by it we understand simple utilitarianism or the morality of benevolence) and even the highest and most intuitive doctrine of an absolute distinction between right and wrong. In fact, for a true morality, we want the doctrine of conse-

[1] Cf. *Exam. of Util. Phil.*, chapters I., XV., XVII.

quences, considered in this light, to aid us against arbitrary distinctions between right and wrong; or, which is the same thing, against *another* doctrine of consequences. When people will deprive us of our ideal in the one direction, we must seek it in the other. Paley tells us, in effect, that virtue is doing the will of God, not as His will or from regard to Him, but because He will punish or reward us. Our feelings revolt against this description of virtue and human motive: then, when we are told that God's will is the happiness of all, we ask why it may not be our will too? why, if He (with reverence be it spoken) is allowed the free morality of consequences, that is, the independent desire of others' happiness, we may not be so also? why we *must be* slaves, *must be* selfish?

The error of Dependent morality is in its denial of *Right* meaning anything more than *Useful.*

The reason why the view of morals which I have described in the first sentence of the above paragraph is erroneous, has been made plain, I hope, in what I said some time since, and in the example which I have given of Bentham. The error of what has been called 'Dependent' morality, from this point of view, does not consist in the assertion, to whatever extent, of the importance of looking to the useful results of our actions, but in the assertion that the doing this must exclude the notion of there being one kind of action (whatever it is) which we ought to do and choose in preference to others. Supposing useful action to be the right and proper action, still in calling it right and proper we add something to the notion of its being useful; and it is the assertion of this which constitutes, from this point of view, 'Independent' morality, so far as Independent morality is the true.

The selfish morality of conse-

The morality of consequences, in so far as we mean by the term a system of morality which looks at all our action from the point of view of its probable consequences to *ourselves*, is something entirely different. If we use the term 'dependent' in reference to anything on this system which is real morality, we should call this selfish morality 'doubly dependent,' or morality with two steps of dependence. We do what is right because it is generally useful, and we do what is generally useful because it is our private interest to do so. There is in this denied, not only an independent sense of, or care for, right, but also an independent (*i.e.* self-transcending or unselfish) regard for utility.

quences is doubly dependent.

But on this I have for the present said enough.

CHAPTER VII.

DUTY.

I AM going to consider now an aspect of the first ideal which has not as yet distinctly come before us. And I will begin by saying a few words on the relation of this first ideal, the faciendum, to the second, the desirable, or supreme good.

The 2nd ideal is subordinate to the 1st, not vice versa.

Though the possibility of the existence of good or happiness may be a necessary precondition of right action, and the second ideal might thus, abstractly considered, be prior to the first, yet the first would still be the higher ideal, for we might possibly consider the second as subordinate to it, whereas we cannot do the opposite. I mean by this simply: there may be a good or happiness which we *ought* to desire, rather than another: here the second ideal comes under the first; but the first cannot come under the second. If we say that among different things which we ought to do, one is *better* for us than another (on any other ground than as being more what we *ought* to do), we are clearly descending from a higher to a lower ground, and introducing considerations which have no business to come in. The same appears in this way: we may be certain that anything which we ought to do is desirable for us; but we have no business to say, that because a thing is desirable for us, therefore it is what we ought to do. This last consideration is of great importance, as we shall in various ways find.

It will be at once seen that between an ideal work to be done (or the first ideal), and an ideal happiness (say) to be gained (or the second ideal), there is a great difference in *this* respect, viz. that as to the second anyhow, we are free agents. If there is a happiness possible for us, and we make no effort to gain it, and therefore do not gain it, it is our own loss, and that is all that is to be said. The conduct which would have led to this happiness may be described, if we like to describe it so, as our proper or appropriate action, or the action fit for us or belonging to us, as what we were intended for when we were created, or in various other such ways, rightly or wrongly: but still, if it was in view of our own happiness only that we were to strive towards this ideal, folly is all that we can have been guilty of, or can be blamed for in neglecting it. In view of this ideal, we are in all respects free.

We are free as regards the 2nd ideal.

Still it is plain that the more ideal we make it, the more, that is, we mean by it 'something which is good for us' rather than a distinctly conceivable happiness, the more do we bring it near the first ideal. But they can never, as ideals, coincide. There can be no obligation upon us to choose, when what is chosen is chosen simply as our own good. Our own interests, as such, are our own concern, and nobody else's.

How do we stand, as to freedom of this kind, in reference to the first ideal—what we should or ought to do?

We are bound as regards the 1st ideal, though the sense of obligation varies with different persons and in respect to different actions.

The answer to this question must virtually involve an account, in the higher regions of thought, of that which is meant by the term 'moral obligation.'

I believe that the ideal is formed in a very different way by different persons, in a manner varying indeed from all but perfect freedom to entire want of freedom in our action. At a future time we may see how this difference comes about. At present we will see if there is any general statement which can be made about it.

We may say of anything which suggests itself to us as the thing which ought to be done, I choose to do this, I do it because I like it: and in this felt freedom of choice may lie a great part of the merit and nobleness: but still there is a call to us in a different tone from that in which we are called to act for our own happiness, a call the not listening to which is a different kind of thing from the not listening to the call to labour for our own happiness, which latter we are free to do, if we are willing to dispense with the happiness.

On the other hand, we may say of a thing suggesting itself as above, I feel I *must* do it, I feel I have no choice: and so difficult is it to get at the bottom of our minds in this, their richest and noblest part, that sometimes, just where there is the most evident, and the most thoroughly felt, freedom of choice, we have most the feeling that we must do the thing, that the call upon us cannot be resisted. Where we are most our own masters, we are more energetic masters of ourselves than anything could be to us.

Every one, it is probable, more or less, according to the nature of the action, feels to have a different degree of freedom along the scale I mentioned above, and will use different language: it is noble, worthy, meritorious, to risk one's life for another, it is proper to give to the poor, it is incumbent on us to refrain from stealing; but though each thus feels along the scale, the amount of freedom or non-freedom felt by each will be widely different.

Roughly, it may be said, that the risking our life or another is a thing as to which we are free, that he refraining from stealing is a thing as to which ve are not free: though this only corresponds very oarsely, it is probable, to what people actually feel. 3ut of this more another time.

Virtue has reference to the whole of the 1st ideal, duty to the more binding part of it.

To the extent to which we feel ourselves, as ,bove, not free, the first ideal takes to us the form f an ideal law or rule, or, as it is commonly called, *luty*. On account of the division of action in the nanner which I have mentioned just above, it is ometimes considered that 'duty' is a term less extensively applicable to good action than 'virtue' is: it s virtuous to do our duty, and not to stop there, but o go on doing good beyond it. This language, as I ıave just said, is only roughly significant: I hope to ınalyze a little more fully both the terms and the eelings in our mind which they indicate.

The relation to each other of the notions 'duty' ınd 'virtue' may be exhibited in another manner in ome respects more accurate and important than this onsideration of virtue as duty-doing and something nore.

Four characteristics of duty considered as ideal law.

Duty being an ideal *law*, may be said to have our main characteristics attaching to it under this ıspect: (1) it is conceived as distinct and explicit; 2) it takes cognizance, not, for merit, of any risings ,bove it, but only, for demerit, of fallings below it. We may fail, that is, in our duty, but we cannot do nore than our duty; so far as we do so, we leave the ıotion of duty and must use some other language. Thus while virtue is a scale rising indefinitely upvards, duty is the top of a scale descending downvards. The science of duty is the science of offences ıgainst it. Again, duty is more or less, ideally at east, personal in two senses: it involves (3) the giving up of our own interest to that of another, and (4) the consideration of a third party with an enforcing power. When, however, we consider these characteristics, all taken from law, as belonging to duty, it is with qualification of the following kind. Duty is not a different thing from virtue, it is another aspect of the same ideal, the faciendum or rightness. At the same time, for certain portions of good action, the notion duty is the more applicable notion: for certain portions, the notion virtue. It is our duty not to steal, and it is virtuous, but we should hardly think of calling it so: it is virtuous to devote our lives to philanthropy without thought of self-advancement: the notion of duty would not here be so applicable. But again: there are cases in which the notions of duty and virtue are both applicable, each in its own special way. Take *gratitude:* the word 'duty' belongs to it, because special occasion has been given for it by the person who has benefited us; we are not free: the word 'virtue' belongs to it, because the manner of repayment is indefinite, and we may carry it out to any extent: it is not something which can only be offended against, but something which we may indulge in and carry out as we please.

Duty is virtue capable of precise statement as to the object and the thing to be done.

I have given these examples to illustrate the nature of the exactness, definiteness, particularity, by which the notion duty, in a great degree applicable to the same conduct as that to which the notion virtue is, is yet, as a notion, differenced from it. With such qualification as the above, duty may be considered to be virtue to the extent to which virtue can be precisely fixed for us, both as regards the thing to be done, and the party to whom it is to be done.

I will anticipate for a moment an after-matter of

consideration, to this extent: it will be said that the notion of duty here given is exceedingly complicated, that this is clearly no case of an ideal naturally formed by people for themselves, but a complicated notion produced in them, it may be, afterwards by drilling and education; an imaginative application to their feeling and individual conduct of the outward or general law under which they find themselves. On the subject of notions or feelings caused in us by education, I hope to speak afterwards more generally. But I would wish it to be observed here that this notion, and many others like it, though taking many words and a long time to describe, are not in reality complicated. This simplicity in fact, with complicatedness in description, belongs to much of philosophy of every kind. Good philosophy, of whatever description, is something not far off from our mind: it relates constantly to portions of our consciousness which from their apparent simplicity and triviality we think not worthy of notice: and then when the philosopher laboriously attempts to put this into words, it looks to us like something very complicated and a long way off, and we puzzle ourselves to understand it as if it were some foreign language or an abstruse mathematical theorem. This is very likely neither our fault nor that of the philosopher, but simply a fact. It is very possible that, even to represent distinctly to ourselves the things most intimate to our consciousness, we must go this long way about. And when there has to be understanding between two minds, and we are being helped or guided in the doing this, such apparent complication or circuitousness becomes still more necessary. After all, when we come to understand the thing it seems ridiculously simple, and we despise it. But the folly consists in this last.

Is not this too complicated a notion to be a natural ideal?

Simple as it is, we very likely could not have come to separate it and see it distinctly except by some such circuitous process.

The nature of duty illustrated from the nature of Law.

To return now to the consideration of duty under its aspect of ideal law. Law is the determination of the mutual conduct of a number of agents with conflicting interests (by some sufficient power, possessing also authority so to determine it), in view of the advantage of each and of all.

The true definition of law involves four views which have been taken of it.

I have given this long and particular definition of law in order to bring into one line of thought the very various views which have been taken of it.

All conduct is individual. And all conduct, so far as determined by law, is intended to be useful, *i.e.* for some advantage of somebody. Now if, in the above definition, we leave out the centre portion, that is, the consideration by whom the law is made or enforced,—or rather, for we cannot really 'leave out' any portion, if we turn our special attention to the first and the last portion, and consider the centre portion as involved in these,—we get the first of the great views which have been taken of the general nature of law.

Greek view (1). Determination of individual action by mutual agreement of all, for the common advantage.

This is in the main the old Greek notion of law, viz. that it was a mutual agreement of all, by which the action of each was more or less regulated for the common advantage; such agreement being enforced upon each by the power of the whole; but the idea of enforcement, coming less prominently forward since each individual is regarded as a co-maker of the law, a co-percipient and recipient of its advantages, and a co-enforcer of it.

In reality, this describes, to a certain extent, all law, and is a very noble view of it. In all cases of law, the physical power is with the mass of people subjected to it, and it is by their passive consent (so to call it) and more or less of cooperation, that the law is law.

Without however going further in this, I will describe this view of law thus: that it is the common reason ruling, for the common advantage, the conduct of individuals to each other.

If now, instead of the above view, we unite with the first clause of the above definition that portion of the second, or middle one, which has reference to authority, we get the second view of law, which I will call the Roman. I must again call to mind that in each case the other part of the definition is not omitted, but only retires into the background.

Roman view (2). Determination of individual action by submission to rightful authority.

The Roman notion is that of subordination of individuals, not to the community as such, but to the *authority* in and over the community, whatever that may be. By 'authority' I mean power over others, with the supposition of reason existing why there should be such power; and I say 'in and over,' because the community is considered in this view to be a community in virtue of a superior authority regulating its arrangements.

This is the Roman ideal notion of *jus*, which has been followed by a large number of moral writers.

I will briefly describe it thus: that it is the supposition of the same power, which makes individuals what, in a community, they are, determining also their mutual action: power of this nature is authority, because we see reasons why the action of the individuals should be determined in this manner.

Hobbesian view (3). Determination of individual action under fear of penalties regularly inflicted by superior power.

If now in this latter view, we dismiss, as visionary and ideal, the notion of *authority*, and attend only to the very practical or concrete notion of *power*, we get a third notion of law, which has entered largely into moral speculation, and may be called the Hobbesian.

We have here power not submitted to willingly as reasonable, in which case it would be the above authority, but submitted to unwillingly as constraining, or simply a superior force. Of course the constraint must be what is called *moral*, and the unwillingness be indisposition: for the action is still supposed to be done by the individual, though forced upon him. The manner of the constraint is by *penalty:* the language of the power is, if you do not do the thing, this or that is what you will suffer.

Law, according to this view, is the determination of individual action by superior power, and by the way of penalties, no account being taken of any reason suggesting the law, or any advantage aimed at by it. It is of course supposed that the law is *general* in its operation, applying to a number of people, and that it is more or less steady or continuous: these considerations are in fact the only thing which causes this notion of law to differ from ordinary force.

Absolutist or Patriarchal view (4) adds to Hobbesian that the superior power is supposed to act for the general good.

If however to this third view of law we add the last particulars of the original definition, viz. that the force which I have just been describing is exercised honestly for the supposed advantage of each and of all subject to the force, we get a view of the nature of law which to many will seem a correct and complete one: the difference of it from the complete definition of law which I gave being in the omission of the notion of authority, or, what is in some respects equivalent to that of authority, the notion of agreement on the part of those subject to the law. This may be called the absolutist legislative view.

Of these four views, the first and the second bear a considerable resemblance, if we understand the *reason* of all, in the first view, to differ from the mere *will* of all as authority differs from power. Between these two views on the one side, and the third view on the other, the important point of distinction is this: that *they* recognize motive to obedience *other* than penalty, whereas the third does not. According to the earlier views, the essential point about law is that it is an arrangement or order, such as is indicated in the Greek term νόμος: according to the third the essential point about it is that it is a command. According to the earlier views, the motive to obedience in the mass of the individuals subject to the law may be considered to be agreement with it, or acknowledgment of the reason which suggested its enactment: and though of course penalty must exist, for there must be (by the definition) sufficient power to enforce the law, yet the need of such enforcement is in a manner exceptional: it is not looked upon as the chief or only stimulant to obedience.

Relation between these different views.

In the third view, those subject to the law are supposed to have no further concern with it than to obey it under penalty.

The fourth view is a return to the earlier views, in so far as it supposes the law to be intended for the advantage of those subject to it and therefore reasonable (for this is the proper purpose of all law), not necessarily appealing to penalty alone. At the same time, since on this supposition the law is arbitrary in the making of it, though not arbitrary in the purpose, and since there is no recognition of authority, as distinct from power, in the making it, those who hold this view are very likely to be strong maintainers of the third view, as regards the making of the law: they regard the law, however good may be its purpose, as having no force, except in virtue of its penalties: if they had had the making of language, the words for law would not have been such as imply order or arrangement, but such as imply simply command.

Application of the four views of law to the notion of duty.

We have now to see how these different views of the nature of law enter into moral philosophy, and what relation they bear to the notion of duty.

The notion of duty owes its distinctness partly to Roman Law,

The distinctness of duty as a philosophical notion is owing to the Roman view of law, and to religion. It existed in the Greek mind and language, as in all, in such terms as δεῖ, τὸ δέον, &c.: but the Greek philosophers, and the Romans who followed them, do not seem distinctly to have separated the consideration of duty, as an ideal, from that of virtue: they did so to some extent, in reference to the entire of duty, in speaking of a man's ἔργον, &c., and in reference for instance to the details of duty, in speaking of suitable conduct in the details of life, τὰ καθήκοντα, translated by the Latin *officia* (*opificia*), mutual services or relative duties: but the question of the obligation by which all this is bound upon us, which differences the consideration of duty from that of virtue, was not much entered upon by them.

The Romans have been considered an un-ideal people, but their ideal *jus*, at least as they began to consider it when somewhat of the Stoic philosophy mingled with it, was a very noble one. I will not dwell on it, but will make some extracts which will show their notion of it[1].

and partly to Christianity.

Nor will I dwell, now, on the development of the notion of duty which arose from the Christian religion: both the Jews and the Romans were in a preeminent degree, though in different ways, law-loving peoples; and the notions of duty which lasted

[1] The extracts were not given, but would probably have been taken from such sources as Cicero, *De Legibus*, Bk. I. and II. c. 4. ED.

on through the middle ages belong in part to the Roman law, in part to the Old Testament.

Hobbes in narrowing duty to obligation enforced by penalty

When the time came for these notions to be routed out, as everything after those ages was, the work was done by Hobbes, and his manner of doing it was simply the introducing what I have called the third view of law instead of the two earlier ones: the Hobbism or Hobbesianism, which for a long time was the main object, whether of attack or defence, on the part of English moral philosophers, was simply the consideration that the obligatoriness of right action is the only matter of importance about it, and further that this obligatoriness is simply the requirement of obedience under threat of penalty.

de-idealized the 1st ideal as Epicurus did the 2nd.

The Hobbists stand to the various forms of anti-Hobbism, in reference to the first ideal (or the notion of something as what we ought to do), in much the same relation as that in which the Epicureans stand to the Stoics and the schools descending from them, in reference to the second ideal (or the notion of something as what it is desirable that we should aim at). The notion of the summum bonum was very early de-idealized or positivized, and it was considered that nothing could, with any meaning, be considered to answer to this description except tangible, measurable, describable, pleasure. Though the notion of the faciendum did not so readily lend itself to this process; still we find here a similar de-idealization of the first ideal, in the form of *duty*, effected by Hobbes; and *virtue*, the other form of this ideal, has suffered in the same way, as we shall see in a future chapter: the machinery in both cases being the same as that employed by the Epicureans in the case of happiness, viz. a conversion of motive or altering the purpose of action.

Effect of Hobbism on religion

The Hobbistic view was not, any more than the

and morals. Its opponents attacked (1) its account of obligation, (2) its narrowing of duty to obligation.

Epicurean, opposed to religion, as religion is, and always has been, understood by many. What it affected was, not religion itself, but the elevation and generality of view taken, whether of morality or of religion. It was opposed in two ways, as we may say; by stoutly maintaining, in application to morals, the earlier view of ideal law; and by bringing into more prominence the other form of the first ideal, or the notion of virtue. These two views met different portions of it: the one disputed the account of obligation; the other disputed the assertion that obligation (however understood) was all that morality was concerned with.

Illustration from Paley's account of keeping our word.

For a simple illustration of this: Paley's answer to his question, Why am I obliged to keep my word? is an example of Hobbism: I should be inclined to answer it by saying, uniting the language of the two classes of anti-Hobbists, I keep my word for other reasons besides being obliged to it, and by being obliged to it I mean something different from what you mean.

What then do I mean?

Further view of duty as an idealization of Law: it prescribes mutual action in accordance with the relations in which men stand to each other.

Before answering, I will recall to mind the beginning of the general definition which I gave of law, viz. that it is the regulation of the mutual actions of individuals, *i.e.* their conduct towards each other.

These individuals, as they stand independently, are each in his own set of circumstances, having done this or that, &c.: the law, taking note of a certain number of these circumstances, classifies them, and prescribes with respect to the individuals, how they are to act towards each other accordingly. It finds, or puts (it matters not to our present purpose which term we use) individuals in certain relations one towards another: and it prescribes mutual action according to these relations. These egal relations were called by the Romans *jura*, as hey called the whole supposed mass of the relations, r the ideal law, *jus*. Each individual had, if we nay say so, his own particular *jus*, that is, his network of legal relations, with befitting conduct, owards those about him. In later language it nas been more usual to make a division and to peak of rights, claims, dues, when the relation is onsidered to make a person the proper object of ome action for his advantage, and on the other hand o speak of duties or obligations when it is *his* ction which is limited or determined, the advantage being for the other party.

General law or *jus*, itself an ideal of human action n respect of particular circumstances in which people are found or placed, and with which law is supposed to be concerned, is still further idealized into duty, the standard of mutual human action generally: general duty is the universal system in which each individual has his particular duty to do, as well as his particular *due*, which each should render to him.

It is owed not merely to the 2nd party but to a 3rd part, the guardian of the law.

Another characteristic of duty which I mentioned is its being *personal* in a twofold sense, as owed, not only to a particular person, a second party, but also to a third party, the authority and power (ideal perhaps) enforcing the law. In other words, in respect of the performance of our duties to the second party to whom they are actually due, we are what is called *responsible* to a third party, the guardian of the law, to the extent to which we consider that these duties are portions of a general duty, or real and actual law. We are in the first instance under obligation, bound by the law, to the second party, to do the duty: and then, in case of failure, we are bound or liable to the enforcing or third party, for the forfeiture.

Paley neglects the obligation due to the 2nd party.

Turning now to Paley's question, Why am I obliged to keep my word? it will be observed that, on the Hobbistic view which is his, no notice is taken of what I have called the actual obligation, or the obligation in the first instance, viz. to the party with whom word is to be kept. This, as we have seen, belongs to Hobbism, which interprets obligation as simply dread of penalty. But it is not in accordance with the natural notions of men, so far as language suggests them. The duty or debt, the obligation or tie, is to the second party. We are under obligation to the person with whom we are dealing to keep our word to him: we are responsible (in Paley's view, to the divine law) for the performance of this obligation.

Hobbism and Utilitarianism both make particular duty depend upon general duty.

I mentioned before two resemblances between Hobbism and Epicureanism, or, more strictly speaking, an analogy and a connexion: I will mention now a resemblance between Hobbism and Utilitarianism in general (*i.e.* as the word is now commonly understood), even if the Utilitarianism be quite un-Epicurean.

It consists in this: that in both of them the question of relative duties, or of particular duty, is considered to depend on that of general duty: the relative and particular, to the extent to which they are considered at all, are considered simply to be consequences of the general. And just in the same way we find Paley here failing to notice that the word obligation implies a tie to another party, or that duties are owed to somebody.

Distinction between jural and non-jural views of morality marked by the recognition or denial of particular obligation.

The recognition or non-recognition of this latter consideration divides moral philosophy into two manners of thought. That which recognizes this particular obligation we might call the jural: that which does not, the non-jural. Hobbism, Epicuanism, and Utilitarianism, meaning by this latter ord the morality of general benevolence or of the reatest happiness, belong to the latter class. This one reason for their blending readily together: nd in fact, utilitarianism, as now frequently understood, includes all the three.

The particularity or definiteness of duty sometimes resides in the party to whom it is owing, as duty to parents;

I will mention also another thing about the articularity of duty. In a sense, all duty may be alled *relative: i.e.* the notion of it implies a certain elation between the two or more parties whom it oncerns, beyond the fact that they are both human eings or sentient creatures. But relative duty, in more restricted sense, may be considered to designate those cases where the particularity or definiteness, which makes the matter in question duty ather than virtue, belongs to the individuals, and ot to the thing: whereas there are a large class of ases in which, though there is always some reference the individuals or two parties, the particularity r definiteness belongs specially to the thing owed r due.

This will be understood better when I come to peak of justice: but I think a little illustration will nake it sufficiently clear now.

sometimes in the thing, as the duty to speak the truth.

When we speak of our duty to our parents relative duty), the definiteness of particularity, which belongs to the duty as such, has reference to he individuals or parties only, for *what* we owe to hem is very indefinite, though it may be generally escribed; and it may be expanded or indulged in any amount, in this respect not answering the haracter of duty: it is duty on account of the definiteness of the parties. On the other hand, when e speak of the duty of truthfulness, the parties are carcely more definite than they are in respect of enevolence: we owe truthfulness to everybody:

but the thing is definite, and hence the notion of duty is applicable to the one in a manner in which it is not to the other. We cannot be truthful as we may be benevolent, less or more, or qualifiedly. It may be a matter of little consequence to a man that on some occasion we break our word to him, and it may be a matter of great consequence to a man that on some occasion we refuse to risk our lives for him: still in the former case we wrong him, in the latter we do not: the cases are matter of different consideration from that of the greater or less advantage resulting from them.

I will now summarily describe duty and obligation: the answer to Paley's question will I trust appear.

Definition of Duty founded on definition of Law.

Duty is the ideally right, or that which should be done, in so far as we consider it determined for us, and the principle which we suppose to determine it we call 'the moral law.'

I use purposely the very vague word 'principle' here, for this reason: that that to which it applies, the moral law, is understood by different persons quite differently. The reason why it is thus understood differently will appear from what I have said above: it is because people understand such very different things by the term 'law.'

In accordance with the view taken of law, Duty will be 'public spirit for the moral universe' (1),

If we suppose 'law' to be order, arrangement, system, the result, or rather the expression, of a harmony, concurrence, agreement, of a number of members capable, in whatever way, of such agreement, or imaginatively supposed so; then duty is the great law which the members of the moral universe, if we may so speak, impose upon themselves: it represents the comprehension by each of his place and his work as it stands related to the work of the whole; each as one of the whole, feeling himself to be a co-imposer and co-vindicator of the w, and, as such, ruling his own self, as individual his interests and disposed to care for himself alone. uty in this view is public spirit: public spirit not r a nation, but for the moral or sentient universe.

If we suppose 'law' to mean a rule or system of dividual conduct, laid down not by arbitrary power, ut by authority (for which *authority* I would briefly ssign three constituents, title, wisdom, and good-ill); then duty is the intelligent and willing bedience of the members of the moral universe to omething which their minds seem to present to hem as possessing the above characters: they feel heir action in this view not free, and yet it is not onstrained: they are, concurrently, ruled and ruling ver themselves; obedient, but glad and proud (so o speak) of their obedience.

or 'willing obedience of the moral universe to that which possesses authority over it' (2),

If we suppose 'law' to mean a rule for individual ction, of which rule we know nothing more than hat, if we do not obey it, we shall be punished, then uty is bare, perhaps unwilling, obedience to something which we have no interest or pleasure in, but which we are afraid to resist. The moral law is hen a yoke imposed upon us by the Deity (Paley), r by society and public opinion (some Socratic interocutors and several philosophers in later times), or y arbitrary power in general (Hobbes).

or submission to arbitrary will, whether of the Deity, or of society, or of power generally (3),

To the extent to which we add to the last supposition, that there is good purpose in the imposers f this yoke, we make a supposition in accordance vith the fourth view which I gave of law, and this s what is generally done by utilitarians who hold Hobbist views. Duty in this view is submission to he constraining power, whatever it is, combined with nore or less of sympathy with the purpose which that power has in its constraint. As if Paley should say, hat virtue (or duty) is the doing good to men, &c.,

or it may be the last united with approval of the end for which the power is exerted (4).

in prospect of the reward and penalty affixed, but still with *some* feeling that God's purpose is a good one, and His wish for the happiness of His creatures what we can enter into and appreciate. It is obvious, that if the added supposition in this case is carried to a great extent, we come very near the second supposition again, as I mentioned in regard of law.

The full idea involves all these.

I have thought it would conduce to clearness to put these various suppositions separately, in accordance with the four views which I gave of law, and will now say about them, that in my view they all belong to the notion of duty, which is made up of them, just as I said in regard to law, that all the special views which I gave of it seemed to me partial, the proper general definition including them all. To different people, the notion of duty will present itself very differently: but if we are to give a complete account of it, I think we must unite all the above.

Responsibility implies the possibility of penalty.

With respect to the third of the suppositions above, that of *responsibility*, or liability to punishment for failure in duty, it is what will be repudiated by some, as applicable to ideal duty, as earnestly as it is maintained to be all that duty means by others. But it is maintained, and I think correctly, by Butler and others, that there cannot be the feeling of obligation (jural or ideal, as the second view presents it) without *something* in addition of the feeling of responsibility or liability to possible punishment in the event of violation of it; the feeling of desert of punishment, generating the feeling of expectation of it. The admission of this, in its due proportion, does not really weaken the second view at all. With duty, as with good and living law (so far as simple habit does not determine), it is consent, and sympathizing obedience, which is the state of the mass of those who obey: penalty is the influence in failure of this: where penalty has to do all, and consent does not exist, the law is bad, or condemned as worthless[1].

Our view of obligation will correspond with our view of law.

According as we conceive the nature of the moral law, we shall conceive that of moral obligation. We feel our action in a manner bound or not free: what is most present to our minds in this feeling may be the claim which the other party has on us; the thought of his having been aggrieved by us makes us feel distressed, or angry, anxious to make amends to him, or disgusted at the sight of him: or, again, what is most prominent to our minds may be the claim which the authority by which the law is enacted has on our obedience, and the offence we have committed against this authority: or what we feel most may be our responsibility as a matter of trust, or responsibility simply as liability to punishment: and there may be other kinds of the feeling, because other conceptions of the law, besides all these. In speaking of *conscience*, I shall discuss these feelings a little more. And also I hope to discuss, in another chapter, what philosophers would call the *objective value* of these—imaginations at first we will call them—of a moral law and moral obligation: a part of such a discussion must be, how far one manner of imagining or conceiving the moral law and moral obligation is more true, more points to or expresses fact, than another. I could not help doing this already a little in criticizing the notions of law: but I have not as yet said anything as to the manner in which these conceptions may suggest, or imply, or prove, or help to prove, real facts or relations as to our *moral*

[1] This seems to me to be expressed too broadly. The law may find no consent, not from its own worthlessness, but from the worthlessness of the subjects. In such a case law may still be useful as a 'schoolmaster,' gradually to instil higher principles of action. Ed.

being which physical observation could not suggest to us.

Reason for treating duty under the head of aretaics instead of making a distinct science of 'deontics.'

I divided the whole matter of moral philosophy into two sciences, which I called aretaics and eudæmonics, not into three, adding to these a science of duty (deontics or deontology). I refrained from doing this, because, as I have explained, virtue and duty, though different, are in the main only different as different aspects of the same thing, viz. the first ideal or that which should be done. According, however, as we take one or the other aspect, there is, as will be found, a good deal of difference in our treatment of the ideal when we go into detail and apply it to practice. I shall endeavour always to make clear which view we are taking.

CHAPTER VIII.

ON THE GENESIS OF VIRTUE: ITS EMOTIONAL ELEMENTS, BENEVOLENCE.

So far the discussion has been carried on from the side of the ideal.

IN all that has preceded, it has indeed been with sentiments of the mind that we have been dealing, but not in the manner in which I propose dealing with them in this chapter. Hitherto what I have considered has been this: that the imagination comes into our mind that there is, or may be, a conduct, or a kind of action, which we ought to choose, or which it is proper for us to choose, rather than other kinds; that there is, or may be, something that is worth our aiming at. Perhaps we imagine at the same time that one or another kind of conduct *is* the proper conduct, and one or another aim the worthy aim: conduct that is useful, that is honourable, that is conscientious, or whatever it may be, commends itself to our *imagination*, (so at first to call it). These various kinds of conduct thus presenting themselves I have called 'ideals': standing at the head of them are those very general ideals which I have called the first and second; that of deedworthy conduct, or the 'faciendum,' and that of choiceworthy aim, or the 'bonum,' good.

I have entered partially into the question, how far these 'imaginations' are to be considered as imaginations only, or how far they are to be considered as indications of real fact of some kind: whether that fact be the existence of something independent of us; or whether it be that thinking in this way, imagining thus, is our nature. It makes little difference which of these latter views we take; for imagining by rule and law and in virtue of our nature is the same thing, in other words, as thinking rightly; and thinking rightly, as I mentioned in regard to perception, is the same thing as perception of truth of existence viewed from another side.

Moral philosophy is nothing if not 'ideal'; for the reason of its existence is our having a notion or imagination of what should be: and therefore whatever else may belong to it, the discussion of these ideals, what is the meaning of them, what conduct they indicate, must belong to it: and this is the main or important part of what I have called 'aretaics.'

This chapter leaves the ideal ground, and deals with practical aretaics, considering what, as a fact, men think and feel about the known thing, virtue.

We must remember however that when we speak of forming these imaginations or ideals, this is a very imperfect description of what goes on in our minds: it is merely a convenient abstraction for the purpose which I have hitherto had in view; viz. that of considering the nature of the ideals formed; just as we talk, summarily and conveniently, of seeing a prospect, though the process which we thus describe is a most complicated matter, and a volume might be written to describe the process which we thus shortly characterize. I shall in the present chapter say nothing about imaginations or ideals: I shall consider virtue as a thing understood, and shall not discuss how it is to be defined, or what are its limits: just as, to take the above instance, if I were desirous to analyze what goes on in us in sensation, I should consider that everybody knew what 'seeing a prospect' was. I shall consider simply that the word 'virtue' has an understood meaning, that virtue is a fact in the world, that some men practise it, and others understand that they practise it: I shall consider what, as a matter of fact, men do think or feel, about this other fact, virtue.

This way of considering things might be called, if we cared so to call it, experiential or observational aretaics, in distinction from the ideal aretaics with which we have been dealing hitherto.

The three great characters or features in, or circumstances about, human nature which go to produce or constitute virtue, are benevolence (using the word in the loose sense in which it is ordinarily used by moral philosophers), the sense of duty, and the love of excellence: or, bringing the description of virtue a little nearer, we may say: Virtue is benevolence, more or less stimulated and regulated by the accompanying sense of duty and love of excellence.

The three features of human nature which go to produce virtue are benevolence, sense of duty, and love of excellence:

If we bear in mind what has been said about the first and second ideals, and the two aspects of the former, we shall perhaps recognize these again in what I have been saying here. To the extent to which we do our action for a purpose, the disposition to do it for a good purpose is what I mean here by benevolence, and we have here the second ideal, viz. what is to be aimed at. But purpose is not everything about action: and the choice of good purpose needs a stimulus, so to speak, beyond the good purpose itself: it is here that come in the considerations of the sense of duty, and the love of excellence, representing the two aspects of the first ideal. By the love of excellence, or the desire of excelling, I mean to indicate the effect upon us, in our character as active beings, of the presence with us of a number of beings active like ourselves, into whose feelings we enter; just as by benevolence I have wished to indicate the effect upon us, as sentient beings, of a number of beings sentient, or feeling, like ourselves, into whose feelings also, in *this* way, we enter; the

corresponding to the second ideal and the two aspects of the first ideal.

effect, that is, so far as it acts towards virtue; or that portion of the effect which aids virtue, in distinction from a (possible) portion which hinders it; or, which comes to the same thing, the surplus effect in this direction, so far as it exceeds that in the other.

The term 'benevolence' is used to express our feelings of good-will.

I will proceed first to analyze further what is contained in the very loose expression, 'benevolence.'

The different feelings which we have, or may have, associated with the thought of other people in general, or of particular people among them, may be classified in a great number of ways: perhaps the simplest division is into feelings of good-will, and feelings of ill-will; feelings, that is, accompanied with desire of the other's happiness, or the opposite.

The feelings of ill-will are not instinctive.

It may, I suppose, be laid down as an axiom, that it is only feelings of the class of good-will which are natural, in the sense of being what I think I may for the present purpose call, without danger of misleading, by a term which I am very shy of using, *instinctive.* We have instinctive loves, but no instinctive hatreds. It is only good-will (if I may borrow for a moment a logical expression) which is of the first intention: ill-will, whatever abundance there may be of it, is of the second intention, and springs up upon occasion arising.

This is not saying much more than that our original feelings are in harmony with the rudimentary principle of our active intelligence, viz. that good, or happiness, is the purpose of action; that the two belong to each other, or ideally fit. It may be doubted whether we could really even conceive native, or unoriginated and unoccasioned, ill-will, such as the Paleian supposition of a Creator making teeth for the purpose of their aching: that is, whether such a supposition does not destroy all meaning in the words *make* or *organize.*

Great variety of instinctive feelings of good-will:

The feelings however which we have thus classed together are in no respect of the colourless and nearly neutral character which the term good-will might indicate, but are, many of them, of a most intense and vigorous character.

To counterbalance this, these feelings have more or less of a merely animal or unintelligent character, associated with the good-will: and, corresponding to this, the indulgence of some of them may degenerate into a merely animal enjoyment.

Hence the dealing, on the part of moral philosophers and teachers, with the strongest sources and forms of good-will among men, has always been perplexed and difficult. The entertaining them to a high degree is a self-indulgence needing, as much as any other self-indulgence, to be restrained by reason and elevated by thoughts of duty and virtue.

compre-hended under the single word 'love' in English:

Our language (or, it may be, modern language) is perhaps fortunate in having, for purposes both of common life, of morals, and of religion, the single word 'love' for that which the Greek, for instance, expressed by several different words, signifying, in fact, several different feelings; feelings, in regard of which it has been often necessary, in a moral view, to use language *for the purpose* of keeping them asunder; but feelings which are so related to each other that their separation in thought is in some respects injurious. Thus the change from the more colourless *ἀγάπη* and *caritas* to the designation of earnest good-will by the same term by which we designate the instinctive and partly animal, but at the same time highly imaginative and idealizable, affections; and the absence of a variety of terms denoting various kinds of these affections:—these perhaps enable us, both on the one side to look at good-will in a warmer and livelier light, and also on the other side to avoid confusing and degrading, under the name of mere desire or ἐπιθυμία, morally only to be restrained, feelings which are themselves of a highly moral character, and main aids to virtue.

but embracing a scale passing from ἔρως through στοργή, φιλία and φιλανθρωπία, down to φιλοζωία.

Under the general name of 'love' we comprehend in English, first, the intersexual feeling which belongs to all animals, and which, in the case of man, is such a main object for his imagination to dwell upon, refine, and idealize: second, the congeneric feeling, or family and kindred love, also instinctive and belonging to all the higher animals; varying greatly as to its instinctive character according to the different relationships with which it is concerned, as maternal, paternal, filial, &c.; in many ways closely resembling the last, and expressible, in this view, in words which include it, like the Greek στοργή, but becoming less instinctive or less marked by animal sensation, as it becomes more general, and widens from the specialness of the last to the generality of that which follows.

The third feeling which the general term 'love' may be said to comprehend, is in some respects wider, in some respects narrower, than the last: it is that φιλία or lovingness which creates, so to speak, a kindred and brotherhood, or the feelings belonging to one, where nature has not made one. I have not called it 'friendship,' or 'friendliness,' because those words, like all moral words, by frequent complimentary use (and it may be added, in the case of the former at least of these terms, by frequent commonplace and moralistic enlarging upon), have lost much of their warmth and force, like the word 'benevolence' itself. I would rather call it *companionship*, or *comradeship*; not that *presence* is a necessary constituent, but something like community of views or action is. Into ancient ethics, as we may see in istotle, this feeling, as an aid to virtue, entered more largely, and with reason, than it has done to modern.

The fourth feeling is the last but one, generalized to φιλανθρωπία or regard for the happiness of all en: and I should not myself hesitate to add, more nerally still, a φιλοζωία or interest in the happiness all sentient beings.

These are in sum the natural feelings of good-ill: what I mean by 'natural' will appear more fully a moment, when I speak of the feelings from which distinguish them. There are, as I said, no natural elings of ill-will; but there are a set of feelings nding that way which more or less accompany some the above feelings of good-will, and which I will otice.

Such of these feelings as are of an appropriative character are liable to produce secondary feelings of ill-will, and even in themselves are not exclusively productive of good.

All the above feelings which are, in any degree, a separative or appropriative character have more less connected with them other feelings, perhaps neglect and depreciation, and, what is of more conquence, of that class which we call jealousy. All elings of this kind, it seems to me, spring from a ouble source, or rather have two characters united them: the one, the general disposition to self-gard, the other, the tendency to look upon others rivals. Now when moralists and others speak of e benevolent affections, or often when religious achers speak of love, they are apt to speak as if ese represented something steady and uniform, ther dull perhaps and neutral, and all productive good. In reality, the term, or any similar term, a kind of general expression for a mass of feeling ost *un-uniform* and irregular, often most intense and thusiastic, by no means even itself always productive of good, and constantly attended by accompaniments, such as I have alluded to, productive of some of the worst evil and wrong that can be. Affection of good-will that is distinctive (and none that is forcible or warm can be otherwise), has a double dark side, one towards the non-subjects of it, the other towards rivals in the affection: we constantly hear the supposition of marvellous effects to be produced by general benevolence or love, while in our conception of the feeling we strip it of all the earnest and enthusiastic elements which make its force.

Still on the whole these *natural* feelings of good-will supply the main stream of virtuous sentiment.

It may then be considered, that the natural benevolent affections, thus understood, with abstraction made, to such extent as is necessary, of their bad accompaniments, are the first and most copious source of that stream of sentiment which, united with other joining streams, and being directed, as to its course, in various ways, forms virtue as a feeling within: leading to conduct, as I have mentioned, for public rather than for private good.

Besides these there are the *occasional* feelings of good-will springing up under special circumstances: in consequence of the condition of others as happy or unhappy (1).

From *natural* affections of good-will, as I have just now used the word, I shall distinguish what, for my present purpose, I will call *occasional* ones: these are, in the main, of two kinds.

They have respect, either to the condition and circumstances of the persons with the thought of whom they are associated, or to the position of such persons in relation to ourselves, as, for instance, our benefactors or the opposite.

The sympathies or sympathetic emotions, which are the feelings of good-will belonging to the former of these divisions, pour into the general current of virtuous feeling a stream scarcely less in amount than that contributed by what I have called the natural affections.

Sympathy is more easily moved in the case of unhappiness.

The text, 'Rejoice with them that do rejoice and weep with them that weep,' has been often commented on, with the observation how much more dificult the former of these precepts is than the latter; and those who, like Butler, trace Divine purpose in the organization of our moral nature, consider that there is a reason for this greater disposition to compassion, than to *congaudence* (so to speak), because the former is more necessary, and more useful. That there does exist this greater disposition, appears from the word 'compassion' itself: which means properly what we now express by sympathy, but on account of the much greater occasion for its application to sympathy with suffering, has come to mean that alone. In fact the word sympathy, which has been adopted into its place, is rapidly following in the same direction.

Besides the feelings of good-will, feelings of ill-will may arise both at the sight of the happiness and unhappiness of others.

Quite consistently with Butler's view of the case it is possible to consider how it comes about that we have less sympathy with joy; that is, what are the secondary causes to which this fact is attributable. Feelings either of ill-will or of good-will are possible at the sight either of the prosperity or the suffering of another. In the case of prosperity there is the well-known feeling envy on the one side, and on the other the feeling of congaudence, which does not appear to exist in practice sufficiently to have a name. In the case of the suffering of another, there are in like manner the feelings of good-will, pity, and of ill-will, ἐπιχαιρεκακία, pleasure at the suffering of others.

That it is difficult to know how, exactly in these circumstances, people do feel; that they cannot always even tell themselves, may appear from the manner in which Rochefoucauld's maxim[1], more pointed than Lucretius' lines[2], has been considered

[1] Dans l'adversité de nos meilleurs amis, nous trouvons toujours quelque chose qui ne nous déplait pas.

[2] Suave mari magno turbantibus æquora ventis
E terra magnum alterius spectare laborem;
Non quia vexari quemquamst jucunda voluptas,
Sed quibus ipse malis careas quia cernere suave est.

to embody a great discovery or perhaps a revelation very humiliating to human nature.

Such ill-feeling arises from looking upon others as our rivals for happiness: but the feeling is usually mixed.

There exists in our mind doubtless, together with a disposition to sympathy, a disposition acting exactly in the opposite direction, which arises from a generalization, so to call it, of the notion of our each having his individual interest, and of life being a conflict of such interests, so that we are not so much co-pursuers of happiness as rivals for it. Something of dissatisfaction or uneasiness is the *primum mobile* of human nature: the natural outlet for this is in action for happiness (our own in the first instance): where it is not absorbed in this, it may to a certain degree take the form of jealousy of the happiness (or supposed happiness) of others. This is a feeling which, darkly and undefinedly, is very wide-spread. It is what men hate and are ashamed of, suspect in themselves and others, but do not like to confess: it is what more than anything prompts that sort of feeling of self-disgust or self-abhorrence, which I imagine to be not uncommon with all at certain moments, and which in religion becomes repentance: it is the feeling which gives the reality which they have to notions of the corruption and depravity of human nature: it is the feeling which with many gives special point and sting to calamity and misfortune, making them distrust pity, as being in reality a sort of covert triumph over them. It is the feeling which makes it plausible for some to say, that men really hate, do not love, each other. Being, as I have described it, a kind of going astray, a turning sour, as it were, of another feeling which is meant to be absorbed in action, it is usually strongest in the least active minds: and hence also it is most likely to exist, and most likely to be observed, in societies where there is not a great deal of active energy, but a great deal of self-observaon, and comparatively idle inter-communication. nd because in general people naturally try to nother it and keep it to themselves as much as ossible, so far as it does exist, therefore there is ways a special pleasure, on the part of those who re for such pleasure, in the bringing it to light, and ny smart utterance of it has the character at once oth of a discovery and of an acknowledged truth. Where this disposition is strong, the man is of course oth envious of the prosperous, and unsympathetic, not worse, with the suffering. Where it exists in ight degree, the feeling is rather a tendency at the ght of others' prosperity or suffering, to recur to the hought of ourselves: then, without envy, the sight f the greater prosperity of others may cause a pang, nd quite consistently with abundant pity, something ay be felt of self-congratulation at the sight of uffering. It is this last state which Lucretius in is qualification of what he says seems to wish to xpress.

I feel inclined to say, that perhaps our feelings f joy altogether are, upon the whole, less intense, s feelings, than our feelings of pain: and if this the case with the primary feelings, of course it ust be the case with the sympathetic or secondary nes.

Pity is a more powerful agent than envy.

Pity and envy are both great agents in life: if we se the word 'envy' loosely, we might hesitate to ay which was greatest: in which case all we ould say of this class of sympathies would be, that counterbalanced the bad disposition to look upon thers as rivals for happiness, without leaving any urplus on the side of virtue. But under the notion f envy, we ought not to include those feelings of ctive emulation in which there is really no ill-will, ut only a strong feeling, on occasion of another's rosperity, of our own want of it: if we exclude these, envy, though a great poisoner of life, is in no respect a powerful agent in it like pity.

Pity, however, is but one form of the very wide and various feeling of sympathy with others. Sympathy is the emotional imagination: through it, the feeling of others, whatever their condition or circumstances, becomes part of our emotional consciousness, and excites action as if it were our own primary feeling, action, of course, to *their* benefit, not to ours.

The other class of occasional feelings are those which rise out of the behaviour of others towards us (2). Such feelings are gratitude, forgivingness and their opposites.

The other kind of 'occasional' feelings of good or ill-will, as I called them, has reference to the position of people in relation to us, as having, for instance, done us good or harm. There is complication about these, and I shall touch upon them again in speaking of justice.

When persons have done us good we feel and practise gratitude, indifference, or ingratitude (for this latter word has more generally a *positive* meaning), and when they have done us ill we feel and practise revengefulness, indifference, or active forgivingness, the returning of good for evil.

Gratitude is of two kinds, connected either with justice or kindness.

Perhaps I shall be understood best on this subject, by saying, that there are two entirely distinct feelings of gratitude possible: the gratitude which is connected with feelings akin to justice, which I shall speak of presently: and the gratitude which is connected with feelings akin to kindliness, and in the case of which the benefit done to us has generated a love on our part to the doer.

I have put this rather broadly, and I do not mean but that most gratitude is compounded of these two feelings, and possibly they may never exist quite separate: but I think it will be seen that gratitude is concerned with the two.

This may be put simply thus: one man's gratitude may be of such a kind that the feelings which compose it are such as would make him, if the other party had done him ill instead of good, revengeful: another's may be of such a kind that the feelings composing it would make him, in such a case, forgiving.

The latter is the one with which we are now concerned.

It is only of gratitude in its connexion with kindliness that I will speak now; and there is no doubt that from this source a vast amount of good-will is contributed to go to the constitution of virtue.

Other occasional feelings spring out of other relations.

The relations of benefactor and benefited, and of injurer and injured, are only two out of the countless relations which circumstances may bring about between men: and I have spoken of the feelings belonging to them only as an instance of such relative feelings.

On the whole the occasional feelings tend to increase benevolence.

Each such possible relation suggests, and constantly produces, its appropriate kindliness: men love each other, not only because they have *been* benefited, but because they *have* benefited or because they *can* benefit; because they are strong and another is weak, because they are weak and another is strong, and for a number of reasons endless to recount. Of course all these relations may, and sometimes do, generate ill-will and not good: but I think the mass of good-will generated by inter-relation among men is the greater. This, also, will come under our consideration again: I will only say now that the best witnesses on this side seem those who have most tried to depreciate human nature: somehow or other, human nature seems to have the gift of turning its selfishness to kindliness, and its mutual hostility to sociability; it is kindliness which is generated in sum, and on the whole.

I have thus endeavoured to sketch roughly the 'benevolence,' which, stimulated and accompanied by the sense of duty, and the love of excellence, constitutes virtue. We are now to examine these, and see how they act on the benevolence.

APPENDIX ON BENEVOLENT IMPULSE IN ITS RELATION TO VIRTUE[1].

Virtuousness defined.

Virtuousness is the disposition to take an interest in the welfare of others, and to postpone or sacrifice self-indulgence and self-interest to their good, whether this latter be the public good, or particular kinds of good of particular individuals, to whom regard of this kind may be due from us.

Its objective aspect, utility.

At the basis of all virtuous action, viewed objectively, that is, if we look at it by itself and abstractedly from the agent who does it, is its *usefulness*, or its being conducive to some real welfare. This it is, which makes action in one way more desirable than action in another.

Its subjective aspect, generosity.

But again, at the basis of all distinctively virtuous action viewed subjectively, that is, looked at as done by the agent, is its usefulness *to others* or to the public and society. I say distinctively virtuous, because it is not the case that all action which is not virtuous is the contrary or vicious. As between action which is useful and that which is injurious, there is a great deal which is useless or resultless, so between action which is virtuous and that which is vicious there is a great deal which, of itself, has no moral character at all. The useless action, as so much action lost and wasted where all ought to be useful, may be regarded as injurious or wrong. And in a similar view, the action which has no subjective moral character, which is done without any virtuous purpose or any accompaniment of conscientious feeling, may be regarded as wrong or vicious in so far as we think that all action, all life, ought to have conscientiousness or virtuous

[1] This Appendix is taken almost entirely from a MS marked V, which is in some respects an earlier draft of the present treatise. The commencement anticipates what is said in the next chapter about the intellectual elements of virtue, but the bulk of it is occupied with the fuller exposition of the elementary feelings of benevolence which were treated of in the last chapter. Ed.

principle mixed with it. Conscience, with some, supplies *purpose* to life, with others, supplies no more than restraining rule. Its nature, as I have described it, is to supply the former as well as the latter. It is difficult to use the words 'right' and 'wrong' in respect of the *extent* of the applicability of the feeling of conscientiousness. But that is a very low degree of *virtuousness* where conscience does no more than guard from wrong action, and does not animate and stimulate to right.

The cardinal virtues.

In order to action bearing this character of *self-transcending* usefulness (so to call it) which makes it virtuous, two kinds of power over self are needed: the one the power (various in its degrees of consciousness and deliberation) of forgetting, neglecting, denying, ourselves: the other, the power of controlling and governing ourselves. It is in the amount of these two dispositions that consists, in the main, individual elevation of character or excellence. The first nearly corresponds to the ancient virtue *ἀνδρεία*, which ethical language has rendered by 'fortitude', but which in many particulars is more akin to our notion of *generosity:* the second is the ancient virtue of *σωφροσύνη*, soberness or self-control. These are the conditions of *self* preparatory and necessary to that self-transcending usefulness or attention to the interests of others which is the ancient *δικαιοσύνη*, and is the more complete and finished virtuousness: and the three together form the three great moral prerogatives of man, the three great elements of that moral nature which raises him above other animals. Put together with the intellectual prerogative of prudence or wisdom they form a famous quaternion, the character of which later ethical language has in some degree disguised in calling them the four cardinal virtues.

Utility should guide without checking generosity.

These different dispositions have reason and value of their own, and yet it is true to a certain extent, that the importance of utility in actions is a paramount principle, and should exercise a restraining power even in regard of *them*. In our nature, we may say, provision is made for the doing of useful actions not by one principle alone, but by many various principles, which act, in this view of their action, in an irregular manner, some of them rarely reaching the mark, others very constantly going far beyond it. It is by this that our nature is rendered complicated as it is: and whether we are better beings or not, certainly we are more interesting beings and good with a greater variety of goodness, than if we had had an exact utilitarian sense, *i.e.* instantly knew the proper useful action to be done and instantly did it. The objective rightness or usefulness of action becomes multiplied subjectively, (that is, when it is transferred to the mind and feeling,) into goodness or virtuousness almost infinite in variety: the mistaken effort to do right leads sometimes to the doing things which, we may almost even say, are better than right: actions which are wasted in the universe so far as resulting usefulness is concerned, lives nobly sacrificed, sufferings voluntarily undergone, are felt as what least of all can really be called wasted, and most thoroughly have a moral value. Still, before such action, the thought of utility, where it may be, should come in: though there should be action of this kind, usefulness of result should be desired likewise.

Division of ethical systems in accordance with this twofold aspect of virtue.

The action thus according to good dispositions and the action which would be determined upon by calculation of reason for useful purposes, do not in all particulars correspond: and under these circumstances there are two ways in which Ethics may tend. There may be a tendency to think lightly of the value and trustworthiness of dispositions, and to try to bring about a calm consideration, upon grounds merely of reason, (or as it would be called by those holding the opposite view, a cold calculation,) of the utility of the probable results. Or there may be a comparative inattention to these latter, and a pleasure taken in the action, whether its results are useful or not, as an exhibition of the virtuousness of the character, and of the possible nobleness of human nature.

Utility neglected by Plato and Butler.

The ancient moralists probably paid too little attention to the utility of the action as of importance in respect of the regulation and estimation of the dispositions. In Plato and in his follower Butler, there is, as I have already hinted, scarcely sufficient information given as to the principles, or law, or whatever we may style it, in accordance with which reason (or conscience) is to direct the rest of the inner man. Failing information on this point, one does not see, for instance, why the reasons of different men should not direct their several kingdoms or systems differently: to say that it is on principles of reason itself is vague, and is saying little. Plato however, I suppose, would conceive that reason directs by reference to an ideal of what perfect man should be: Butler again, that conscience does so by reference to a law of God of which it is itself the vehicle, publisher, and witness. In neither of them however is this point clear. Only it *is* clear that they neither of them think much about a regulation of the dispositions, as to their strength and amount, by a consideration of the consequences, as to utility, of the action which they would engender.

And by Aristotle. His defective account of virtue.

Aristotle attributes the same importance as Plato to the dispositions of courage (or generosity) and self-control, and may be said to give (in different language or under a different metaphor, from those used by Plato) a theory which substantially resolves the whole of virtue into the latter. In respect of the different dispositions which man may have, virtue in his view, is the having them in the proper amount or proportion: reason judges or fixes this amount. It is obvious that this is not saying much. Some dispositions perhaps we ought not to have at all, others in a very large amount. Aristotle accordingly takes account of those dispositions only, which it is considered we should have in some measure: as to them we should avoid both excess and defect, keeping in the middle between them; this middle however not being a spatial or geometrical middle, but very likely nearer to the one point than the other; reason finding it where it is. Now as reason must be supposed to be that which fixed whether we should have the disposition at all, so here again reason fixes the amount which we should have of it: and the question arises, what is reason supposed to look to in fixing these? Reason, in general, must be supposed able to assign *reasons*, in particular, for its proceeding: for what *reason*, then, is one special definite amount of the disposition which leads us to face danger to be called a virtue, and named courage, while both a greater quantity and a less quantity are to be called vices, and named, as such, rashness and cowardice?

It requires to be supplemented by a reference to some external standard.

I do not think that Aristotle gives any answer to this question, otherwise than by that appeal which he continually makes to human judgment and opinion. And this answer is not sufficient; for ethical science, though taking account of human opinion, still ought in the main rather to lead than follow it. The real answer, I apprehend, must be sought in two directions, both of them different from this: one in the direction of an ideal of human character, so far as we are able to form it, or of a divine law of human action, so far as we have reason to suppose that such exists: this is the way of Plato and Butler: the other the way of examination of the consequences of the actions which arise from the dispositions, and the pronouncing accordingly, that that amount of fearlessness which, looked at generally, is likely to produce useful action is virtue, while a greater or less amount, not being likely to produce such action, is not so. When we talk of *reason* acting, unless there is a rule or law at hand for it to go by, it is evidently by such consideration of consequences that we suppose it to act. The whole theory then of self-government, self-control, avoiding excess and defect, having dispositions in their right amount—however we may express it—cannot stand by itself: it has necessary reference to some external or objective considerations: and these considerations, to be found to a certain extent in the supposition of a divine law guiding us and an ideal of human character commending itself to us, yet are more fully and more specially to be found in *utility*.

However, the difference in value of dispositions even supposing them unregulated, that is, supposing reason, with all calculations of consequences, were away, is perhaps recognised by Plato and Aristotle both, but in any case by Plato. The portion of the soul which is active for activity's sake, without any view to ulterior enjoyment, which struggles with opposing difficulty, and finds its pleasure in effort (the *θυμοειδές*) to which most specially belongs the disposition of generosity (*ἄνδρεια*)—this, with the dispositions flowing from it, independent of any regulation of them by reason which might have to do with consequences, is itself of a noble nature, and is a virtue, or, in the language which I have used, has moral value. We have here two lines of virtue which sometimes, as I have said, will not coincide: when this is the case, and we are calmly judging or framing a moral system, regulation by reason on proper consideration of consequences is what belongs to the higher region of thought, and is more essentially moral than any impulses can be, however noble. But we destroy man's nature altogether if we do not take account, and full account of the worthiness and moral character of these impulses independently of reason.

I have mentioned that human conduct is compounded internally, in various degrees, of principle and impulse. In other words, the primary desire (so to call in general the original spring of action) rarely acts immediately to influence conduct, but commonly is mingled in the thought with various other things, and these together result in the *will* or *resolution* from which the action proceeds.

Will is a resultant of principle and impulse.

In speaking of desire as a spring of action, we must consider it to consist of two elements, the one, the imagination of an object as desirable and as absent, the other, the feeling of restlessness or desire of action itself. This is a very old and popular analysis: the springs of human conduct, says Gibbon, are the love of pleasure and the love of action.

The primary impulse is to action as much as to pleasure.

I do not know whether it is of consequence how far we consider the proper germ of the resulting will to be this restlessness or irritability, rather than the other portion of the complicated desire or impulse. The mere restlessness however, or inward demand of action, cannot be called 'will'; it is at best but the embryo of it, till it is attached to an object of desire.

Action is not the object of moral consideration unless in the mental process preceding it, mere desire has become converted into *will* by the mixture of something of imagination, deliberation, and choice. Otherwise the action is what, in our proper language, is called *involuntary;* that is, possibly with consciousness, but without *deliberate* consciousness; not on purpose; not with consciousness as of things done of and by ourselves.

Action becomes moral as impulse passes into will.

Defect of consciousness in action may be the subject of moral condemnation in so far as it is to be considered that there should never be action without such consciousness. A high degree of consciousness or deliberateness is called self-possession: a low degree of it, with much vehemence of feeling, is called 'transport', or by various similar mames.

The two ingredients of will may coexist in various proportions.

With respect to the provinces of reason and feeling (or passion) when we enter on action, the language from the beginning of ethics has been, under all sorts of metaphors, the same, ascribing the moving power to the latter, the guiding power to the former. Under these circumstances what is described as a strong will, would signify a mind in which both of them existed in great amount, so that a great

Strength of will implies a high degree of both.

deal of deliberation could coexist with vigorous action. In this case there is what we call resolution or determination.

Moral character is injured by defect of either, but in most men there is a preponderance of one or other.

With regard to what is desirable as to the proportion in the mind of these two elements, ethical science has not much to say, only neither must be deficient. A man in whom impulse or feeling is deficient, is called 'hard', even if he be virtuous: a man in whom principle is deficient is called 'weak', even if he, in a way, be virtuous. He is less likely however to be so than the other. The virtue of the former is unsatisfactory, but real. That of the latter is specious, but untrustworthy. The words in almost all languages point us to this: *κακία*, *vitium*, are in original signification this same 'weakness'; *ἀρετή* and *virtus* mean strength. In thus arguing from the history of words we must of course bear in mind that it is more or less a general rule in language for ethical terms to degenerate in their application, arising from the tendency of men on the whole, to speak of such things cautiously, considerately, and indulgently, rather than strongly and exaggeratedly: still, that there is importance in wrong-doing being expressed by a term which once meant weakness, is marked by virtue being in a similar manner associated with strength.

There cannot then be virtuousness without any conscientiousness, but there may be without a very great deal: that is, the same result in action, which in some proceeds from conscientiousness, may proceed in others from the happy following up and cultivating a happy temperament as to feeling: while the state of mind, though very different in the two cases, cannot be described in the one as worse than in the other.

And where there is conscientiousness, it will generally happen that it is largely mixed with feeling. I have on purpose described it rather barely, in order that the different elements which result in good conduct may be more distinctly understood: but in moral life these different elements go together, and form an organization or a new whole.

Difficulty of determining goodness of action.

Rightness or goodness of action is not a thing which can be decided absolutely. There are problems of moral difficulty which may probably be pronounced insoluble. One of the *real* and *wise* reasons for the disposition which people have often had to refer such cases away from themselves to others who may be supposed competent to form a good judgment, is, that it is probable that no judgment come to will ever be entirely satisfactory to the framer of it (if he be a good one), who has looked at the matter on all sides, and is aware of the objections against, as well as the reasons for, his judgment. The agent therefore is more likely to act with full persuasion in his own mind, when there is added to his own feelings on the subject confidence in another's judgment, and when his own resolution is not weakened by the continued recurrence of doubts and objections. In any such difficult questions, there needs the strong overruling feeling which I suppose a judge must have, that a judgment must be come to, that reasons must be found to distinguish some things, some line of conduct, from other alternatives, as the best and, if not satisfactory, still the least unsatisfactory. Some one line of conduct must be chosen to pursue. This, chosen as it best can be, is for the agent the absolute faciendum or right thing to be done, in spite of all the accompanying unsatisfactoriness. But looking at it in the general, it is very clear that it is not thus absolutely right or good. It is its being under the circumstances the best, that makes it the absolutely right for the doer at that time.

Still greater difficulty of determining goodness of character.

But, difficult as it may be to determine goodness of action, goodness of character can much less be absolutely decided on. It is like beauty of form or feature, with regard to which in the abstract certain absolute principles may be laid down, but which affords, as it is met with, endless scope for variety of taste and of principles of judgment. The notion of *rightness* suggests to us one thing right or to be done, as against many wrong, or not to be done: but in application to disposition and character, virtuousness is as various as viciousness. And in comparing different virtues, or forms of virtuousness, together, as to their relative importance, it is hard to find any certain principle on which to go.

In what sense it is true that love is the temper of virtue.

Love, if by the term we mean such love, *e.g.* as is indicated by St Paul in the Epistles to the Romans and Corinthians, may be said to be the temper of virtue, and to produce virtuous actions without any intervention of conscientiousness, intellectual principle, or reason. But the form in which this has been often put is very erroneous. Love, to do what St Paul thus describes, is no simple feeling or primary impulse: it is an exceedingly complicated result, development, production, of a course of feeling and action; which result the Apostle here calls ἀγάπη, or love, but which might not have been misdescribed in other manners. When people say that the Christian religion removes morality from other bases, whatever they may be, to fix it on that of love, they do not always sufficiently reflect what they mean. If they mean here by 'love' any simple feeling or impulse, they are much in error. The love which does all the noble works, and possesses all the noble qualities, which St Paul and St John enumerate, is clearly a special temper growing more and more out of the Christian mental discipline and Christian inward life: what Christianity does, is not to give any new basis for morality, but to supply means for the engendering certain new tempers of which this ἀγάπη, or Christian love, is the principal, which are likely to be more powerful agents for virtuous action than any tempers which can exist independent of Christianity.

In Plato justice takes the place of Christian love, though he allows moral importance to ἔρως:

With Plato, justice, which, he says, consults the interests of others, is put to a certain extent in the moral position in which St Paul puts love, when he describes this latter as working no ill to his neighbour. But a very important by-place in morals is filled in Plato, as all are aware, by passionate love, or ἔρως. His thoughts in this respect very much penetrated the ancient world. Christianity, which in some things showed sympathy with him, did not in that.

As Aristotle does to φιλία:

Aristotle's main or direct system takes less account of attention to the interests of others as distinct from our own than does that of Plato. He however, like Plato, has what we may call a by-place, but an important place, for *love*, not however ἔρως, but the love of attachment and companionship, lovingness or energetic friendship, which with the Greeks indeed was often passionate too: for the Latin 'amicitia' and our 'friendship' represent a colder feeling than the Greek was. Aristotle's two books of the Ethics about φιλία, though important in the ancient world, still were not so much so as Plato's thoughts on the subject of ἔρως. But it being a wider form of love that he spoke of, there is, in some points of view, more ethical importance in what he says.

And the Stoics to φιλανθρωπία.

The Stoics introduced the notion of what we should now call an universal brotherhood, an οἰκειότης, or kindred of the whole human race, a φιλανθρωπία, or general love of man.

The doctrine in this respect which was preached by our Lord and his Apostles was common with Christians to the Stoics.

'Αγάπη and 'caritas' used to express Christian love.

The Christian writers make slight use of the term philanthropy, or love towards man, greater use of the notion φιλαδελφία, or brotherly love, to represent the mutual affection within the Christian family. But the word they chose to represent the Christian temper which I have spoken of was not ἔρως or φιλία, which indeed were preengaged, the former in a less worthy, the latter at least in a different application, but ἀγάπη. I suppose the early Latin translators were influenced by a kindred feeling in avoiding 'amor' to represent it, and using 'caritas.' Our translators, undecided between the mediævally-consecrated, and the more significant word, have confused us by giving to represent ἀγάπη, according to the place and author, both 'charity' and 'love.'

The Christian and the cardinal virtues.

Charity or love then, in the Christian dispensation, is a Christian temper, exercised in the main towards men, but in certain respects towards God also. Being this, it was very reasonably described in the mediæval ethics as a theological virtue: two other Christian tempers mentioned along with it in 1 Cor. xiii., 'faith,' and 'hope,' being considered to constitute two more such: and the three forming what we may call a Christian constellation; holding a higher place than the pre-Christian constellation of virtues, the Platonic quaternion or cardinal virtues. The seven together formed, in the middle ages, the frame for systematizing virtuous feeling and conduct. Love is the principal theological or Christian virtue, and therefore the principal virtue altogether.

Conscientiousness and love the two sources of virtue.

Virtue may be said, as something existing in the mind, to have two sources, one in conscientiousness, the other in kindly feeling, the streams from which unite to form virtue complete. Moralists, determined to shut their eyes to one of these sources or to the other, have in general gone on with a weary battle. Those of them who are determined to make out that the motive for men's association is fear of each other, and therefore desire of each other's protection, shut their eyes to the mutual attraction which nature furnishes in all the various forms of love, which would, so far as we are able to see, bring them together even if they had nothing, any of them, to be afraid of. These various feelings of love are, as it were, the nutriment provided by nature for the developing moral nature, while moral principle, partly formed out of these feelings, is infixing itself. Suppose that the reason why men should come together in society were only the not very high one of mutual protection, and that we were to attribute no value to the elevation of intellectual and moral nature which results from their society; I think we may doubt whether their intellectual perception of this reason would have overcome the mutual repulsion which there must have been, if they saw in each other only rivals and probable enemies. Nature has brought them together and enabled them to protect each other by conquering any tendency there might have been to this repulsion through an opposite principle, the attraction of love.

One-sided moralists confine their view to one or other.

The different parts of kindly affection, or love, fall in with the different parts of relative duty, and, even in the absence of conscientiousness, would secure the performance of a good deal of this, while, in the presence of conscientiousness, they reinforce and facilitate it. Things are best, as I have said, when the two fitly concur. Conscientiousness by itself is dry and cold. Feeling by itself is occasional and variable. The element of self-transcendence or self-sacrifice which conscientiousness brings adds on its side new worthiness and beauty. On the other hand, the spontaneousness, the absence of effort, the genuine willingness, which there is in feeling, brings a worthiness of a different kind. There is a kind of native intolerance in us due to contraction of sympathy and limitation of intellectual view, from which it results that few persons see moral beauty in both these things, conceiving it must exist only in one, or only in the other. There hence arises (for there are few persons more intolerant than ethical systematists) a continual contest between the moralists of duty and the moralists of feeling, the *officiarians* and *emotionalists;* while anti-moralists adopt, in conjunction, the views of each on the subject of the other, finding in the morality of duty a want of spontaneousness, in the morality of feeling a want of reason. "So far as we do right because it is our duty, we do it as something forced upon us, as something which, except for its being our duty, we had rather not do, the action is therefore not genuinely ours:

oral obligation is thus constraint. So far as we do right ecause we like it, there is no merit in it: it is like the stincts of the animals, and does not belong to our rational ature: we do it not deliberately and of purpose, but one appens to be led by his tastes to it, another not to be, hereas the action which we do deliberately and of purpose that which is really ours."

Surely it would be better to accept the nature and life of an as complicated than to be determined to simplify it in ese various intolerant manners. It is not necessary, except the logic of a systematic moralist and the limited comehension of his sectarian admirers, that because we do ght as our duty, and as under obligation, therefore right is hat we certainly should not do otherwise, and what must disagreeable and forced upon us. Nor again does it folw, because we find ourselves drawn by some of the kindly fections as unconsciously, as almost irresistibly, as some imals, *e.g.* by their maternal instincts, that therefore these me affections and actions according to them, may not as ell be commended to us by our reason for the purpose hich they answer and the good which they do.

Love seems to consist in the main of (1) pleasure in the ciety of its object, (2) pleasure in the thought of its object, and (3) pleasure in the thought of the pleasure of its oject: and of course the converse of these under opposite rcumstances. Three characters of love.

There seem also in the main to be three kinds or types of ve: *φιλία*, or love of association and companionship, *στοργή*, family affection, and *ἔρως*, or sexual love. Three kinds of love:

To begin with the last of these, as the most definite and stinct: it is a natural passion, making itself strongly felt the organization. It belongs to all animals, in most cases ith them obeying very definite instinctive laws according the species, and producing often in them a violence of mper and action quite exceptional as compared with their eneric habit. It is in some cases with them, as *e.g.* in most irds, associated with a certain degree of family affection nd pleasure of association and companionship, but in the reater number of cases, even of the higher organizations, no respect so, but perfectly independent of both of these. ἔρως, in animals:

Nor does it appear in any of them to be associated with anything like what we may call imagination, or particular observation and distinction of the object of it.

ἔρως in man. In man the natural character of this passion is to shew itself in conjunction with all that is thus wanting to it in animals. As in other cases, in the comparison of man and animals, so in this, there is with man little of that very definite instinctive limitation which there is with them: but, to counterbalance this, the passion tends to unite itself strongly in man, not only with the στοργή which we shall soon speak of, but with the rational and distinctive elements of his nature. It gives occasion to a stirring of his imagination greater than any other cause of exaltation and excitement can produce, and in conjunction with this it animates the feeling of enjoyment in sight, talk, and association, and increases the feeling of sympathy, in a manner which could not exist under any other circumstances. Where this is the case, and in the better sort of natures, it is probable that the passion itself hardly makes itself consciously felt otherwise than by its intensifying effects upon the whole nature; and its distinctness is lost in the variety and vigour of the imaginative action which it helps to excite.

Not properly an appetite. There seems to me but little significance in classing it among appetites and putting it with hunger and thirst. If we consider them as the types of appetite, appetite is an indication of a want of nature which must be supplied for the health and existence of the individual. This is only the case, or anything like it, with regard to the passion in question, in cases where the mental organization is in some way very defective, and the corporeal, through want of self-control, in a state unworthy of man. Where the tendency to society and sympathy and the imagination are active and as they should be, they will absorb the passion into themselves without allowing it to degenerate into appetite.

Its connexion with the imagination. It is evident that the association of this passion with imagination introduces dangers nearly as great, if of a somewhat more honourable kind, than what would arise from its being, as in animals, bare appetite. But the moral teacher in this respect must look at human nature as it is. Three parts out of four of elegant literature and of art are concerned, one way or another, with imagination as connected directly or indirectly with this passion. It is at the age, when character is being fixed, when purposes are being formed, and when the intellectual powers are, taking one thing with another, at their strongest, that the inflaming of the imagination from this cause usually takes place. And the steps, whatever they may be, to which it leads, are generally such as are felt through life.

Moral dangers arising from or associated with it.

We may accept it then as natural that some such stirring of the imagination should in some way or other take place, and count it as a blessing in comparison with the infinite degradation which results to the character in cases where the passion makes itself felt, and where there is neither moral self-control on the one side, nor the elevating, and to a certain extent diverting and absorbing accompaniments I have spoken of on the other. If once the coarseness or carelessness of companionship causes the passion to be looked on as an appetite which, if it is felt, may be satisfied, many of the best chances for future imaginative elevation and nobleness in the character are gone. A coarseness is introduced where delicacy and refinement are necessary, not simply for the goodness of the moral character, but for the clearness, and vividness and elevation of the imagination: the most promising shoot for future nobleness is cut off.

I shall not dwell here on the manner in which this coarseness of what should be the best part of the mind, is likely to be multiplied tenfold by the associations which it leads to, when what man's imagination has in its noblest flights taken pride in exalting, is viewed in desecration and degradation,—desecration and degradation which the author of them must abundantly participate in, through his own sympathy and consciousness, so long as there is anything left in his nature to degrade.

Not in itself stronger than there is occasion for.

Even where the imagination and higher parts of the character are in exercise there is of course no occasion possible in life in which more of reason is required for the purposes of consideration and foresight, than this, in which so many things occur to render the exercise of reason difficult. On the other hand, supposing the feeling to be associated with the imagination and under due self-control, as it should be in man, we shall not probably consider that it is stronger than there is occasion for in reference to the whole of life which follows it. If it is strong, there is a demand for strength of feeling to correspond to the closeness and intimacy of that particular relative duty which it concerns, the mutual duty between husband and wife. In man's various moral nature the early provision of it is intended not to be exhausted and done with, but to fill the moral being in such a way as to influence the whole of after life: the merely emotional feeling of passion and devotion which might of itself evaporate, is preserved and rendered continuously active by its being incorporated in the conscientious feeling of duty.

Στοργή in animals and in man.

Family affection, or στοργή, is a feeling extending along a scale from maternal affection, which is an instinct of the strongest kind, till in the affection of brothers and other kindred it widens out into more general forms of love. Here, we seem to see an instance how, as instinctive feeling and duty generally coincide, so they do not *necessarily:* and the greater complication and worthiness of the life of man, as compared with that of the animals, wants considerations of conscience to be superadded to those of feeling. Nature, in regard of animals, makes great provision for the weakness of youth: little, if any, for the weakness of age. The former it cares for: the latter, its work being done, it does not. Correspondingly, when nature transfers its animal dealings to man, there is a vast provision of instinctive affection to support the relative duty of parents to children, and by no means so much to support that of children, grown up, to parents, weak and old. But old age, though not dear to instinctive or lower nature, is eminently dear to social or higher nature. Morality has two characters, one falling in with instinctive affections, the other supplementing them. It is in the spirit of this latter that regard for parents and regard for old age has ever been a special point of positive morality. It is as important a matter for life and for society, and as important a relative duty, that parents should take care of their children, as that children should honour their fathers and mothers, but we do not so commonly find it included in schemes of relative duty such as the Decalogue or the 'Duty towards our neighbour.'

Four kinds of association among animals.

Besides these markedly instinctive associations, there are the less strong ones concerned with general friendliness and companionship.

Of such association among animals there are various kinds, principally perhaps four:

1. Association of community or with the appearance of political organization, such as that of bees. This rather takes place, it would appear, low down in the animal scale, arguing less complete individual distinction and independence. It is one form which is taken by the as yet insufficient detachment of individual existence from common: and it furnishes a figure of what, in the highest moral existences, reason tends to produce; namely, a conscious reabsorption, to a certain extent, of individual interests in the common. Political association (bees).

2. Gregariousness, which is not real sociality, or rather which furnishes us an image of what sociality would be, were all individuals (speaking generally) similar. Sociality is founded on difference as much as on resemblance. Society in general as much depends on difference in the individuals who form it as social economy on difference of employments. Gregariousness.

3. Congeneric attachment or recognition, which seems to exist at least in all the higher kinds of animals, giving them a different feeling towards individuals of their own kind from that which they have towards creatures of any other kind. Feeling of kind.

4. Familiarity, habitual proximity, or *consuetudo*, which seems to bind together almost into a real friendship, and without any regard to kind, creatures the most dissimilar. Consuetudo.

There is another kind of animal association, more like human association in some respects, and much more like human association as viewed by some moralists, which nevertheless I have not thought fit to reckon with the others: I mean that joining together for the purpose of taking their prey which seems the nature of some animals (wolves for instance), and would indicate a high degree of reason. But I do not think it would help us in what is my business now, the comparison of human affections with those belonging to animals. [Cooperation in hunting prey.]

All the different characters which I have mentioned as belonging to animal association belong to the association of man with man, together with several more.

All human kindly affection is *discriminative*, that is, it attaches itself to some individuals in distinction from All found in man combined with discrimination.

others. The discrimination depends partly on reasons personal to him who feels the affection, partly on reasons general, or good for all. These two kinds of reason are often closely involved together, leading to intellectual error, which may be of importance, or which may not be so.

Love may spring from a general or a particular cause.

The love produced by gratitude, and the love produced by moral admiration (a particular, and a general reason), are probably not of themselves very different in kind: that is, the difference which there is in one instance and another of love of the above kinds, depends, in each case, upon the particularity of the circumstances which have caused it. It is action that is to the benefit of men that moves our moral approbation: and this benefit being by sympathy made ours, the moral approbation thus felt is very similar in character to the feeling of gratitude. On the other hand, we cannot help (more or less) generalizing kindness to ourselves into goodness and worthiness in our benefactor: it is in the nature of things that we should. Though in this we may be often, intellectually, wrong, it is what we could not wish, within limits, otherwise.

Love or affection, in the main, bestows itself,—and speaking broadly bestows itself right,—in the manner which I mentioned when speaking of its accompanying relative duties. But in individual instances it is by no means certain to bestow itself right, and the providing, as far as possible, that it shall do so, is a great part of moral training.

It is an advantage to morality that the two are often blended or confused.

The confusion between love for individual, and love for general, reasons is in reality a very great advantage in morals, though at the first sight it perhaps does not seem so. On bare principles of reason we shall perhaps be told, that we ought to love, not our actual brother, who may be no better than other people, not our benefactor, who may be good to nobody but us, but the man whom for his goodness everybody should love, who is in his way virtuous and kind to all. But it is the producing this same affection in different ways which (always of course within limits) makes the strength and value of it. It is produced by felt benefit to ourselves, it is produced by familiarity and companionship, it is produced by knowledge of good deeds: this latter marks specially what should be loved on grounds of reason, but the bestowing the affection in the other ways is no injury to this, for by it a character of warmth is given to the whole affection, and love as caused by moral approbation is all the better for it.

We ought to love what is worthy of love and what is not worthy of love both, in different ways and for different reasons. What is not worthy of love in general is often worthy of it from *us*, as I have said. It may be said to be a moral provision of nature on the side of good, that the sensation of being loved and thought well of by any is elevating and beneficial. It is a provision by which good is gained from circumstances which no doubt give rise to much harm.

General esteem and love a strong natural help to virtue.

For the misbestowal of love and, as a consequence of it, the attributing moral approbation (or what is equivalent to this) where it is not deserved, *does* of course do much harm. It is hard to give any moral precepts as to which people will not, in their eagerness to make morality simple, exaggerate their applicability and so destroy their value. This is preeminently the case in regard to all precepts tending to diminish the *discriminativeness* of the kindly affections. The great moral provision made by nature for the securing virtue in the world, is the approbation and, more than approbation, love, felt for the virtuous. Every good and virtuous man is, in his measure, a benefactor of all: and nature has to a certain extent provided that all shall love him as such. This is the real moral notion of 'merit.' One reward which virtuousness looks to, and may look to without losing its disinterestedness, is the kindly feeling of men: and virtue, when considered as the object of this, is called, in the moral application of the term, 'merit.' The position of the virtuous, in this respect, is like that of the man who does a kindness to another: if it is done on account of an act of gratitude expected, of a kindness in return, it is no proper kindness, it is interested. But if it is done on account of the good it will do and the pleasure it will give, with full anticipation, as well, of the feeling of gratitude on the part of the receiver, this does not make the action interested: under many circumstances it makes it the better, the kinder. And so in respect of virtue and the love or approbation of men. As well say that no man cares really for another's good because all men value gratitude, as say (as moralists have occasionally done) that virtue or kind action is nothing real, is not done for its own sake or loved for its own sake, because men value the love and approval with which it is welcomed.

How far affection should be under control of reason.

The bestowal of love or affection is not a thing to be entirely subordinated to reason, or it ceases to be what it is. It must have much in it that is accidental. But it must in some degree go by reason: feeling is to some degree matter for self-possession and direction. Kindly affection is founded on opinion about the persons whom it concerns. That this opinion should be entirely wise and correct, does not matter: but it should not be too much otherwise. The relations of life perplex the intelligence in judging of people, and ought to be allowed to a certain extent to do so. But beyond this, the being led away by accidental associations and by insignificant particulars in our opinions about people and affections towards them, is the source of a vast deal of mischief and a vast deal of vice.

CHAPTER IX.

GENESIS OF VIRTUE: ITS INTELLECTUAL ELEMENTS, PRINCIPLE.

Feelings of good-will require to be controlled and reenforced by principle before they can be called virtuous.

At the beginning of the last chapter I defined virtue as benevolence stimulated and regulated by the sense of duty and love of excellence. We have seen what is meant by the loose expression benevolence, and have now to consider how this is affected by the other things spoken of.

Considering then benevolence as above described in its relation to virtue, there has to be said the following: first, that it wants something before it can be called virtuous itself: and next, that even if it were entirely virtuous in itself, it needs to be reinforced by something besides itself.

In the first place, simply impulsive action, or action on feeling only, would not lead to virtue, or the public-spirited action which I designated by that name. The benevolent impulses themselves would want direction and management from what I will call principle, not to mention that we should be moved by a great variety of impulses besides those of benevolence. Man is thus a being whose virtue has two distinct features belonging to it, good impulse and self-control: I mean by the vague word principle whatever it is that brings about the latter.

It is to emotion, from its nature, that the *starting* of action mainly belongs, while the controlling of emotion belongs to intelligence.

Principle in itself is always good.

Principle in one sense is always good, in another sense it may be good, neutral, or bad: or, in other words, it is always good in so far as it is *principle*, though in the particular case it may be wrong, and the self-control which it generates may be perverted and misapplied. We shall probably see this more plainly when we come in a moment to speak of distinctively moral principle, commonly called *conscience.*

Human virtue a compound of principle and impulse.

In all *human* conceptions of virtue principle and impulse concur, and must do so. The being of purely good impulse, without need, and without possibility, of good principle, is, in the Aristotelic phrase, ἢ θηρίον ἢ θεός, which means, that this is a state of moral consciousness, if we are to call it so, which we cannot at all picture to ourselves. Again, if we imagine a being of purely good principle, or rather, a being whose virtue was of principle alone, we should either have to suppose him without impulse or feeling or with none but bad: neither of which suppositions would represent what we call virtue.

Virtue being thus compounded of principle and impulse, is voluntary partly with the voluntariness of premeditation and deliberation, and partly with the voluntariness of spontaneousness: it is self-command and self-mastery, and yet not something which, with whatever view, we merely force upon ourselves: it is good impulse, and yet not merely the unreflective result of our emotional organization.

Increase in virtue is not the same as the formation of mechanical habit.

When we picture to ourselves increasing virtue, we consider the struggle involved in the self-control or principle as continually diminishing: but we cannot really picture to ourselves our ideal of perfection in this respect, for if the self-control (which loses meaning without the supposition of something to be controlled) entirely vanished, then we should have come round to the supposition of a being inferior to man in one respect, that his action, however good in result, was simply spontaneous and without the higher form of will, the premeditative and deliberate. There is no meaning in choice of virtue without some degree of supposition of possible choice of vice.

The process of increasing virtue, in which the struggle which results in self-control is continually diminishing, is called by philosophers the formation of moral habits: and it is highly important that those who speak of these should remember that the process is not in any respect the extinction of reflection and principle, which would be the falsifying the moral nature of man and making him, morally, an inferior kind of creature, however he might, individually, become a better creature of his kind. Moral philosophers, in their desire of explanation and simplification, are probably more in danger in this respect than ordinary men. The ordinary view, from its point of inferior exactness, seems to allow distinctly enough, the difference between mechanical and moral habit: there is danger lest philosophers, in their desire of greater simplicity and exactness, should confound them.

Benevolence needs principle, first, to regulate it:

But not to dwell on this: benevolence, in whatever degree it exists, wants *principle* before it can be conceived to constitute virtue: that is to say, it must be regulated in various respects: some benevolence would be wrong, not as benevolence, but as coming into the place of what would be right; and there must exist in the mind not only the feeling that this regulation of it is desirable and necessary, but also the power, the self-mastery, required to bring it about.

On the various respects in which benevolence, if we wish it to result in virtue, must be regulated by principle, I will not linger. In the benevolence which is virtue there is more or less a definite aim or purpose (that is, an ideal, as I called it, of the second kind), a conception formed of the happiness which we wish to promote, and of the manner in which it is to be promoted.

There is in such benevolence also a feeling of very great importance which I have yet to speak of, that of fairness and justice. And more generally, the notion of duty which I have discussed at length, comes in: comes in, as respects what is now before us, to determine the objects of the benevolence, and to ensure account being taken in it of those relations among men which I have spoken of.

second, to reinforce it:

But, in the second place, besides that benevolence, to whatever amount it existed, would not, without principle, constitute virtue, it would not, without principle, exist in sufficient quantity to produce or account for,—not to say the virtue which the world wants, which is not the matter of our present consideration,—but the virtue which the world *has*.

as against self-regard.

In speaking of benevolence or good-will, I have spoken also of the feeling which is directly opposite to it, ill-will: but I have not spoken of the feeling (so to call it) which, though not thus directly opposite to it, is a far greater counter-worker of it, viz. self-regard or self-engrossment.

This latter is of two kinds, according as there is or is not applied to it such principle (as I just now explained the word) as is consistent with it and does not destroy its character.

Self-regard may itself be under the control of principle, in which case it

Self-regard, without such principle, is self-indulgence; with it, it is that which is known by various names, in later moral philosophy as self-love or rational self-love, in common language either (with blame implied) as selfishness or self-interestedness, or (in absence of blame) as prudence. The term 'prudence' is itself a term of praise or the supposed name of a virtue: it may be exercised on behalf of others as well as on behalf of ourselves: it represents in fact all the lower portion of that which I have called principle: I mean by 'lower,' all that portion of it which is intellectual only, as distinguished from what is moral. When prudence is exercised for ourselves only, it is a virtue in so far as it is *prudence* (as I said about principle in general): in so far as it is for our own benefit alone, it is of no moral account.

becomes prudence: otherwise it is self-indulgence.

The work of moral principle is threefold: first, to make benevolence, as above described, prevail over self-regard and self-engrossment; second, to regulate and govern the benevolence, in the way which I a short time since mentioned: and third, to elevate, stimulate, govern, and discipline, the individual dispositions in accordance with the above.

And of moral principle (all these divisions are to be taken very generally, for *exact* classifications, in a subject such as we are now dealing with, are a mere appearance) there are two forms: one more definite and precise, which we will call the sense of duty: the other more aspiring, but at the same time more vague, which we will call the love of excellence.

Two forms of moral principle.

The sense of duty goes by the name, with a large number of moral philosophers, of *conscience*. The word 'conscience,' at first signifying what in legal phrase is called 'guilty knowledge,' then the notion, not far removed from this, of self-condemnation for some particular offence, came at last to signify what we may generally express as 'the mind acting morally': judgment of actions or possible actions as portions of, or contraventions of, duty, *i.e.* as in accordance with, or in opposition to, the ideal moral law.

Sense of duty, or conscience (1).

There is the same difficulty in regard to this as in regard to perception.

In the case of conscience on the one side and the moral law on the other, the same thing is to be said which I have said in each case where we speak of perception on our part of anything, viz. that we may consider the reality and truth either to be on the subjective side, and to consist in rightness of thought or judgment, or to be on the objective side, and to consist in the fact, that that which is supposed to be perceived presents itself to us as it is: which of these two we do is of no further importance than in respect of their comparative facility of consideration; the only thing of importance being that we must know *which* we are doing, and avoid a confusion between the two.

Some, as Butler, take the subjective view, and speak of conscience; others the objective, and speak of the moral law.

Of these two views that which may be called the subjective has been taken by those moral philosophers who speak much of conscience and little of the moral law, or who consider conscience itself to be that law: virtue, as Butler would describe it, is the acting according to conscience (or the moral mind) judging rightly.

Of what importance, however, are these two latter words? and why is it not sufficient to say, that virtue is acting according to conscience?

How far is it true that action according to conscience is right action?

We may say so altogether or absolutely, upon one supposition: and without any supposition, we may say so approximately, and with a degree of truth.

The supposition is, that we consider the operation of anything and its ideal or proper operation the same thing. On this view, 'according to conscience' would mean 'according to conscience judging rightly,' for it is the function of conscience to judge, and in mentioning it, we suppose it to discharge its function properly. It is on this view that philosophers speak of *reason* as an authority in morality, or in fact, that we use the words 'acting according to reason,' 'reasonable,' at all: for reason may, actually, be wrong as well as right, judge mistakenly as well as correctly; and when there is any danger of mistake from taking the ideal view, a philosopher like Aristotle is careful to take the *actual* one, and to say ὀρθὸς λόγος, *right* reason. It is in the same way that we speak of conscience judging rightly.

But without any such supposition, and simply considering how conscience actually does judge, there is an approximate truth in our saying that virtue is acting according to conscience, in this double way: that conscientiousness is one step of virtue, and the person who makes the one step is likely to make the other, and to be *rightly* conscientious, careful, in theological language, to have his conscience well informed: and next, that without the supposition of such special care, conscience, when put in exercise, is more likely to judge right than wrong: its wrong judgment will be the exceptional.

Butler describes virtue at one time as conscientiousness, at another as benevolence, without showing the relation of these to each other.

Butler may be said, not to make two virtues, but to give two different forms of virtue, which ought to fit together, and to be shown to coincide, but whose fitting he does not sufficiently describe. His two forms of virtue are 'conscientiousness,' and 'the acting according to the public, rather than to the private affections,' or, as he has also called it and I call it here, 'benevolence.' He has given what we may call two moral philosophies without any account of their relation to each other. I conceive, that in giving what, as they stand in him, are two moral philosophies, he is right: but that there wanted more account of their relation, and attempt to make them one.

He shows that conscience

It is a part of this, and probably a part of the reason of it, that his account of conscientiousness is

has authority over impulse, but not that it has authority over prudence or principle of any sort.

not sufficient: he gives no reason why *moral* principle, or conscience, should be superior to *intellectual* principle, or prudence. The account which he gives of the supremacy of conscience is applicable to all of that which I have called principle, and in fact, is only one particular, new, and striking form of the universal account of it. Everything in our nature is to be supposed for a purpose, and if either a faculty whose function is to review does not review, or if its judgments of reviewal are unregarded, it is as good as if it were not, and there is something wrong about it. Every faculty, in its function, has given to it authority for its function, and the supposed supervising faculty has the authority to supervise. But this applies to reflection, or as I have called it *principle*, of all kinds: and we want to know why *moral* reflection has authority over other kinds of reflection.

Let us take then the stream of virtue composed, so far as we have seen as yet, of the various concurring streams of benevolence: let us see what is contributed to it by conscientiousness; and whether that which is so contributed is of such importance as to deserve to be considered the main stream.

[Danger of personifying abstract terms.]

I use the word conscientiousness rather than conscience, and in the same way I shall often use the word virtuousness instead of virtue in general, and speak of forms or kinds of virtuousness instead of particular virtues, because I prefer to use terms which on the face of them, are plainly no more than abstract, the old abstract terms having been realized and personified in a very perplexing way. Men are conscientious or virtuous in the same way as they are physically black or white: the terms may express imperfectly what it is wished to express, but there is no puzzle about them, no question as to what region of thought they belong to; and conscientiousness or virtuousness is at once understood to be the abstract substantive of the corresponding adjective.

Conscience is one form of imaginative sensitiveness.

The word conscientiousness may be applied in a wider or narrower sense, but I am now going to use it in the narrower. I mean, it might mean simply sensitiveness: we might, if we liked to widen the use of the word, speak of a conscience of benevolence, and, in a way which I shall speak of presently, of a conscience of honour. There is a kind of self-judgment, taking account of benevolence alone, in reference to any past failure of benevolence on our part. Independent of any feeling of right and wrong, without anything that can be distinctly called self-condemnation, past unkindness on our part may be remembered by us with pain; and the thought of the suffering which our unkindness may have caused, may dwell in our minds most unpleasantly. That this is a different thing from conscience is clear from the consideration, that this feeling of the consequences of our act may exist in cases in which the unkindness (so still to call it) is justified by our real conscience or sense of duty. Conscientiousness thus is not simply sensitiveness in general: not simply the imagination in application to our actions towards others, but one form only of such.

Distinctively benevolent action involves principle akin to, but not the same as, conscience.

Again, in acting from benevolence only, without, or almost without, anything of what I have called principle, we may form ideals for action, and exercise our imagination in this way also. I say *almost*, because the acting for an ideal does always involve something of principle or force exerted by the mind on itself: it makes the action to some extent distinctively intellectual. The amount to which it is intellectual depends upon how far the force, which keeps us from wandering from the ideal, is the imaginative presence to our mind of others' sufferings or pleasure, that is, a matter of feeling and the same kind of thing as stirs our benevolent impulse, or how far, on the other hand, it is a resistance, from other quarters than this, to those temptations and distractions from occasional impulse or otherwise, which will always make acting for an ideal an effort. Speaking generally, a person who is to act distinctively for a benevolent ideal must not be too distinctively benevolent. That is, he must conceive benevolence in a large way which would be disturbed in some degree by being too keenly alive to the details of it. I mention this simply philosophically, without any insinuation : each of the two manners of benevolence is good in its way. The thing which I am saying, put in an exaggerated way, has been made a subject of reproach to supposed professional philanthropists : again, an exaggeration of the reverse view has been made a reproach against emotional impulse. I have nothing to do with these.

Conscientiousness or moral principle differs from benevolent sensitiveness and idealization by having reference, in the first instance, rather to what *we do* than to what *others feel*.

Our active nature conjoined with our social nature suggests that pain is not to be inflicted on others, just as, conjoined with our sentient nature, it suggests that it is to be avoided for ourselves.

It will be remembered that I said some time since, in speaking of pain, that its being what we ought not to inflict seemed to me quite as much a part of what I may call the instinctive definition of it, as its being what we do not like to suffer. It is commonly assumed, that its unpleasantness to ourselves or rather, its *to-be-avoidedness* is an immediate feeling (as no doubt it is), and its *not-to-be-inflictedness* a secondary feeling which can only come to us after observation, on our part, of it in others, and sympathy with their suffering under it. This does not seem to me so. Our nature is, as I have tried before to describe, in itself, in its very rudiments, active and social as well as sentient : *i.e.* we are, to start with, different beings, ı every portion of our make, from what we should e, not only if we were going to grow up stones, but ' we were going to grow up in a world where motion ras impossible or in a world of necessary solitude.)ur active nature superadds *this* to our simply sen-ient nature, that pain is instinctively felt by us not nly as unpleasant, but as to be avoided; in other rords, that uneasiness causes movement: our *social* ature, superadded, widens this into the more gene-al feeling, that pain is to be prevented, *a fortiori* ot to be caused or inflicted: there does not need xperience of pain in others, and actual sympathy rith their suffering, for this: the supposition of their esemblance to us is, if anything is, instinctive. We nd thus, from the very first, a determinant of our ction beyond ourselves, a restraint, as it were, laid pon it.

Thus our nature supplies an original moral restraint: which seconds the benevolent impulses.

It is simply an expansion of this principle, when re find ourselves possessed with the notion that, in urting others, we are doing that which action is not or; that such action is improper action, not the action hat should be; that, as hurting ourselves is what ac-ion is not for, and we call it unwise, so hurting others s what action is not for, and we call it wrong. The wo notions, of that which we should not do, and of he causing pain to others, are thus from the first in ur nature combined: and thus, for the constituting 'irtue, we have not only the mass of affection which have spoken of and called benevolence, but we have he notion of restriction or determination of our own ction, and that *to* actions which are benevolent, and *gainst* actions which are contrary to these: we have n fact the stream of principle, of *should* or *ought*, flow-ng into that of benevolent emotional impulse, to nake virtue.

Importance of

Some notion or assumption of this kind was, I

this consideration as explaining the relation of conscience to benevolence;

think, wanted by Butler, to make it appear how or why conscience (moral principle) determines action in the direction of benevolence rather than any other way. If virtue is made to consist at one time solely in conscientiousness and at another time solely in benevolence, it ought to have been explained how it is that, as a matter of fact, right moral judgment does determine our action in the direction of benevolence.

and also the authority of conscience.

Some consideration like that which I have given seems required, to tell us not only how it is that benevolence is the conduct to which conscience impels us, but also why conscience is to be looked on as something in human nature which should be thought highly of, rather than as a weakness of it. Why is the virtuous view, that conscience is to be honoured, to be preferred to the vicious view, that "conscience doth make cowards of us all," that conscientiousness, and the habit of taking ourselves to task as to what we do, is a foolish weakness, that consideration for others is a foolish weakness also? It seems to me, that the real answer to these questions is contained in the consideration that our very notion of pain is, as much, that it is something wrong to inflict, as that it is something which it is well or wise to avoid: in this way we have from the first the conscientious feeling leading us to direct our action so as not to inflict pain, in the same way as we have the prudent feeling leading us to avoid it: and thus both conscientiousness and consideration for others are provided for in our nature from the first, and cannot be considered as weaknesses into which it may fall.

Conscience aids benevolence by restraining what is opposed to it; the prevention of pain being a more positive idea than the

The impulsive maxim then, or axiom of benevolence, Love all in their degree ('in their degree' marking the different nature of the affections which I have spoken of), becomes reinforced by the maxim of principle or conscience, less emphatic in its contents but more emphatic in its enforcement of them upon us, Hurt no one, *neminem læde.* production of pleasure.

Conscience is, as I described, another expression for the sense of duty; and it will be remembered that I said that the notion of duty differed from that of virtue in its generally negative or prohibitive character; guarding against offence, rather than pointing to heights of aspiration. This is apparent in what I have given as the general maxim of moral principle here. In speaking of the nature of pain and pleasure, I shall endeavour to show how it is, that *pain* is, as it were, the *positive* consideration, and that pleasure, as it is called, does not suggest the effort after it for ourselves and for others, in the same immediate way in which pain suggests the effort against it, and the disinclination to inflict it. In the same way, as regards duty, possible offence against it is the positive consideration. Conscience is not a stimulating, but a restraining principle.

Conscience is moral imagination, not merely moral judgment.

Still, as I said about duty, that it was an ideal, so principle, as I have described it, may almost be defined, as acting by an ideal. Conscience is commonly described as moral judgment: it might more widely be described as moral imagination, including judgment where judgment is required. Each act of conscience, as some moral philosophers have put the matter, is a moral syllogism: there is a contemplated action, as minor premiss, referred to a general principle, as major premiss. In reasoning, the syllogism is only the conclusion of a long process of preparation in the way of consideration of the subject, determination of premisses, &c., just as a trial in law is the conclusion and final result of a long process of investigation, search after evidence, &c. This previous consideration, in reasoning, is the work of imagination. In the same manner conscientious judgment is the result of a process of moral imagination: there are principles in the mind, which correspond, in the subjective view we are now taking, to the objective particulars of the ideal moral law, or duty. The right information of the conscience is the same thing, in the one way of speaking, that the discovery what the moral law says upon the subject in question, is in the other.

The 2nd form of moral principle is love of excellence.

I will not however say more on conscience just now: I shall speak of duty in the next chapter from a slightly different point of view, and we may have to refer again to the sense of duty, or conscience: I now proceed to the love of excellence.

Our social nature enables us to sympathize with each other's thoughts and purposes, as well as with pleasures or pains.

Man's sociality consists in his being born into society with a number of beings who are not only co-sentient with him, but co-active: and in his having a nature correspondent with this. He is imaginatively aware not only of their pains and pleasures, but also of their thoughts and purposes. The former of these kinds of imaginative knowledge we call sympathy, and have spoken of it in treating of benevolence: the latter has no word to express it, not coming much into common consideration: we will for the moment call it co-intelligence: though, as it is a form of sympathy, I shall sometimes speak of it under that term.

Our moral, like our intellectual, judgments are formed in imagined sympathy with the judgments of others.

I have already said of how much importance the known or supposed sympathy of others with our thought is in respect of our notions of truth. In the same way, all our conscientious or moral judgments are formed in imagined sympathy with the judgments of others. The fact that this is so, has sometimes been perverted to signify that conscience is nothing more than a representation to ourselves of the probable judgments of others, that thus it is no individual judgment, and only a cowardly abdication of our own authority over ourselves, a *mis-subordination* of our conduct. But this is only in close analogy with our intellectual judgments. When we judge even in a simple matter of sight, as *e. g.* that such a tree is green, we may be said implicitly to make the assertion, that others think so too, or would if they were in our position. If anything led us to doubt this assertion, we should doubt the tree's being green, in spite of our eyes. For we see, as it were, not with eyes of our own, but with all men's eyes, and if anything made us think we saw with eyes of our own distinctively from this, we should not have the faith in our senses which we are considered to have. When anything leads us to test our knowledge from what I have called the subjective point of view, that is, whether we see rightly or correctly, or however it may be, we instinctively have recourse to what is the real meaning of truth from *this* point of view, viz. what I will call ideal or right thoughtness, towards which the thought of our fellow-intelligent beings is an approximation.

In analogy with this, our conscientious judgments also are always made in the imagined company of our fellow-moral beings. We encourage ourselves with their imagined approval, (even with no thought of actual knowledge on their part), and reproach ourselves with all the imagined authority of their common voice.

The importance of this imagined union of the general moral judgment with our own we shall see more fully directly. But I turn first to something else.

Our active, joined with our social, nature

We are all, by our very nature, each other's rivals in action, *i. e.* the action of one stimulates another. This may be said to be hardly more than another way

makes us rivals, not only for the ends of action;

of expressing the union of sociality with activity. This consideration, in some respects, acts in the direction against virtue. There is in the world a great deal of conflict of interests, and this notion of rivalry with each other leads to an imaginative generalization of this partial conflict, *i.e.* to a sort of half-formed notion that another's happiness is a loss to ourselves. This is the disposition to vague general grudging, sometimes called envy, and not uncommon. I have already said something about this rivalry for happiness.

but in action itself.

Were action really to be considered a necessary evil, only existing in the universe on account of the insufficiency of happiness, this mutual rivalry would probably all act on the side of vice. But, as it is, action is as natural to man as enjoyment, as much a pleasure as a pain: and we are each other's rivals in action independently of being rivals for the object which the action is to gain.

This is the rivalry in merit which is so powerful an aid to virtue.

Hence arises that rivalry, as I will for a moment call it, in worth, merit, or moral value, which is a main mover of the world, and a far more efficient agent in aid of virtue than rivalry of interests is a difficulty on the other side. This rivalry in worth is not a mere dispute as to which shall have the most of men's approbation, but a stimulating of the good in one by the thought of the good in another.

Real worth is the fact which is tested by actual excelling and supposed by estimation.

The words signifying 'virtue' in modern languages have been transferred or translated from ancient philosophy without independent life in themselves, but the notions from which the old terms started were all, more or less, of *excellence* or comparative worth. What may be called the *fact* of excellence is worth: the *test* of it is actual excelling, or comparison: and the *presumption* of it, or a presumption for it, is estimation.

Worth consists in

I have discussed 'moral value' above, and the conleration of worth must go upon the principles laid own there. A man's worth in the universe is his use-lness taken in connexion with the personal qualities hich cause or accompany that usefulness, not his use-lness alone, even supposing we take a very elevated ew of the nature of usefulness. The high estimation r instance of *courage* among the Romans, which used 'virtus' to represent, in conjunction, both urage as worth, and worth as courage, was not lely because courage was, in a state of society like eirs, what the state most wanted, but because they, ke all men, had an independent admiration of urage.

usefulness combined with certain personal qualities.

The test of worth is actual excelling, and here we me to that rivalry of which I have just spoken. The valry or contest for superiority or excelling is a force f great moment in the world, both for evil and for ood. It is different from the conflict of *interests*. his latter arises from our sentient nature; and not nly to the extent to which it exists, but also to the xtent to which it is imaginatively expanded, it is ltogether a difficulty in the way of virtue, though an nportant field for virtue to exercise itself in. The valry for *excelling*, on the other hand, in the main ne of its operation, is more an aid than a hindrance o virtue: men, as active beings, are rivals of each ther in many efforts and pursuits which are unworthy, ut in more that are worthy. There are however a ariety of subsidiary feelings most of which are *against* irtue: these are suspicions, jealousies, chafings under efeat or inferiority, sour regrets, and other feelings f that nature.

Men are rivals for that which tests worth.

I mentioned some time since, that active or unoc-asioned ill-will from one sentient being to another vas hardly conceivable. If we are to imagine then a eginning for moral evil or wrong, we shall probably

This rivalry though mainly favouring virtue yet

easily passes into evil in the form of ambition.

look for it in the conflict of interests, and the rivalry connected with that. If we suppose a state where this is not possible, we shall still have remaining, for supposition, the rivalry for superiority which is an incident of the co-existence of any active beings. Accordingly, when people have theorized about the beginning of moral evil, *this* is what they have very commonly supposed: and the way in which it has been expressed has been by saying, that the mother of all offence, the arch-sin, is pride, or, in Wolsey's language, ambition. It is here that there seems most readily possible a passage from good to evil, a sort of transmutation of the one into the other.

Effects of a right ambition.

For it is clear that ambition, in so far as it is a desire to excel another in pursuits or efforts which are proper for both, has nothing in it of evil, but is, on the contrary, a most powerful agent on the side of virtue and good. Our sociality, *i. e.* our living in the society of fellow-moral beings, is not only an occasion for benevolence, but it is (and that independent of mutual estimation, which I shall consider directly) a most powerful stimulant to action: the thought of companions in the same endeavour communicates courage, animates enterprize, and makes moral action quite a different thing from what it would be if we were solitary actors.

Danger of thinking too much of the estimation of others:

It requires however a considerable effort of abstraction, though one occasionally very necessary, to consider the effort only without the estimation, or, in other words, to consider our fellow-moral beings only as fellow-combatants, and not at all as witnesses: we had better therefore proceed to that which I have spoken of as being a presumption of excellence, viz. estimation.

I mentioned some time since that, so far as their derivation goes, the words expressing excellence are very likely to express, in the first instance, the estimation of it, as is the case for instance with the term 'honestus.' If we want to express anything so abstract as the ideally right, we must do it through the medium of some metaphor (as it is frequently called) or, more properly, through the medium of something different from it, nearer to us, and less abstract[1]. Of course then we are always liable to the charge, that this latter is really all that we mean, that we have nothing in our minds beyond. And it is difficult to meet the charge: for, to express what we have beyond, we can only use some other metaphor, and so fall under the charge again.

Hence it has been often said that the *praiseworthy* means really no more than the *praised*: that we have no means of knowing what sort of conduct is worthy of approval, except by seeing what generally *is* approved: and that in fact there is no meaning in talking of worthiness, beyond this. The notion, that the conduct which goes by the name of virtue is entirely a result of man's love of others' approbation, that the term has in men's minds nothing else corresponding to it and means nothing else, has been widely held, and has taken various forms. If, when anything of this kind is said, it is still allowed that men praise what is praiseworthy, and that therefore the fact of their praising virtue is an argument that virtue is in itself, independently of their judgment, worthy of praise, then what is said really is that men are actuated by an inferior motive in doing that which it is well they should do from any motive; that they are

Of confounding the praiseworthy with the praised.

Some philosophers have held that virtue is nothing more than love of approbation.

[1] The author was in the habit of using the word *dianoematism* to express this universal law of language. See his (posthumous) articles on Glossology in the *Cambridge Journal of Philology*, vols. IV, V. As an instance of fallacious reasoning grounded on inattention to this law, it may suffice to refer to Mr Matthew Arnold's examination of terms expressive of *existence*, in the *Contemporary Review* for Nov. 1874.—ED.

doing right with a very imperfect conception of what they are doing, and, though looking upon virtue, mistake the outside and dress of it for itself, possibly with disadvantage to their practice, possibly not. If, on the other hand, people do not regard general praise as a sign of a thing being praiseworthy, but stop at the fact of the general praise, then there arises the view of virtue which treats it as *conventional.*

Thrasymachus' view that it is ἀλλότριον ἀγαθόν.

The rudest form of this view is that maintained against Socrates, that men wish others to be virtuous, while wishing, if possible, to avoid being so themselves; that everybody therefore praises virtue, in order to induce his neighbour to it, that being what is to his own interest; that hence there is universal praise of virtue, with universal desire, in each one, to avoid the practice of it; that with some, the love of the praise conquers this desire, and these are the virtuous.

This makes virtue result from universal viciousness, as Hobbes makes benevolence result from universal hostility.

The thing may be put, and has been put, in a great many other ways, and on all of them the same sort of thing is to be said which has been said on the Hobbistic notion of duty, to which this is the counterpart in respect of virtue. It seems to me, that those who, in the interest of natural theology, look for skilful contrivances on the part of the Creator, could find none more skilful than this, were the world such as philosophers of this kind consider. It goes further than the simpler Hobbistic notion, of universal mutual hostility producing universal kindness: if everybody can injure everybody, it is the best policy *for all* that nobody should injure anybody. But in this notion of virtue we have virtue in a manner existing without itself—existing, and not existing. It is the effort on the part of each to escape being virtuous himself, which produces such virtue as exists. In order to avoid it himself, everybody praises it in others; and this universal praise has its effect on some: hence virtue. The contrivance is admirable.

But why are men really to be supposed thus double-minded, and to praise not because they do like, but because they do not?

Virtue is really approved with the feeling that it is worthy of approval.

Without however going to any such extent as the above, almost all philosophers who are jealous of intuitivism are more or less driven to Hobbistic views on this part of moral philosophy, and are thus liable to the same censure as the above. When people are said to be influenced to virtue by what, in the language of many philosophers, is called the moral sanction, this moral sanction is often described as the general approbation of the thing to be done, as virtue. Now with what view is this approbation given? If those who approve approve because they think the thing ought to be approved, they must think also it ought to be done, and must themselves feel, more or less, the disposition to do it, though, in the particular case, this disposition in them might be overcome: then, speaking generally, the person who is supposed to be influenced by this moral sanction will be influenced also by the feelings which produce (in the supposed approvers of the thing) the moral sanction, and will himself approve the thing in the same way that they do: and this is the real moral sanction, rather than the other second-hand one, however as a fact, as no one would dispute, this latter may come in aid. I said just above, 'speaking generally,' because doubtless there are many particular cases in which the individual himself would not have the feelings which cause the approval in others: but where this is so, it is not any *moral* sanction or influence which moves him, but respect or care for others' opinion.

Any other view is

If, on the other hand, those who describe the

untrue to human nature.

moral sanction as above will not allow that the approbation of virtue, in the approvers, is determined by their feeling that it is worthy of approbation, then their view is really that which I mentioned before, though not rudely expressed like it. They must hold that there exists an opinion, resting at best upon nothing, resting possibly, like that, on the feeling in the approvers that the thing approved is *undesirable*, not desirable.

All notions of this kind, to whatever extent carried, of people making, in whatever manner, interested or heartless or unmeaning conventions by which individuals are influenced to what is then called virtue, are evidently untrue to human nature, and do not represent any fact. The approbation of others is in many respects a most powerful influence on the side of virtue: but when it acts as a really moral influence, then it is united with an approval by the man himself of the thing which the others approve, and this is conscience.

As imaginative sympathy combines with the thought of our action as right or wrong;

All the various attempts which have been made to discredit virtue because it is what is highly esteemed among men, seem to me founded on error. I have described how the fact, that our conscience judges in conjunction with the imagined judgment of others, is not a moral weakness, but a part of our nature and of our manner of judging altogether, intellectual as well as moral. I will speak now of some feelings cognate to conscience, in which this character, of reference to the imagined judgments of others, is *more* prominent.

and as kind or unkind;

I mentioned that benevolent sensitiveness made a sort of conscience, *i.e.* that we think about, and think over, our conduct in respect of it, not properly with self-approval or self-condemnation, for that would belong to our real conscience, but with pleasure in the imagination of the pleasure we may have caused, and pain in the imagination of the pain we have caused, or the pleasure we have refrained from causing: brooding and imagination in these respects will produce a benevolent sensitiveness, in a manner very analogous to that in which reflection and moral judgment will produce conscientiousness.

so it combines with the thought of our action as worthy or unworthy, without destroying the independence of such thought.

Similarly, we may form an ideal to ourselves of—excellence, I might say, worth, worthiness: none of them express with sufficient wideness the notion. It is superiority without reference to any as surpassed; praiseworthiness or admirableness without reference to actual admiration. Almost every one, from the highest to the lowest, forms some sort of ideal of this kind. The degree of moral importance of any such ideal depends upon two considerations: how far what it is concerned with has really moral value, and how far it is—not disengaged from the thought of others' actual estimation of us, for that it cannot be nor would it be well it was, but—with a strong root of self-judgment and self-trial in ourselves independent of this.

This is the sense of honour and shame.

Favourable estimation of a man by others on grounds of excellence, worth, or superiority is called *honour* of him, and a man who is in such a position is said to be honoured or to be in honour. The regard on a man's part to his own self-judgment in the above particulars, in conjunction with the imagination of the judgment of others about him, or, which is the same thing, his care for a *deserved* estimation of this kind by others, is called 'a sense of honour.' And if he acts at all systematically in this respect, or has an ideal law, rule, principle of this kind to go by, this is called, in reference to him, honour, or the law of honour. More generally, the same notion is expressed by self-respect, or a regard to character.

The opposite condition to a man's being *in honour* is his being *in disgrace,* and the state of mind of feeling disgrace is called 'shame.' 'Shame' indeed is a word of earlier, more positive, and wider signification than honour. And for this reason I shall often call what I defined above as the sense of honour, in its wide application, the sense of honour and shame.

How this differs from, and resembles, conscience.

It is more difficult to distinguish the sense of honour and of shame from conscience, or the sense of duty, than it is to distinguish benevolent sensitiveness from that. The sense of honour has the appearance of being a higher feeling than the sense of duty, in so far as in some respects it is freer, and there is not in it any thought of penalty, or dread of that kind. On the other hand, it is lower than the sense of duty, as there is certainly more imaginative reference in it than in that to men's opinion and judgment: it is therefore less individual and self-held; it has less hold of real moral value or merit; it is more likely to be fantastical and conventional; it stands more apart from benevolence; it is more occupied with our relation to our equals, or to those equally strong with us, than to the weaker: and hence the ideal law which it sets before us becomes often strangely at variance with that of duty.

The frame of honour is self-respect.

But the sense of honour and shame, as to the *manner* of its acting, is exactly a conscience like the sense of duty: it judges, controls, supervises, if we are to use such language, exactly as that does: it judges of law and fact, *i.e.* reminds us that we have done such and such a thing, and tells us that we have been wrong in doing it, exactly as that does: it is a moral reason, and syllogizes, as that does, bringing particular facts under a general principle.

The sense of honour and the sense of duty coincide to the extent to which, keeping strictly to the term 'honestum,' we identify the honourable with the right. To the extent to which we identify it with the 'beautiful,' (supposing the word καλόν ambiguous between this and the honourable), for the sense of duty or honour we have a kind of elevated æsthetic sense: on this another time.

Failings in regard to self-respect.

Adopting now 'self-respect' in reference to the sense of honour as the analogous term to conscientiousness in reference to the sense of duty, we have three ways of possible wrong about it: (1) a man may be deficient in self-respect, or, supposing him to have it, it may be to a great degree unregarded, or not powerful; just as conscience, with all its *de jure* authority, may not have actual power: or, (2) a man's self-respect may, like his conscience, be mis-informed: he may act strictly from considerations of honour, but may have an exceedingly bad code of honour: or, (3) his self-respect may be of a bad kind, bad in the manner of it, mixed with bad feelings: we shall see how.

Self-respect is essential to virtue and may not be sacrificed like self-indulgence.

One of the many ways, true, if not over-stated, in which virtue may be described, is that it is the substitution of one kind of self-regard for another; the substitution of self-respect for self-indulgence and self-interestedness; of regard to character (*i.e.* actual character, of which repute is an image or mark) for regard to pleasure and advantage. It is as much a part of virtue to foster self-attention, in this point of view, as it is to restrain self-attention, in the view of enjoyment. If this is forgotten, there is a danger, greatest perhaps in the cases in which the impulse to virtue is the strongest, of what we might call the suicide of morality by some such supposition as this: "the end which I want to gain is, by the allowance of all, a worthy and a noble one, one which is worth any sacrifice: what matters it what *I* do, one individual like me, and why should I not sacrifice to it myself, my conscience and character? Why should I not gain it by crime? There is then a noble end gained, and to counterbalance this there is nothing but *my* moral self-ruining; what am *I* in the universe, that this should be of any count? Is not moral self-sacrifice of this kind even nobler and worthier, because greater and more difficult, than any other kind of self-sacrifice[1]?"

Utilitarianism would lead us wrong here.

On any kind of utilitarianism, or supposition of the moral value of actions being all in their results, I do not see what answer could be given to this, except the following: You must take care that others do not imitate you in this particular, for if they do, that very powerful motive to virtue, regard for character, will become depreciated. To which the man would rejoin, No fear, there will not be many like me: it is an emergency, and *I* feel how much I am sacrificing: depend upon it, regard for character and reputation will always be powerful enough in the world: well if it is not too powerful. The man who feels like me its value, who knows what he is doing, has a right to sacrifice it.

Self-respect is the opposite of selfishness and helps self-sacrifice:

The proper view seems to me to be, that self-respect, or regard for our real character (as distinguished from reputation) instead of being, so to speak, a very elevated form of selfishness, so as to be a matter in which a sacrifice of self could possibly be made, is really exactly the reverse of selfishness, or self-interestedness, if we take even the widest and highest views of this. Our own moral individuality is a matter of entirely different nature from our individual

[1] The name 'Danton' is written by the side in the MS., no doubt with a reference to the famous words '*que mon nom soit flétri, que la France soit libre.*'—Ed.

nterest, and is not a thing which, like that, can possibly be matter of sacrifice. It is very well to put ur individual interest in the scale against a mass of ublic interest, and sacrifice that: but the putting ur individual virtue or moral being in the scale gainst the same, and sacrificing *that*, is another natter. No amount of the one will in reason bear lown the other. To the extent to which we feel the romotion of the public good our duty, we shall, in eason, feel the force of duty in general, and not acrifice duty even for that.

Moral self-maintenance then, so to call it, is the emper of virtue, exactly in the same way as selfbnegation or self-sacrifice is with reference to indulgence and to interest. And the way of this selfnaintenance is by conscientiousness and self-respect; y the existence, *i. e.* of such feelings, and by their ffectiveness for action.

because it raises us above the care for our own interests.

Self-respect thus, as well as conscientiousness, to he extent to which we consider them different, brings n a large reinforcement to the stream of virtue. Its peration is, to encourage feelings and conduct of that ind which I described as having moral value according to the first ideal, not the second, the value, *i. e.* ot of utility, but of self-transcendence and self-sacrifice. Conduct which has this kind of value has far nost usually the other kind as well (the converse not eing true); for conduct which I just now called elf-maintenance, care for our moral self, is more or ess the same thing as superiority to the care, in any ndue extent, of ourself in the point of view of indulgence and interest. Hence the aim or purpose of ction transcends self in the same degree in which the moral principle is firmly self-rooted: care for our own *moral* being involves no conflict of interest, appropriates nothing which anybody else could have, does not subtract (or at least need not and ought not to subtract) any time or labour from others' utility, but directs conduct to this from another side, and gives an additional value and energy to the conduct which is for it.

The ideals set before us by conscientiousness and self-respect may be erroneous.

Conscientiousness and self-respect are both kinds of what I have called *principle:* this we have seen: and they both idealize, *i. e.* act very much by the way of imagination, fill our mind with, or set before our mind, an ideal of conduct which we consider ought to be *our* conduct: particular conduct suggested to us we judge one way or the other according to its conformity to this ideal.

But is this ideal, in either of the cases, always a good one?

There is no doubt but that it is often far from being so, and where this is the case, both conscientiousness and self-respect become ministers of vice and wrong, not of virtue. In themselves they are still each good, as I have already said in reference to conscientiousness: the acting by principle is good, and the man is in a way which ought to have led him right; but owing to circumstances, particular indeed, but by no means very unlikely to occur, it has led him wrong.

This is more often the case with the ideal of self-respect than with that of conscience;

I explained before why a man's being conscientious makes it more probable than otherwise that he will act right: and exactly the same may be said of self-respect.

It is commonly considered that the sense of honour and of shame is a less sure guide in conduct than conscience is. This is so partly in one respect which I shall treat of soon, viz. in the manner of the feelng: is it so in the view of the ideal law or ideal of onduct, which it supposes, being more likely to be a alse and bad one?

It probably is, but still there are various things which must be considered as to this. When conscience has been written about, it has been generally, ven by the best philosophers, with a strange inattention to the distinction between the *ideal* view of onscientiousness, in which conscience is supposed to e properly performing its function, and the *actual* iew of it, as it exists in men, associated with all orts of error. The Republic of Plato with its ruling eason, and the Butlerian system or constitution with onscience for its regulator, never admit the possiility of the reason and the regulator going wrong, r what is to happen then? But it is clear that one f two things must be the case. If Butler means by onscience the ideal conscience, necessarily right, then nen's actual conscientiousness, the conscience in each f them, is quite a different thing (for it is often in rror), and in that case there is a wide field of moral hilosophy which he quite passes over, which should onsider the relation of the actual conscientiousness o the ideal conscience, and the means by which each s to know whether his own individual conscience ells him right. If, on the other hand, Butler means y conscience the actual conscience or conscientiousess of particular men, then there is entirely omitted y him all that large subject which is called by theoogians the *information* of conscience: and what is of nore consequence (for in general a writer is not to be lamed for what is *not* in his book, unless he proesses to give it), the descriptions of the authority or ightful supremacy of conscience lose very much of heir point and meaning. The authority becomes xceedingly untrustworthy: it is a judge requiring

still conscience needs to be informed, if it is to guide us right and have real authority.

supervision, a sentinel who wants a sentinel over him: and hence the question, as difficult in morals as in politics, about the right of resistance to this authority, and whether conscience really ought always to be obeyed.

Honour has more reference to opinion and is liable to be conventional and capricious.

While honour has been idealized by some philosophers in a manner not very different from conscience, many more have set themselves to describe the evils of its action when wrongly applied, a thing which has been but little done in the case of conscience. Not to dwell on the fact that honour has become a cant term among many persons professing to be guided by it, so that any true notions of it have been superseded by mere conventionalities, it cannot be denied that considerations of honour are more capricious, more liable to error, than anything which can be called conscience; and this mainly on account of the greater reference in them to opinion, or, which is the same thing, on account of the greater strength and intimateness of the individual feeling which really lies at the root of the other, though both, in different degrees, associate themselves with opinion. The individual feeling is of the same kind in both; it may be described as 'regard, not for self (except for *doing* right), but for others:' in duty or conscience it is simpler, plainer, less aspiring, more intimate.

How conscience and sense of honour are educated.

Our sense whether of duty or of honour is, with each one of us, as to the particular circumstances of it, the product of our particular individuality, of our education, of the companions we have had, and of the life we have lived: by all this each sense is educated or informed: but still there is something in each sense which is the same with everybody. Of training and education I hope to speak hereafter.

There remains now to speak of conscientiousness and the sense of honour as to the *manner* in which they exist in a man; I mean as to the particular nature of the feeling, and what feelings it is associated with. What I have just said has had reference to the *application* of the feeling, or its content, as some might express it, *i. e.* the conduct which it urges upon us: but independently of this, there may be a very great difference in the feeling itself; more especially perhaps in the case of the sense of honour.

APPENDIX ON CONSCIENCE AND HONOUR[1].

Three kinds of moral reflexion: Self-interestedness (1).

Let us proceed now to consider the nature of introversion of the mind, or consciousness, or reflexion, not in its intellectual, but in its moral bearing.

The simplest, readiest, and most superficial thought about one's self, is about one's own enjoyment and provision for one's self,—what I have called above, self-care. If it has however much of the character of *thought*, it would be better called 'self-interestedness.' This sort of reflexion furnishes of course sometimes self-congratulation, as on occasion of success; sometimes self-reproach, as on occasion of failure by one's own mistake.

Self-estimation (2).

Another sort of thought about one's self is what I will call self-estimation. By this I mean that consciousness which is concerned with the various feelings, good or bad, of pride, vanity, shame, modesty, and many others of the like kind. This sort of thought about one's self furnishes, as we know, often much of self-congratulation and pleasure; often, again, much of self-reproach and pain, and that of the bitterest.

[1] In the last paragraph of the 9th chapter, it is said that 'it still remains to speak of the particular nature of the feelings of conscientiousness and honour, and of the manner in which they are associated with other feeling:' and, in the original MS., the following loose jottings appear at the end of the paragraph: 'Is it like pride, or like what? Discussion of the feelings of pride, vanity, &c.' I have thought it well therefore to supply from earlier MSS. what the author intended to insert here. The first passage is taken from a course of lectures marked II. 1.: this is followed by a quotation from an older MS., of a somewhat fragmentary character, marked *b*; and this again by quotations from MSS. *G* and *Q* forming part of a long series intermediate in age. The commencement of each quotation is marked in the notes. In bringing together a number of passages, written at different times upon the same subject, it is inevitable that there should be a certain amount of repetition and want of order; but each passage seemed to me to contain something of independent value, and I did not feel justified in making the alterations which would have been required in order to fuse them into one whole. Ed.

Both these kinds of thought about one's self are natural as to the fact of them, but as regards the form and detail, they are almost entirely the creatures of education and custom.

Conscience (3).

Conscience is a feeling, on the whole, intermediate between these two, but containing in it elements not belonging to either. Self-reproach arising from the first of the feelings I mentioned is in the main of the nature of fear; so is the self-reproach arising from a guilty conscience: self-reproach arising from the latter of these is of the nature of shame; so again is that of conscience. Again, there is in the reproach of conscience self-blame for a failure: this is the same sort of blame as prudential self-blame, but it is for a higher nobler cause: it is failure and coming short of the right, instead of failure as to the useful. Similarly, on the other hand, there is in the reproach of conscience a sympathetic self-condemnation, by which I mean a self-condemnation accompanied by the feeling that others, to the extent to which they know what we know, condemn us likewise, and if they knew all that we know, would condemn us altogether. This is a feeling closely analogous to the general feeling of shame, as we shall have to see; but it is more pointed and particular; it conveys to us the idea not only of failure and disgrace, but of astonishment at and shrinking from ourselves, that it should be so. And conscience contains in it the element of sympathetic feeling in another way belonging to it alone. It is the pleading and remonstrance in our imagination of those whom we may have wronged. It is the imaginative putting ourselves in the place of others.

Conscience distinguished from the practical reason.

Conscience, as it is usually treated by moralists, is looked upon in its medium state of neither self-approval nor self-reproach, but as an inward voice, indicating to us, on the occasion of an action presenting itself, what is its moral character, whether good or bad. Conscience clearly does this, so far as it does it, by the incipient tendency to the self-approval or self-reproach, by the anticipating of the one or the other, according to what we do under the circumstances. Conscience is said to be the reason acting morally; but it is this only properly for ourselves, and on a real occasion for action, and the term is not properly applied to general moral judgment on occasion of action of others, or action merely suggesting itself to our imagination. No doubt, with certain qualifications to be mentioned, the judgments of these two are likely to be in harmony, and it is by the education of the moral judgment that the conscience is to be made what it should be: but the extension in this manner of the word conscience has produced many practical inconveniences, which we shall see.

Sympathy enters into our idea of truth, both intellectual

In regard of all the forms of introversion of thought, or reflexion, it is a matter of interest and importance to ascertain how far there enters in sympathy with the imagined judgments of others.

As to this, it is first to be considered what is the meaning in any case of our judgments being supposed to be independent of the presumed judgments of others; and next what is the real nature of *shame*.

Intellectually, the presumed accordance of our judgment with that of others is one of the two great canons of conviction, or feeling of truth, the other being that the judgment is what we can certainly *act upon*, with expectation of such and such results. One definition of truth which we instinctively give to ourselves is, that it is the common thought and conviction of rational beings: or in other words, a part of the definition of truth is, that what is true for one intellect is true for another. Reason removes us from a region of particular and wilful thought into one in which the thought belongs no longer to us alone, but to united intelligence. This is in some respects what is meant when we are told of the submission and bowing down of the intellect to nature and to fact, the giving up the idols of individuality, and the yielding ourselves to truth. In this respect, the advance of knowledge in the individual is his entering more and more into the commonwealth of rational beings: it is intellectually an *unselfing*, a gradual passage from thoughts, distinct, separate, and individual, to thoughts more than sympathetic, really common and identical. The true is something fixed and limited independently of us, and in entering upon it we quit our own will, as we are aware that others do also; their wills otherwise being individually various. In their common judgment, therefore, we take them as not speaking from themselves, but from the truth independent of them.

We must thus bear in mind, that in regard of truth of any kind, one part of the conviction of it in ourselves consists in our supposition that others, though they may not perhaps think as we do (for they very likely do not know the circumstances, or may be mistaken), yet still judge in a manner which would inevitably make them think so, if they knew what we know, and were in the same position as we are. All certainty is thus fortified in our minds by the imagined sympathy of others in our thoughts, and it may be questioned whether without this support we could individually maintain it.

Whether we care much, or do not, for the particular opinions of those whom we are actually concerned with, depends very much upon our particular disposition: but supposing we maintain in our minds our own opinion against theirs, the question whether we maintain it as true, or simply as ours, depends very much upon how far in our imagination we appeal from their judgment to a more general and higher judgment. If we feel that our judgment is true, we feel that we cannot be alone in holding it, but that we are in sympathy with universal reason.

and moral.

Imagination therefore of the judgment of others is more or less a necessary part of the judgment of ourselves, so far as we conceive this judgment of ourselves to be sincere and true. And the growth of conscience, and of our observation of the consequences, and therefore of the character of actions, is accompanied from the first by a growth also of thought of the opinion of others.

The simplest form of regard for other persons' opinion refers to our own merit.

The first and readiest form of judgment of ourselves and idea of others' judgment of us is in reference to the comparison of us with others, as to one form or another of merit, excellence, and superiority.

In regard to this, it is important for us to remember that though we may fix independently what are the proper points of human excellence and merit, the τὸ καλόν, the *honestum*, yet that which measures it, and gives it in one respect its special character, is the fact of one man's excelling or being superior to others. And as the morality of feeling is in danger of erring on the side of weakness, the morality of justice on that of over-exactness and yet insufficiency, and the morality of reason on that of selfishness, so the morality of freedom and honour is in danger of erring on the side of rivalry, comparison, and pride.

The number of words expressing modifications of feeling connected with our judgment of ourselves, and our thoughts of others' judgment of us, in reference to our possession of supposed points of excellence or superiority, and our doing things generally well or ill, is in all languages very large.

There is also much complication in regard to the degree of truth in the judgment, the mixture of judgment of oneself with regard for the judgment of others, the sort of bearing and action which the judgment leads to, and much besides.

Αἰδώς is the natural feeling connected with such regard for the opinion of others.

The first feeling of this kind which I will mention is the general one of *αἰδώς*, or regard, respect, reverence for opinion and custom and the judgment of others. Aristotle makes this regard for others' feeling a sort of *fear*, comparing it with actual fear or *φόβος*. This moral or imaginative fear is a real passion, attended with the bodily *πάθος* of blushing, in the same manner as actual fear is attended with paleness, shivering, and its other accompaniments. We might make a scheme of *αἰδώς*, similar to that which might be made as to actual fear, *φόβος*, and fix the proper place between impudence and bashfulness for the virtue of moral courage, as we should between rashness and cowardice for the virtue of simple or actual courage. Aristotle is rather disposed to place the mean, as with actual fear, nearer the side of boldness, answering to what we should call moral courage; but we shall probably consider that there is at any rate another virtue nearer the other extreme, which we should call modesty. This it is which is *αἰδώς* or *αἰσχύνη*, as a good quality. There is not however much resemblance between the two kinds of fear, so to call them, between the Latin *vereri* and *metuere*. They have in common something of the nature of restraint, but not much besides.

It belongs especially to youth.

Αἰδώς, as shame, is, in one shape or another, an instinctive feeling of the growing intelligence. It is evidently a feeling answering to and fitted for a state of understood comparative ignorance in the presence of others supposed to be wise and experienced: it is the graceful awkwardness of expanding and inexperienced intelligence and feeling, corresponding to the same facts as we see them in the external frame. The eyes and the judgment of those supposed superior and wiser are thus naturally shrunk from, and, in default of knowledge as yet unformed, opinion and custom are, may be foolishly, reverenced: the fact of this being so is one of the main sources of the ductility and docility of man's mind. There can be in the youth but little intelligent self-confidence, for he is but little tried and known even to himself: and in the absence of it, he is eminently the creature of association or companionship, and of respect. The first is the habitual modifier of his mind, the general stiffener of it in its pliability: the second, the 'ingenuus pudor' of the Latins, is what indeed large classes of society are almost compelled by their circumstances to grow up without, but the loss of which can probably never be made up to them.

This *αἰδώς*, or respect for the feeling of others, is a complicated sentiment, for there is in it both a feeling of its reasonableness and of the real superiority of others, and also more or less, and that growing, a feeling on the part of the youth of an independent judgment of his own, partly in harmony with, partly protesting against, what he considers others to think. Except that, as I have said before, so far as he does protest against it, and believes he is right in doing so, he of necessity believes that he has wiser others on his side.

Points in which conscience differs from *αἰδώς*.

Conscience differs from this *αἰδώς*, or respect for the feeling of others, in so far as (1) it is full and felt self-judgment, however in harmony with the supposed judgment of others, and however this judgment of others may have gone to form it: (2) it is concerned not with the comparison of ourselves with others (whether or not the thought of others may have suggested this feeling), but with things which are considered to have their reason in themselves, to be binding: and it is accompanied thus not simply with fear of others' judgment, but with actual fear of results and consequences: and (3) it is connected, by feeling and sympathy, with the judgment of us by a person in a peculiar circumstance as regards us, viz. in some way or other injured by us.

Conscience appears in the very first beginning of intelligence in the last of these three ingredients, and gradually forms itself in regard of the other two: in regard of (1) chiefly through means of the *αἰδώς* above mentioned:

which in this respect goes to generate a habit of mind beyond and above itself: in regard of (2) conscience gradually forms itself from the habit of exercising the reason and judgment and of observing mutual rights and claims, which the experience of life, bringing one into all sorts of relations and collisions, will suggest.

The third feeling here by which I have supposed conscience to differ from shame or *αἰδώς*, is one however which in a certain degree may be said to belong to them as well as to it: where this is so, *αἰδώς* is not much short of general moral sentiment. Αἰδώς and δίκη in this point of view are not far from representing subjective and objective, free and definite, morality. Αἰδώς as used by the Greeks was made to comprehend more or less all the elements of conscience: it was in fact the feeling of relative duty, a feeling of special regard for each person according to his circumstances; regard as such for the unfortunate, for those who have benefited us, for elders and superiors. It had also a very strong religious reference, and in this way came to possess in a certain degree the ideas of definiteness of obligation and fear of punishment, which more properly attach to conscience. But the general fact which it represents and which the Latin *pudor*, our 'ingenuous shame,' does not go beyond, falls short of conscience in the main by the three particulars above mentioned.

Conscience then involves (besides a regard for opinion or reputation) self-attention or self-examination, attention to the fact of duty or rightness, and sympathy. The more developed conscience is, the more do these three latter tend to supersede the former, upon which they may very possibly have been in point of fact actually built.

The education of conscience involves accordingly the right management of consciousness, a good eye, judgment and knowledge as to actual duty, and the cultivation of feeling and sympathy.

Feelings connected with *αἰδώς*.

I have mentioned that the number of words expressing modifications of feelings of self-estimation &c. is in all languages very large. Those expressing modifications of feelings of conscientious self-judgment are by no means so numerous. The former are more conspicuous in their action, and are in practice more powerful movers of human affairs;

the latter, though there is really a great variety of them, are more inward and individual.

The general principle of action which is concerned with αἰδώς, self-estimation or regard for opinion, is what we generally call 'honour.' The character formed upon it is noble and generous. The feeling in the mind corresponding to the distinction of actions into honourable and otherwise is highmindedness or self-respect, μεγαλοψυχία.

How complicated: pride and vanity.

I have mentioned that one great complication of feelings of this kind arises from the different manner in which self-judgment, and thought of the judgment of us by others, come to be mixed. Another complication related to this arises from the comparative strength or weakness of the character in which the feeling is. According to the disposition, the feeling of self-respect and care for honour has more in it of the feeling of value for credit and reputation, or of the feeling of value for self-approval and self-congratulation. Where the feeling of self-respect becomes vicious, either by being excessive as regards other feelings, or by being too much a matter of thought and attention, such misdevelopement takes the form of pride and vanity. The distinction between them cannot be very accurately drawn, but in a general way we mean by the former word the feeling as it is self-dependent, self-satisfied, to a certain degree unsocial, connected with a strong will and a strong nature; and, by the latter, the feeling as it leans, more or less, either imaginatively or in fact, on others, and is connected thus with a nature more social probably, but less distinctive and individual than the other. A special complication arises in case of disappointment, when we sometimes find regard for others' opinion disguising itself under the form of the most frantic opposition and contempt.

Self-confidence and modesty.

Other forms of abuse of the feeling of self-esteem have relation to future action, and are of the nature of self-confidence. This may be actual or moral, may have relation *i. e.* to φόβος or αἰδώς: in the former case it is presumptuousness and rashness: in the latter, impudence, insolence, arrogance, haughtiness, according to the circumstances of its exercise.

High-mindedness or self-respect is, as the words imply, right self-esteem, but it does not follow that the estimation of self which it involves is actually a high one. Where it is not, and yet the feeling exists, there is what we commonly call modesty.

Humility, diffidence.

Humility is a simple low estimation of one's self; it is modesty considered independently of the feeling of self-respect. When practically thought of, it is mostly looked upon in a negative light, and considered as the absence of, or opposite to, pride.

In reference to future action, modesty and humility are closely akin to diffidence and self-distrust, qualities which though attractive for association are on the whole disadvantageous for action. Aristotle, in his practical view, and with the feeling of a Greek, which certainly in these respects differed much from ours at present, depreciates all these qualities. His μικροψυχία is little other than the Christian humility.

Three features of honour; freedom, distinction, genuineness.

As the principle of honour rests mainly upon the comparison of man with man, and the idea of excellence and superiority, the fact of individuality is brought out very strongly by it; and with this there are three feelings associated, those of freedom, of distinction, and of genuineness or truth.

Freedom is shown in regard of it, sometimes not in a good way, by wilfulness and caprice, but most chiefly by the readiness and willingness to give and to sacrifice; which is called, according to the greater or less intimateness of the things it is concerned with, munificence, liberality, generosity, devotion, self-sacrifice, &c.

Distinction is the basis of the desire of fame and glory. The idea of it gives to man's individuality a value in his own eyes, which may have a bad effect on his character. The feeling is associated more or less with the thought of the feelings of others about him, in a manner to which applies what has been said about pride and vanity.

Genuineness, or truth, of course lies at the root of all real feeling of honour. In the cases, not perhaps unfrequent, where the man knows that the self of him which others honour or think highly of is something quite different from his actual self, as he knows it, there is no real self-estimation at all: he is simply playing a part; and his own estimation of himself, whatever it may be, is something quite independent of others' estimate of this his mask.

Abuses of honour.

There is very much needed in morals a word corresponding to the inelegant but useful word 'selfish,' to express the temper of mind which leads to a man's actions being much under the guidance of a strong self-judgment and self-opinion, when this is of a nature rather concerned with honour than with obligation and conscience. For it is obvious that honourable action shades off into the wrong (just as prudence, or proper self-care, shades off into selfishness), in a direction which, according to the circumstances and the character, we should call that of pride, wilfulness, harshness, or various other like terms: there is then a self-assertion which is wrong, in whatever way, and in whatever degree. I should like to call this by the name of *selfliness.*

Further examination of the distinction between conscience and honour:

I mentioned above that one difference between the feeling of *αἰδώς* and conscience was the fact that the latter had in it more of distinct self-judgment. But in a strong, noble and well-bred nature, honour is as much an individual feeling, as real self-conviction, as little fluctuating with the partial judgment of others, as conscience can be. Each of them in this way is a genuine and individual sensitiveness which, being, as such, discriminating, we may call a sense, if we like it. Only they are neither of them native, except as regards certain rudimentary principles: it is from association, instruction, and habit, that they have grown to discriminate in the way they do: they are the sense of many worked by these into the one.

in regard to their authority,

The great and important distinction between conscience and the principle of honour as a guide to action lies in the greater definiteness of the former, owing to its association with actual law, with definite rights and duties. Conscience is a continual inward voice to us, telling us that we are not free. How, as a matter of fact, this feeling of obligation in us may take its origin, is what I am not at present concerned with: we may suppose it a matter of education, of our being brought up under discipline and government, constantly told that we ought to do this and ought not to do that, &c. This may be so, and then the feeling of 'ought' and 'ought not' might become naturalized and self-fixed in the mind, just as regard for the judgment of others may gradually change into an habitual judgment of ourselves. Conscience grows, none can doubt, and is not natural and authoritative in the sense of being from the first complete and mature. What there is natural in it arises from its representing, without instruction, the great principles of our nature, which must exist alike in all, and from its growing with instruction. Its authority arises from its being our moral mind made what it is by reason; from its being the voice of reason in us. It possesses authority, not as conscience but as reason. It is not our feeling it, but our understanding it as an expression to us of reality independent of us, which makes it our duty to obey it.

in regard to the idea of punishment.

The relations of the principles of honour and of conscience to the idea of *punishment* are altogether different. With the former the idea does not enter in. There is an impulse to do the right act: if it is not done, the punishment lies in the fact of its not being done; not in any feeling of grief that it has not been done, though there may be such; for this is felt and understood as nothing like punishment; in fact, punishment is in one way or another reparation, and on the principle of honour what is done wrong is understood as once for all, and irreparable. Punishment, were it possible, would be desired.

Conscience, starting from solider and lower ground, supplies simpler and more generally acting motives, and is enabled thus practically to act in many cases where the other would vanish and fail. The being not our own masters, but being under obligation, supposes punishment, and the fact of punishment recognizes the existence of fear. Instead of the vague feeling of degradation resulting from offence, conscience supplies a distinct feeling of demerit, guiltiness, and consequent fear. Our education and life under law among men has made us feel that the same is likely to be our position in the great commonwealth of reasonable beings.

Three characteristics of conscience considered as the moral mind.

Conscience is the moral mind, a part of the sentiment or feeling of the mind as to action and life in general, but distinguished from the rest of this (1) by being limited in the range of actions which it concerns, viz. those of which it can be said that they are right or wrong; (2) by being very precise and definite in its judgments upon them, and having reason to go upon in them; and (3) by leaving in the mind, in cases where it is not attended to, a sense of guilt and indebtedness, and of something deserved and coming.

Conscience is formed and grows like all the rest of the habitual sentiment and feeling of which it forms a part, except that owing to its connexion with reason, more direct instruction and more definite inoculation of principle is possible with regard to it than with regard to the rest.

As a feeling, it is different in different individuals.

Conscience, *as it is felt*, is susceptible of many of those varieties in the manner of it which have been described in reference to general self-estimation. Though the substance of it must be a strong feeling of personal self-judgment, yet this, according to the temper, will be accompanied with more or less of thought of, and fear of, the judgment of others. Independency also of the conscientious faithfulness as to self-judgment in particular cases, there will be as to habitual action more of self-confidence and boldness, or more of fearfulness and self-distrust, according to the individual temper. A good conscience may sometimes be an anxious and depressed one: the stings of one not so good may be accompanied with much of sanguineness and hopefulness. And in the same way there is much variety in the amount of brooding and self-attention which conscience gives rise to.

Conscience is moral judgment, but it is more especially moral memory.

Conscience, viewed as the moral mind, is not only the moral judgment for action to be, but it is the moral memory and experience as to action which has been. This is indeed true of mind in general: it is a record of the past, and a power for the future. It is by experience and teaching that we learn in everything: and our moral judgment or faculty now is what it is in consequence of what it has gone through in conjunction with what has been taught it. This idea of the moral experience is the original one, in respect to morals, of the term conscience. It is in this sense that we speak of a good, and a guilty or bad conscience, or of conscience being purged. On the other hand, when we speak of its being informed and enlightened, we mean by it the moral judgment.

One point in which conscience, as the moral mind, differs from simple intellect, is that what its experience tells of *lives* for it in quite a different way from that in which the experience of the intellect can be said to live for *it*. To a certain degree the way in which we have arrived at our knowledge, lives in our mind still, but only to a certain degree: forgetfulness is as necessary for knowledge as remembrance: if we had always to preserve in our mind all the abortive guesses and mistaken observations we have made, we could have no systematic knowledge at all. But the moral experience is a record of actions which have their reality and their value,—*i. e.* their merit and demerit,—independently of the result which in the mind they have led to. Our intellectual history has no significance except as to this result: our moral history has concerned others as well as ourselves, and has been right or wrong, meritorious or guilty towards them; this is a real fact of which our experience is the impression.

The content then of conscience, in this view of it, is our own moral history: on the other view of it, what it contains is a view of life and of our proper action, the result of observation and instruction: it is the producing of this which is the informing the conscience. The moral law is an impression or transcript of life as it should be: and our moral mind, inward moral view, or conscience, should be an impression or transcript of this moral law. It is in this sense that conscience is our law, a law to *us*. Its authority over us is not derived from our feeling it, but from its being *to us* the outward authoritative law, the way in which this comes to us. The informing the conscience is really only instructing the mind in the actual outward law.

The sense of honour is a development of the sense of freedom, which is an element in perfect moral action.

[1]Moral action, as perfect, is the acting (1) for good ends, (2) by good rules, and (3) with good feelings,—or, intelligent, orderly, unconstrained.

The freedom of action which is involved in (1) and (3) is as necessary to make action moral, as the control which is involved in (2).

The feeling of *honour*, or *honourableness*, is a strong development of the feeling of *freedom*, balanced by a strong consideration for the imagined opinion of others, when our own sympathizes with and justifies it.

It answers to trust, and is felt as pain at the thought of trust deceived.

Honour, as a feeling, is the reactionary feeling to *trust* or confidence, placed, or imagined to be placed, in us, by others. It is the accepting the fact of others making us a law to ourselves, when they might impose law upon us, and the determination to justify the confidence thus shown.

[1] The quotation from MS. *b* commences here.

The pangs of the conscience, so to call it, of honour, are nly one part of the pangs of conscience in general. The magination paints, and the reason justifies, the feeling of isappointment and contempt with which those who trust us ould look upon us, if they knew we had done what, in such case, we are ourselves conscious of having done.

The root of all society is communication of feeling and nowledge, and upon this communication rests all sympathy nd all personal feeling. These all therefore involve trust, nd wherever there is trust, there is a possibility of deceit; here is no power to prevent the party trusted from taking dvantage of the other.

In all these cases therefore the feeling of honour comes in ith the freedom above spoken of, and acts (as described) hrough the imaginative consciousness. The first and main hing thus that honour is concerned with is deceit. The reat organ of communication is of course language, and the ypical or most marked form of deceit is verbal falsehood. The hearer trusts the speaker; and, so far as the particular ommunication is concerned, is in the speaker's power. This ower to deceive makes the dishonourableness of deceiving elt so strongly in minds capable of such feeling, that the onsciousness of falsehood, even in cases where it might appear ustifiable or right, is almost unbearable.

Shame is the fear of others' estimate.

The feeling of moral fear, shame (*αἴδως*, *pudor*), or consciousness, exists in reference to the simple estimation of us y others, independent of any consequences of that estimation. I call it *moral* fear, but it is also a corporeal passion, no less han physical or actual fear, producing blushing, as the other roduces paleness. This is noted by Aristotle[1]: where consciousness (so to call it) produces paleness, it has mixed with t actual fear, or fear of consequences. This moral fear is oncerned (besides the exercise of our freedom above mentioned) principally with two other sets of circumstances. These are:

It is associated with certain bodily instincts and with the consciousness of moral weakness.

(1) Certain corporeal feelings and animal instincts, with which it is associated physically, *i.e.* by nature arbitrarily, as it would appear, and independently of reason. The tendency to this instinctive shame or concealment we see in many animals which approach the rank of man.

[1] *Eth. N.* IV. 9. 1.

(2) Circumstances of moral weakness and self-indulgence, arising from want of self-control and of higher purpose. To a certain extent, what has been said above about truth may be brought under this, the keeping of our word being viewed as strength of mind in contrast with the weakness of yielding to the temptation of breaking it.

Reason for its association with bodily instincts.

We may suppose the feeling of shame associated in the manner in which it is by nature with certain particular animal instincts, for the purpose of giving the reason, or moral power, a special or additional hold over them, which is needed on account of some of them being far stronger than any other instincts of nature. And generally the feeling of honour or shame or moral fear, may be said to attach itself to the exercise of reason and the less self-regarding feelings, so as to enable them to prevail over indulgence and the more self-regarding feelings.

There are three distinct points of view from which men judge of themselves and their actions: viz. (1) as to their prudence, (2) as to their justice and benevolence (or rightness in general), and (3) as to their honourableness.

Three kinds of conscience corresponding to three genera of vice.

Corresponding to this we have three cardinal genera of vice: viz. (1) Vices of selfishness, or selfish prudence. (2) Vices of weakness, or self-indulgence. (3) Vices of pride or false honour. And similarly three kinds of conscious, rational, controlled or deliberate action, all of which tend to restrain the self-indulgent or impulsive parts of nature; three forms, we may say, of *conscience:*

(1) the *prudential* conscience, or judgment of our actions as affecting our own permanent welfare:

(2) the *moral* conscience, or judgment of our actions as affecting the welfare of others, of the public, of mankind, and as judged of by any power or authority which may have that welfare for its care:

(3) the conscience of *honour*, or judgment of our actions as bearing a character in our own eyes and in those of others.

All these different kinds of inward judgment, involve in their character of judgments or reviews of action, a difference or supremacy of nature above human facts or principles which lead more directly to action, and which are the objects of the judgment. Butler's idea of the rightful supremacy of conscience applies to all of these.

Ground of the superior authority of the moral conscience.

The special prerogative of (2) the moral conscience is that it has an authority over the two other forms of conscience, as well as in common with them over the impulses. It has this, because it represents our position more truly than either of them do. It may come into error through misinformation, or through misplaced action: but in the other two there is very likely to be, though there need not be, an error involved from the beginning. In (1) the error, that we are, as regards the entirety of our action, all to ourselves, with no one else to consider, as if there was no one else in the world. In (3) the error, that we are really free, with no law over us or duty incumbent upon us, so that what we do right we do simply because we choose it, that there is a merit therefore in it, which is represented and measured by our opinion of ourselves, and by the imagined opinion of us in others. On the other head (2) suggests to us against (1) purposes for action beyond ourselves, and against (3) the fact of right action being incumbent upon us, not merely done because we like to do it. It is evident, that (2) in this case approaches much more nearly to (3) than it does to (1): in a good many cases there being no difference in regard of the *action*, whether it is suggested by (2) or (3), only in the feelings accompanying it. But this difference of feeling in some cases, where the action is the same, will lead to a difference of actions in other cases.

How the imagination enters into each kind of conscience.

All the forms of conscience, so to call it, are very much associated with imagination. In respect of (1), the imagination generalizes from the particular desires an ideal unity of happiness, which it more or less looks forward to and dwells on. In the same way also it expands the personal feeling, or creates an enlarged personality, and makes us feel, as a part of ourselves, all that investiture of property, family, &c. which we consider and call *ours*.

In the same manner, in respect of (3) the imagination converts our feeling of personality into a reflexly conceived *character*, which we look at, but look at, so to speak, with the eyes of others, bringing to bear thus upon it a general judgment. The actual character which we bear in the individual minds of others we have seldom means of knowing; but between this and our imaginative judgment there lies generally the common character which we bear in the world, so far as we form a subject of interest or conversation to others. This, our good name, so far as it is one, is recognized by the law usually as a sort of property, which no one has any business wantonly to injure.

In respect of (2), the imagination idealizes the happiness of *others*, and gives us by sympathy an interest in it as ours, in many respects in a similar manner, though with different objects, from the way in which it acts as to (1): while as compared with (3) it idealizes our character and the merits of our action as seen by impartial judgment, with this difference, that the judgment is one conveying with it the idea of authority, and consequently of possible future penalty.

There are actual facts corresponding to all these imaginations, though what the exact facts are we cannot readily determine, and the imagination gives to them, in many respects, their dress and colour.

Influence of custom and education on conscience.

All the forms of self-judgment are very much associated with *custom*; and, what is to a certain degree the same thing, they are all, as to their particular form, generated by life and action, and are susceptible thus of education and training.

In regard of prudence, foresight, and value for property, this is most evident: it is the tone of society which nourishes it so far as it exists, and very great pains are often taken by educators to produce it.

The conscience, or sensibility, of honour is stimulated and cherished in some societies very much as that of prudence in others: great pains are taken to instil and guide it, and to nourish a value for reputation and glory for their own sakes.

The moral conscience is, in the manner of its generation, training, and nourishment, very similar to these others; differing from them in its roots lying deeper and its being in consequence more really universal, in its being higher than the one, and less capricious than the other.

The moral conscience combines sensibility and reason.

In its perfect state, it may be defined as a habitual, though not necessarily explicit, accompaniment of action, of the nature of a sensibility to the character of the action as good or bad, right or wrong, the mind being always ready, in the event of the action being perceived to be one of them, or rather and specially, in the event of its being perceived to be otherwise than right, to give some reason to itself why it is so. It is thus not proper to call it a moral sense, inasmuch as it is mixed with reason, and, like everything which has to do with reason, is the result of growth and development, and may possibly be erroneous and tell false. On the other hand, it is, as existing and developed, a sensibility, not a simple operation of reason. The questioning of every action in detail by reason in the course of the doing of it, would produce, even if well meant, a sort of calculated action very different from moral action as it is actually done.

Different kinds of conscientious sensibility.

There are thus two circumstances or conditions of moral conscience; (1) consciential sensibility, or an habitual attention to, and care for, the rightness of our actions: (2) consciential deliberation, or the consideration, as to a particular action or habit, whether it *is* right or wrong, with reason rendered to ourselves. We call a man *conscientious* in whom the sensibility is strong, and *scrupulous* in whom it is too much so. There are, however, two steps in the process, and therefore two elements in the sensibility: there is the anxiety to be sure of what is right, and the determination when known to do it. It will frequently happen that the one of these elements of conscience is more strongly developed than the other: thus, a man's scrupulousness as to being sure of what is right may prevent action altogether, even in cases where it is quite certain that, whatever may be right, to do nothing is wrong. Or conversely, a man's scrupulous determination to act according to his conscience may be of such a nature as to preclude any misgiving as to the possibility of his not being right in his judgment.

Different kinds of conscientious deliberation.

Again, consciential deliberation may be of two kinds; (1) as to the rightness or wrongness of a *sort* of actions, or habit, the fixing, in this respect, a general rule or principle: and (2) as to the rightness or wrongness of a particular action arising out of a conjuncture, or (which is the same thing) how, in such particular conjuncture, we may or ought to act. This latter part is more especially *casuistry*.

Consciential deliberation again goes in what we may call two steps; the first, answering to that idea of the inward process which gives rise to the word conscience, is the consideration how the common judgment of men would view the matter, or, which is the same thing, what we ourselves should think of the action if we saw it done by another. The second and more important, answering to the idea of the inward process as being practical reason, is the consideration of the fact upon which this common judgment must be supposed to rest, *i.e.* whether there is anything to enable us to conclude as to the will of God in regard of the action, and otherwise, whether it is natural, fair, kind, and honourable.

For conscience, when we speak of it as the moral guide of action, or as what we should act according to, is the law of right and wrong as it exists in our minds, or as it is *bona fide* understood by us. But no true conscience can exist (though many of the good effects of it may) without the idea on our part of there being an eternal law, or absolute right and wrong, and of its requiring effort also on our part to know and understand it. A part of true conscience is of necessity consciousness of our having done our best to know the right.

The law of right and wrong, as objective and real, is independent of us, and may be digested into rules, and observed in this form as a matter of fact, from whatever motive, without the intervention of any consciential perception of it. But in order to be applicable to the various circumstances of life, it needs to be, and as a matter of fact it is, worked into the mind by experience and training, in such a manner as to become, what it has been called above, a sensibility, of which account can be given, when called for, by reason, or a habit, *habitus*, ἕξις, of the mind, still with the same provision as to reason.

It is not simply a habit in the sense of custom, nor can it by training be made to take any form indifferently, because experience goes to it as well as training. It is a gradual generalization of the good feelings, noted as good by reason, into one indistinct mental idea of right and good, accompanied with a perception also, more or less vivid, of the fact, that there are reasons in the reality of things why they are good or should be done, and that the general feeling of men goes with us in considering them good. The practical conscience or moral self-judgment contains in it thus the elements of natural feeling, of custom, of reason, and of sympathy.

Sound and unsound consciousness.

[1]A feeling in its substance similar to what we call conscientiousness spreads from it in the direction of religion into a desire of pleasing God (to use religious language), and commending ourselves to His judgment, and, in the direction of common worldly action, into what is called honourableness of feeling or conduct; we use the term conscience in regard of the most definite obligation and what is most exhibitable in law, but the feeling of general honourableness is quite as real as that of conscientiousness, and quite as necessary to take note of in morals. The definite judgment of ourselves which we call conscience, is contained in a sort of general atmosphere of what it is hard to describe in words, self-attention, self-respect, self-maintenance, value not for our own good name with men, but for our character with our own secret selves. There is an imagined sympathy with others, an imagination *i. e.* of their opinion about us, on the supposition of their knowing about us what *we* know, *not* of their opinion about us knowing what *they* do; rather, if it is true conscience and self-respect, it stoutly maintains its independence against this. Unhealthy consciousness is the uneasy consideration of what people with their half knowledge and imperfect judgments are thinking about us: sound consciousness and honourableness is an assertion to ourselves of our independent judgment of ourselves, with the feeling that this judgment is in sympathy with the substantial moral standard or judgment of others, though the actual exercise of this moral judgment by them in our case may, from their defective knowledge of the facts, be very wrong. Conscientiousness and honourableness often involve therefore much of imagination, *i.e.* imagination comes in aid of the maintenance of the independence of our own judgment against the actual judgments of others, by helping us to rise from these to sympathy with the true moral feeling of others, of which these judgments may very likely be mistaken exercises.

Honour may be a kind of religion.

It has often been observed that honour has constituted, with those who have made much of it, a sort of religion. The meaning of this is, that the lofty ideal standard of honourable character, according to which the disciples of honour have, often with much self-sacrifice, tried to maintain their conduct, and in regard to which they have always felt sure of

[1] The quotation from MS. *G* commences here.

the true sympathy of mankind, has been to them very much what the religious man finds in the glorious aim which he proposes to himself, of carrying out what he believes to be the will of God, of the reference of himself to the divine judgment, of the struggle towards a moral ideal, which is as it were a shadow of the divine perfection. In both, the resistance to unworthy gratification and the maintenance of independence against weak and unworthy compliance are fundamental.

Independence essential to honour and conscience.

This independence of the moral judgment and the volition consequent on it, with the constant feeling however that it is in real sympathy with the truest and deepest feelings of mankind, is an essential part of moral action: it belongs to what is called its freedom. The assertion of the individual will is a part of the morality both of action and of judgment. "I am at liberty, so far as any force is concerned, not to do this honourable action, many people would not: many people even would not think it honourable, that is, would not enter into the idea what 'honourable' means: but I will do it because *I* feel it would be honourable, and I am quite sure that in my doing so all those whom I should wish to sympathize with me, all the best part of mankind, would, if they knew what I do, sympathize."

Honour and conscience may both be mistaken.

On freedom I will not say more now; but one word about conscience and honour as mistaken. This is what they may both be, one really almost as much as the other; and there is one special respect in which they are both liable to be so. Independence, self-assertion as we may call it, is, as I have said, a special part of each of them: the peculiar province of both of them lies out of the region of actual law, with its sanctions and penalties: they may each of them become, and sometimes have become, the watchword of a particular understanding and sympathy among a particular set of people, which understanding may be moral and in accordance with actual human law, but may be the reverse. In these cases as in all, conscience is indeed the better of the two; but there is a considerable degree of resemblance in the results. Paley has given a sort of satirical description of the law of honour, by which he means a certain understanding among fashionable people, leading them to a course of conduct quite different from that to which morality or actual law would lead them: it is an understanding involving mutual confidence, and amounting to a law having for its sanction honour and nothing else, the essence of such honour, as I have said, being independence and freedom. It is, as he describes it, a bad understanding, but there is no reason why an understanding among men with honour for its sanction should be bad, and many such particular understandings are good. If you look at many books, which in some degree perhaps now, but more especially two centuries ago, ridiculed some forms of religion where the word 'conscience' was much in use, you will find acting according to the law of conscience satirized very much in the way in which Paley satirized acting by that of honour: some parts of Hudibras you may take for an example. Mistaken conscience may be supposed to establish a separate code among those who understand the same thing by it, and this possibly in some points immoral, just in the same way as mistaken honour may.

Conscience is self-complicity.

[1]Consciousness or conscience, in its most general and widest present sense, is self-dividedness or self-doubleness.

The origin of the word is primarily from its moral point of view, and its first meaning is self-complicity or self-accompliceship, of evil in the first instance, but possibly also of good.

The reason of this prominence of the idea of evil seems threefold: (1) that failing in obligation is both more common and more important to others than merit, or the exceeding of obligation; (2) that fear, with which the sense of self-condemnation is likely to be connected, makes a deeper impression, and dwells in the mind more than hope, with which merit would be connected, (3) that complicity, as a thing between two people, is in a sense a secret held against others, while association in good is more likely to be a public and unconcealed matter, not a subject for *conscientia* between the two.

Relation of conscience to memory.

The relation of conscience to memory is two-fold, according as we are considering the nature of the mind itself, or the nature of knowledge.

The mind is a *qualitied* unity, the pattern or origin of unities. Quâ qualitied, we may consider it as quasi-extended,

[1] The quotation from MS. *Q* commences here.

having contemporaneous variety, several different things existing at one time, and making up one whole: but quâ unity, which is the truest view of it, its variety is in time only, it has no extended or contemporaneous variety. In this point of view, instead of being made up of many parts or faculties, it is one thing passing through a succession of states.

Every act of intro-spection involves memory.

The word 'reflexion' supposes as to its *dianoematism*[1] that the natural or direct action of the mind is from within outwards, and that this operation is susceptible of being reverted, and the contrary process performed. Of course this, as in fact the word *retro* or *re* itself, implies time as well as space, and reflexion will mean a turning back in point of time as well as a turning backward in space. But if we translate the consideration of the mind from spatial to temporal language, and convert compositeness into successionalism, every act of reflexion is seen to be an act of memory. The very idea of personality is in this way closely involved with memory, so closely that some philosophers have entirely absorbed the former in the latter.

In self-consciousness proper there is a double exercise of memory.

Self-observation or introspection is thus memory in a sense in which direct outward observation is not; but being thus memory as observation, it is still more memory as knowledge.

Action is not of itself conscious or self-conscious, nor is outward observation; where consciousness exists, it is something superadded, and there are two thoughts in the mind, one backward, the other forward. Actional or direct thought is objective and unconscious, simply regardful of its object or end: so also subjectivity in itself is unconscious: consciousness arises when the subject is objectified as knowledge; nor does even this in all cases give rise to that which we properly call consciousness. There is, for instance, the common process of *unconscious* thinking about one's self; in which we

[1] The Author was in the habit of using the term *noëm* to denote the word as thought, in distinction to *phone*, the word as spoken: *noematism* he employed more generally as equivalent to 'meaning,' and *dianoematism* was the term by which he expressed the original metaphor involved in all abstract terms. The process of forming a *noem* he denoted by the term *unification*. See his posthumous papers on *Glossology*, printed in the Cambridge *Journal of Philology*, Vols. IV. and V. ED.

form a sort of idea of ourselves as individuals like others whom we see and act with, and think about ourselves as about them. This is in point of fact becoming, what we very speedily do, *cosmocentric* instead of *autocentric* in our knowledge: it is what reason naturally leads to and makes us.

True consciousness, or reflexion, only arises when we bring together into one observation this previously remembered or known self, and self as the subject of some particular remembered feeling or act.

Consciousness has been distinguished from conscience for the sake of convenience:

The general *noem* 'conscientia' is now practically divided by philosophers into two parts, which we in English call 'consciousness,' and 'conscience,' meaning by the first intellectual introspection, such as we are able to make, and by the second, moral introspection, reflexion or judgment, the word having drifted to this noematism from its early one of moral self-complicity or self-accompliceship. The distinction of the two, or rather the distinct unification of the first, is, I should think, in origin English: it exists in German, perhaps after English example; the philosophic term *bewusstseyn* standing beside the old moral term for 'conscientia,' *gewissen;* but I think it does not generally in other languages.

but is never really separated from it.

Now though it is very convenient for philosophic and investigatory purposes to unify the noem 'consciousness,' and suppose the existence of a purely intellectual self-knowledge or self-observation, I am inclined to think that, in an analysis of the mind, we do not really find such a thing to exist, and ought not, as matter of fact, to suppose it. Man, it is to be considered, is essentially a moral or active being, and intellective properly, mediately and subsidiarily to this: and though his intellectiveness *expatiates* by curiosity as I have described, and part of its essence and effectiveness lies in this expatiation, yet intellect is felt to be dependent and subordinate at both ends,—dependent on the limitations which fact and reality supply to it for its substantial interest, and dependent on its conceived applicability to possible action for the concern we take in it. Moral relations we of necessity conceive as prior in time, and posterior in purpose, to anything which is appreciable by, and concerned with, intellect alone. Now self-introspection or self-consciousness is a thing which concerns our whole nature, and has no special relation with, is not in any way like, any particular process which is intellective and which we may call knowledge. Knowledge, or knowing, is in fact simply the qualifying of an old idea by a new observation, or, if we like it, the dividing off a new unity from an old: self-introspection is nothing in the world like this. The knowledge or feeling of our personality is *moral*, the base of our moral or active being; we may, of set purpose and with effort, accompany our outgoing intellectual processes with this, and we may do this for philosophic or intellectual purposes, and when it is done for these we may call it consciousness: but there is nothing intellectual in it.

Man's nature being primarily moral, every introspective act is accompanied by self-judgment.

It is on account of the nature of man being thus primarily moral or active, and not intellectual or speculative, that reflexion or self-consciousness, whenever it arises in practice, is accompanied with self-judgment, or an application of the idea of right to the operations of the moral being, resembling the application of the analogous idea of truth to the results of the intellectual. In consciousness of ourselves as willing and acting, the idea of whether the thing is right or not comes to us just as, in thinking of knowledge or imagination, the idea comes whether it is or is not true: the idea is not in either case definitely before us till it is drawn out and made a matter of thought; but when we attend, we become aware that there is a *judgment* both in self-consciousness and in objective knowledge, will in the one case, and conclusion in the other, being supposed or assumed to be according to right, and to truth, in such a way that if they are not so, the feeling strikes us painfully. Both right and truth, as either objectified and abstracted, or defined and measured, are exceedingly complicated and elaborate ideas; but they enter substantially, the one into every reasonable or reflexional volition, the other into every perception, and constitute in each case a judgment.

In a supposed primary perception, where a sensation is decomposed and knowledge is taken by the subject of the object of it, it is not correct to say that any knowledge is taken by the subject of itself. Such knowledge might be taken, but we are not to suppose that it is, any farther than as the moral being may be considered to wake up simultaneously with the intellectual. Otherwise the subject comes no farther into notice or sentience than as discriminated from the object, the object being what is noticed, and the felt subjective unity not dwelt upon, but only transferred or counter-attributed to the object. The subject, when it is itself matter of notice, is no longer subject, which term has only reference to sentience and knowledge, but is person or moral being.

Have brutes consciousness? There is no doubt but that, if we mean by consciousness merely subjectivity as the base of knowledge and of sentience of pleasure and pain, they have: consciousness in this sense is the differentia between animal life and vegetable. At the same time we know that they have no reflexion, the real *conscientia* in its wide and old noematism: how is this?

Brutes have subjectivity,

For one thing, in the same way as we have seen before that they have no general ideas, it may be said that they have no reflex general idea of themselves or their own being, which would make them *persons*. Such a reflex objective general idea is what would arise after the ideas gained of other individuals similar to ourselves: and since they have not those, of course they have not this. The absence or incapability of general ideas would of itself thus mark them as unmoral beings, or not properly persons, since subjective morality presupposes intellectiveness.

but no reflex general idea of their own personality.

It is a question whether all conceivable intellective beings, by the fact of their intellectiveness, are also moral? The question seems to me to be analogous to that, whether all sentient beings, by the fact of their being sentient, are also intellective? The answer it seems to me in each case should be, that they are capable of intellection, and capable of morality, rather than intellectual and moral. The sentient being, by the fact of his existence, has a relation to everything else which exists, and his sentience may be conceived such, that this relation shall not only exist, but be made sensible to him, which is knowledge. Similarly the intellectiveness of the intellective being supposes the possibility of his knowledge of all the inter-relations and mutual fitnesses of moral beings with whom he could come into contact: and action according to such would be morality. At the same time, as in the case of the sentience before, we must suppose his intellectiveness not simply general, but specialized and adapted for the gaining of such knowledge. In man therefore, just in the same way as the possible general sentience, by which he might be made aware of his relation to everything else in the universe, is modified, for knowledge, by all sorts of limitations, concentrations, definite sensibilities and powers, the whole apparatus of the human mental organization: so for morality and moral action, the general intellectiveness requires to have definite directions given, and limitations set to it. The result of the outgoing mental organization, the rule of judgment in it, is what we call *truth:* the result of the introspective or reflective moral constitution is *right.*

Man differs from brutes, both morally and intellectually, rather in impulse than in faculty.

Intellectually I cannot find that the brutes differ from us by any particular faculty, or by any separately conceivable power: they differ by a tendency, an impulse, which I have elsewhere spoken of, partaking of curiosity and imagination, the tendency in fact to dwell on the perceived and known as something of interest in itself, independent of the occasion of the knowledge and use of it. Just so I conceive the moral difference between man and brutes to be a difference of impulse and tendency, rather than of inward sense or faculty. Right is probably not a thing of a nature to be cognizable by anything like a separate sense, but it is a relation, or fact, in regard of which it may make all the difference in the world between kinds of creatures, whether they have an impulse or tendency to note, attend to, and care for it or not. I cannot but think that in man there is such an impulse, giving him his distinctive moral nature, as the previously mentioned impulse gives him his distinctively intellectual one.

There is a special moral impulse in man.

Consciousness proper then or reflexion may be considered from the first as something of a moral nature, involving moral judgment and an obscure intimation therefore of a rule to judge by. Were there no impulse to attention to right, such as I have spoken of, reason *might* indeed, in its nature, supply the materials for moral judgment in reflexion; but in the vast extent of the possible applicability of reason, with the importunacy of appetite and the likelihood of the connexion of reason with that, it is doubtful how far moral considerations would be attended to. In fact, that they are attended to very much more than, supposing a mere unstimulated deduction of them from reason, they would be, may appear from this, that conscience or moral anxiety is a much more common phenomenon in the world than, if we judged of the world from the idea which the writings of the specially rational moralists would give of it, we should conclude it to be. I do not mean conscientious acting, but anxiety of one form or another about the matter, quite different from any care or anxiety about intellectual truth. Such anxiety, whether folly or not, is a fact, and often exists without any reference to religious considerations: now if morality were a matter simply shown to us by reason, I cannot think it would exist in this way. It seems to manifest to us a special call, in some way or other, to considerations of this kind.

Different degrees of consciousness in action.

Reflexion of this kind, involving moral judgment, produces what I have called a self-dividedness. Self-consciousness may exist in any degree; and according to the degree in which it exists is the nature of the exertion of power or of the action modified. We may conceive a continuous scale from the most perfect involuntariness to the most complete double-mindedness, or self-observation, and criticism on each particular of it. At the one limit, the involuntary, our personality may be said to vanish, the action is no longer ours: at the other, our individuality vanishes, and such an entire self-possession may be conceived as would make us two beings rather than one.

Along this scale we might distinguish three kinds of action:

(1) Spontaneous action, or action on impulse,
(2) Considerate action, or action on principle,
(3) Reflexional or self-conscious action.

These only differ in degree, and after Aristotle's fashion we might say that the middle sort was the best and the most proper, for with the first we have no security for its being moral at all, and the third, if moral, is yet probably defective as action, and can hardly be otherwise than hesitating and weak, much of the power and attention, which should go to the action, going of necessity to the reflexion upon it.

CHAPTER X.

DISTRIBUTION OF ACTION CONSIDERED FROM THE IDEAL POINT OF VIEW.

In this chapter it is assumed that action is determined solely by its end.

I HAVE, for convenience sake, all along used the term 'action' as a general term to express any proceeding on our part which is the result of will, and can possibly have a moral character. Action, as I have used the term, includes in itself its negative, or, forbearance to act, when this is the result of will: it includes also internal action, or any effort of our will upon our own feelings or inward man.

There is a great difference between the meaning of the term 'action' as thus applied generally to life, behaviour, bearing, conduct, and its more restricted meaning as expressing something definite done for a definite purpose. What we do, in the wider sense of the term 'action,' is done in an infinity of different manners; never quite without thought, and always with something of will mixed with it, and always, in so far as there is this thought and will, with something which may be called purpose: but with the utmost variety of degree of deliberation, and the utmost variety of impelling or accompanying feeling. The more restricted sense of action, if we include in it the negative, or forbearance to act, differs from the other, mainly in the attention given by us to the definite purpose, and the non-attention to the accompanying circumstances or feelings. We may call this more restricted sense of the term 'action' the real sense: in that case, when we speak of our moral life as made up of actions, we use what philosophers call an 'abstraction': we take a particular view or make a particular supposition: a thing very constantly necessary, in philosophy, to be done, and not misleading, if we remember that we must not apply our results to actual life without taking account of the considerations which we had, for a particular purpose, neglected.

In the present chapter I omit all attention to accompanying feelings, and consider each action as done for its purpose, taking nothing else into account about it. Very few actions are really done in this way, but some are: and, with the proper additions, our considerations on this view will be useful generally.

We may say, to begin with, that the *purpose* of each action is some good, or if we like to use the term, some happiness; under the following qualifications.

If we mean what we say to be absolutely and universally true, we must be content to consider our proposition convertible or identical, *i.e.* to mean by good or happiness, no more than the purpose of action. Except on such an understanding there is much of action, as, for instance, revengeful action, which has no good or happiness for its purpose.

All native action tends to good.

All native action however is for something which is good or happiness in itself, independently of its being so in the above way as purpose of the action, and all action which has value in the result is for good or happiness also, similarly understood.

By saying that all *native* action is for happiness, I mean that it is either self-regarding or else benevolent, not malevolent: I expressed the same thing in a former chapter by saying there was no such thing as native ill-will.

It may be considered a principle in our nature independent of morality, that action should not be lost or wasted: *i. e.* that it should be useful; though some action not useful may be, as we have seen, *morally* valuable, and in that way not wasted. Nature makes a provision in the first instance for the usefulness of action by giving us no native ill-will: as we pass on to *non-native* feelings, we ourselves must take care that our action is for good or happiness only, *i. e.* is useful.

Utilitarians change this generalization into the rule of human life; neglecting the complication which arises from diversity of interest.

It is this principle, barely and by itself, which some philosophers consider the cardinal, or even the only, principle of morality. So far from this, it cannot properly be considered a principle of morality at all. I have mentioned that the existence or possibility of happiness, and the possibility of acting so as to promote it, may be considered a necessary precondition of morality: and in the same region of thought as this, the principle that action should be useful, or should be calculated to produce *some* happiness, may be considered a part of our notion of action. But this principle is anterior, logically, to the supposition of our being social beings, or of there being any others whose happiness we may promote besides our own: and it is not till *this* supposition is made that morality begins or becomes possible. The moral value of actions may sometimes consist, as we have seen, in their non-utility—in the negation of utility to ourselves. It is with the variety of individualities and interests that morality begins. It is in the additions which we have to make to the above proposition, that action should be useful or should promote happiness, that morality consists. We have not only to ask ourselves the question which I will reserve for another chapter: what sort of utility? what sort of happiness? but we have also to ask ourselves another question more important still, which I will discuss in this chapter: viz. *whose* happiness? *whose* utility?

Our own first, says one philosopher, next that of our relations, next that of our friends, finally that of all the world. By 'first' he will mean, first in consideration, and to the greatest degree.

In a very rough way, this does probably represent actual human conduct. That, in order of consideration, things go in some degree in this manner is evident. We feel our own wants, pains, and desires with an immediateness which we cannot share even with those nearest to us. And unless we take care of ourselves, to some degree, first, we could not, if we would, take care of anybody else.

Pope's rule of preference is wrong in identifying love for self and love for others.

Those philosophers who have gone upon the basis of actual emotion and sentiment, without examining it very accurately, have generally taken this view. It may suffice to give the lines of Pope:

> Self-love but serves the virtuous mind to wake,
> As the small pebble stirs the peaceful lake:
> The centre moved, a circle straight succeeds,
> Another still, and still another spreads;
> Friend, parent, neighbour, first it will embrace;
> His country next; and next, all human race;
> Wide and more wide, th' o'erflowings of the mind
> Take ev'ry creature in, of ev'ry kind.

The important thing to be attended to about this, is, that there is really no analogy between what is here called self-love, and the love of any one else. The word self-love, and other such words, are formed upon the notion of such an analogy: but it is altogether misleading. The above lines do represent with a certain degree of correctness the way and the different degrees in which comparative care for others' happiness should exist, *after* the chasm between self and any others is passed. This is because there is a degree of resemblance in the different feelings described, which allows of the speaking of them, with meaning, as constituting a diminishing scale. But neither actually nor ideally, neither looking at what *is* nor at what *should be,* is there, or can there be, any resemblance between our love of self, so to call it, and our love of any one else. I do not mean that the former is necessarily greater than the latter: it might be, and often is, so far as there is any meaning in speaking of comparative magnitude, even less: but it is quite different in kind. It is only by a very ill-applying metaphor that we can speak of self-*love.*

The point, or real significance, of the above lines is, that in the love which we have, and should have, to kindred, as compared with the love which we have to strangers, there is mingled something of the feeling with which we regard ourselves, something, to speak loosely, of selfishness. And, proceeding the other way, we learn to love, it may be said, by taking an interest in the welfare of our kindred and those near us, and we apply what we have learnt, in a less degree, to those not near us or strangers: the necessary moral care being, that the increase of love to kindred should, by application, increase the love to strangers, not, by engrossment, diminish it. The truth of all this is, that our love to kindred is composed of two elements, a selfish one and a loving one, and thus has two aspects: but it is the loving element, not the selfish one, which breeds love to strangers. The selfish element causes our love to kindred, on account of its double character, to bear some resemblance to the feeling with which we regard ourselves, but it does not, in the other direction, make the feeling with which we regard ourselves bear any resemblance to the loving element of our love to kindred. It is the assumption that it does, and that thus love to kindred has the same relation to general love, as self-love has to love to kindred, which makes the falseness of the lines. But reflection soon satisfies us, that self-regard or self-engrossment is against all love of every kind, against love to those nearest as much as against love to those farthest: it has no tendency to expand, as love to kindred has: it is what all the kinds of love oppose and diminish.

It describes correctly though vaguely the scale of preference amongst others.

The philosophy then which the above quoted lines generally express gives us no rule as to the distribution of our action for happiness between ourselves and others in general, *i.e.* as to the comparative degree in which we should care for ourselves and care for others. All it says in reference to this goes on a false analogy. Amongst others, it gives us vaguely a comparative scale of action or of care, what I will call a scale of preference.

A different line has been taken by some philosophers who have thought less of the emotions, and more of the happiness, which is the definite object of the action.

Bentham's rule of equality fails in both cases.

Thus Bentham in the famous maxim "each to count for one, ourselves included" gives a principle of supposed equity or fairness. The view expressed in Pope's lines he would admit as roughly representing fact, but fact which, in his view, morality ought to correct.

Of Bentham's view also it may be said that it roughly represents fact: in the actual world, preference and equity are engaged in conflict; but morally, it is of less value than the preceding. It has importance as a correction of the other, but has less importance than it.

The other gave an account, to a certain degree

true, of the comparative degree of care due from us to different individuals among others, though it did not give a true account of the comparative care due, as between ourselves and others in general: *this* does not give a true account in either case.

It sounds well to say, we should take no more care of ourselves than we should of any one else: but it does not sound well to say, that we should take no more care of our father or our wife than we should of any one else.

But in regard of the former of these, though it may sound well, that is all. The two relations, that of ourselves to others in general, and that of one individual amongst others to another, are no more comparable in this case than they are in the preceding one. To say, as a general rule of conduct, that we should take the same care and thought for ourselves that we do for each other, as much, no more, has simply no meaning. There are certain definite circumstances, there is no doubt, in which this rule of equity, so to call it, is the true one. There is something to be divided: let us divide it equally. We are on the deck of a steamer going down, and can be saved only one at a time. Even here every one sees the principle will hardly hold: the noble-minded gives place to others, the cowardly tries to press before others: there is no meaning, and no virtue, though it may be a convenient arrangement, in striking an Aristotelian mean or balance between the generosity and the cowardice. The virtue is in the regard for others: with the virtue there is mixed, in each, a certain amount of regard for self: it is likely that where there is more of the former there will be less of the latter: virtue has nothing to do with any relation of equality or otherwise between the two, but simply with the abundance of the former. The latter is not virtue ; but neither is it vice, except so far as it stands in the way of the former : it is simply, as I expressed it before, of no moral account.

The Scripture rule compared with the rule of preference, and the rule of equality.

It will be said, that the Scripture precept 'Love thy neighbour as thyself' both recognizes the above 'equity' as the rule of conduct, and also exhibits an analogy between our love for ourselves and our love for others, which I have said does not exist.

But really it neither implies such an analogy, nor does it recognize equity as the *rule* in the manner above, but only as a general consideration.

So far as the precept, Love thy neighbour as thyself, is understood to indicate a Benthamic equity, *i. e.* a relation of equality between the two loves, it must regulate our love for ourselves as well as the others, and have an understood supplement, viz. 'and thyself as thy neighbour.' But the precept is manifestly of the same kind, and commends itself to men's approbation as being of the same kind as many others, such as, Love your enemies, Love all men as brethren. On this principle 'Love your enemies,' *i. e.* 'Treat them as friends,' must be understood as having the understood supplement, 'and treat your friends no better than your enemies:' 'Love all men as brethren,' will have the supplement, 'and your brethren no better than other men.'

Now when precepts of this kind are accepted as they have been by human nature, as showing to it its duty and its feelings, it is evidently not in that view of them which we are here considering. The passages will to a certain degree bear putting into the form of the preferential system which I gave at first : in which case we should read them thus, Give to your neighbour, or spread over him, some of the feeling which you have for yourself, to all men some of the feeling which you have for your brethren : even to your enemies (here however we change the sign and almost lose the view) some of the feeling which you have for your friends. But they will not bear putting in the equalitarian form—strike a balance between yourselves and your neighbour, between your friends and your enemies, between your brethren and men in general: they have nothing to do with quantity.

Nor will they do well for the preferential system given previously, as is manifest from the different manner in which each must be observed: 'Love thy neighbour as thyself,' means, Diminish your care for yourself, and care more for your neighbour: 'Love your enemies' (it being supposedly your friends that you do love) means, on the other hand, do not diminish your love for your friends, but love your enemies too; it is here that appears the want of analogy between the passage from ourselves to any others, and the passage from one to another amongst others: and clearly love for friends has no tendency to suggest love for enemies, as love for kindred might suggest love for non-kindred, but the contrary. In reality, human nature accepts these passages as describing, vaguely but pointedly, an ideal to be aimed at: try if you cannot come to care for your neighbour, as a regular thing, in something of the same proportion in which you naturally and inevitably care for yourself.

However, I do not mean to say but that the precept, 'Love thy neighbour as thyself,' implies equity, real equity, as a very important consideration. The manner in which it does so may be seen best by comparing another precept with a strong reference to equity, 'Do as you would be done by,' 'Do to others as ye would they should do to you.' Whatever reason of equity exists for taking the former passage exactly, applies in the same way in this. But we see at once it can mean no more than, Do not act towards anybody without the thought what you would like if you were in his place and he in yours. It is only in a very moderate degree that this (one form of the consideration of equity) can regulate action: the juryman must take care that he does not allow his feeling how much he, if he were in the prisoner's place, would like to hear 'not guilty,' to influence him: and in the same way, 'Love thy neighbour as thyself,' does not imply any real putting of him in our place and ourselves in his: it implies that we should not forget that happiness is as dear to him as it is to us, and pain as painful: such remembrance will have its influence on our action, though it is only one consideration in regulating it.

Question examined here from the ideal point of view.

I will endeavour to make out the principles upon which action is really distributed, and to examine what share is taken in the distribution of it by each of the two considerations above mentioned, that of preference, and that of equity or equality: and I will do this in reference to two views, or two stages of view, of the manner in which we act or may act: the one of which I will call the moral or ideal, the other the jural: and I will examine what relation these two views or stages of view have the one to the other.

By 'action' in the above I mean all the particulars of our life and conduct, in so far as we have any purpose in view of these, and assuming that this purpose is somebody's pleasure or welfare, our own included: and the point under examination is *whose* pleasure or welfare this is or should be, in what degree that of one, in what degree that of another. We might say instead of action, if we pleased, thought, care, interestedness.

In this chapter I will discuss the question from the moral or ideal point of view.

The equalitarian rule is a foreign addition to the utilitarian system, which suggests simply the pursuit of our own happiness.

The division of our action between ourselves and others in general is regulated on the principle that virtue, worth, merit, excellence, is in proportion to the extent we act for others rather than for ourselves. Our acting for our own happiness, and our acting for that of others, do not come under the same consideration. The mistake of the simple utilitarian scheme (I mean that which simply considers the important thing about action to be, that it should tend to *some* happiness) is that, to whatever extent it attributes merit to the acting for others' happiness, it must do so also to the acting for our own. The distinction between these two ways of acting seems to me the cardinal point of morals, a distinction which utilitarianism, as a principle, endeavours as much as it can to obliterate. It may indeed not attribute merit in either case, neither to the acting for others' happiness nor to acting for our own : it may not recognize the notion of merit, and think it only a result of education, a late human conventionalism : it may view all action for any happiness as alike useful and good. If this is so, it seems to me that Bentham's principle of equity, given above, is an arbitrary superaddition on his (in fact on the general utilitarian) supposition of action being for the greatest happiness. In spite of the mention of 'the greatest number,' it seems to me that the direct tendency of all thought of this kind, if only anybody could be considered really to hold it (which I question whether anybody ever did, in spite of utilitarian attempt at system), would be to make action self-regarding and selfish. Nay, I question whether it *ought* not. So far as we can abstract 'action for happiness,' or look at action, in each case, as effort for some definite happiness, considering the human, doubtful, view which we must have as to what is happiness, and the importance of making sure that our action is not wasted but produces *some* happiness—it almost seems to me that the most reasonable course, even with the view of being sure of producing the most happiness, and even in spite of the addition 'of the greatest number,' would be for each to take care of himself, and be sure of making *himself* as happy as he can. "Mirato ingentia rura; exiguum colito." Look widely around and *wish* well to others: but, mindful how likely dispersed effort is to be lost, and how ignorant you are of their feelings and circumstances, concentrate your felicific effort where you can make tolerably sure that none of it will be lost, and let *your* production of happiness be on your own ground, *your* contribution to the sum of happiness, your own happiness.

Answer to supposed utilitarian objector.

I am well aware that many other considerations, in reason, enter in here, and that every man's pleasure depends very largely on the pleasure of those about him, and is most intimately complicated with it, so that he could not produce happiness for himself alone, and in trying to produce it for himself, he would have to do this through the process of producing it for others. This complication of different sorts of happiness, and of different people's happiness, together, represents the reality of human life: and moreover, there is something besides this; viz. that happiness does not really offer itself as a distinct and definite object to be striven after or produced, as all our present hypothesis supposes, but is, in various ways, too fugitive and intangible. All this I shall have shortly to speak of, upon the subject of 'happiness.' But the view which we are taking now, as to action being directed in each case to some definite happiness of somebody, though a hypothesis and an abstraction, is a view which people often do take and which it is convenient to take: and since it is assumed as the foundation of the utilitarian moral philosophy, many questions, having reference to utilitarianism, must be discussed upon this view. If it is the utilitarian who urges what I have said in the first part of this paragraph as an objection to what I have said in the last paragraph, he is really meeting an objection to his view by abandoning his view altogether. The principle of utilitarianism is that human happiness may be made distinct and exhibited distinctly, with measurement, as an object for action, and that morality is the production of as much as possible of it. It is replied: We are so much more likely to be able to calculate, with accuracy, our own happiness than that of others, that probably, for the mere production of quantity, it would be best each should attend only to his own. Though others may answer, the utilitarian must not, 'No, for happiness is indistinct and complicated, cannot be exhibited distinctly or measured: when trying to produce the happiness of others we constantly, without intending it, produce our own, and if we work distinctly for our own we are sure not to be able to gain it.'

The independent value of self-sacrifice must be recognized before we can lay down a rule for distribution of action.

The distribution then of our action between ourselves and others in general is given us by the principles of moral value which I discussed some time since: viz. that that action has most moral value, or most virtue or merit, in which there is effort for the happiness of others accompanied with postponement of our own: that in reality both these elements must to a certain extent go together, (since consulting the happiness of others is, to a certain extent, always self-postponement, or employing otherwise effort which might have been for ourselves:) and that actions which are done for the happiness of others, have their highest merit as they are done with the most of self-sacrifice or self-devotion.

There will be more then of thought, care, and effort devoted to others' utility and others' good, according, in the first place, as we have more of that which utilitarians rightly praise, value for human happiness, imagination how it may be best promoted, ideals of it floating before us, and much more of this kind; accompanied, according to our temperament, with more or less of emotion, and sympathy with seen or imagined misery: and, in the second place, according as we have more or less of the feelings which belong to self-forgetfulness, self-postponement, self-devotion, and which have the most special *moral* value or merit. 'Generosity' is perhaps the most general and expressive term for this kind of feelings: but it hardly expresses the feeling belonging to the highest and worthiest acts of the kind, for which, I think, we should deem it insufficient: and it has also associated with it notions not necessarily connected with actions of this kind, and leading perhaps sometimes to misconception.

This self-sacrifice is the same as the Greek ἀνδρεία.

The ancient ἀνδρεία, *fortitude* or manliness, may be considered to be this 'generosity', with great reference to these associated notions, and with but little reference to the good to others which the self-forgetfulness might be likely to produce. The word 'generous' in English is usually applied to self-forgetfulness for the cause of others: the Latin 'fortitudo' had a wider signification, or perhaps it rather signified self-forgetfulness, absence of fear, when honour or shame was in question. Still both it and the Greek ἀνδρεία expressed a character of mind which is essential to the exercise of a high and large benevolence: for the valuing the imagined result is not enough, unless there exist also the disposition, and the capacity, to make the effort and the self-sacrifice.

The proportion of care which we should devote to ourselves and to others cannot be determined by considerations either of equity or preference.

As between ourselves, then, and others in general, and with reference to our conduct as a whole, there is no place for any considerations either of equality or of preference. No morality can tell us any proportion in which we ought, respectively, to care for ourselves and for others.

The bidding of what I will call *bare nature*, by which I mean nature as the inferior or ordinary reason (distinguished from the higher reason, or aspiration and imagination, and also from emotion), the operation of which is simply to take cognizance of our own condition, circumstances and wants, is to call upon us simply to take care of ourselves.

Self-preservation is the instinct of which self-sustentation (to be spoken of however also in another quite different view) is the rational development.

With the vast majority of mankind, the great mass of their thought must, by the mere necessity of the case, be devoted to self-care, modified indeed, and extended, in a manner which we shall shortly see. In such cases, it makes little difference whether we consider that life altogether and the whole laying out of it should be modelled upon moral principle and upon considerations of virtue, or whether we consider that self-care must be the main modeller, virtuous principle only coming in to restrain from wrong, to animate with more or less of good feeling, to elevate with more or less of aspiration and ideal.

The life, or its laying out, would have on either view to be very much the same: self-care must be the leading feature of it: virtue would on the latter view παρεισελθεῖν, come in on a second thought, as a corrector; on the former view, virtue would be the first thought and the leading principle indeed, but, like some Oriental despots, would have to be content with its superiority, and to give up the actual conduct of life to the inferior principle, reserving only to itself the same degree of intervention or correction as on the other hypothesis. Still, the mere acknowledgment of its superiority is noble and elevating.

Our first duty is αὐτάρκεια; when that is secured our duty is to give all we can to our neighbour.

The degree then, in which we *should* care for others, is the degree in which we *can* do so: making certain in the first instance, that our life is not of such a kind, as to lay upon them the necessity of taking care of us. This is the other view of self-care or self-sustentation to which I just now alluded, in which it is one of the first, if not the very first, of duties, for it is one without the performance of which we shall not be able to perform any other. It is no use to think of bearing the burdens of others if we begin by making ourselves, or leaving ourselves to be, a burden for them to bear. The first condition of good or worthy action for help of others is such a condition of *αὐτάρκεια*, self-helpfulness, independence, as shall enable us to call our action our own, and so give us the right to dispose of it: this by itself, with many, will of necessity fix a considerable portion of their action upon themselves.

All that I am saying now goes, it is to be remembered, upon a hypothesis which very imperfectly fits to the facts: for in fact all our life, in most cases, is a web of self-care and care for others, mixed and often indistinguishable. All this in its place.

I said that, in respect of the apportioning our care between ourselves and others in general, considerations of equity do not enter in as regards the whole of our conduct, or our conduct on the whole: I might have said, our conduct to others *in general.* I have to explain what I mean by this.

The rule of equity is applicable as between oneself and one's neighbour only in points of detail.

There is a sentiment of *fairness* as between ourselves and others, in the same way as there is a sentiment of fairness in respect of our conduct as between two parties. But this regards *particulars* of our conduct and particular persons: it has no bearing on our conduct as a whole, or on the question between us and others in general. It is flagrantly, and plainly, only in regard of particular circumstances and particular people that we can make the supposition upon which utilitarians seem to suppose that our whole conduct can be regulated, viz. Here are two parties, myself, and whoever else it may be: I will act, in any transactions between the two, as if they were two parties independent of me; as if neither of them were myself. No doubt there are many occasions in life in which fairness of this kind is required: but it is treating moral philosophy as if it were a matter on which people might say just what they pleased, to talk of regulating our whole conduct, as between ourselves and others, by it. It takes for granted certain already existing relations between us and others, which will come before us shortly: till then, it cannot be applied, and is mere words. Fairness, with any meaning in the word, implies conflicting individual interests: but the existence of individual interest at all, implies a transgression of the Benthamic or unmeaning fairness, according to which we should take the same thought, and no more, for ourselves and for each one else, or count ourselves for one only, like any other, in the universe.

Fairness consists in refraining from taking an undue advantage of another in any matter in which we are rivals: it is no unfairness to work for our own bread rather than for his, though it is self-preference.

All this, however, will be better understood after

I have spoken, as I shall now do, about the distribution of our care, or our action for happiness, between different individuals amongst others.

It is applicable generally to determine the distribution of action amongst others.

In respect of this, fairness or equality may be said to be the natural starting-point or foundation: all individuals who may be the objects of our action, are, as a matter of course, to be treated equally or similarly, except so far as reason may appear for the preferring of some to others. But besides this, equity may possibly come in afterwards, in a manner more important, as a restraint upon over-preference, or mis-preference.

But requires to be qualified by the rule of preference in answer to the call of opportunity or obligation.

Probably the two main principles of preference among objects of our action are these two: want, or opportunity; merit, or obligation.

In the last chapter I spoke entirely of feeling or emotion: in this, I wish, so far as I can, to leave it out of account. It is by putting together these various abstractions or partial views that we shall get, so far as we can get, a general view of human nature.

Opportunity illustrated from the case of mother and child.

Let us then leave out of account family affection, i.e. as a reason why we should care more for kindred than for others: I think the simple existence of the family relation, as a fact, is a sufficient reason why preference should be given to kindred over others. Putting this more generally, the various descriptions of benevolence or goodwill, which I went through in a previous chapter, indicate or suppose various relations of fact, which (even if we supposed the feeling, the goodwill, not to exist) would show opportunity and need for care, and thus, as facts, call for care, i.e. preferential care. Supposing there were no such thing as maternal love, the mother and infant are, as a matter of fact, in such a position the one towards the other, that the mere fact, if we were beings who acted in that way, would demand that same conduct on the mother's part which maternal love now ensures. I mean, of course, supposing a general goodwill, of which the direction has in some way to be determined.

The fact of the relation fixes the particulars of duty.

This, which I have called the demand of fact, is the same thing as what I have already spoken of under the name of duty. The fact, *i.e.* the relation, or relative position, as a matter of fact, does not give the notion of duty, but, supposing this to exist in general, it supplies the application and the particularity of it. If we are such that nothing calls upon us to help others, if we have no ears for such a call, then of course this relation will not call: but if our nature is prepared for the call, that is, if we possess the general notion of mutual duty, then the relation or fact gives the call, or fixes the *particulars* of duty.

The existence of what are called in moral philosophy 'relative duties', *i.e.* duties from father to child, from child to father, from brother to brother, &c., is in reality a call to us for preferential care or action for happiness in the case where such duties exist. The nature of the care or action is generally indicated by the relation, or, which is the same thing, readily suggested by the mind. The description of the duty owed, is, in many cases, little more than the same thing as describing the fact of the relation.

The relation is, perhaps, a simply natural one: perhaps, as that of friends, it is a self-created one: in this case the want and opportunity are self-created, but do not the less exist.

We come next to relations which imply merit or obligation: it might be better to style them generally 'relations of occasion' in accordance with the language used in a former chapter. Some of them, in any case, come best under this title: but it is not of consequence.

An action is not necessarily right because there is a call of obligation to it.

The important thing about relations of this kind is, that the conduct which the relation, as a fact, suggests to us is not necessarily virtuous, though it comes, in a manner, into moral consideration; in other words, that the conduct, which, so far as the relation goes, is reasonable, may not be the proper conduct.

Obligation is usually founded on some previous disturbance of relations which calls for redress.

The chief relation of this kind is the position in which any one stands towards us in respect of previous conduct, either on his part or on ours. He has benefited or injured us, or we have benefited or injured him. The consideration of the setting right the inequality (in the language of the ancient philosophers), or readjusting the disturbance thus created, suggests in the former case, on our part, benefit or injury to him; in the latter case, on our part, expectation of benefit or injury from him, and, so far as our conduct is concerned, desire to redress the injury we have done, and to injure if our benefit is not repaid.

This is what bare equity or fairness, justice (the first time we have used the word) as ἰσότης or equality, and as διορθωτική or *expletrix*, the redresser of inequality, would suggest: but there are two exceedingly important considerations to come in.

In such a case our action must be governed not by justice alone, but by considerations of utility,

The first consideration is that with which I have started in this chapter, in the same way as I started with the consideration of benevolence in the last, viz. that it is the nature of action to be done for the production of some good or happiness: action exists in the universe as a means of producing something wanted; action is possible in the universe in virtue of there being capacity for good or happiness, which the action can supply. Utilitarians have with reason complained of the manner in which this principle has been often assumed without acknowledgment by their opponents. When, in consequence of mis-action past, there is call on the principle of reason as *fairness*, for action which is intended to produce not happiness, but pain, there is a counter-call on the principle of reason as *utility* (*i.e.* reason looking to the good result of actions) against such action, as what ought not to be. What I am now speaking of, it is to be remembered, is the *fact* of the relative position of the parties, and the consequent suggestion of reason. As reason is divided against itself, so also is feeling; the intellectual feeling of fairness, of which I shall speak in a moment, is very strong on the one side, and in aid of it are various malevolent feelings; while there is benevolence, in whatever degree of strength, on the other.

and also of a rivalry in honour.

The second consideration is that we are rivals of each other (as I have before mentioned), not only in interest, but, in a different and more important way, in merit and excellence. I put the thing here rather coarsely and broadly on purpose. These two rivalries (of interest and merit) act in opposite directions; and elevation of nature, the Aristotelian magnanimity, depends upon the degree to which the latter prevails over the former. In the rivalry of interest the party who has injured the other is the superior; that is to say, he has gained an advantage: in the rivalry of merit the party who has conferred benefit is the superior: and on *this* ground it is not he that desires the repayment, but the other party. Similarly, forgiveness of injuries is a moral triumph to the forgiver, and a humiliation to the forgiven: and in the interest of virtue, what we have reason to fear is sometimes lest it should be only too much felt so.

'Injury' and 'benefit' are of course however very vague expressions. To take injury: there are two great heads of it, insult and wrong, which stand, in reference to what I have been saying, on a very different footing: but still what I have said applies in general.

Manner in which action is influenced by these three considerations.

In respect then of that relative position of two parties in which there has passed between them injury or benefit, the suggestions of bare fairness are qualified by the double consideration, of utility or benevolence, and of superiority or merit. All these concur to enforce gratitude, which, as I mentioned in the last chapter, may be urged upon us by very different motives. On the other hand, revenge is urged by mere fairness, while it is always opposed by benevolence and the desire that our conduct shall be beneficial and useful, and ordinarily by magnanimity also. If we have been the benefactors, mere fairness, careless of feeling, suggests offence at failure of repayment, while benevolence and magnanimity suggest the contrary. If, on the other hand, we have injured another, fairness, benevolence, and magnanimity all concur to enforce restitution, redress, contrition, and more or less increased goodwill.

In the first and last cases indeed, secondary feelings of a terrible nature sometimes come in, instead of the above-mentioned secondary feeling of increased goodwill. Men hate those by whom they have been benefited, as odious creditors; they hate those whom they have injured, as likely to be nursing feelings of revenge.

The love of fairness compared to the love of truth.

Though I am in this chapter concerned mainly with the intellectual view of fact, yet as just now in the case of benevolence, I cannot entirely escape notice of feeling, and I will say a few words here on what I have called the intellectual feeling of fairness.

I described, some time since, the analogy between the moral desire to do right, or love of duty or virtue in general, and the intellectual love of, or value for truth. The love of fairness, which I am now speaking of, is the same thing as this desire to do right, in a particular application and in a more definite shape: and on account of this greater particularity and definiteness, it is in special analogy with the love of truth.

The love of fairness means first, the desire to ascertain how interest, on our part, happiness, advantage, should be distributed, balanced, apportioned between two parties in a particular case; what is due to the one, what to the other: and next, the desire that this knowledge may be acted upon, both by the parties and by others concerned. The desire to find out this, is in fact the same thing as the intellectual thirst after truth, with the addition, that the practical feelings, the sympathies and care for good and happiness, are strongly enlisted in the case. And then, when this has been ascertained, there comes the anxiety for its being acted on, and the corresponding dissatisfaction or displeasure, often most intense, at its not being so. I have called this love of fairness an *intellectual* feeling, because it has nothing at all to do either with benevolence or with any æsthetic feelings: the feelings with which it most readily associates itself are the semi-malevolent feelings; it tends to produce rather indignation at wrong than any sympathy with happiness. This is because that which is fair is considered the normal state, something natural or which ought to exist as a matter of course, capable of exciting dissatisfaction if disturbed, but giving rise to no particular satisfaction in its existence. The peculiar intensity of the feeling which springs up at the sight of wrong done is owing to the wounding of the sense of fairness or equity, analogous to the wounding of the sense of truth, combined with the more emotional feelings of pity for the sufferer, and aversion for the inflictor of pain.

For right distribution of action, the principle of particularity has to be combined with those of equity and preference.

I have here been going out of my way to speak a little about the feeling of fairness, which, like other feelings, often exists more or less arbitrarily, and errs in various ways. I am now rather concerned with fairness as a fact, or, which is the same thing, with what the feeling of fairness, which should follow fact, should be.

Our conduct to different people should be regulated, in other words, our care for them apportioned, on three principles combined: proper preference; proper fairness, or absence of preference; and proper particularity.

Our duty to kindred, for instance, has, as we have seen, this character, that more interest is to be taken in them than in others, in other words, that our action, as useful, is engaged as it were to them, before we have right to the general disposal of it; and also that the nature of our action towards or for them is determined by the nature of the relation: it is different according as they are parents, according as they are children, according to what they are. The principles of preference and particularity both come in.

On the other hand, the principle of equity or fairness exists, to prevent over-preference and mispreference. It exists, as between the preferred and the non-preferred; and as among the preferred.

How far it is true that benevolence is an extension of self-love.

I mentioned that our preference, in care and action, of kindred and others standing in similar relation to us, is a feeling which in some respects resembles self-preference, or has selfish elements in it.

In one point of view, it *is* an extended self-regard: and this is important for various reasons.

The view that all benevolence is an extension of self-love, which, as I said, roughly represents a real fact, does so in this way for one; that, as affection to kindred and friends, if we compare it on the one side with simple self-regard, may be called benevolence, so, if we compare it on the other side with philanthropy and the wider desire of human happiness, it may be called selfishness. To this is to be added, that many really selfish elements associate themselves with it, while, exactly to the same degree in which this takes place, benevolent elements mix with our selfishness: an interchange takes place: we think of those whom we love with selfishness; we are ready to sacrifice ourselves for those we love. The greater part of the selfishness or self-interestedness which exists is of this character: it is very far from being mere care for our single selves. But then, correspondingly, our love for those connected with us takes a selfish character: our reputation, our success, our pleasures, are bound up in them.

Conflict of relative and general duty.

So strongly is this the case, that carrying relative duty too far, as against general duty, is an offence against duty altogether, as great as the neglect of relative duty would be; and within the limits of relative duty itself, there is duty to be maintained which is not relative. Undue preferences in families, as amongst children for instance, is one of the most fertile sources of evil and trouble.

The principle which, in these respects, is to be set against relative duty is, what we may call in general, fairness or equity: as we are considering it now, it is vague and without very much meaning: its meaning will come to it chiefly at a later stage of consideration, after we have supposed people existing in a definite social state under law. Still it *has* importance in the earlier stage: we owe duty to everybody: in some respects all are to be treated alike; no one's happiness should be matter of indifference to us.

What has been said as to the wrongness of over-care for kindred, &c., applies in the same way to the *occasional* relations which I have spoken of, of benefactor and benefited, &c. Gratitude is a stronger call upon us perhaps even than family affection; but still one which, like that, must have its law and limit. Nor, if we have injured any, shall we do any good by violating fairness in some other way to redress the wrong.

But enough perhaps of relations which suggest a preference, in our care, thought or good-will for one over another. There are other relations which suggest our action in particular cases, some of them most important: and I will here discuss one which is perhaps the most important of all.

The duty of truthfulness.

This is the relation of trusting and trusted.

By our nature, we are, to a certain extent, a sealed book each one to others: we can keep our thoughts to ourselves, while we can say what we please. And besides this, our will is exceedingly fluctuating and uncertain; we constantly do not know our own mind for the future.

Now if we have given occasion to any to trust us, so as to regulate by this trust in any way his mind and thought, our action is pledged by this or engaged to him in the same way as I mentioned in respect of relative duty, and much more definitely. And independent of any act of ours, in virtue of our mere nature as men, we give occasion to others to trust what we say as expressing our thought: and hence truthfulness is an inevitable duty of speech. I suppose, if we individually could, in any way, let each person know that we were an exception to human nature, and that we wished it to be universally understood that what we said did not at all necessarily, though it might, represent our thought; in this case, there would be no duty of truthfulness for us, because our speech would not be human speech, but would be only sound without meaning. As it is, the most untruthful speech is human speech, because it is understood as addressed to people who more or less trust us, and because it has, ordinarily, one of two purposes, either to express the man's mind, or to mis-express it and deceive: it is not human speech unless it has some purpose in relation to understanding.

It is best viewed as one aspect of faithfulness.

The proper moral aspect of truthfulness seems to me to be that it is one case of the very wide duty of faithfulness to trust, which alone renders possible the correspondent virtue of trustfulness; the two together constituting almost the highest prerogative, the greatest glory, and at the same time, the greatest pleasure of human nature.

Truthfulness comes more simply thus, as a branch or case of faithfulness, than as a branch or case of 'openness,' which latter, as virtue, is a matter of difficult consideration.

There is no more occasion that we should wear our heart and mind on our sleeve, than that we should turn our heart inside out, and live in public, except so far as others may be benefited by our openness, or as it may affect their action; or, on the other hand, except so far as any reserve or incommunicativeness is the result of fear. Our minds are, by the necessity of our nature, individual, and very often what is in them cannot be communicated, because such communication is a double process, involving conditions on the part of the listener as well as on the other side.

The action suggested to us by the above relations, and other similar ones, constitutes duty, or the law of duty, as to its particulars; or, if we like so to express it, it gives us the contents of that law of duty, the ideal of which we form to ourselves in the manner which I described in a former chapter, which, so to speak, we imaginatively impose upon ourselves, or imagine as binding upon us.

For the application of duty we need a system of positive relations.

The law of duty, in so far as we consider it not an ideal presenting itself to our imagination, but as something actually existing, or which has existed, or which might possibly exist, as an understood and more or less obeyed rule of conduct among men, is called natural law or the law of nature.

But, as a rule of conduct, though it *has* thus contents or particulars, it is evidently exceedingly vague.

Before it can be applied to any extent, there is quite a different set of considerations upon which we have to enter. We have to consider men as existing, as in fact they always do exist, in certain relations to each other more complicated and more definite than those which we have as yet considered: they are what are called positive as distinct from moral relations, and the system of them is what is called positive law. I shall more generally call them jural relations. The law of duty has to be applied to the conduct of men to each other, in reference to these relations; to take cognizance, both of the manner of the formation of the relations, and of men's conduct in them. These will form the subject of our next chapter.

APPENDIX ON DISTRIBUTION OF ACTION IN REFERENCE TO EXISTING LAW[1].

Justice has reference to three stages of law, law of the state, of humanity, of God.

JUSTNESS, in the highest degree of abstractness or general application to which we can trace the word, is indistinguishable from fairness, fitness, rightness.

Between this point of abstractness and the most definite understanding which can subsist among men as to the most accidental relations, there is a continuous course of possible relation and action, which we may divide into three regions, commencing from the lowest:

(1). That to which applies particular and express human law, with its definite authority and penalties.

(2). That to which applies general and unformalized human law, *i.e.* universal, public, or (more or less) general opinion.

(3). That to which applies conscience, imaginatively representing to us a more general and higher opinion or judgment still, viz. that of all possible intelligent and moral beings, to which our intelligence and moral judgment, so far as they are true and right, must be conformable. Natural religion concentrates this judgment into that of God, and revelation makes it definite, and makes known to us the particulars of it.

There lies thus always an inward or moral appeal from express human law to universal human feeling, and from (apparent) universal human feeling to our own conscience,

[1] In the preceding chapter the Author had proposed to consider the principles on which action should be distributed, first, from the ideal, and, second, from the jural point of view, and also to examine the relation of these two views to each other. He has completed the first part of his task, but has left only the merest sketch of the second and third. I have thought it better therefore to insert here a discussion of the same subject taken from an older MS. marked *Series* 3, incorporating in it one or two paragraphs from the later sketch. ED.

as representing to us, in the only way practicable, the law of universal intelligence or of God.

Definition of law.

The definition which I gave of law some time back will be remembered: it is the restraint or regulation of the acts of individuals, in view of the advantage of each and all, by sufficient authority and power. The authority, recognized by the common reason, distinguishes it from mere violence: the power, acting upon individuals by penalty, where necessary, distinguishes it from mere custom.

Duty in regard to actual law.

Duty is concerned with actual human law in three ways: it regulates, to a certain extent, the making it: it enforces obedience to it as actual law, except in cases where it is contrary to duty itself: beyond such obedience, it regulates action in conformity with the relations which actual law has introduced.

The law determines rights and duties in accordance with the relations established by it.

In considering relative duty as it exists in society and civilization, or under actual law, we have to consider individuals as *clothed*, so to speak, with various circumstances and conditions. The simplest view of these is to call them rights and duties. Duties exist as we have seen prior to any actual law: the term 'rights' was introduced in later jural language to express the circumstances of the party to whom duty was owed, signifying the same as claim, call, due.

The purpose of law is to regulate individual action, but the manner in which this is done, in all actual law which is in other than its rudest stage, is not by mere isolated injunction, but is by the recognition of individuals as in various relations to each other, or by the placing them in such relations, with certain things which each must do and which each may claim; and then saying to individuals, If you do anything inconsistent with, or offending against, these arrangements, you incur such and such a penalty.

Law is thus an authoritative distribution of action.

Law is thus an order, νόμος, or distribution of men in a society: that is, it is an authoritative distribution or apportionment of a certain portion of their actions for them.

This general distribution is the sum of a number of less general distributions, or arrangements as to the things people may claim or must do, and these arrangements, in so far as they are brought into being by the actual law, are called 'institutions.' An actual society is abstractly a congeries of such institutions.

Sources of the authority of actual law.

Actual law is, at no one time, without its authority, *i.e.* power accepted by reason as right: but the authority which there is for it at any one time is, in a measure, accidental: that is, the authority which there is for it at the particular time, is representative more or less of three separate things, (1) of the superiority of the whole society to each individual member of it: (2) of the superiority which there is in the *continued* society, as existing in past and (prospectively) in future time, over the collection of individuals at any moment: and (3) of that general government of all intelligent beings by God, which is the moral law. The form of the representation is in a great measure accidental. The power and reason both come, more or less from each one of the things which are represented.

Its embodiment is often accidental.

Primâ facie, the *power* is in the whole body; but practically, the power at any time is very much according to the accidental grouping of the members, and the third consideration supplies an additional element of *moral* power the practical effect of which is very great. Primâ facie, again, the *reason* (the business of which is the consideration of the good of all) is in the whole body: but practically some will be better judges of this than others, and experience will very probably have suggested certain ways of selecting such judges, as well as the best means for judging, and for carrying into effect their judgment.

Bare power is changed into authority by the recognition of relations on both sides.

When it is said that, of particular law, the authority at any time is a matter of accident, what is meant is that it is equally authority of whatever sort it is, and whencesoever it has come; the two elements of it as authority being power and recognition. Practically, in many cases, authority or *legific* competence has begun in bare power; and law, so to call it, that is, such regulation of action as there has been, has been simply the result of a struggle between two parties, in which the weaker has yielded. Sociality or political life has been the gradual conversion of this state of things into one of mutual understanding and consideration: bare power has become authority by the prevalence of the feeling on the one side that obedience to it is a duty, and on the other that the exercise of it is not meant for private benefit, but for the benefit of all.

Growth of law from custom.

Law grows of itself, like language, and passes from one

state to another. Much of it begins in the form of custom: and, of the great and important parts of it, there are few which, as a matter of fact, have ever been established as the result of previous deliberate discussion. They have established themselves gradually: one and another has been convinced of the utility of a practice, it has been imitated, and has grown by more or less general assent into a custom: and then such customs have authoritatively established themselves as law. Such discussion as has come, in human experience, on these greater points of law, has hence been of defence and attack, rather than of previous consideration of advisability. What has been deliberate has been sometimes repeal or alteration of the great principles, but more generally various development and modification, with addition of smaller accompaniments.

The main framework of law existed prior to enactment, which has merely served to define it.

In speaking therefore of law as something enacted, we have to consider that the great framework of law in any system has (speaking generally) never been matter of proper enactment, but has had its authority in a great degree independent of such: what enactment it has had has been a formal expression of something previously existing. When we speak of the institution of property, we do not mean that property is a thing which has ever been historically instituted: the human race has never been without it. It is, historically, an universal human custom, made definite, in various ways, by particular law. Deliberation or previous discussion as to the establishment of cardinal institutions of this kind would have been impossible, in the same way as a previous discussion, on the part of any number of men, whether they should adopt the practice of language: the possibility of orderly organization for the previous discussion involves the existence of the institution.

The primary essential of law is that it should conform to human nature.

Keeping then in remembrance this, that, historically, much of law has never had an express purpose, we may say that the purpose of law is the public utility, and that law is good in proportion to its utility, that no law which we are certain is useful can be unjust. But in respect of law there are three things, justness, utility, naturalness, very closely complicated together. And the first which we have need to notice is *naturalness*. Naturalness expresses both primary justice, as the word is applicable to laws, and primary utility.

The justice or utility of a law can only be determined in reference to its naturalness.

Before we can settle as to particulars, what is just, or not unjust, and what is useful, we must have before us the facts of human nature to which justice and utility are to be referred. A law that the wife should support the husband would be unjust, because nature has made man the stronger of the two. A law that female children (or a certain portion of them) should be destroyed (as enacted in Rajpootana on grounds of presumed public utility) would really be unuseful, as doing violence to those primary facts of nature to which all utility must be referred. We must therefore have given to us the great outlines of law from considerations of what is *natural* to man, and then law may be developed on the principle, that whatever is for the general good, including the maintenance of these as a part of it, and is not contrary to the higher law of rightness, is what should be.

Bases of legislation, family and property.

The two great bases of legislation, in all human experience, have been *family* and *property*, the one going with the other: and these again are results of two facts belonging to human nature, one, that man in society, speaking generally, can produce or add to the whole stock of wealth more than he wants, at least for his immediate and individual use: the other, that man is not *insulated*, *i.e.* that the *self*, whose interest self-regard makes him seek, is not divided by a definite boundary from the not-self, in rivalry with which he seeks it. As the body is, for sensiveness, at once a part of ourselves and of the physical external world, being the medium between the two, so family stands between a man's self and the society, at once a part of both. The two facts (of the gaining power of men and the needs of the helpless part of the family) are clearly correspondent: the law says no more than nature does in saying the community will help you to preserve what you gain, on condition that you use your gains in support of those whom you ought to support. Both, in different ways, shall belong to you.

Inequality of property is natural

That the institution of property is in this manner *natural* for the human race, *i.e.* was what, considering what men are, could not fail to take place and what human experience could not fail to ratify, has not probably been disputed. But it might be considered that the existence of separate property was a primæval abuse, necessary perhaps in early ages, but one which civilization might be expected to rectify; that mutual trust, the great character of civilization, might increase to such an extent that the stock of property might without injury be held in common: or in any case, without going so far as this, it might be considered that the great inequality of property, which would very likely develope itself, is what law, in the interest of all, might check. The inequality which does develope itself in this respect, and which seems more and more to do so the higher the economical civilization is carried, is a thing, in some respects, painful to contemplate; and it is a great hindrance to moral civilization. But so far as human experience goes, it seems as if a high economical civilization or a large population (which can only exist on the supposition either of this, or else of a very low level of material welfare on the part of the mass) cannot arise or be kept up without the full allowance of such inequality. The inequality of property which arises in a comparatively uncivilized time, from preoccupation and superior strength on the part of some, though this cause acts with diminished force in the advance of civilization, yet is reinforced from another source, in the exceeding inequality of commercial success, and the tendency to accumulation in particular hands which commerce involves. This again arises from the same fact of the superiority, if we are to call it so, of one man to another, the result of such individual superiority being continued in families. Many efforts have been made, at one time or another, to cause by legislation comparative equality, but their result has always been as yet to paralyse commerce and industry (upon which the national support depends) and in this way to prevent the increase of property in general, while the existing property has only changed hands, without any greater equality than before being at all secured. It appears as if human nature was such, as not to allow the stretching of the cord of mutual trust too tight. It is the union of the feeling of it with an equally strong feeling of individual liberty, enterprise and interest, which alone seems able to produce that amount of exertion which is required to make nations prosperous. It is not only human selfishness but individual independence, which revolts against equalization: inequality of property is only one form of that general variety of condition, which seems a necessary part of human nature. And man, though rising above most of the brute animals in having the idea of a community to work for, and in the fact that there are some of his race with whom this will be a sufficient stimulus, yet is not so far raised above them as that it is sure to be a sufficient stimulus for all. The stimulus of individual necessity seems to be still indispensable.

The incidental evils of inequality may be to a certain extent obviated by poor laws:

It may perhaps then be considered as what human nature, at least as interpreted by and known from human experience, suggests as one base or primary provision for law, that each member of the community should continue undisturbed in the possession of what is his, as the representative of a former pre-occupation; and that he should also be allowed to enjoy the fruits of his abilities and industry, to whatever amount they may accumulate, and whatever degree of inequality of condition may result from such accumulation. The law of England is honourably distinguished at present in doing what the law certainly ought to do, viz. providing that this inequality shall never go so far as to admit of really unsupported destitution. In a complicated society, where the soil is all appropriated in such a manner that independent support of life is entirely impossible, there is doubtless a right in each individual to support at the hands of the community to this extent; it is a part of the common law of mankind. The community says to him, Instead of the aboriginal and barbarous ways of gaining your bread which are now not possible, we open to you a thousand others: if these are all, for whatever reason, impracticable for you, then we will support you: more particularly we charge ourselves with your support in those times of sickness and old age, which barbarism cut short or neglected.

In England such a provision is fitting and equitable, not only from the general complication of society, but also from the difficulty and expense of moving from one place to another where support may be more easily obtained.

and by emigration.

It has never been the condition of human nature, nor ever could be, that every man should claim, as his right, a ready-made society to be born into, with all the advantages which could arise from the previous labour of others in his behalf. If men are so fortunate, well and good:

if not, they have only to do what their forefathers have done before them, and make a place in the world for themselves. Property rights in England are representative of former movements, emigrations, and occupations continued through many generations: it is competent for those who are born into a pre-occupied land to repeat such movements in other lands. So it is thatnew communities are established and civilization extends.

Legislation in respect of family, which is the other great primary matter of law, is parallel and correspondent with that in respect of property.

The economical unit of a state is the property of each member of it, and the social unit is each family, to the members of which that property is, speaking generally, common.

The family is the social unit.

Legislation about property is, so far as necessity goes, chiefly concerned with its relation to the family, and with its (wrongful or rightful) passing from one hand to another (which indeed includes much of the former).

Legal connexion of family and property.

Historically, much complication has arisen from the association of property with service to be done, which is what we call the feudal system. But without entering into details of law, we have merely to speak of a few facts of society with which it is concerned.

The first family relation is that of husband and wife.

The experience of mankind shews us as facts, which have existed in nations to some extent civilized, polygamy, and a terminable monogamy so to call it.

Permanent monogamy is the natural form of marriage association.

But one special condition of civilization and human improvement is "concubitu prohibere vago," and the experience of civilization may be taken as leading us to think that neither of the above is so far a remove from it as is desirable. Our previous ideas of human nature would tend the same way.

The feelings which should lead to the marriage association are of such a nature, that unless concentrated on one, they can hardly have that elevating, higher than sensual, character, or produce that entireness of union which it is a fact in human nature that they do have and produce. And, under either of the above-mentioned conditions, the family can hardly exist in the manner in which it should, considering its importance as the foundation-stone and rudiment of society.

Hence religion with which these primary relations of human society have always been a matter of special care, and the Christian revelation in particular, has drawn the marriage bond and the restriction to one very tightly.

One reason for dissolution of marriage is expressly allowed by Christianity, and there are others besides which might be considered valid: but in dealing with this subject it must never be forgotten, that the loosening of the marriage tie is the loosening of society altogether. To say that nothing can authorize exceptions may be too much; but the engagement bonâ fide till death do part seems as much an anchor of civilization as of religion.

The legal position of the sexes should conform to their natural differences. Error of Plato.

The relation, as to power and property, between husband and wife, is a matter upon which laws have varied and nature has not apparently given principles so clearly: but perhaps it may be said to have given this, that the idea of moral similarity of the sexes, the keystone of Plato's education, is fallacious. *Mind* has given rise to a possibility of difference which destroys the analogy in this respect between man and the brute animals, even supposing there were in their case, which may be doubtful, that similarity of sexes which Plato assumes. That human society derives much of its interest and value from the moral difference between the sexes, is what we should hardly now hesitate to say, and surely human experience is with us. Each needs and helps the other.

That law then should recognize a difference between the sexes, is no more than its expressing a natural fact: and if this is to be considered a political inferiority of the one, it is an inferiority surely balanced by the social influence, power and importance on their side, which there is no doubt but that it greatly helps, and with the best result.

Naturalness is justice and utility in the first degree.

I have briefly discussed these two heads of legislation by way of illustrating the manner in which we have to proceed in making, defending, or altering laws. We have to attend first of all to what is natural, which is known partly by the examination of the circumstances of the physical nature of man, and partly by an observation of the experience of mankind about it.

Then, when from these first principles we have fixed the purposes and parties to which definite utility and justice are to be referred, we may discuss what is just or useful as to details.

In respect of any of the first institutions of society, such as marriage, the details of its usefulness may be exhibited; but the examining whether it is useful or not almost of necessity involves a fallacy. For there is assumed in the process that society, constituted as it is upon it, could have existed in anything like the manner it does independently of it. What these are useful for is not the improvement only, but the very existence of society.

Justice and utility in the second degree.

Passing on from this framework, the test of a good law, as to detail, is that it is useful, and not unjust. In this second degree usefulness means, in the main, conduciveness to the stability of that first framework which we have alluded to, which, as has been said, gives the principles to which utility is to be referred. And justice here means fairness among the different individuals whom the law concerns, on the supposition of that framework, which determines their relations, and consistently with it.

Legal utility and legal happiness.

We shall shortly discuss the idea of *happiness* and the nature of utility as referred to that: at present we will say that happiness is an idea not definite, and that legal happiness (that to which utility as predicated of laws, refers) must be taken to mean the possession and enjoyment of those things, which human experience, as exhibited in actual human arrangements, seems to shew man likes. Property and the preservation of it against others, family power, affection, protection, stability, these and many other such things in the eye of all practical law, are not *for* happiness (*i.e.* useful) but *are* happiness, and legal *utility* is the being helpful or contributory to them.

Should the legislator be content to aim at this?

It will be asked, Is law to have no higher purpose than this, and is not the legislator to form his own idea of what will make the subjects of the law happy and be for their good, and to make his laws accordingly?

His aim must be practical as well as elevated.

Theoretically, and to the extent to which we can, with any significance, speak of a legislator and of power on his part, this is so. But practically human nature or political society, in many things, legislates for itself. Of definite or pre-experimental systems of law, a part takes hold, a part dies or becomes inert. It is not what the legislator promulgates, but what he can make the people more or less act upon, which is the law worth considering as such.

The views which determine what laws are to be, should be both elevated and practical: the former character is not likely to exist in the first instance in a mass of people, though it is very possible that when it is once initiated, they may heartily respond to it: large and exalted views belong to the legislator. The latter character, if it does not exist in the legislator, will probably shew itself in fact afterwards, by rendering part of his work useless. While the legislator therefore may form for himself a high ideal of what he would wish his people to be, he must bear in mind, that judging by human experience, his enactments, be they what they may, will one way or another make themselves. There still remains perhaps much that he can do: and the higher the aim in this, the better.

In old times the legislator was an educator.

Legislators, in earlier times, were looked upon as educators, and no doubt they often were so. In respect of actual codes of law which history tells us about, it is often difficult to make sure how much of each of them was embodiment or re-embodiment of what existed before in the form of custom or law, and how much came fresh from the legislator. But the power of individuals for good in this way must often have been very great. It is possible that much of what has been described as the foundation of law may in the first instance have owed its suggestion to individuals, conceiving more strongly than others that which must have been more or less common to the thoughts of all, and with the art of putting it into practical shape and influencing the wills of others in favour of it. In simpler society, a man in character at once representative of others and more high and large-minded might actually by laws effect much in the way of educating and civilization. In the more complicated states of civilization this of course is not so possible. But it is still possible to have, and to encourage in those who are to make laws, elevated views of what those laws may at least *try* to effect.

Society is a partnership not only for

A society is a partnership not only for the purposes of police, *i.e.* for the mutual protection of property, but also for the purpose of helping the common progress, and for the aid which the members may give each other in all which makes human nature better. The law is the action of the society in doing this. In vast societies like some of the states of modern times, with the multitudes of conflicting interests and opinions which they involve, it is doubtless difficult for the general law to effect much more than the keeping of the peace and the maintenance of the above named first principles. But so far as it can act to improve public morals and the general character of the population, it should. And the wish that such means should be found, is one which should exist in the minds of those whose business is to legislate. Without regulating everything and making, as was the tendency of some of the ancient legislation, the society all, the individual nothing, we yet need not take the opposite extreme of considering the partnership and, its expression, the law, simply an evil and a restraint, of which therefore the less there is the better. The law should be not *merely* a restraint, but a means of common action for good.

mutual protection, but for improvement.

Prevention therefore of anything injurious to public morals is thus one thing the law may aim at, and means of effecting it what it should look for. In a more positive way the law should provide for the education of the people and the encouragement of religion; this latter, not only as a part of the encouragement of morality, but as a common paying of the duty which every member of the community owes to God. The distinction of the Sunday from other days is at once a part of traditional and revealed religion, and is an ordinance for the benefit of all engaged in labour. By ancient usage of our country the state itself is considered in some degree a religious union; more or less of a religious character is given to important acts of it; and the law provides, by ancient endowments, for the keeping up of the worship and knowledge of God among the people. This is at once in the highest degree auxiliary to the general purpose of the law, in the preserving the public peace and morality, and in itself it is the highest purpose which the law could subserve. Nor is there any opposition between such action on the part of the law and that individuality of religion, which is demanded by the spirit of Christianity. It would be hard if improvement of faith should lead to apparent godlessness, and Christian communities should fail to do what all other communities have done,

It must therefore make provision both for education and religion.

viz. make their society and their law, so far as they could, a help to their religion.

With the progress of society law becomes more technical, and is looked at with less sympathy and reverence.

In a civilized and complicated community, law as to its form and method, loses certain characters, which in a simpler one it may have, in regard of the education or improvement of the people. It necessarily becomes *professional:* it becomes so vast in detail that principles and leading features are lost: it acquires its own language, which is unintelligible to the majority: it ceases to influence the mind or modes of thought of people, being rather looked on with awe and dislike, and the necessity for paying any attention to it being deplored as a calamity. This progress is gradual: in simpler states of society, the law is an interesting and important part of national literature: long after this, and after it has become to a certain degree technical, the study of it makes, so to speak, a part of the apprenticeship of a gentleman: at last its extent and technicality become so great, as to render even this impossible. How far this progress of things is necessary, we cannot here discuss. It is concerned with morality in this manner. So long as laws continue within the scope of the general mind of the people, they are viewed with an interest and respect which disappear as they become more technical. It is desirable that law should present itself to the minds of people as, not simply offering to their choice the alternative of either a particular course of action or the penalty of disobedience, but as having a claim upon their obedience and regard independent of penalties, for the reason involved in it and the good purposes which it serves. Of course the paying or not of such regard will depend in the main on the substance of the laws, and in a large community and system of laws there must be various laws which one and another will consider unjust, and what ought to be altered. But still, a right view in this respect would surely be very much helped if laws were more distinctly presented before the minds of people: both the reasons for their existence and the manner in which they might be improved would thus be made more apparent. The public reason would make itself better felt, as such, if it were not too much dissociated in manner and language from reason in individuals.

There is a further practical difficulty as to laws of formal procedure. Occasions will continually arise, when these will exactly defeat the purpose which they are intended to subserve. It is when there are no more of them than necessary, when the purpose for which they are intended is definite, that people will be likely to understand that the good which they cause *upon the whole* would not be attainable except at the hazard of the occasional injustice which seems inherent in them.

Duty of those who are subject to the law.

We are naturally led from the duty of the legislator to the duty of those subject to the law. In fact, what we have last treated about makes a transition between the two.

We will speak another time of the difficulties which may arise from the conflict of the requirements of the laws of the land with those of higher or moral law.

The law itself is suggestive of action beyond the law:

In earlier society, the law of the society (not always accurately distinguished from the unwritten custom of it) is considered to furnish at least a general outline of moral behaviour, and to be the first thing to be regarded.

Vir bonus est quis?
Qui consulta patrum, qui leges juraque servat.

both in the way of intension and extension.

But "ad legem bonum esse" can hardly from the first be considered sufficient. The law suggests and, for obedience to it, almost requires a corresponding education and general tone of feeling which, without any express provision, must cause a much wider and completer action in the direction indicated than is demanded by the law itself. Next come, in various forms of philosophy, considerations of virtuousness, excellence, and free good action superior to mere legal obedience and to custom: and often, as in the main in our time and country, the care of influencing and educating the morals of a country belongs to religion, and is considered a part of it.

The wider sphere of good action suggested by the narrower law of the land is both an expansion of it and supplementary to it. The law requires particular conduct on our part towards certain people, on account of their particular circumstances or relation to us: the corresponding virtuousness will consist in the acting, not only by the letter but in the spirit, of such conduct to them, and also in acting in the same spirit, so far as it is applicable, to others, to whom we are not so bound. These two processes, of the intensification of legal relations, and the supposition, so to call it, of moral ones beyond them, must be contemporaneous. The legal obligation of care for our family must be raised into special kindred love, and must further be supplemented by more general love, by the supposition of a moral relation beyond that of kindred. We are to love brethren more, and to count all men brethren: the additional amount of moral feeling generated is to go partly in intensifying the legal or express relation, and partly in extending the feeling belonging to it, as far as we can, beyond itself, to others with no such definite claim upon us. This expanding and supplementing of actual law is in fact bringing it into relation with more general law, or moral feeling.

'Let him that stole steal no more, but rather let him labour, working with his hands the thing that is good, that he may have to give to him that needeth.' This passage is singularly expressive as a general sketch of what moral education should aim at when it takes the definite law as its starting point. The crime or offence is distinct, and the disposition of mind prompting it is so likewise: the thing to be aimed at is to draw the mind as far as possible the other way, to produce a disposition as far as possible different. It is not merely that he may have lawfully what he has tried to gain unlawfully; but that he may have to give *to* others, instead of its being (apparently) necessary for him to take from them. Stealing or injury suggests the idea of its opposite, beneficence or benefit.

Public opinion finds expression in actual law, and is itself a more general form of law with sanctions of its own.

The laws of a nation are a more or less definite and complete expression of a public spirit and feeling which is produced in the first instance by education, using the word in a wide sense, and which afterwards operates to extend and supplement the laws in the manner above described.

The wider law thus generated derives its authority from public opinion; its sanctions are public approval and disapproval, and they are very powerful. To many it will constitute nearly the whole law of their action: by those who think and feel more deeply it will be respected as a representation, though often inadequate, of what is higher than itself, the common feeling of human nature, and also of that which when not inconsistent with this, is itself also valuable, the traditional individuality of the nation.

The common feeling of human

This common feeling of human nature, though indefinite and not easy to fix as to the detail, is yet a reality, and is, in practice, that which most commends and brings home to man the facts of rightness. It is the *jus gentium* or *jus naturale* of the Roman law. It is a law, the authority and penalties of which, in this form of it, are in conscience and human opinion, the former imaginatively representing the second, where this latter cannot itself act. This is the law, certain particulars of which become, in the manner which we have mentioned, the great framework of national law. In those who are able to enter into the idea of it, it generalizes and exalts and supplements the national or public spirit as this does the particular national law.

nature represents a still higher law.

There are certain parts of human conduct, which not entering much into express law, are regulated greatly by general feeling, and refer themselves a good deal to this, without the possibility of reason much more definite being given for them. Of this class is much of what we call decency of manner and purity of conduct. There is much that is necessarily conventional in the details of these, but the conventions, so to call them, upon which the main principles rest, are deep rooted and widely spread human feelings. There is no part of human conduct, the regulation of which more concerns the orderliness of human society and the elevation of character of the individual: and it is this fact together with that just mentioned, that it is harder to give definite reason as to this part of rightness than others, which has always more specially placed it under the guardianship of religion.

Certain portions of conduct, such as decency, are mainly regulated by this higher law.

That which this common feeling of human nature represents is what is understood by the moral or supreme law in its application to man. To the independent reason it is that systematic arrangement of all things (relations of persons included) upon which the rightness of actions depends. This system, to the eye of such reason, has of necessity one Author, who is concerned to maintain and vindicate it, and from whom therefore penalty for infringement of its arrangements may be expected.

This law is the supreme moral law of which reason informs us:

The conscience and feeling of man presents from a different side this same feeling of a law, the violation of which is anticipatedly punishable. Human and conscientious disapproval or condemnation is felt not as the punishment, but as the presage, the warning, the indicator of it. The offender has not only offended against human opinion and law, for

and to which conscience bears witness.

which men and his conscience hate and torture him, but he has offended against something which that opinion represents, and for which offence punishment from somewhere beyond man, a Nemesis or Ate, indistinct sketches of a real future judgment, await him. Law is the establishing of rights, and the righting of wrongs; human feeling indicates to us, more or less distinctly, what the rights are, and at the same time anticipates, more or less distinctly also, the manner in which the wrongs done in violation of them will be righted.

Actual law supplies a very incomplete scheme of moral action.

In the view which we have been taking, obedience to the actual law is looked upon as the lower limit of moral duty, but, in a manner, as representative of the extent of it: so that it in some measure directs towards what general conduct should be.

This however it can only be very imperfectly, even taking duty in its most positive or objective form. For the law has to be very definite, and in this way, it may have to pass over conduct which may be more injurious to society than many of the crimes which it punishes.

A code of morality is impossible.

And all that large part of morality which is concerned rather with the constant outgrowth of tempers and dispositions than with definite actions is one to which considerations from actual law have no direct application. A man without doing any special action which can be considered an offence against family duty, may make all those about him miserable: without being dishonest, he may be oppressive.

We have to judge of right or wrong by general opinion variously criticized.

Objective morality, or the rule and law of proper conduct and of a good life, is not anything which can be expressed in any sort of way in a code or system. For the forming, mentally, some sort of method of it, the consideration of the great heads or subjects of actual or particular law may be useful, in the way which we have mentioned: but, besides that they themselves are with difficulty systematized, they are incomplete as an index to morality. And if those tangible relations of human beings which law can attend to are so large in number as the great extent of particular law shews them to be, how infinite in number must be the relations which morality is concerned with! Practically, the book to which we each one of us have to refer, to discover, as to a particular action or line of conduct, whether it is right or wrong, is the general opinion of our age and time variously commented upon, interpreted, or criticized, by the more immediate circle in which we move, by the books which we have read, and by the view of life which our past or present circumstances have given to us. Of the nature of this general opinion, and of the degree to which we *ought* to consider it right or wrong, what we should follow, or what we should rise above, we shall speak again. But for the *direct* practical purposes of human life, systematic morality is of no use. What it *is* of use for, is to enable us rationally to judge and criticize the public or general opinion which of necessity is what we first refer our conduct to.

The chief use of systematic morality is to criticize general opinion.

From the first we compare, and must do so, our conduct with the conduct of others, and our judgment on that conduct with the judgment of others.

The object of systematic morality is to give us rational grounds on which to make these comparisons. The actions, succeeding one another in infinite number and variety of life, cannot be classified under heads. Life cannot be lived by rule, or it is not life. As well might we make it our business to classify the different possible movements of muscles, limbs and body, and for the sake of our health determine to be always making some movements and never others; irrespective of the fact that movement is for purpose, and that, if we are to live and act, a continual complicated movement must always be going on, our business therefore (as to the body) being to learn to make this in the manner which shall be most healthy for us.

CHAPTER XI.

THE ANATOMY OF WRONG-DOING.

Moral terms are applied to actions, feelings, dispositions, habits:

ALL proper moral terms are descriptive adjectives applicable to actions; or to transient feelings, which I shall call feelings; or to permanent feelings which I shall call dispositions; or to permanent feelings steadily influential upon the will, which I shall call habits.

Each good moral habit is a particular kind or branch of virtuousness, as each bad moral habit is a kind of viciousness. Virtuousness and viciousness, and again virtues and vices, stand in a rude kind of opposition to each other, like pleasure and pain, or pleasures and pains. I say 'rude,' because the general opposition, between virtue and vice, is, like that between pleasure and pain, of a very imperfect and inaccurate kind: the particular oppositions are, like those of propositions in logic, of very various sorts. Sometimes a man must have the virtue or the vice; as he must be either just or unjust: sometimes there may be a middle ground; as a man may be an ordinary character, neither courageous nor cowardly; sometimes (in Aristotle's view always) there may be a second vice which stands in a more point-blank opposition to the first vice than the virtue does, as in the opposition of rashness to cowardice: and so probably in various ways besides.

most properly to actions and habits.

Morality is properly concerned with action, and therefore the most strictly moral terms are applicable nly to actions, and to habits which, we have seen, re closely associated with actions. Feelings may e good, but, as being transient, cannot be called vir- uous; and dispositions, if they are properly called irtuous, are such as cause action, or are habits. Vir- uousness is a continuance of good feelings, and an xercise of good dispositions.

As we have seen, language presents us with ames, in abundance, both of virtues and vices. Most commonly, I think, it will be found, it is the irtue which has the positive or, more properly, ffirmative name, the vice the negative; even where, upon the whole, it is rather the virtue that has the egative character and the vice the positive; as in ustice and injustice.

Tendency of language to give prominence to good dispositions and bad acts.

However this may be, certainly the reverse is he fact in regard of single actions. To describe bad ctions, we have a great many terms of loose and varying application, from all sorts of metaphors; but we have no general name for a good action, like the Stoic κατόρθωμα.

I must here call to mind what I said before, that he term 'action' in its wide sense must be taken to nclude forbearance from action, when opportunity or emptation occurs.

Action thus generally spoken of, may be conveniently divided in two ways: according as it affects ourselves or others, and according as it is action or forbearance to act, activity or inactivity.

Inactivity of itself, the neutral state, is good or bad according to the kind of action from which we consider it to be an abstinence.

Forbearance to act may be immoral:

Abstinence from bad action affecting others is harmlessness: abstinence from bad action of any kind s innocence.

Inactivity or indolence, *segnitia* or *ignavia*, is

abstinence from action, considered as blameable partly in the view of the action abstained from being good, partly in view of action, as opposed to inaction, being of itself proper for man.

proceeding from self-indulgence or from cowardice.

The two chief causes for such inactivity are self-indulgence and cowardice; the inactivity is either voluptuous, or inert and timid: there is a want of principle and self-government, or there is a want of courage. Self-government accordingly and courage were counted by the old moral philosophers so important, that they were made to constitute two of the four great divisions of virtue.

Inactivity in some respects may be coupled with very great activity in others, as I shall explain more fully in speaking of character.

Broadly, setting aside the very large mass of action in life which must, from the nature of things, be devoted to the care of ourselves, and which, as I have said, we may call of no moral account, action *beyond* this may be considered good if for the benefit of others; not good if for our own benefit when it might be for theirs; not good if for the injury of others; good or meritorious if for our own loss, rather than theirs.

Inactivity prevents us from being self-seeking or actively selfish, prevents us from injuring others deliberately, prevents us also from benefiting them: possibly it may lead to conduct which, looked at in reference to others, is virtue; and it is very likely to lead to conduct not at all injurious to them, and not in this way wrong.

Self-indulgence is wrongly described as a breach of duty to self.

A great mass of the conduct which it expresses, and of similar conduct, all self-indulgence, for instance, is wrong as being, in the language of some philosophers, against duty to ourselves. This is not a good expression: we may, and must divide or double ourselves in imagination for various purposes, as *e.g.* we ourselves judge ourselves: but to imagine ourselves as having claim upon ourselves seems absurd. Wrong self-indulgence is offence against the general law of duty as distinguished from offence against particular relative duty, in which the other party is marked and clear. This law of duty, which I have described, is ideal, and is considered by us to be owed to God, in so far as we are religious: failing religion, it is a due on our part imagined or believed in, according to what our views of the moral universe are.

It is easier to classify wrong actions than right actions.

Bad conduct has been classified, by law, so far as it is amenable to penalty; by theology, so far as particular portions of it are considered as more or less a hindrance to salvation. Good conduct, independent of there being less reason for its classification, is also more difficult to classify as being freer and wider. Conduct which can be classified is that which has reference to duty: and duty, as I have said, though markedly positive and affirmative in certain cases where the other party is distinct, yet as regards the mass of it is, in particulars, negative or prohibitory. Conduct which has reference to an ideal for imitation or effort cannot be classified. Hence the tendency in language to notice and name good dispositions, and bad acts. Hence also it is simpler to anatomize wrong-doing than right; and probably the simplest way of doing so in the first instance, is to ask, Do you do to others all the good you can? And do you refrain from doing them any wrong, harm, or injury?

Vices of inactivity.

The causes which make us inactive when we ought to be doing good to others, may be roughly summed up in the three dispositions which I have just now noticed, and which may be called in general indolence or idleness, cowardice, and self-indulgence.

The two latter of them are, as I have mentioned, the opposites of two of the old cardinal virtues, and may be called cardinal vices. The first, according to its kind, would come under one or another of these.

Vices of activity.

The circumstances under which we are active in doing harm to others may similarly be considered as coming under three great heads, though we cannot speak of there being any particular disposition of mind accompanying each, which we could call a vice. Active offences, or crimes against others, would then be classified as offences of maleficence, offences of simple injustice, and offences of unfaithfulness.

Maleficence proceeds from the desire to revenge supposed injustice.

By 'maleficence' I mean the attempt to give pain, as such, to others. This can hardly arise, deliberately and in a mature mind, except from revengefulness; in which we must include, in some degree, jealousy and envy, which produce a sort of half feeling of injury done to ourselves by the person envied. Combativeness indeed, love of pursuit and conquest, love of exercising power, and other feelings of these kinds, produce a certain amount of capricious cruelty, in which more or less pleasure is felt at the mere infliction of pain; but scarcely as a matter of deliberate purpose.

Acts, offences, and crimes, of revenge justify themselves to the person committing them as acts of justice, and indeed are constantly felt as such: it is this mixture of a most powerful sentiment, and one so associated with virtue, which makes them so terrible.

By simple injustice I mean when pain or loss is inflicted by us on others, not for any pleasure taken by us in their pain or loss as such, but in order to pleasure or benefit to ourselves ensuing from it. I use the term injustice rather more widely than we commonly use it, about as widely as we commonly use injury. I mean the causing of harm to others for our own advantage, whether this is done by our action or by our failing to act, if this is deliberate, not arising from mere inaction, of which I have spoken before.

Injustice divided into wrong, legal and moral, and unkindness.

Roughly, we may divide the hurting of others into wrong and unkindness. Fairness, the instinctive form, or fundamental feeling of justice, is a feeling of tremendous power, but very rudimentary and blind. This feeling, in the first instance, inspires and commands law and custom, regulating mutual conduct; and then itself submits to be commanded and regulated, to a certain extent, by what it has thus inspired; and thus there grows up the feeling of justice in society. A certain amount of wrong, such as can be laid down clearly and with profit to the community, is fixed and forbidden by law, and is legal wrong. Outside of this there is a large margin of conduct in some respects of the same nature as this, which may be even more keenly felt as wrong, but which, either from defect in the law, or from the matter not being adapted for legal enforcement, is not legal wrong. All this wrong is violation of duty, which duty, in order for the conduct to be a wronging of others rather than simple unkindness, must have, more or less, the characters which I described as belonging to proper duty: that is, there must be definite parties to it, it must be clear and particular, it must appear as in some way incumbent, and much besides.

By unkindness positive (unkindness negative, *i.e.* neglect to take trouble to do kindness, belonging to inaction) I mean the giving pain when the hurt is not of such a nature as to be called a wrong done, even when we speak of a moral, as distinguished from a legal, wrong. It is a violation of justice, understood in its wide sense, as the social virtue, the general duty due from one man to another. Of course, justice, as thus understood, may be described as the whole of virtue, and in fact, more than any other particular virtue, it has been so understood: but in reality the same is true of any one of the great virtues, or great heads of virtue; in many respects, instead of calling them divisions of the whole of virtue, it would be better to call them sides or faces of it.

Pleas of injustice.

Offences of injustice justify themselves to the doer probably in one or other of the following ways. If slight, they are sometimes excused, as of no consequence, what will be but little felt by the sufferer; at other times, as what there will very likely be opportunity to repair. Sometimes (by a curious kind of borrowing from maleficence, which, as I have said, appeals itself to justice or fairness) the excuse is supplied through a momentary supposition of universal mutual hostility—the man would do to me what I am going to do to him, if our places were reversed, and he had my opportunity or temptation. In the gravest cases, most probably the self-justification is helplessness—the motive, the temptation is so strong—I cannot help it.

In all these cases of injustice, it will of course be remembered, that what is just in one view may be unjust and unkind in another. Legal non-injustice is compatible with very much undutifulness, and with an infinite amount of unkindness. And besides this, the duties may be contradictory and conflicting. Of such cases I do not speak here.

Unfaithfulness the worst case of injustice:

I distinguish offences of unfaithfulness from those of simple injustice by the fact that the person injured trusts us, and is therefore more vulnerable by us.

They will be considered generally the worst of all. This is on account of the ingratitude and cowardice which, in addition to the injustice, they more or less involve.

They are however cases of injustice, and may be divided, as we divided those of injustice, into legal, distinctly moral, and more general, fraud or betrayal; only with this consideration, that the moral portion of unfaithfulness involves more guilt, in comparison with the legal, than is the case with injustice.

In one point of view, unfaithfulness might be considered better to represent all wickedness, or the essence of wickedness, than injustice; in so far as it more than the other unites in itself the two elements which go to wickedness, that of injury to others, and that of self-degradation.

is partly owing to *ignavia:*

All that unfaithfulness which is opposed to steadiness and constancy in friendship and association, belongs rather to the inactive portion of vice, and is probably the worst instance of it. This portion of unfaithfulness is what stands in the most flagrant opposition to the old virtue of ἀνδρεία or fortitude and courage, and is the worst description of the old 'ignavia.'

generally accompanies offence against relative duty.

All relative duty is sure to be accompanied with much of trust; and offence against it, as involving betrayal of trust, is worse than simple injustice. Duty to friends, *e.g.*, which I placed among relative duties, is such, that its violation is almost entirely of this kind.

Breach of promise.

Unfaithfulness to agreements and promises, the opposite of 'keeping one's word,' is that form of unfaithfulness which has had most attention given to it.

An engagement or promise is a pledging our own future conduct to another, so that it morally belongs to *him*, though of course it is *we* who must actually do the thing.

Unlawful engagements are not to be kept.

It is clear that an engagement to do what is not lawful, *i.e.* pledging what is not ours to give, is no more binding upon us, as to our doing the thing itself, than our giving to any one the property of another makes it the property of the receiver. If we have given any one another person's property it must either have been in fraud or by mistake. Supposing the former, we have already committed an offence, and that against two parties, against the engagee, in the case of the unlawful engagement, and against duty, the law, or the public: but we should only make the offence worse by trying to maintain the property as the property of the now unlawful possessor: we must repair the wrong, as we can, towards both parties; towards duty or the law, by non-performance of the engagement; towards the engagee, by whatever equivalent, or more than equivalent, may possibly indemnify him for the wrong we have done him. If it has been mistake, there has been no offence on our part in the first instance, but there will be in persistency, and we have got ourselves into a great difficulty.

Two feelings which should accompany an engagement.

To an engagement there go on the part of the engager two main feelings; persistent absence of fraud in intention; steadiness of effort in performance. It is not well therefore to make engagements where we cannot reasonably rely on ourselves for the latter; though the fact of the engagement, if we are right-minded, will be a most urgent motive to us.

What is prompted by benevolence and self-respect in

There are two kinds of feelings on our part which will impel us to the fulfilment of a promise or engagement which is for another's benefit: one is of the nature of self-respect, and is closely allied with the feeling of justice or fairness, the feeling namely of dislike of failing in what we have pledged ourselves to do: the other is the feeling of benevolence towards the engagee, who will not only have lost what we have promised, but to whom the loss of it will be a double loss, he having counted upon it, and probably regulated his conduct accordingly. I will call to mind here what I mentioned in the case of gratitude, viz. that there go to it two feelings, one of which, under other circumstances, would dispose a man to be revengeful, the other the opposite. In the same way here: the disposition which urges a man to be faithful to his promises may be of such a nature as shall equally impel him to be true to his *threats:* or it may be the opposite, and such as under given circumstances would make him forgiving, and not disposed to be true to his word.

regard to keeping engagements.

Considerations from the morality of benevolence or utilitarianism are necessary here against the simple morality of justice or duty; and are valuable even against possible delusion in our common thought, and in respect of some of our reasonings about religion. Being true to our word is not necessarily pure virtue, or all of it virtue; any more than being a hearty friend is. A portion of the feeling which goes to the former is such as may, in a different relation, make us unforgiving, as a portion of the feeling which goes to the latter may make a man, in a different relation, a good hater. 'Be true to your promises and your threats' is the same morality as, 'Thou shalt love thy neighbour and hate thine enemy.' But in the minds of many of us I think there lurks, if not a feeling in ourselves that we ought to do what we have positively said we will do, even if it is to another's disadvantage; yet at least a kind of respect for the person who does act in this

Promptings of benevolence needed to correct the other.

manner: and in respect of religion, we seem to think that promises and denunciations on God's part stand in the same relation to his truth and the keeping of his word; that any hope of his relenting in the carrying out of his denunciations is equivalent to a doubt of his faithfulness to his promises.

There is no moral obligation to fulfil an engagement which is only productive of unhappiness.

But in reality, faithfulness is not a relation between us and things; it is a relation between us and persons, the fulfilling of an indebtedness on our part to them for their benefit. The fairness, equality, truth, correspondence between deed and word, which may all be associated with very strong feeling on our part, is yet not of a properly moral nature unless it is applied in the interest of benevolence or the production of happiness, which is the business of all action, the basis, in the sense of precondition, of all morality. The performing of action which produces no happiness or does no good, *a fortiori* of action which produces only unhappiness, for the simple reason that a word passed may be kept, is the subjecting moral considerations to a kind of unmoral fate or necessity: and faithfulness is not of this nature: the indefeasibility of word given is not the inevitable action of a machine or mechanical force. What qualification there is to this we shall see perhaps in a moment, when I speak, as I am going to do, of mechanical truth.

Truthfulness.

Faithfulness, and in a certain degree faithfulness to engagements, might exist, even if we had not the power of speech, nor consequently of writing: but, of course, our having these enables engagements to be much more definite. That part of faithfulness in engagements which refers to the meaning what we say in them is called truthfulness. Truthfulness however of itself, has properly reference to that which is the proper use of our power of speech, the communication of thought from one mind to another: our word is the expression or representation of our thought in the hearing of another. The important thing about truthfulness is, not necessarily the transference of the whole thought in our mind to another, which is in many cases impossible; but the transference of thought in such a manner, that there shall be no wrong supposition on the part of the receiver as to the character, or place in our mind, of the thought transferred.

Openness, or the making our thought common to others, stands in the same relation to truthfulness as the simple, semi-moral feeling which I spoke of in reference to faithfulness stands in to it: and we must add to the feeling which we have as to openness the feeling besides, that speech is an action on our part which, like all action, ought to be useful or productive of happiness, and very strongly ought not to be the opposite; that it ought to do good, and not to do harm. Truth and openness are the subjects in regard of which the careless and thoughtless language, in which moral subjects are most usually spoken of among men, have their fullest play. The moral feelings of each person are exceedingly imperfect, associated with much wrong feeling, and there is very much said and done which comes to the knowledge of some individuals and ought not to come to the knowledge of others and ought not to be public; and while this is the case reticence is quite as important a duty as truthfulness; even those who talk so foolishly about openness, when they think for a moment, are perfectly aware of this. Of course, supposing reticence and reserve were impossible, and each could see into his neighbour's breast, one most powerful support of evil disposi-

Reticence is as much needed as openness.

tions, the manner, viz., in which people are able to withdraw them from the judgment of their neighbours, and keep them hugged and cherished in their own breasts, would be removed. But the removal of it would do no good, if along with it were removed, as might probably be the case, all care for others' judgments. Without going so far, or near so far, as to say that complete mutual knowledge would produce mutual contempt,—I believe in many respects its tendency would be the opposite way—we may yet say that men's self-respect and mutual respect belong, as things are, to a state of mind which would indispose them to make their every thought public, and would make them hold back in some degree from the thoughts of others. But independent of these considerations, the world could not go on if, with the limited knowledge which we have of one another's thoughts and feelings, there were not combined a very extensive ignorance. There could be really no intercourse among people, and no knowledge of each other: thought would be impossible, and there would be nothing to know. It would be as if, to make more light and brightness in the world, we were to abolish all the material objects about us on the charge of their intercepting the sun's rays: we should have no reflection of those rays, no colour: for the sake of the light we should be abolishing every thing we might see by it.

The real merit of openness.

The real praise of openness is of two kinds: the man is to be praised, who has nothing in himself to conceal, and who keeps (and is in a position to keep) nothing to himself for his own sake: the man is partly to be praised, and still more to be loved, who *trusts* others, because he, often at some hazard, kindles good feeling in them which would not otherwise exist, and is thus a producer of virtue and a binder together of man to man. It is this trust which is the foundation of the charming openness and unreserve of youth. In both these cases, it is to be observed that a moral consideration supervenes, besides the simple intellectual one of the experience and thought of one mind being open to another mind.

Truthfulness is faithfulness, from the one side, to the communication by speech from mind to mind: the correlative faithfulness from the other side is trustfulness or disposition to give credit and believe. Offence on either of these sides is treason, in various degrees, against the great bond of human society. Truthfulness is the disposition to give correct information. Trustfulness or believingness on the other side is the disposition believed in, or supposed to exist, by the speaker; which belief on his part is one main ground of his own disposition to tell the truth.

Trustfulness in the hearer is the corresponding virtue to truthfulness in the speaker.

The general principle on which we must go in regard to knowledge is that it is a benefit to the person who possesses it: doubtless in many cases it is not so, yet it is hard for us to judge where it is not; and consequently, when we have not the option of silence or doing nothing, but must either give knowledge or deceive, deception is an injury to the person deceived; it is a case of injustice or wrong to him, and not of simple injustice, but of unfaithfulness, because it is presumably a betrayal of trust or belief.

Three grounds of the duty of truthfulness:

Truthfulness as a duty rests thus in the first instance upon these two pillars conjunctly, the one, the consideration that speech evidently exists as a means for community of thought among men; the other, when it appears, as we have seen, that this community cannot be, and (as men are) had better not be, complete, the consideration that we have a

nature of speech: trust reposed:

trust reposed in us by the person desiring information, which we may easily violate, and which, the more easily we may violate it, calls upon our conscience the more imperatively not to do so.

and self-respect.

Truthfulness however as a duty rests in the second instance, and most fully, not upon these feelings themselves, but upon a feeling derived from them.

A man's words are the most simple and natural expression of himself, and are taken to be so. His actions are the actual putting forth of his character, but his words are taken as the sign of it. It is taken for granted that they naturally follow his thought, as instantly and inevitably as a dog's howl follows (if it can be said to follow) your treading on his foot: if they do not do so, there must be some motive. The motive might be the advantage of the person spoken to; but it is considered of course more probable that the motive is the advantage of the speaker. The motive is much more likely to be either of the nature of fear, or of the nature of covetousness. And our lips are our own: a man's speech is so thoroughly in his own power, that his betraying trust in this particular is looked upon as the most complete sign that there could be of want of courage, and also as the taking the most contemptible and unworthy advantage of others that could well be taken.

The feeling of self-respect and the love of substantial truthfulness are so intimately associated, both in a man's thoughts of himself and in his imagination of the thoughts of others about him, that they come to be in a manner the same thing. The man has the feeling about himself, and the feeling that others have the feeling about him, that if he is untruthful in his words he is not to be trusted in anything; and the man who feels himself not to be trusted, and not trusted by others, is without the greatest guarantee of virtue.

I used deliberately just now, the words 'substantial truthfulness.' I will explain why.

Regard for truth may pass into a superstition.

In speaking of faithfulness to engagements, I said that, unless somebody was interested for good in an engagement made, the words of themselves carried no force. On this point there has often been a superstitious feeling in men's minds, the removal of which is highly important, in the interest of morals.

Cases of conscience under this head.

We are not really bound to our threats as we are bound to our promises, and the mistaken self-respect which tends to induce us to stick to them is what benevolence and a regard to the purpose of action should triumph over.

What is to be done as to speaking the truth, first, in cases where the matter is trifling, next, in cases where our speaking the truth must evidently be injurious, either to the person spoken to, or to some other parties, especially if we are bound to them by special duty, or to ourselves, in certain flagrant cases where the person has no right to put us to the trial of answering? Granted that in all these latter cases we may be silent, if that will answer the purpose; but may we deceive?

Substantial truthfulness is not opposed to the use of imagination.

I have mentioned these various cases not with the view of going into them but for the purpose of saying in regard to them this. Reverence for the spoken word, in the way I just now alluded to, seems to me *all* superstition. But in respect of truthfulness, there is a religion as well as a superstition; and the religion seems to me weakened and degraded by being carried into superstition. The abolishing, for the supposed sake of truthfulness, imagination out of thought and language, whether it be in the form of figure and metaphor, or of fable and story, or of filling up and expanding fact by the supposition of what might be, would speedily, if all were to practise it, render truthfulness valueless by the extinction of knowledge, to which this imagination is the road. We may talk with as much of mutual untruthfulness as we will, provided we understand each other in doing so. Truthfulness is one side of the communication between mind and mind, to which speech is but the means: whatever aids this communication is the real and substantial truthfulness.

No summary rule can be given to decide cases of conflicting duty.

The application however of the consideration, that what is said or done should do good, and not harm, is met in the case of truthfulness by a real religion, as it seems to me, not, as in the case of engagements, only by a superstition.

The association of word with thought in a character of real self-respect is so intimate, that the utmost you can probably teach is silence, and that with difficulty, while conscious falsehood is all but impossible. In the case therefore, where important utility, or marked duty of another kind, conflicts with truthfulness, there arises the most painful conflict which can arise in the mind of man. It is the misfortune of such conflicts, that instead of being considered in the frame of mind which properly belongs to them, viz. the seriousness and anxiety which any right-minded man actually brought into such circumstances would feel, they have been first rather coldly and heartlessly digested into system, and then been made a mere ground for fighting and mutual depreciation between one moral teacher and another, or moral teachers in general and those without thought at all. When such cases arise, they are real conflicts; that is, neither the clinging to truth nor the desire to do the other good, or fulfil the other duty is to be depreciated. If Effie Deans had been hung, I suppose we should not have blamed Jeanie Deans, nor should we on the other side, I suppose, blame the man who misdirected the murderers pursuing his father. I do not see how we can say in general, for such cases, either that truthfulness, in this extreme, is a superstition and what must yield, or that it is a clear and distinct duty to which everything else must yield. Each case must stand on its own merits.

APPENDIX ON MALEVOLENCE[1].

The sight of others' pain may be productive of pleasure in five ways.

There are many ways, we will say five, in which Rochefoucauld's maxim has some truth.

There is something not disagreeable to us in the sufferings of others:

(1) On account of the feeling which I will call here rivalry between us and them for happiness, or jealousy of their happiness.

(2) On account of the thought being brought home to us that we are free from the suffering, or that we are at least not worse off than they.

(3) On account of the opportunity afforded us for action and for helping them, and the pleasure taken in doing this.

(4) On account of the quasi-superior position in which we are thus placed, and the idea that the sufferer is likely to envy us, and to wish that he were in our position.

(5) On account of the imaginational interest taken in looking on effort and suffering, and on the calling forth of human feeling and power, when we are ourselves unaffected by, and independent of it.

Jealousy of others is caused by self-dissatisfaction.

The basis of the half-felt and undeveloped jealousy of the happiness of others, which is apt to burst into life on occasion, as momentary ill-will, and to produce that *subnote* of pleasure in the suffering of others which Rochefoucauld's maxim is generally considered to refer to, is a sort of discontent and dissatisfaction with ourselves and our own happiness.

There are, in our minds, two general and vague feelings of a very different nature which nevertheless continually confuse themselves together: the one, an unbounded desiringness, arising from the manner in which our imagination runs beyond our power and condition; the other a

[1] The Appendix is taken from a MS. volume marked IV. 2, which consists mainly of short essays and notes on moral questions.

feeling of fairness or, more properly, of pain at anything which we consider violation of fairness.

The feeling of fairness is misused to heighten the disappointment incident to boundless desire.

This second feeling ought, with any rightness of judgment on our part, to correct the first, and the efforts of moralists have always been to make it do so, and to urge upon us the consideration that we ought not to wish to engross all happiness to ourselves, but should be contented to take our share as things go. The second feeling however, being in general the less strong of the two, instead of acting to restrain and keep in order the other, is usually overborne by it and pressed into its service, and there is generated more or less an under-feeling in us, not only that we have not got all we want, but that it is hard and unfair upon us, somehow or other, that we have not. In the general half-latent state of this feeling, there is no direct comparison of our lot with that of others; for if there were, it would often rather correct the feeling, it being clear, in almost every case, how many others must be more hardly treated still. But, the feeling thus lying smouldering, often before we have time to think, the news of others' suffering kindles it into a momentary blaze; and our latent self-pity or repiningness, our, in fact, unreasonable and unconfessed envy of others, has for a moment a weight taken off it, and is relieved by tidings of calamity to them.

Variety of ways in which the individual's consciousness of unhappiness may be affected by the thought of the unhappiness of others.

Moral ill, or badness, may be said to be generated only from actual ill or pain, if we take care to consider that the mind has the power of *making* actual ill or pain where it does not at all necessarily exist. Desiringness, uncorrected and untempered with other feelings, will of itself produce it. Imperfection of condition, or *wantingness,* is regarded as loss or privation, and loss or privation as suffering, producing discontent or repining, and this again jealousy and envy, and this ill-will, anger, and hatred.

If we go back to an earlier point than that which is taken when we say that the non-disagreeableness of the sufferings of others is a mark of the malevolence of human nature, we might say that it is a mark rather of the unhappiness of human nature, not necessarily, that is, of actual unhappiness, but of the feeling or supposition of it. The sight of others' suffering is an illustration that we are not alone unhappy; this wide and universal theatre contains more woful pageants than our unhappiness furnishes. When we observe on the one side the moralist maintaining the benevolence of human nature against the man of the world, maintaining its malevolence, we should observe on the other side that the prescribed moral maxim for comfort in unhappiness is to observe that others are unhappy too, while we constantly have people, speaking from feelings and from life alone, saying to us that this knowledge and sight does not diminish their unhappiness, but increases it. The sort of unhappiness, unsatisfiedness, or felt imperfection, which is the experience of individual human nature, has the unhappiness which is in the world and in others for the congenial object of its view, and is variously and complicatedly affected by it; it is rebuked, encouraged, soothed or half comforted, embittered, interested, and affected even in more ways than this, according to the mind in which it exists.

It is probable that all native and original ill-will,—native and original, that is, in so far as it does not arise from any distinct ulterior purpose of good to ourselves—is connected with a perversion of the feeling of justice, making it appear to ourselves that we have some cause of complaint and wrong against the person towards whom it is felt, or against somebody or something which benefits him unduly and more than us. This is the manner in which the sort of rivalry for happiness which exists among men turns sour, and becomes productive of malevolence. The feeling of hopeful effort, which is the life of life, and which naturally measures itself, in one way, by concurrence and competition with others, is, like that of desiringness which is its source, properly inconsistent with, and almost contradictory to, the feeling of delight in fairness which is the source of that of justice. But in a similar manner to the other it subordinates this latter to it, and makes us think that what we aim at gaining is our right and what we ought to have; and then, since our success measures itself in one way, as I have said, by that of others, success on their part seems so far failure on ours. First the feeling of disappointment is produced where there is no reason for it: then this again becomes a sort of feeling of being wronged.

The existence of this feeling of fairness is important to observe. It is quite distinct from the feeling of conscience or right determination of our own conduct; the mis-application of it, in the manner which we have just seen, being one of the things which this latter has often most to guard against. At the same time it is of course much associated with it, and helpful to it.

There is no native ill-will. It springs in all cases from an imagination of wrong received.

Moralists, it appears, have been wrong, both on the one side in disputing the existence of pure ill-will, and on the other in considering it native in the same manner in which pure good-will is. Ill-will is perhaps always a form or mode of *vindictivolence*, i.e. is connected with a feeling of ourselves as somehow wronged: whereas good-will on the other hand, is by no means necessarily a form or mode of gratitude: but ill-will undoubtedly exists *pure* in so far that it is felt for no purpose of good to ourselves.

It appears therefore that there may be pure and intense hatred or ill-will entirely disinterested as regards the future, but not entirely disinterested as regards the past, *i.e.* not uncaused by some feeling akin to injuredness.

The lines of Lucretius need not be understood of malignant pleasure.

The lines of Lucretius seem to refer mainly to the fifth source of pleasure particularized above.

The sight of others in labour and danger is interesting, and on the supposition that we are unable to give active help ourselves, and that we hope their escape, this interest may have more in it of a pleasurable, than of a painful nature, without supposing anything of positive malignity in the spectator.

APPENDIX ON JUSTICE AND TRUTHFULNESS[1].

Distributive and corrective justice.

Justice consists in making preferences where they should be made, and carefully abstaining from making them where they should not be made. Using Aristotle's distinction, *distributive* justice teaches what preferences should be made; and in virtue of this, might be taken to teach when preferences should not or need not be made; while *corrective* justice restores equality or sets things even again, where conduct has been determined by preferences uncalled for or wrong.

The notion of justice then simply as fairness or impartiality, that is, neither as relative duty on the one side, nor as recompense on the other, is something intermediate between the two Aristotelian notions. It might be considered a case of the first, or the basis of the second; the former, because equality is itself a relation; the latter, because to set things even when disturbed, we must have given to us what constitutes their evenness.

The former is the manifestation of the feeling of duty, the latter of the love of right.

The two Aristotelian kinds of justice are most markedly distinguished from each other in a subjective point of view, that is, in the temper of mind belonging to each. The temper belonging to the former we might call 'the feeling of duty;' that belonging to the latter, 'the love of right.' The former is of a more constant, uniform, ever-ready nature: the latter is less uniform than the other, because not regularly called out, but when it is called out, is stronger and more energetic.

The action of corrective justice must be controlled by benevolence.

When we speak of the temper of justice, and compare justice with proportion, equality, or other intellectual notions of this kind, it is to be remembered that justice, in so far as it is morally valuable, must fulfil the condition

[1] This Appendix is taken from the MS. marked V. It contains a fuller discussion of some of the questions touched on in Ch. xi, treating especially of 'commercial credit,' 'vows,' 'prevarication,' which are noted as points for further consideration at the end of the MS. of that chapter. Ed.

not only of satisfying the intellect, which is what these notions of proportion and equality belong to, but also of satisfying the description of the objective value of the action of a reasonable being, namely, that some good is produced by it. From this it follows, that when the balance has been disturbed in the direction of more good being done by any one than he was called upon to do, the moral call for the setting this right is not absolute, but only subjective, affecting particular people: on the other hand, when the balance is disturbed in the direction of ill being done to any, there is an absolute call for the making up the good which has been failed in, but there is not a subjective call on the sufferer to repay evil to the doer. To put this more plainly. If in speaking of fairness in relation to recompense and repayment, we think only of notions of equality, evenness, &c., we shall be in danger of supposing, on the one hand, that revengefulness is a duty in the same manner as gratitude, and on the other, that it is the duty of individuals not directly interested (as for instance the state) to reward gratitude in the same way in which it is their duty to punish wrong. As it is, the duty of repayment of good is a private or particular one: the duty of repayment of evil is a public or general one. Speaking without reference to feelings of love or friendship, which I have not here to do with, it is equally to our private honour to be in no man's debt for favours, and to be above taking revenge on any for injuries. And this action for intellectual fairness on the one side, and against it on the other, will in each case be produced by the same feeling, which I have described as the first basis of all action, viz. the desire that it should be devoted to some good or welfare, not simply to the production of ill and pain: for if we suppose for a moment that happiness of our own resulted from such production, that is a feeling which we should rise above. The obligations therefore of justice in regard to ourselves, are to gratitude only, and not correspondingly to revengefulness: in regard to others, while we have no call to take upon ourselves the rewarding of their benefactors, we are called upon to punish those who have injured them.

Vengeance for private wrong is thus left to the community; gratitude for private benefit to the individual.

When duty between two persons is failed in, there is, besides the loss to the sufferer which he may do his best to regain, a bad or hostile disposition on the part of the offender which it would be revengefulness in him to punish, but which others (as the state) may punish, and should.

Moral advance in the individual shows itself in the increase of indignation at public wrong, and of gratitude for private benefit.

The *feeling* which lies at the bottom of justice *compensatory* or *corrective* is *resentment,* not in the sense in which Butler uses the word, but in the more general sense in which it was used at an earlier time, as applied both to good and evil—a quick sensitiveness to benefits and to injuries. Till corrected (if not by natural kindness and love) by the feeling about action of which I spoke, the tendency of this sensitiveness is probably to revengefulness in the same way as to gratitude, and to what we call 'taking offence' for wrong done to ourselves, as well as to moral indignation for wrong done to others. Moral advance consists in keeping up the feeling, and cultivating it, on the side of gratitude, and extinguishing it on that of revenge: and again, in keeping it up as moral indignation on behalf of others, but extinguishing it as readiness to take offence for ourselves.

Different kinds of justice:

Justice, as I have said, consists equally in making distinctions or preferences where they ought to be, and avoiding them where they ought not: and it is because this description has so many different aspects that there are so many different kinds of justice.

observance of relative duty, (1)

Justice, as 'attention to duty,' is regard to 'jus,' or to those relations of nature and usage which determine a large portion of our action from one to another.

impartiality, (2). Difficulties in respect to this.

Justice as 'impartiality' is an important pendant to this regard to *jus,* and is indeed frequently in direct antagonism with it. There are many difficulties connected with its practical application. Those moralists who have come forward as advocates of impartiality in opposition to what they have called sinister interests, have often not sufficiently considered that the public interests would be quite as badly off (in fact considerably worse) if these interests, which only become sinister when they get out of their place, were in any degree less powerful motives of action than they are. The difficulty in the case of impartiality arises not only from the strength of the particular adverse interest, but from the difficulty of determining what are the cases in which impartiality is called for, and what, in such cases, is the proper impartiality. Where impartiality, as it not unfrequently does, becomes a passion, and where conscientiousness in this direction is wrought up very highly; and where moreover, the way and limits of impartiality are not distinctly marked out, in the manner in which they are with judges or administrators of law; dread of supposed self-interest and of partiality constantly leads to mistake and cruelty; and we want strength of mind to conquer the fear of partiality as much as for any other purpose. Impartiality, as it should be, is a public virtue of a very high order: partly from the difficulties mentioned; partly from the facility of censuring conduct which concerns it, while at the same time it would not have been easy for the censurers to agree upon the right conduct; and partly again from the fact that what is called partiality is often the most readily suggested line of conduct, and therefore where the agent can neither satisfy himself, nor hope to satisfy others, with a different conduct, he naturally adopts this.

It is in reference to its character as impartiality, and as being 'no respecter of persons,' that justice is drawn blind. The often quoted and very curious passage of Leviticus will be remembered, 'Thou shalt not countenance a *poor* man in his cause.' Justice might perhaps better have been drawn with many eyes to see the difficulties which from opposite directions beset impartiality, and of which sinister interest is one only.

Honesty, (3).

Justice as *integrity* or *honesty* is, speaking generally, impartiality between ourselves and others, in so far as the word 'impartiality,' in this acceptation, has meaning. It assumes that we pursue our interest, and others pursue theirs: and what it consists in is, that in the course of this, we should take no undue advantage of them.

Honesty compared with honour as a help to virtuous conduct.

There are many analogies between the *honesty* of business and the *honour* which belongs to a very different set of associations, and is counted rather an aristocratic and military sentiment. Trustworthiness is the prominent character in both. It suited both Paley's particular temperament and the feeling of the age in which he wrote to depreciate the latter, as what was very much a matter of convention, and scarcely more likely to lead to virtuous conduct than to vicious. Remembering the duels and gambling of those days, one should not be too severe on Paley for this. But we must remember, that the matter-of-fact sentiment of justice, as integrity or uprightness, is itself a very insufficient guide to virtuous conduct, resembling the sentiment of honour in this point of view as in many others. It is consistent with much of harshness and cruelty: nay, the tempers associated with it seem sometimes even productive of such; the same strictness and severity which the man enforces on himself being exhibited in his requirements from others. Nor again is it inconsistent with covetousness: it does nothing to preclude the taking the most cruel advantage of others in dealings (of their necessities, for instance), provided only that there is nothing in these which is actually dishonest. And what is or is not dishonesty has to be settled, in respect of many particulars, by usage and convention, for it could not be otherwise.

With all these disadvantages, so far as we expect it to lead to perfect virtue, it has, like honour, singular advantages as urging to virtue: it takes continually the form not of a mere restraint, but of a passion, and developes a sensibility in respect of commercial honour, as keen as can be developed in respect of honour of any other kind; so that commercial credit, character, good name, is counted as dear as life itself.

The degree of mutual confidence which must exist, and does exist, in order to the carrying on of complicated commercial transactions, might well astonish the unprepared spectator. This mutual confidence, and mutual justifying of such confidence, is in fact the basis of all civilization: society is founded on mutual truth.

Honesty as concerned with contracts.

Justice, as honesty or integrity, has relation to that part of law which concerns *contracts*, and to such usages and circumstances as bear more or less a resemblance to this. In respect to justice of this kind also we have to remember what I said a short time since as to the usefulness of actions, and that justice is only a virtue in so far as, along with it, we keep in mind this. We are *servants*, not *slaves*, to our word: that is, in keeping it, we must go by reason, and take to our aid intelligence.

An engagement, which binds us to the benefit of the person with whom it is made, does not bind us to his prejudice.

Difficulty arising from the application to this of the idea of utility.

There is of course a good deal of difficulty about all this, arising chiefly from two sources: the one, the value, as we may express it, of our own word; the other, the possibility of difference of opinion between the other party and ourselves as to what is for his benefit.

Particularly as regards the sense of self-respect attaching to truthfulness.

I have before spoken of what we may call the *passion* for speaking truth, the love of truth for truth's sake, and the almost impossibility felt by a high and generous nature, of doing otherwise. Conscientiousness, as I described, has a double aspect, outwards and inwards. Speaking the truth, in the former aspect, is the transferring something external to our neighbour for his benefit: in the latter, it is the transferring to him something as *our* sentiment, a part, as it were, of ourselves. Now, however much the rule I mentioned just now as to action being useful applies to the conscientiousness of truth in the former aspect, we find it hard to apply it in the other. The setting something before others as our thought, which is not our thought, is not simply misleading others and betraying their confidence, which for benefit to them we might possibly be led to, but it is the doing this through the way of a sort of abuse, prostitution, degradation, of *ourselves;* it is our own sentiment which has to be falsified for this benefit to them. *There* is the difficulty.

Danger of superstitious reverence for the letter of engagements.

It is from a generalization of this feeling that there arises in men or bodies of men that noble value for their word which sometimes degenerates, as among the ancient Romans, into a sort of superstition. The feeling of the Romans in this matter was a compound of the highest honourableness with the driest technicality. They worshipped words and formulæ, and considered sacredness to be in them, instead of in the meanings of which these might be made the vehicle. Now in reality, both language is imperfect, so that it is almost impossible for a man to say what he does mean without being in danger of saying more than it; and thought itself is complicated, so that it is difficult for a man to be sure of saying all that he does mean. This being so, it is very important that the worship (so to call it) paid to the language of our word should be intelligent, not superstitious, and that the inward feeling which I described before should not be merely externalized (losing constantly in this way a vast deal of its value) into a verbal particularity. Truth is not in the words, but in what the words mean. The value for the truth, and the value for the words which contain the truth, are two entirely different feelings.

The obligation to execute threats of evil is not the same as that to promises of good.

This kind of reverence for the mere thing which has been resolved, or uttered, or denounced, without thought of the interest of any, leads vaguely to a good deal of unwise thought in men's minds. In this view, threats and denunciations are equally binding with promises. There arises from it a notion of obligation being simply absolute, without a second party at all, even a divine or ideal one. Supposing the word given by a king of the Medes and Persians of former time to have been more than usually foolish, and absolutely unproductive of benefit or pleasure to anyone, it puzzles one to know to whom he would have been supposed under obligation to perform it, or whose business it was to enforce it. Even in regard to religion, there is sometimes, I think, a tendency in people to forget the immeasurable difference between this kind of keeping one's word and the faithfulness which really belongs to our idea of God: hence they speak as if they thought that past denunciations had laid God Himself under a force or stress rendering it difficult or impossible for Him to forgive, instead of the past denunciations and the present difficulty both arising from the same continuing cause, the hatred which God feels for sin, in spite of His love for sinners. And among ourselves, this wrong regard for what has been once said is not unfrequently a perpetuator of the worst and most unforgiving passions: people may have every disposition now to better conduct, but what they have once said they seem to think they are wrong in departing from, even for confessed benefit to all parties.

It is not obligatory on any to continue to mean the same, in whatever manner he may have declared it, unless the interests of some one else are involved in his meaning. There is no signification in a man binding himself to himself. Religious vows are made to God, and He, as supreme sovereign, is supposed concerned in the keeping them. And in respect to His continuing to mean the same—that He always does: and yet always differently according to changed circumstances, as change of disposition and needs in those with whom He is dealing: His meanings at any time are wider than we can follow, and no revelation, by means of any denunciation, of His justice, can preclude the exercise of His mercy.

Difficulty of determining whether the keeping of a promise will be for the advantage of the other party.

An engagement binds us to the benefit of the other party, not to his prejudice. If then we find out, to our own satisfaction, that a thing which we have promised to another would really be a disadvantage to him, are we free from our promise?

In all conduct, to a certain extent there must be the supposition, that every man is the proper judge of his own interests. Where there is an engagement, this is in a much higher degree the case. The duty of not keeping an engagement claimed by the other party because the fulfilment of it would be to the injury, not the benefit, of the other party, can only arise when we are in that sort of superior position, as to knowledge, in reference to the other party, which destroys his independence against us, and puts him under something like tutelage.

As a rule *his* estimate of advantage must be taken.

Advantage must be taken at *his* estimate, not at ours, except in extreme cases where he is plainly not a proper judge, as in the case often supposed by the old moralists, of the promise of a sword to a man, who afterwards becomes mad.

Perhaps the rule ought to be extended beyond such extreme cases as this, and certainly should be extended very much further, if it were not for one consideration in regard of all promises, which is, that we have no right, speaking generally, to give the management of our action out of our own hands, and yet we are not, and cannot be, fit judges in a cause in which we are ourselves concerned with another. Promise of any kind therefore embarrasses action, and often embarrasses it hopelessly. Moralists and casuists have, like lawyers, to reason on the supposition of there being, if it could but be found, a clear way out of a difficulty, whereas often there is none.

Ambiguity of the phrase 'a promise is not binding.'

When it is said that a promise is not *binding*, the language is sometimes misleading. The phrase is a confused expression 'for we must not perform it,' and 'we may perform it, but need not,' which are quite different things. What it suggests, is the latter of these. And, owing partly to this association, there is a constant jealousy of any discussion, about promises, as if the saying that any one was unlawful (after it had been made) was always something in the interest of the promiser, something which he would have wished.

It may be our bounden duty not to keep a promise.

The putting the question about promises in this form, whether they are or are not binding, constantly suggests to people that there need not be so much discussion on the matter, for people might always settle it by giving the verdict *against* themselves. Binding or not, if people have promised a thing they had better perform it, we shall readily be told: and with reason, provided only there has been no flagrantly unfair advantage taken in the procuring the promise, and provided it is not more wrong to perform than it would be to fail.

Case of promises obtained by force or fraud.

The case of promises procured by deceit or compulsion is one of moral difficulty. The law would declare them invalid, and not only this, but would use its utmost efforts to make individuals treat them as invalid: for faith kept with crime or among criminals is a strength to crime, and in this way a disadvantage to society. On this view, a promise made under compulsion, for instance, with the deliberate intention of violating it, would have nothing in it wrong. Rather, the keeping such a promise afterwards would be wrong. On the other hand, if the individual is a man of honour and of his word, all this must be very painful to him. The limit between outwitting and deceit, between urgency and compulsion, is not easy to draw, and even if it is quite distinct, a man might say he would rather abide the worst consequences of his own foolishness or weakness than break his plighted word. The highest honour has consisted in a man's attributing the same value to his word under all circumstances, whether uttered under compulsion or not, and refusing to say anything which he did not think and mean, and was not prepared to execute.

No rule can be made where our own interest only is concerned.

I do not see therefore how it is possible to lay down any moral rule about the performance of a promise made under compulsion when it affects a man's own interest alone. The making such a promise and failing to perform it is equivalent to the telling a lie. If the promise is made with the intention of the breach of it, that is a lie already; in any case the whole process amounts to one. A lie under compulsion is pardonable to the same extent to which a promise under compulsion is invalid.

We may not keep a promise to the injury of others.

When promises affect the interests of others besides ourselves and the party to whom they are made, care needs to be taken about the word 'binding,' in the manner to which I have alluded. A thing which is wrong for us to do, in any manner, is not made the more right by there having been a promise made to any, on our part, to do it. We can only give what is ours to give: and this is a second rule about promises, besides their being for the benefit of the second party, that they can only be taken to apply to what is lawful, and what is fairly in our power. Of a promise of what is not ours to give, it is more correct to say it is no promise, than that it is not binding and should be broken. Instead of saying we should break an unlawful promise, it is more correct to say we have no right to do wrong because we have promised it. If we have gained anything by such a promise, we have gained it by false pretences, and nothing now can help that. If we must injure one of two persons, either by wronging one or breaking our word to the other, the latter is the alternative which we must choose.

Perjury.

The all-importance, for society and civilization, of mutual confidence, has been the reason why the sacredness of obligations has always, in the early mind of men, formed a department, and a principal department, of religion. Oaths are promises (or declarations) with express reference to this sacredness. The notion goes back beyond the supposition of actual divine personality to the conditions of such. The gods themselves are not free from this bond. It is the subjective feeling which I have spoken of, of untruth and unfaithfulness being with the honourable man something impossible, embodied in the supposition of a sort of material or fatal impossibility. It is a superstition thus, in which the purpose and meaning of the engagement are lost in attention to its form. The gods are themselves slaves of their promise, and their fiercest vengeance is reserved for breach of faith in men. The lowest circles of hell are for treachery. Both treason and felony, the two names in our law, feudally derived, for capital crimes, have for meaning 'breach of faith.' Perjury is breach of faith expressly plighted in a religious form, breach of oath.

Lawfulness of oaths.

The relation of oaths to promises is simply the relation of religion to common life, and thus our rules with regard to the use of oaths must depend upon what we think, in these points, as to religion. If common life were what, ideally, it should be, religion would lose its separate significance by being all-pervading: correspondingly, every promise would be more or less an oath, because we should be always acting in reference to God. As common life is, it is felt to be a gain that religion should preserve a certain character of solemnity, except so far as, pervading common life, it can elevate it also; the tendency of things of themselves being to spread religious notions through common life and language, in a lowered form, as matter of universal recognition; a consequence of which is that the former lose their force and meaning without elevating the latter. This takes place, in regard of oaths, when they are applied to trivial declarations or engagements, and also when the language of oaths is used as a simple strengthening of common language—a thing which (according to the laws which govern the changes of meaning in words) it soon ceases to be, frequently losing at the same time all outward sign of its origin.

Besides, then, that there should not be misuse of the language of oaths, there should not be too great frequency in their use: but should they be used at all?

Scriptural argument.

Our Lord forbids swearing, and requires the use of simple language unstrengthened by religious references, in the same manner as He forbids the resistance to evil, and requires the turning of the second cheek to the smiter, the giving to him that asketh of us, and the lending to those who would borrow. There has always been difference of opinion among Christians as to how these precepts should be interpreted. A test of the propriety of the interpretation of a particular part, is of course, the applicability of the same manner of interpretation to the whole. The precept about swearing, however, being rather on the surface, and not, speaking generally, very difficult of observance, has been considered by some bodies of Christians as what ought to be obeyed literally (as it is called), while the others are not to be obeyed to the same extent.

Moral argument.

Independently of this, it has been considered by some

that the practice of occasionally strengthening our engagements and declarations by a religious reference is really not of advantage to morals, as tending to give an idea of two sorts of such engagements, one more binding than the other, whereas the bindingness is complete, and as great as it can be, in either. That an effect of this kind is produced in some ignorant minds, cannot, I think, be doubted. The whole matter, however, is a case of the general relation between religion and morality. Religion and morality, with misjudging minds, sometimes injure each other instead of benefiting, and the thought is mistakenly suggested that either would be better if the other were away. An oath is usually in form a solemn prayer, and, in ordinary suggestion, it is an acknowledgment of dread of the divine vengeance (with us, punishment) in case of breach of the engagement. The more distinct the engagement is made by these additions—the more, that is, the other party is likely to be induced by it to rely upon it—the more is this punishment, in case of breach, to be dreaded. There is nothing in this to suggest that truthfulness in other cases is a matter of slight importance: on the contrary, the suggestion is that truth, more than any thing else, is under the special sanction of religion, and that we give prominence to this sanction where it is of more than usual importance that the truth should be accurately stated.

In what sense promises are to be understood.

The rule for the *understanding* of promises or engagements is given clearly by Paley: they are binding in the sense in which the promiser understands the second party to have understood them. The ground of this is simply: thepromise is the common understanding. Words used as vehicles of a promise (or declaration) must have one meaning, in the same way as they must in logic for an unfallacious conclusion. The words mean what the two parties agree in meaning by them: if they do not mean the same by them, no intelligent promise has been passed: if the promiser has two meanings, one his own, which he means to keep, and another, which he is aware is held by the person to whom the promise is made, there is *equivocation;* and this, which in logic is bad reasoning, is in morals bad faith. And as it is the promiser who has to act on the promise, the performance of it has to be guided by the best supposition which he can make of what was the common understanding between the parties.

The rule is not free from difficulties, chiefly arising from this, that the words, like language in general, have a meaning of their own in common use, distinct (in the notion of it) from the meaning which either party may attribute to them at the time. Appeal, on the part of the promiser, to individual construction of the words of the promise as opposed to usual construction of them, is the fountain of abundant bad faith. It is true, he cannot generally in such a case say, with any face, that he thought at the time that the opposite party interpreted the words as he did; but still there is difficulty.

Justice as candour, (4).

Not to dwell longer on justice as integrity, there are various other forms of justice; one is justice as *candour*, readiness to make allowances.

This is not far different from justice as equity, or fairness of mind, in that sense in which the notion approaches to that of good nature, easiness, facility. The Greek *ἐπιείκεια* has the same sort of variety of application. It will be better, however, to speak rather of this at another time as a temper.

CHAPTER XII.

ON PLEASURE AND PAIN.

Three kinds of pleasure and pain.

In this and the following chapter I shall speak of what I have called *eudæmonics:* and I shall treat first of that which may be considered a subordinate branch of it, *hedonics,* or the philosophy of pleasure and pain.

For my present purpose I shall divide pleasure and pain into three kinds or portions, as follows:

Feelings of comparative undisturbance (1).

The first kind of pleasure is that which, after the suggestion of such terms as well-being, welfare, &c., we might call *well-feeling,* and I think this name will make my meaning clearer than any description. I will not pretend to say how far it can be considered to be pleasure at all: that depends upon how we use the word 'pleasure': but I mean by it the feeling, so far as there is a feeling, which accompanies a normal and healthy state of mind; a feeling expressly not attended to as a subject of distinct consciousness, because the attention is supposed to be given to whatever we are interested in, or employed about; but a feeling which accompanies this interest and employment, or, if we prefer the language, which is itself a portion of the interest, coming into distinct consciousness, as self-enjoyment, only slightly or occasionally; otherwise we should have to recognize it as a different kind of pleasure.

Well-feeling opposed to discomfort.

Corresponding to this pleasure there is pain which we must not call ill-feeling, that expression existing already in a different application. The term 'ill', though vaguely opposite to 'well', has been much less used than 'well' in un-moral application, and we do not talk of ill-being and ill-fare, as we do of well-being and welfare. The kind of pain I am speaking of now is the feeling which we may suppose to accompany an imperfect performance of function, not distinct or violent, but vague and general: we might call it discomfort. The essential character about it is that, as in the case of the pleasure, there is no local consciousness of it, or attention, other than slight or occasional, to the painfulness of feeling.

Different views as to the pleasureableness of such well-feeling.

I expressed a doubt as to the propriety of giving the name of pleasure to that which I described in the previous paragraph: there is not so much doubt as to the propriety of giving the name of pain to what I have now described. We may suppose that, midway between them, there is a neutral point of entire undisturbance, and that the first feeling represents a slight though general disturbance in the direction of pleasure, the second, a slight though general disturbance in the direction of pain. People will probably express themselves differently on this matter according to their own feelings. One will say, the supposed pleasure of health is nothing more than undisturbance, or unconsciousness in this particular; it is no pleasure at all: distinct consciousness of any kind is with few exceptions a disturbance in the direction of pain: the supposed well-feeling is only neutrality, the second feeling is real pain. Another will say, so far from the pleasure of health and mere life being no pleasure, it is the intensest of all pleasures; a pleasure in comparison with which any pleasure of disturbance is nothing. It will be observed that, in the first of these views, pain is much more a reality or a fact in the world than pleasure is. The second view is more suggested to people, I think, by the sight of the pleasures of other people or other creatures than by their own experience; the reason being that, for an observation of this kind in a person's self, there is required a distinctness of consciousness or attention which is rather inconsistent with the absorption of attention in the employment, or the play, or whatever it is, which is supposed to cause the intenseness of the pleasure.

Pleasure and pain of this first kind is pleasure or pain of *undisturbance*. As I have mentioned, this term may not be strictly accurate, and I use it subject to an abundance of discussion like the preceding. In any case the disturbance either way, or in whatever way, is slight, vague, and general.

Feelings of disturbance (2).

The second kind of pleasure and pain (for here we may speak of them as a true pair or couple), is pleasure and pain of *disturbance* where the disturbance from a normal state is marked and distinct. What I mean will appear as I proceed.

Distinct corporeal pain is a particular state necessarily involving consciousness or attention of the whole sensitive being, a state coexistent with, associated with, or belonging to, a particular physical modification of some one or more of the nerves which are capable of such modification. Distinct corporeal pleasure may be defined in the same manner. The *fact* distinguishing the one from the other, whatever it is, is simple and ultimate, incapable of definition. The *result* of the fact is, that the one we like, the other we dread.

There is disturbance of the normal feeling in this, coincident with local disturbance of the nerves.

Pain or pleasure of disturbance, more generally,

is a state of the sensitive being similar, as to the simple undefinable fact which constitutes it, with its results, to the above described, but not necessarily accompanied by any local nervous disturbance.

The pleasures and pains which may be called mental rather than bodily are those which are connected with imagination in the same way as the others are with direct sensation. It is of course to be remembered that both sorts affect the whole man. Pain is properly of the mind, though caused (in the first sort) by something distinct and definite in the body; and in the second, or imaginational, pleasures and pains the body is constantly affected, and that sometimes in a very strong degree. Tears and laughter, blush and paleness, shiver and glow, trembling and stupor, are the results among others of such affection. These, in the old language, are various forms of the *passion*, or changing corporeal state, of which the *affection*, or changing mental state, was the mistress and occasion.

Enjoyment opposed to suffering.

I shall take the liberty in the present chapter of appropriating the word *enjoyment* to signify what I call pleasure of disturbance, and the word *suffering* to signify what I call pain of disturbance.

As regards the body, there is a greater capacity for suffering than for enjoyment.

Enjoyment and suffering arise from our having, in our mental and corporeal organization, distinctly provided susceptibilities or capacities for them.

So far as the body goes, there is much more suffering possible than enjoyment. [1]For, speaking

[1] Paley's argument on this point in his *Natural Theology* is entirely fallacious. The body is in no sense a magazine of possible pleasure to us, as unhappily it is a magazine of possible pains. If the organism does its work, there is pleasure for us in the work done: if it does not do its work, there is want of pleasure, or pain, in the work not being done: but independently of this, there is a possibility of pain for us in the organism with its sensations, which is not balanced by any possibility of pleasure. If our teeth do their work of eating, we shall have pleasure; if they do not, perhaps because they can get nothing to eat, we shall

loosely, each sensor nerve or nerve of sensation is a special or separate capacity for pain: in fact, such capacities in the body are infinite; wherever there is disturbance of the normal state in the wrong way (and there may be any where), there is, probably, pain. Whereas it is only in the case of a very few of the sensitive nerves that there can be disturbance in the direction of pleasure. Every sensitive nerve is a nerve of possible distinct pain; the nerves of possible distinct pleasure (in the palate, alimentary canal, &c.) are limited.

Use of this capacity for suffering.

I am speaking now, it is to be remembered, of eudæmonics or hedonics, and the view which I am taking, like each view which I have taken, is a particular abstraction, or partial view. I leave out of account, as much as I can do so, man's having an active nature, though it is in relation with that that all this possibility of pain stands, and that it has its value in the universe, a value far greater than that of enjoyment. What I have called enjoyment might be very greatly diminished, without the state of things in the universe differing much from that which exists at present: there would still exist the kind of pleasure of which I have spoken already and that of which I am going to speak: but, so long as there exists the possibility of anything going wrong in the universe, pain, or the *feeling* of this going wrong or disturbance, is a matter of vital necessity, and the universe could not do at all without it.

have pain: so far there is a balance of counter-possibilities. But independently of this, if they ache we shall have pain: unhappily there is no sensation of *counter-ache* or possibility of pleasure in them outside of their work: the alternative is only between non-sensation and pain. There is no doubt that any argument in reference to Natural Theology, which is based on a consideration of the organism alone, will go the other way from Paley's. The argument is in fact a painful difficulty coming home to the feelings of all, and Paley's smart *conclusiunculae* are quite unavailing against it.

The mental capacity is as great for enjoyment as for suffering.

Though, so far as the body is concerned, there is far more possibility of suffering or pain of disturbance, than of pleasure of disturbance or enjoyment, this is not the case with imaginative pleasures and pains. Here the capacity both ways is very great, and the capacity of enjoyment probably greater than that of suffering. On this, however, I will not dwell now.

Feelings of want and satisfaction (3).

The third kind of pleasure is of the nature of disturbance, as enjoyment is, but it differs from enjoyment in that it always implies a preceding want either real or supposed. It is the feeling which accompanies the satisfaction of such want. I will call it by the name of gratification.

Desire and gratification.

The word 'want' I use here, as I have done before[1], to express *a fact:* the want may exist, felt or unfelt: the feeling of this want as a want, is what we call 'desire' (though there may also be desire without the real fact of want, owing to our power of imagination): upon the want follows, if it does follow, another fact, satisfaction of it (or imagined satisfaction, if the want is only imagined): the feeling accompanying the satisfaction (or imagined satisfaction) of the want, is what I call gratification. Gratification is to the desire what satisfaction is to the want.

Desire is pain in so far as it is consciousness of want. Gratification is the replacing of this pain by pleasure. But desire may be also itself pleasurable through the anticipated possession or attainment of the object desired; and if it is followed by effort to attain it, there is a further pleasure in this, as in all action for a purpose which is free, *i.e.* which is not attended by an opposite feeling of fatigue, or of wish to be engaged in something else. Some of the ancient philosophers considered that gratification was nothing more than the restoration of an equilibrium. They compared

[1] Cf. Appendix on *Want*, p. 27.

desire and gratification to the filling up of a vessel with holes, or (we are not more plain-spoken than Plato) to itching and scratching, leaving no result in the way of surplus pleasure. In this they confine their attention too much to the moment of gratification, though even as regards that, there is no meaning in speaking of equal amounts of pleasure and pain. But I shall have more to say on this further on.

Distinction between gratification and enjoyment shown in case of food.

A ready illustration of the difference between enjoyment and gratification may be taken from our feelings in respect of food.

When the bodily system needs support, the want makes itself felt in corresponding desire of food: and the gratification of this desire by the satisfaction of the want is a pleasure perhaps of a very intense kind. Besides this, the nerves of the tongue and palate are so constructed, that they give at the same time a local pleasure quite distinct from the other, though associated with it by nature, for various useful purposes. But either may exist without the other, and constantly does; there may be keen pleasure in eating an old shoe if one is starving, or on the other hand in tasting an exquisite wine, though there may not be the smallest degree of thirst or previous desire for it.

We are then, it will be seen, capable of pleasure, as distinct from simple well-feeling, in two ways: the one to the extent of our susceptibilities of pleasure, or we might say, our voluptuary senses, amplified by imagination, so far as we may consider the imagination of a being without faculties for action: the other, when to these are superadded our activity, and our imagination as connected with this, and correspondingly, *want* also, as a fact in our nature or the universe.

Though in fact combined, the

The difference between enjoyment and gratification will I think be best understood by our making the

two are not necessarily connected.

two suppositions, so far as we can, first of our being without the possibility of the one, then of our being without the possibility of the other. I say so far as we can, for our nature is *one*, and the different portions of it all fit, or belong to, each other: and the making these abstractions, or taking these partial views, is only to a certain extent possible: *i. e.* when we suppose the *absence* of any element, our real supposition is the existence of only just so much of it as is necessary to keep our nature barely going.

Enjoyment belongs to our sentient nature, and is not preceded by a sense of want.

The first supposition then will be of our possessing great and various susceptibility to pleasure without any desire or feeling of want, *i. e.* without any independent, or spontaneous, feeling of pain at the absence of it. I mean by 'independent or spontaneous,' this. We may suppose, to a certain extent, memory of a past consciousness of pleasure, contemplation, itself accompanied with pleasure, of the possibility of our repeating the consciousness, and effort on our part to reproduce it. But the supposition which we must exclude is, that of a pain at the absence of the pleasure, going along with the susceptibility to it, when such susceptibility is not in exercise: except so far as we may call an imagination of the agreeableness of the presence of the thing a pain at the absence of it. We have by means of the nerves of the palate and tongue, an intense susceptibility of the pleasure which we call taste: but this susceptibility implies no want or pain when that which would give pleasure is absent: our palate does not feel in pain at the absence of nice savours, as it feels in pleasure at the presence of them. This perhaps may be understood best by the case of smell, because there the confusion caused by the feeling of hunger will be avoided. It is the same with the ear and music.

All these are pleasures of our simply sentient nature, in the service of which, indeed, our active nature may be by imagination engaged, but to which it is not at all essential. The circumstances of such pleasure and pain are that there is a condition of neutrality or undisturbance, during which (except for memory) there exists no consciousness of such susceptibility to pleasure and pain, nor (except for memory) any knowledge of the existence of such: this neutrality may be disturbed either way. It is quite easy to imagine our nature infinitely richer than it is in susceptibilities of this kind. Add more nerves and intensify the memory, and we might not only sympathize acutely with every chemical process going on in outward nature, but putting these feelings together, might have a knowledge of it in comparison with which our present coarse and rude acquaintance is nothing. Only we could not multiply pleasures of this kind without multiplying possible pains. And, on the other hand, we might diminish these susceptibilities very much, without making much difference as to our happiness. Many people get on very well without any sense of smell, and others without any feeling of music.

Our active nature is involved in gratification, which is preceded by sense of want.

The pain and pleasure concerned with the facts of want and satisfaction, are of different nature. We might suppose some local cause entirely to destroy our power of special taste, and that there only remained the knowledge that some things were good to satisfy our hunger, others were not: hunger, *i. e.* a want and the feeling of a want, might still subsist in all its force; there might still be intense pain in the feeling of the want, if it were great, and intense pleasure in the gratification, or feeling of satisfaction of the want, even if there were no pleasures of taste at all.

The two sorts of pleasure or pain are constantly in fact mixed or superadded the one to the other: but there seems to me little difficulty in perceiving their difference. There are two conceivable, quite different, ways of multiplying possible pleasures: the one by multiplying susceptibilities of pleasure, which may be titillated or set in action, the other by multiplying desires which may be gratified, and correspondingly wants satisfied. In both cases, we multiply pains or possible pains along with pleasures. These two kinds of pleasure may or may not go together. As on the one side the pleasure of taste will go very well with the satisfaction of hunger, so on the other side the feeling of hunger is very likely to be accompanied with imaginative pictures of this or that manner of satisfying it. But this imagination is not the hunger, any more than the nervous pleasure of taste in the palate is the satisfaction of it. If the hunger is very intense, it will destroy, by overwhelming, this latter, leaving no possibility of distinct attention to it.

Butler assumed that all pleasure was gratification, his opponents that all pleasure was enjoyment.

The exclusive supposition of one or other of these two kinds of pleasures and pains, is what is in substance done by a certain set of moralists, more or less called selfish, on the one side, and by Butler on the other: the former suppose only pleasures and pains of enjoyment, Butler only pleasures and pains of gratification.

According to the latter view, the object of desire is the thing of which we are in want, and such pleasure as arises is from the gratification of the desire by the attainment of the thing. According to the former view, such desire as there is, is for the pleasure which we picture to ourselves in the attainment of the thing, and the desire for the thing is only in order to this. The word 'pleasure,' in strictness belongs to the former view, the word 'desire,' in strictness belongs to the latter. The first set of philosophers, insufficiently, define *desire* to be the feeling which prompts and accompanies our effort after pleasure: the effort, in the mass of cases, is not after pleasure, but after some *thing*. Butler, insufficiently, defines pleasure to be the feeling of gratified desire: there may be pleasure without any want or desire. But Butler is the nearer the truth, in fact more confused than wrong, joining desires (or wants) and susceptibilities under the common name of faculties.

Butler was wrong in denying that action might be simply with a view to attain pleasure.

I will just mention by the way that, for the particular purpose for which Butler discusses this matter, he seems to me to overshoot his mark on the one side as much as he convicts his antagonists of overshooting theirs on the other; or at least not quite to keep in view what I suppose his point. Putting the thing roughly, his adversaries say All our conduct, even what we call benevolence, is selfish and interested: it is all done in view of the pleasure which will redound to ourselves. He answers: None of our conduct is selfish or interested; it is all done in view of the gaining certain special objects, whatever they are, the gaining of which will indeed give us pleasure, but what we desire is the object, not the pleasure. In one point of view, which we shall see directly, the taking up ground, as Butler does here, exactly opposite to that of his opponents, is of great importance. But the doing it thus roundly tends to obscure two important distinctions. The first is, that we have both these ways of action: at one time the imagined pleasure, at another time the thing, is the direct object of desire; only that this latter is much the more important part of our action. The second is the distinction, all-important as to morals, between conduct which is self-regarding and conduct which is outward-going or public-spirited: this distinction may exist with regard to both parts of our conduct, both that which is for an object and that which is for imagined pleasure: the object may go no further than ourselves, the imagined pleasure (of our own) may be the giving pleasure to others. It may indeed be a question what is really to be thought of the latter conduct (the benevolence of the selfish philosophers): on that there is much to say, which I will not say now.

His opponents were more wrong in denying that action might be with a view to attain some object independent of pleasure.

Butler's opponents however are far more wrong than he is. There is no statement more thoroughly untrue and misleading than the constantly repeated one, that what people, as regards the mass of their life or the sum of their thought, are wishing for and acting towards, is pleasure, or happiness as a function and derivative of pleasure. They are *expecting* pleasure in the attainment of their various objects: but what is before their imagination, the *object* of their action, what they are *desiring*, is all sorts of things, and the mass of action in pursuit of these things is what we call life. I do not deny that a part of our action is for distinctly imagined pleasure: but we desire many things in virtue of our nature and not as a practical conclusion from having found them enjoyable; and all the most important desires are of this latter nature; that is, the parent of these more important desires is spontaneous impulse, a faculty seeking its object, in Butler's language, not the remembrance of past enjoyment. It is not correct therefore to describe pleasure, the enjoyment and the remembrance of it, as the spring of action: it is but very slightly so. No catalogue of pleasures, however complete, would at all represent the actual happiness of life. Columbus's desire to discover America, and Newton's desire to discover the secret of the heavens, the gratification of which desires we must conceive to have given to them the intensest pleasure, we cannot suppose to have been excited by the remembrance of the pleasure which a small exploration will have given the former, or the solution of a problem the latter: they had their rise in the nature of each, and supposing Columbus and Newton had never felt pleasure in their lives, and did not know what it was, so as to desire it, they would have been as likely to desire these things which they did desire, the impulse to which was a part of their nature.

Even if we combine love of pleasure and of action, this does not give a complete account of human motives.

Of all professions, those to *practicalness* are generally the most empty, and never was any philosophy less practical than that which would make pleasure the universal object of desire and action. It is convicted of unpracticalness by the ordinary non-philosophical view, simply expressing itself: men plainly see the love of *pleasure* will not account for life: if we are to have it, we must at least add to it the love of *action*. But neither pleasure nor action express the real direction or pointing of our desire, though we may resolve this, in a manner, into them, as into two co-ordinate lines. Our nature, bodily and mental, has various wants, which wants are indicated to our consciousness by the feeling of them, or desire, and are indefinitely multiplied by imagination: these wants are of *things*, to speak roughly: before the attainment of the thing, there will have to be action in the pursuit of it; after the attainment, will come, if it does come, the tasting or enjoyment of it: but it is neither the pursuit nor the enjoyment which we *want*, but the thing. Our imaginations indeed are likely enough to picture to themselves as well both the excitement of the pursuit and the pleasure of the possession: but the moving force is neither love of pleasure in general, nor love of action in general, but particularly determined desire.

Hedonometry.

No doubt the utilitarians are justified in saying that, in the laying out of life or the determining of action, there is and must be a great deal of comparison, in the imagination of different pleasures or kinds of pleasure: the doing of this well may be of the greatest importance. Of two pleasures choose the greatest (supposing there is nothing else to be considered) is a very natural pendant to the rule, Of two evils choose the least.

But how far is this comparative hedonometry, so to call it, possible, in the first instance, and desirable if possible? I am inclined to think that the various assertions which have been made as to pleasures differing only in intensity and duration, have been the result, partly of want of sensibility, partly of want of elevation of view, partly of a desire to give a slight shock, as paradox does, and partly of that pleasure in depreciating the higher parts of human nature which arises, not surprisingly, from the foolishness which is occasionally talked about them.

Those utilitarians who have looked a little deeper than Paley or Bentham cared to do, have been obliged to admit a third difference in pleasures and pains, in addition to those of intensity and duration.

Those who admit difference of quality in pleasure must abandon the exact comparison of pleasures.

They have said that we must take account of *quality* as well as of quantity. But it is evident that in doing this they must give up the direct hedonometry which Paley and Bentham contemplated, for it is quantity, not quality, which admits of being gauged or measured: they must even give up, as generally applicable, the very moderate measurement implied in such a phrase as that 'of two pleasures choose the greatest': to which they will have to add, Look at your kind of pleasure, as well as at your magnitude.

But in thus giving up the notion of directly measuring pleasures one with another, do they not give up all that recommendation of utilitarianism which arises from its being a good definite and practical guide of action? Is it a more real and easy thing, in this way, to compare pleasures than to compare virtues?

They say it is, because it is matter of experience. We can estimate, they say, the pleasingness of pleasure in the only way in which we can estimate anything, by experience: we can find out how much it *does* please: *i. e.* how much one kind of it pleases as compared with another: and we may do this by finding how much it *has* pleased: we must for this interrogate our own past experience, and the experience of others, who are competent judges. Fallacy of experience.

I would just call attention in passing, to the point where we make the false step, or where, in its usual noiseless way, the *universal* fallacy of experience, as I will call it, comes in; where we step, in an instant and unperceivingly, over a chasm of infinite depth. It is there where we conclude the degree in which pleasure *does* please, from the degree in which it *has* pleased. For by 'does please', we really mean, not that, as a fact, it pleases now, or at such a time, or any number of times, but that 'it is its nature to please:' the universality of the proposition is something not given by experience. And in *this* case it will appear, that the universal proposition is not only illogically concluded, but is wrongly concluded in *fact*.

No doubt pleasure is a thing about which we may, and must, if we are wise, ask advice of others and of our former selves, but we shall not therefore consider ourselves necessarily bound to follow it. *They* are not *we* (on the individuality of pleasure I shall Pleasure is a function of individual character.

shortly have something more to say): and we are not what we were: what we found pleasant formerly may not be pleasant to us now. All this is so trite and evident, that we only wonder that this comparative tasting of pleasures by people's experience can ever have been seriously brought forward as a doctrine which was to solve all moral difficulties and give us a universal guide to action. Our palates have the same sort of nerves: and consequently, in the rough practical way which I above mentioned, if there is a new dish, and the larger number of the company like it, I say, I shall very probably like it too: but 'de gustibus non est disputandum,' in matters of pleasure there is no authority, different people like different things, we like different things from what we liked twenty years ago, people in general now like different things from those which people in general liked a hundred years ago; and if we say there are some things which are *worth* liking, which people *should* like, we are adding a new element not belonging to experience, but implying an ideal, and really borrowed from that other part of moral philosophy which I have called 'aretaics'.

CHAPTER XIII.

ON HAPPINESS.

To get an idea of happiness from pleasure, we must start from well-feeling, not from enjoyment.

FOR the consideration of happiness, the proper point of departure is well-feeling, not that distinct pleasure which I have called enjoyment. The opposite proceeding is what may be called an error of utilitarianism, in this way. To utilitarianism, as simply making much of happiness, happiness of one kind is the same as happiness of another kind: but to utilitarianism, as considering happiness describable and measurable, and professing itself, on this account, more susceptible of accuracy, as a moral system, than other moral systems, it is important to start, in considering happiness, from the notion of distinct pleasure;. because then happiness is considered as a mass of pleasures, or a quantity of pleasure, which it could not be if we began in our consideration of it from well-feeling. No one would conceive that *this* could lend itself to anything of measurement, or that we could in any way compare the degree of it felt by one with the degree of it felt by another. It is the accompaniment of a state, which state may be analysed as to its constituent parts, but happiness itself, the accompaniment, is something incapable of analysis. In this view of the matter we cannot possibly imagine the happiness to be the principal thing, so that the state exists in order to the feeling of it. Our feeling happiness, may be a test of the state being the right and proper state; but to produce the happiness, we must produce the state.

Happiness according

The error of modern utilitarians as to happiness, seems to me to arise from an imperfect notion

to Paley and Bentham.

of the manner in which any happiness, deserving to be called such, belongs to life in general. Had they understood this more truly, they would have seen that it is as hard to describe happiness as it is to describe *right*, and that any notion of making morals more simple by building them on the basis of pleasure or happiness is chimerical: while in the attempt to do this all real notion of happiness is destroyed. Of utilitarian conceptions of happiness, Paley's is probably the truest to the ancient Epicureanism; which, to the depth to which it went, had its truth, and was susceptible of very various form according to the mind of the conceiver; but which nevertheless always seems to me to have had a kind of untruthfulness like that of pastoral poetry, to have taken little account of the real movers of action, and the most important feelings. Bentham's conception was of a sort of *legal* happiness; a mapping out of infinitely varied feeling into forms in which it *ought* to arrange itself, French departments or American counties; a process excellent in many respects for the purpose for which he used it, but not at all a real account of man. At present, it seems to me that, in the desire to create a positive or inductive science of morals, there is a disposition, suggested by political economy, to describe the materials of happiness as happiness itself, and to think that some observation, or positive research, will give the manner in which they ought to be distributed. On this I will say a few words.

Economical view of happiness as consisting in the possession of materials of enjoyment.

Wealth, I suppose, may be defined as the mass of the commodities which man more or less urgently requires, and in using enjoys, with the exclusion of some, scarcely indeed to be called commodities, which are common to all. We may thus readily analyse it, and we find the various kinds of it satisfying various requirements, and giving various kinds of enjoyment. We may classify the kinds: and we thus have a catalogue or arrangement of enjoyments at once suggesting itself to us. Wealth is most unequally distributed; some have none, some have much. Here then we find a ready means for increasing man's enjoyment; here we have good action suggested to us, and suggested to us simply as the production of enjoyment.

Action is not merely a means to enjoyment, as labour is to wealth.

Again, according to Political Economy, labour is looked upon merely as the means to the attainment of the one thing in itself needful, wealth. Did wealth exist without labour, labour would be folly. In like manner it seems to be assumed by some moralists that all the happiness of life consists in the play of it, so to speak, and none in the work.

It will be remembered that I noticed as the cardinal point of my difference with utilitarianism in the beginning, that it looks upon man as *fruitive*, or enjoying, in the first instance, and active only in the second instance, because without acting he cannot procure enjoyment. Man, I said, is active and fruitive both in conjunction: and the happiness or successfulness of his nature is in this, that there exists pleasure, his own and that of others, which may serve as an end for his action, and that he has powers of action by means of which he can procure his own and others' pleasure.

There is enjoyment involved in action.

It is the alternation or conjunction of action and enjoyment which constitutes *life*: and happiness is in *life*, not in the fruitive portion of life only, the enjoyment. Man's active powers are as much a part of him as his susceptibilities of enjoyment. The enjoyment *involved* in the exercise of the former is as important as the enjoyment which they are exercised to procure. He would in this way be unhappier if he were happier: his happiness would be further off if it were nearer.

Even economical progress is due to love of action as much as to love of wealth.

It is all this which makes the complicated character and, at the same time, the interest of human happiness, and which makes it constantly impossible for a man to say what is his enjoyment, and what is his trouble. And man's economic circumstances themselves in reality rest upon this, though in considering them we make for convenience an abstraction, and suppose that wealth is enjoyment, and that labour is (so far as it goes) a pain or evil undergone for the sake of it. It is this complication of human happiness which makes the substantial folly of all satires on the Vanity of Human Wishes, or in fact, on the supposed folly of men. It causes a perpetual circular reasoning in all our attempts to estimate pleasure given: we say, it is evident that this thing gives great pleasure, or else men would not take so much trouble to get it; and then again, they take all this trouble to get it because it gives so much pleasure. It seems to me, that if we oppose the total action of men on the one side, to their total enjoyment on the other (not taking into account the fact that often the labour falls to one, and the enjoyment to another), and if we suppose that men then really could and did beforehand estimate the value of pleasure against the labour it would cost, estimating this latter all along as an evil, it is a question whether states of high economical civilization would ever exist. They exist, because along with the love of enjoyment, the sole utilitarian motive, there exists in man an impulse to the exercise of his faculties, or so far to *labour*, as well as to enjoyment, and a capability of rational improvement which suggests to him that it is better to exercise these faculties in the production of what will be useful and enjoyed than in savage pursuits like war. And so men get on to high civilization and to luxury.

As there is one line of moral philosophy thus connected with the study of political economy, and suggesting to us human *enjoyment* as what we should start with or make our first consideration: so there is another line of moral philosophy which is associated with jurisprudence or law, and which starts with the consideration of human *action*. Bentham attempted to reform law by bringing it into the sphere of direct considerations of human pleasure and happiness, so far as I understand, with great profit. But there exists exactly the same necessity for our bringing our views of human happiness into the sphere of jurisprudence, or the science of the principles upon which, as a matter of fact, men have regulated their action. For there we see human life: we see how men understand their own requirements, the purpose of their action, the proper direction and proper restraint of it: a theory of human happiness out of relation with this would be as unsatisfactory as a system of law out of relation with human happiness.

Jural view connecting happiness with action.

And human life, as a whole, consists more in action than in enjoyment. To describe man we must describe his habits of life, the things that he does: his important pleasures are closely involved with these, and hardly describable independently; or, where they are so, are endlessly associated with other feelings: the more distinctly describable and separable a pleasure is, the less it is important. The distinct pleasures are like an animal's fondness for salt or any speciality of that kind, as compared with the pleasures, involved with other feelings and with pain, in its exercise of its faculties to secure its food and gratify its appetite, according to its constantly present impulses.

Life is made up mainly of action, very slightly of distinct enjoyment.

Aristotelian εὐπραξία.

It is not 'the abundance of the things which he possesseth' which makes a man's life, but it is his *living*, his exercising his faculties; his happiness is his εὐπραξία, that word which the Greek moral instinct may almost be said to have made for the Aristotelic philosophy, in which feeling and action are joined in a single notion as they are joined in consciousness, the *life* being in this union of action and feeling: living rightly is the doing what we should, in which doing we feel as we should; and this is the important or fundamental happiness, to which the various separate describable pleasures are desirable, but not necessary, appendages. The Aristotelic philosophy was true to reality in the way in which it looked at these pleasures, and in the way in which it dealt with the materials of happiness. Its εὐδαιμονία, or happiness, was not a function or development of ἡδονή, pleasure; but, as I have described it above, a something more general and deeper, to which this other might be added: not a mere product of the χορηγία or materials of happiness, but the right use of the latter, with full individual action.

Improved definition of happiness.

Happiness then consists, firstly, in living, feeling, thinking, as it is the nature of man to live, feel, and think, especially as it is the best or ideal nature of man to live, feel, and think; secondly, in the pursuit of purposes worth pursuing, especially in the successful pursuit of them, giving rise to gratification; and, finally, in more of distinct and separable pleasure, or enjoyment; or perhaps, which comes to the same thing, in less of distinct pain, the counterpart of enjoyment, and in the lives of many much the readier at hand; in so much that, in such a case, the entire absence of the one would be cheaply purchased with the entire absence of the other.

In man's nature, as I have described, sociality is

not a quasi-accident, but of the essence of it: each feeling bears its imprint. Thus the living, feeling, thinking, as man should, has reference not to the man's self alone, but to his place with others, and his relation to them; and into his purposes they, as well as himself, must enter.

From the above remarks about happiness the following may appear.

Difficulty of arriving at general conclusions with regard to the experience of pleasures.

Moral psychology endeavours to co-ordinate individual experiences; a thing which is, in all respects, difficult, and at least as difficult in regard of happiness as in regard of any moral sentiment. When we are speaking about moral sentiment, of course a man may reply to us, 'I feel no such sentiment': but quite to the same degree, as it seems to me, when we are speaking of any pleasure, he might answer, 'It does not please me.' And when we say, that men are educated morally to think in this or that manner, and that it is in this way that it is determined what their moral sentiments shall be, I cannot see at all why it may not be said to the same extent that they are educated to enjoy this or that, and that thus it is determined by education what their pleasure shall be. When therefore an appeal is made to experience as to what is pleasing, and we are told, Here is real matter of experience, Here is something to found a positive science upon, I am quite unable to see how an appeal can be made to experience as to what is pleasant more than as to what is right. Men seem to me to vary and differ at least as much in their enjoyments as in their moral sentiments; and therefore, besides the consideration that moral science is concerned primarily with an ideal and only with positive science as subordinate to such, I do not see that pleasure offers us a firmer ground for a positive science than moral sentiment does.

Writers who have not had a theory to serve, the simple surveyors of human nature, like Herodotus or Montaigne, have dwelt on the variety and uncertainty of human enjoyment just in the same manner as the utilitarians have dwelt on the variety and uncertainty of moral sentiment and reason among men: moral sentiment is as much fixed in man as anything is. That is, both his moral sentiments, and his views of pleasure and happiness, are developments and exhibitions of his wide and varied nature.

Human pleasure and happiness thus eludes the attempt at exact description and classification of it: and there is danger of mistake and immorality in such attempt, in the manner which I will shew.

Danger of insisting on the experience of pleasures.

It is scarcely possible to attempt to analyze happiness into particular distinct pleasures, without giving a greater apparent importance than they really have, in proportion with the mass of happiness in life, to the distinctly describable pleasures, such as are many physical ones. To give a coarse instance: a man sees put down among pleasures the very distinct physical pleasure of intoxication, and hears it said that it is very intense. He says to himself, 'To think that I should have lived so many years without once experiencing this pleasure! here is one ingredient of happiness which I have quite neglected.' He is told perhaps, 'You will have to pay for the pleasure with pains, with head-ache afterwards, with the danger of falling into a habit which will be your misery.' He says, 'I will try if I cannot, managing the thing wisely, secure the pleasure and guard against the pains,—I think I can.' The real thing to be said to him is, Your truest happiness will be that which will flow from your life itself, and your wisest plan will be to try to make your life such as will furnish such happiness. The pleasure of distinctly conceivable and describable enjoyment, the old ἡδονή or *voluptas*, is something which life might be perfectly happy without, there being quite enough pleasure for happiness *involved*, so to speak, in living, in the moral respiration of desire and gratification, pursuit and attainment, affection and response, which we cannot live for a day without; so that we need not go out of our way to say with regret (except it be in the point of view of curiosity), there is this or that distinct pleasure which I have gone through life without tasting. We have not enough enjoying power to taste every possible pleasure, and the pleasures involved in life are the most fundamental and the best.

It is because of happiness having its groundwork thus in the individual life or mind, that it so thoroughly flies all description, and that we do not, in enumerating particular pleasures, even approach towards a description of it. And it is for the same reason that the experience of one person and another about it cannot be really compared. To a being capable of reading human hearts the world must present a curious picture of people mutually pitying each other, each thinking the other unhappy, and of people mutually envying each other, each thinking the other happy. Even the comparative amount of enjoyment, to different individuals, of the distinctly separable pleasures, cannot be estimated: no man can tell whether different individuals derive the same pleasure from intoxication; no man can tell whether the rich man's champagne gives to him the same pleasure that the poor man's beer gives to him, or whether it gives him a greater pleasure in proportion to the superiority of the liquor: so utterly empty is all the talk about measuring the intensity of pleasures.

Conditions of happiness, internal and external.

The first condition of happiness is then, if I may so speak, to have good faculties for it and, to the best of our power, to keep or make them such. These faculties are in fact the ordinary faculties of inward or moral life in their subjective or conscious aspect: and to have them good in the point of view of happiness is to have them what they should be in themselves, and then to take the pleasure which springs from the exercise of them as it comes. This is that great principle of happiness,—that it is not anything which can be gained by seeking it, that it is not what will bear being looked at in the face. Secondary to this groundwork of happiness (the happiness of well-feeling, of life, of enjoyed and fruitful thought, emotion, and action), is such happiness as may arise from distinct and exhibitable pleasures: and then, as a pre-condition, more or less, for the substantial happiness, though in no respect constituting it, are necessary what I have called the materials of it.

Examination of maxims about happiness:

The common maxims about happiness belong for the most part to the region of what I will venture to call *amphilogy:* that is, they are true, but an opposite statement might be made with equal truth: their truth is partial, and implies such conditions and such an understanding of the terms as does not exclude the opposite statement.

that happiness consists in contentment.

Of this kind is the saying, that happiness consists in contentment.

Relation of this maxim to Stoic and Epicurean views.

This, as we should mean it now, is not exactly either a Stoic or an Epicurean view, but a sort of dilution of either of them, or balance of the two, to suit the common run of the world: it is what they have come to in the currency of ordinary life. With the Stoic the maxim would only be properly true on the supposition of contentment meaning, as it etymologically does, active self-restraint, amounting possibly even to self-denial. With the Epicurean it would not be properly true, because he says that life is to be continually, though not an anxious, yet a real, search after pleasure. Our present meaning for the maxim, viz. 'You have so much material for happiness, be satisfied with that and make yourself happy with it,' would suit neither. The Stoic would say, Do not be resting in and thinking of that: the Epicurean would say, Get more. Nor is human nature, in practice, more satisfied with it than they. There seems to be no alternative between not thinking of happiness, and trying to get more. No man will be content, if he begins thinking whether he is happy or not. Contentment is a passive, not an active, resting in our lot.

Whatever may be natural to man, contentment is not. *Acturience* or desire of action, in one form or another, whether as restlessness, ennui, dissatisfaction, or the imagination of something desirable, is quite as much a fact of human nature as any kind of want or need. Were all appetites and desires satisfied, this would remain. Man wants an object for his activity quite as much as he wants his activity for the support of his life.

It is not in accordance with either Christianity or Political Economy.

'Having food and raiment, let us therewith be content': but neither the Apostle nor the political economist recommend content simply; for it is dissatisfaction and not satisfaction, which is the parent of all idealism, energy, and progress. The political economist has to urge men not to be content short of food and raiment, and that good and substantial, and even not to be content with these: it is the business of the pioneers of commerce to make men feel new wants, that is, to put an end to their contentment: content is stagnation. The Apostle bids people be content with food and raiment, not in order that, having provided these, they may rest and be idle, but because he has worthier work to set before them than the labouring to supply themselves with more of food and raiment, and things like these. It is not the being satisfied or content that he praises, but the knowing when we have got enough of the less worthy good things of life in order that we may expend our efforts on the more worthy.

Does not agree with human experience.

The praise which has been given to contentment belongs, I am disposed to think, to a sort of language which does not represent anything very real among men: it is a neutral state, not to any great extent existent, nor particularly desirable to exist. If a man's thoughts are employed about his condition, he either enjoys his circumstances and employment, and this it is which is such a main element of happiness, or else he dislikes it: if, on the contrary, his thoughts are not so employed, this may be either because he is simply stagnant-minded, or because, as in the case of the Apostle above, there is something else which employs them. None of these states of mind, I think, represent the contentment of moralists, which seems to me to belong rather to the sphere of shepherds and hermits than to man as he is. If St Paul had not had something better to do, there would have been no merit in his being satisfied with food and raiment, and certainly no happiness: he would have been happier in providing himself more of them and things like them, whether he wanted them or not, than in idly meditating on his having enough of them.

The converse is true: discontent is unhappiness.

The truth on this subject of contentment and happiness really lies just the inverse way: it may be truly said that *discontent* is of all the feelings which are not bodily pain, the most essential and evident *unhappiness.* By discontent we mean commonly sterile and repining dissatisfaction. This is quite a different thing from active and energetic dissatisfaction. And it is the poison of all happiness; as envy, which it resembles, is the poison of all benevolence. It is the positive or affirmative feeling, and ought to have had the positive term. The colourless contentment which we spoke of, simply means the absence of it, and should have had the negative term. In a general way, where there is absence of discontent, there is more or less enjoyment of condition, the mind is alive one way or the other: and generally where there is enjoyment there is activity, work is being done: discontent is a kind of mental fermentation or turning sour, without result either in the present or the future.

The maxim is at best only one side of the truth.

The old Stoic view was, in substance, If you have sufficient strength of mind you can enjoy anything: and this, though exaggerated, is truer to reality than the notion of neutral contentment. So far as, by saying that happiness is in contentment, we mean that happiness is to a great degree our own work, we are undoubtedly right. According to circumstances, our best happiness will be either in resting satisfied with, and doing what we can to enjoy, what we have and are, or in exerting ourselves to gain more and be different. Or, most commonly, our happiness will be found in being satisfied in some particulars, restless, stirring, energetic, in others. Accordingly, with exactly the same truth with which we say, Happiness is in contentment, in *restraining* desire, we may say, Happiness is in hope, effort, energy, in *encouraging* desire.

The moral philosopher is in fact as much concerned to encourage *desires* and aspirations, as the political economist to encourage *wants.* The helplessness, listlessness, undesiringness, which characterizes the moral being of so many, is exactly analogous to the economical condition of well-satisfied, *unwanting* barbarians. Few people desire anything of themselves: they copy their neighbours, desire something, wealth for instance, simply because everybody else does.

Contentment is opposed, in a manner, to ambition and to covetousness.

Contentment as opposed to ambition: Ambition is a term which we use now to express the desire, on the part of individuals, to rise and to distinguish themselves, and the desire on the part of states, to gain glory and to extend their dominion.

Between what is commonly understood as ambition, in individuals, and contentment, the question, both as to duty and happiness, is mainly one of temperament: some are called one way and some another. But giving a wider meaning to the word ambition, *all* are called to ambition, to aspiration, to effort upwards, to raise themselves higher, to make themselves better: there is no true living, and therefore no real happiness, without it: the contentment which is opposed to this is *ignavia*, sloth.

as opposed to covetousness. Covetousness means with us now rather the indisposition to part with money than the eagerness to gain it. It is in this latter character however, as the πλεονεξία or φιλαργυρία of the New Testament, that it is opposed to contentment. In a commercial country, the quality of mind which makes a man an energetic trader is a kind of ambition, a trader's ambition: and as against contentment, it stands on the same footing as that. There is no principle upon which we can fix any point as the point of reasonable contentment. The same reasons which may make a man, after having made twenty thousand pounds, go on to a hundred, may act to make him go on still further.

Perhaps I may as well here, as anywhere, say a word or two on the relation of patience and of hope to happiness.

The state of our mind in regard of pleasure, and the fact whether we have much or little of what can be distinctly described as pleasure, is of comparatively little consequence as regards our general happiness, this depending far more upon our disposition of mind as to pain, and upon our disposition of mind as to the future.

Patience under suffering contributes to happiness in so far as it implies a principle of faith.

By patience, as we use the word in English, we mean two very distinct things; one, a manner of endurance of present pain; the other, a manner of looking to something expected.

In respect of the former of these, supposing patience to be a bare self-resignation, and impatience a struggle, it is a question which of the two is a better bearing of pain, and so far as either of them can be said to diminish pain, which does so most. The real reason why, in pains of a serious nature, *patience* is the better of the two, is because of the mixture of moral (or religious) elements in it with the bare self-resignation. Both the old Stoic endurance and the Christian patience arise from a principle which may be called faith: and the Stoic notion, that its being hard to be borne by the individual did not make it in itself an evil, is the same principle which, more rightly informed and made to refer to a divine ruling will, becomes Christian patience. It is the union of self-resignation with faith in something, or far better, with faith and love resting in some One deemed better and wiser than ourselves, which makes patience, as compared with struggle, the side of less unhappiness.

Patience as to the future is a

Patience, as a manner of thinking about the future, might more properly be called non-im-

mean between hopefulness and fearfulness.

patience, impatience being rather the affirmative feeling, and patience the negation of it.

Patience in regard of the future is something like contentment in regard of our circumstances, and is of a very doubtful character, either as a virtue or as a part of happiness.

Imagination, applied to the future, generates in us two feelings, sanguineness or hopefulness on the one side; fearfulness on the other, and so far as constitution determines our after happiness, it is a trite matter that our disposition to the former of these is a main constituent of it.

Patience, as a temper for action, like an Aristotelic mean, moderates sanguineness at the same time that it supplies encouragement and constancy to fearfulness or distrustfulness: it is a kind of fly-wheel to energy. Impatience is a sign, according to the temperament, either of ill-regulated sanguineness or of fearfulness and distrust.

The happiness of life depends greatly on the feelings which accompany desire and pursuit.

It is however in the point of view of happiness that I have to do with these feelings now: and the position of the mind, as to pleasure, in its prospective feelings, is a matter of great interest.

Pleasure and pain are in the greater part of life mixed together in a manner such that we cannot separate them. One genus of pleasure is, as I have described, gratification or the satisfaction of desire: as in contrast with this satisfaction, the desire is pain: but the desire and pursuit is a development of life in us, an exercise of a faculty: as such, it involves the concomitant pleasure of such life and action, the well-feeling as I have called it, and this may be so great, that the desire and pursuit may be, in its way, as pleasurable as the gratification.

The great mass of life is desire and pursuit, for gratification is from the nature of it short-lived as ompared with that: and hence the happiness of life, n one or another, to a large degree depends upon he proportions in which, according to the constitu-ion, desire and pursuit are painful or pleasurable.

The intermixture of fear with hope adds interest to life.

Speaking generally, a hopeful or sanguine tem-erament is in this point of view the life of life; but his is only speaking quite generally, for when we ome to particulars, much presents itself besides. Where there is hopefulness, there is a half-enjoy-nent, by anticipative imagination, all along the ursuit; but, if the mixture of fearfulness tempers his half-enjoyment, it adds to it certain elements, which must be called pleasure, though of a different ind. The life of each one of us, which, while we ead with interest the depicturement of the lives f others, seems prosaic to us because it is ours, ust as the present seems prosaic because it is not he past, is an epic of continually varied interest s to the feelings which it involves; and a course of niform hopefulness would not be the most interest-ng, nor all things considered, I think, the most appy.

Cause of the happiness of childhood.

Childhood and youth are the time of most hope-ulness, and are probably in the mass of men the appiest time, and this because of the prevalence of uch hopefulness: but we are hardly able to say for ertain that they are the happiest, for it is as ifficult to compare, as to pleasure, the experience f one time of life with another, as it is to compare, s to pleasure, the experience of one man with that f another: and supposing they are so, we can hardly ll whether this does not arise from the unnecessary egree in which our imagination, and consequently e vividness of our moral perceptions, stagnates as e become older. 'When I became a man, I put way childish things:' so I suppose it must be with us: but there are some childish things which I think we might keep with us always, at least more than we do.

Maxim that happiness consists in distraction.

The saying that happiness is in *distraction* is not more true than the saying which we have been considering, that it is in contentment. Neither of them do justice to human life.

The latter saying gives the idea that life is so unhappy and so dreadful that it will not bear to be looked at; that we can only be happy when our attention is in some way diverted from it; that, left to our own selves and our own thoughts, we must be unhappy; that happiness is in amusement, labour being one form of such amusement.

This very likely represents the state of mind of a good many, and it has a side of truth in application to all; but it seems to me that the truth which it involves is very limited, and that the state of mind which it represents is one which our happiness rather consists in avoiding. There is a pleasure in distraction, dissipation, amusement of mind; but there is a higher and worthier happiness, where it can be had, in self-collectedness. There is pleasure, of course, of the highest kind, in employment, as distinguished from vacancy of mind: but it is not dealing fairly with this employment of mind to describe it as distraction, and set its value in that character of it. The fact is that the nature of the mind is to be active, and that it is unhappy if it is not active; but its activity is for a purpose, and part of the pleasure is in the fact that it is so. It is not merely pass-time or killing of time.

Pleasure is incompatible alike with perfect conscious-

The relation of *consciousness* to pleasure is one of the most difficult of psychological problems. Without consciousness, we can hardly be said to enjoy: but no enjoyment will stand full consciousness or direct attention to it. Entire unconsciousness is, so far as feeling is concerned, non-existence: in full consciousness the intellect is in operation to such a degree as to spoil or vitiate the pleasure. Pleasure, unattended to, passes by us: if it is attended to, we find ourselves examining and analysing instead of enjoying. The greatest and most important pleasures cannot be fixed or attended to: they are, as I have several times expressed it, *involved*, they are un-analysable constituents of a general state of temporary happiness.

ness and perfect unconsciousness.

The pleasure of success or attainment, gratification of a desire, as I have called it, is one that can hardly be attended to: we cannot say what it is. It is, I think, from this that arises the complaint which is so frequent in men's minds of the disappointing character of all earthly success, while nevertheless it is perfectly plain that they do and have enjoyed it. They ask themselves every now and then what their enjoyment has consisted in, and they cannot tell: yet it has existed. The gratification is passed by, they say, in a moment, then they go to some other pursuit: but in spite of the complaint of disappointment, they know they would not do otherwise were the thing to do again, and they feel the gratification was worth the pursuit.

Consciousness, in its application to pleasure, is of various kinds: perhaps the principal distinction about it is, that sometimes it is rather attention to the particular pleasure, sometimes it is rather general self-collectedness, tasting the pleasurable state, with mental comparison of other states. One question of hedonics is as to the concurrence of pleasures, similar to the painter's question of the relation of colours: what pleasures heighten, what kill, neighbour or concurrent pleasures. But every question of hedonics is at the same time a question of the relation of individual natures to pleasure, or of individual dispositions in regard of pleasure. What is true for one man is not true for another.

Close connexion between pleasure and pain.

The consideration of the relation of consciousness to pleasure brings strongly before us the fact, how near all pleasure is to pain. It is this which has made people so strongly inclined to put pleasure in distraction, or in that strong form of distraction, which is called transport, amounting to entire self-forgetfulness. Yet this transport also has its evident side of pain; it is minor insania: the 'mens sana,' though it may allow itself 'desipere in loco,' is before all things self-collectedness. But self-collectedness is what not all pleasures, perhaps not any, can thoroughly bear. Wherever we put our pleasure, the casting on it the full light of attention throws out its shadow of pain: everything in our inward experience is mixed.

The pleasures of the imagination and affections are constantly mixed with pain.

Not only have the lower and more manifest pleasures their twang of pain, but in regard of the higher and more refined pleasures it is constantly impossible to distinguish pleasure from pain. And yet that in regard to which we cannot make this distinction is nothing neutral, it is eminently pleasure or pain, and felt as one or the other, though sometimes we cannot tell which. This is a good deal the case with the emotions of desire, hope, pursuit: but it is most markedly the case in all pleasures concerned with the affections. The γλυκύπικρον, the δακρυόεν γελάσασα, the joy in grief—this mixture runs throughout the affections, and in fact belongs more or less to most pleasure which is worth having: there are pleasures, so to speak, whose intensity is in their nature, not in the degree of them, and this intensity is what we may feel as a pain. Farther than this, the character of mixed or undistinguishable pain and pleasure belongs to every thing connected with the imagination: the thought of the past or the distant, with which affection is associated, is constantly, I should think, such, that whether it is pleasure or pain cannot be said, and that for the very intensity of the sensation.

Pleasures of malevolence.

What is the character, in this view, of the antipathetic feelings like revengefulness? Moralists tell us not unfrequently that all such feelings are in their nature painful, and the sympathetic pleasurable. But in this they are clearly doing what in moral science is very difficult to avoid, *i.e.* letting a view of what *should be* anticipate in their minds the observation of what *is*. Even with regard to the feelings of this kind which seem least of all to have the character of pleasure, such as envy, we talk, and with full meaning, of *indulging* them, implying of course that there is pleasure taken in them: and how shall one of us judge of this pleasure in another, and prove that the pleasure of conquering the feeling, and feeling kindly, would be greater?

The habit of benevolence cannot be securely built on the desire to obtain pleasure from it.

We cannot then say with justice to any one, straightforwardly, Cultivate the benevolent and subdue the malevolent feelings, for that is the way to enjoy in yourself mental pleasure. If he should say to us, 'I know that with me the indulging in the feelings which you call malevolent, if there is occasion for them, *i.e.* if circumstances arouse them and seem to me to justify them, will be a pleasure,' we have nothing to answer. But we may say, Cultivate the benevolent and subdue the malevolent feelings, for that is the right thing for you to do and, being right, it is what will give you pleasure: and saying this, we are on surer ground. This does not mean that the doing the thing *as right* is the only source of the pleasure, benevolence being supposed not more such a source than malevolence: benevolence *is* such a source of pleasure, while malevolence is not; and it is so, because it is the right thing for us to do, quite independently of whether we think of it as right or not: but benevolence is not genuine benevolence if it is done with an *arrière pensée* or ulterior view of causing happiness to ourselves. And thus, if one should say to us, 'I feel no preference, as between benevolence and malevolence, for the one over the other, but will do whichever of the two will cause me most pleasure: tell me which it shall be,' we can hardly perhaps be certain that, in this view, benevolence is what will cause most pleasure: in fact, an action so done would not really be benevolence. We should have to say to him, Certainly benevolence is what you should choose, but do choose it, if you can, because it is benevolence, or else because it is right; either *i.e.* because it will give so much pleasure and do so much good to *others* (forgetting yourself), or because it is the course of action belonging to you, intended for you, dictated by your nature, expected from you by other intelligent beings (all which are forms or circumstances of the idea of rightness): and that it will be for your happiness you may conclude. No doubt we might say to him also (and it would probably be the best thing we could), Enter upon a course of benevolence any how, with whatever motive, and it will soon commend itself to you for itself, and chase away the *arrière pensée* or selfishness with which you first entered upon it.

Philanthropy can only grow out of selfishness by virtue

This latter, with many moralists, is the entire course of morality, which consists in their view in the transmutation of selfishness (by society and education) into benevolence, the birth from selfish feeling and selfish purpose of an unexpected progeny, philanthropy or virtue. That this process is a fact, there is no doubt; but it is an involved and continuous fact, a part only of what belongs to morality, in no respect the explanation or the sum of it. We may allow human goodness to be transmuted selfishness, if we take account of a transmuting principle: but selfishness has in itself no such self-transmuting or self-elevating power, no germ of such a noble growth. The setting before ourselves our own happiness is not only (as we have seen) a mistake in fact, on account of its not being realizable by us sufficiently to allow of being so exhibited; but besides this, so far as it exists, it vitiates the character of the conduct done for the purpose of it, and prevents it from being what it professes to be. It imparts a character of sordidness to the desire of doing right, and of non-benevolence to benevolence. How shall the stream rise above its source? Morally indeed, as we have seen, it often does so rise, but by a power not belonging to it: and it is the power which does raise it which is the principle of morality, not the selfishness so transmuted. It is a part of the fact that all things belong to all and are fitted to each other; or, if we speak in religious language, it is a merciful provision of the Author of our nature, that benevolence is in this way often developed from selfishness. When moralists use this fact to prove from it that selfishness is a sort of moral principle, they are themselves forgetting, and teaching others to forget, that it is only as selfishness vanishes that morality supervenes; and that, the selfishness not vanishing, the dispositions built upon it remain in their first state of non-genuineness. The world they picture is a world with no free impulse and no absorbing purpose, but all, feeling

of some other transmuting principle.

and action alike, overmastered by self-interest: the world of satirists, not of life.

Malevolence is a perverted feeling of justice giving rise to a morbid pleasure.

The bad passions are often more absorbing, and in this way may conceivably be vehicles of more intense pleasure (if pleasure it is to be called) than the good. They are proofs that, as goodness in human nature (in the manner which we have just seen) is not merely modified self-interestedness, so neither is badness; self-interestedness being, as against this, a good principle, and tempering it, as it vitiates goodness. Badness is, not mistaken, but perverted goodness: so far as we can see, hatred never exists without some reason (mistaken or otherwise) for it; but it may overrun and leave behind its first reason or occasion, and become a feeling as unmixed, on the side of malevolence, as there may exist unmixed feeling on the good side. No doubt feeling of this kind is to be considered morally morbid. Not unfrequently it comes near what we should consider insanity[1]. But the fact that bad-

[1] The consideration of wrong feeling as a moral disease is one which more especially belongs to religion, as it is religion which provides the remedy for it. But observing it as a simple matter of fact, we shall find many striking resemblances between different forms of bad feeling and actual mental disease. Such are the absorbing and almost irresistible force of several malignant passions, which may be described as a real madness, and that not by any means of only a short duration: still more the very marked resemblance between the obscure smouldering feelings which are the root of pure malignancy, such as jealousy and envy, on the one side, and on the other that diseased consciousness which leads the insane to think everyone is looking at them, and to suspect everyone of hostility towards them: similarly the manner in which self-interested dread of the future tends, with the weakening of the mind, to become actual disease, inducing sometimes, in advancing years, a dread of poverty even in the richest: these with many other like considerations tend to show the near alliance between moral badness and mental disease. No doubt something of the same kind may be observed in some forms of mistaken goodness: feelings akin to conscientiousness are capable of a morbid excitement; but on the whole the 'mens sana' is goodness. There are various feelings which might be roused in us by the thought of this resemblance of viciousness to

ness is perhaps a fearful disease of moral intelligence, does not alter the fact of its reality. It may, if we talk of demerit and responsibility in such extreme cases, alter our opinion as to *that*: but still badness is not miscalculating, it is *misbeing*. And the pleasure which it gives will be perverted accordingly. Springing from diseased feeling it will itself be wild and inconsistent, in ways which no sober analysis can follow. "Evil, be thou my good." The reason probably why attempts like that of Milton's to exhibit perfect badness have usually failed, is that there has been generally an attempt to show with the badness too much of consistency, reason, wisdom. These however belong to goodness only.

Maxim that happiness consists in the simpler pleasures.

Happiness has been described as consisting, the main part of it, in the pleasures which are simpler and nearer at hand to all, rather than in those which are more recondite and greater.

Most lives must find their happiness in small pleasures.

This statement is partly open to the objection which was spoken of before as to the impossibility of comparing pleasures together. Whether a man who has had one great pleasure in life but a great many small troubles is to be considered to have had a happier life than a man who has had few troubles but no great pleasure, is a question as indeterminable as that raised by Solon and Aristotle, whether a man can be called happy before he is dead. Still, as great pleasures must of course be excep-

insanity. We must of course take care that the association of the two does not lead us to judge harshly of the latter, but rather to pity the former. At the same time our pity must not degenerate into indulgence or excuse, as though moral responsibility were done away with. The absence of self-mastery which shows itself in the early stages of vicious passion must be met by every existing means of influence and deterrence, and all the more from our knowledge of the impending danger both to society and to the individual himself of entire subjugation and possession.

tional, a happy life must on the whole be made up of small and simple pleasures. And there is a further and more important truth in the statement, one however which opens a rather difficult question.

Ambiguity of the maxim.

The word 'simple' is very vague, and the putting happiness in simple pleasures may either mean a lively appreciation of the coarser common pleasures, as of eating and drinking, or a sensitive and imaginative openness of the mind to such pleasure as may be drawn at each moment from the circumstances around.

The enjoyment of common pleasures is not increased by luxury.

I do not know that it is much worth while to consider about the former of these. These coarser pleasures are eminently natural, and insensibility to them, except on account of the mind being occupied by something better, is no more a merit than, except for the same reason, contentment or undesiringness is. But, for the very reason that they are thus natural, the pleasingness of them is probably very little increased by any attempts at refining and artificializing them. It is not really possible to compare experiences of pleasure; but it is probable, I think, that luxury in the pleasures of the table makes no addition to the actual amount of pleasure enjoyed, but merely dresses this up in a manner supposed to be accordant with wealth, civilization, and refinement. If we say then that happiness is in the simpler pleasures, meaning by the simpler the coarser, there is this truth in it, that for the rich man to enjoy his dinner, he must be able to enjoy it as the poor man does *his*, and that the poor man has in his simple dinner all the important part of the pleasures which the rich has in his luxurious one, if he is wise enough rather to enjoy that, than to envy the other.

Luxury

Luxury is a word of vague meaning in English,

and sometimes means mere self-indulgence. In its ordinary meaning however, in which it unites together the two notions of mere enjoyment and of superfluity, it seems to me that it is in the main something which comes upon a state of high civilization of itself, as it were, and more from human helplessness than of human intention. Advanced economical civilization should go on to what I will call refinement: the superfluity of production and enjoyment, which there is upon the whole, should flower into the higher pleasures of literature and art, of taste and beauty, not merely as something to be admired and talked about, but as something entering into the thoughts and lives of men.

naturally grows up where wealth exists without refinement.

Luxury, as I understand it, seems to me something which comes in the default of these. Nobody particularly wants it or cares much for it: but for the refinement of which I have spoken there are needed much effort and power of mind, which do not exist, and in the mean time money has to be spent, labour to be employed, enjoyment to be had: and so fashion fixes itself upon fine furniture, magnificent dresses, rich tables: these become necessities of a certain rank: they are the same kind of thing as badges or uniforms; there is no reason they should not exist, except that there might be something better: failing that, they are in a manner right: the wrong of them is, that a good deal of them represents labour which produces no enjoyment (for nobody looks at the fine chairs or tables, though they would look if they were not there); but then the question is, what labour, at that economical stage, *would* produce enjoyment: on that I will not enter now.

The literature of luxury is rather considerable, and how little reality of pleasure (I mean of addi-

Unreality and affectation in

the literature of luxury.

tional pleasure for the luxury) there is underlying the luxury, may be judged in some measure from the observation, in how small a degree the luxury of one time suits another. About luxury, it is very hard to get hold in any way of the real feeling, on account of the affectation and falsehood of thought which constantly appear on both sides in the treatment of it. The literature of luxury, say of *gourmandise*, descants upon enjoyments which, it is evident from a moment's consideration, cannot be real, but must be talk alone: it is quite evident that, while what is wanted for enjoyment is the increase of sensitiveness (appetite, but not in too strong a degree, being supposed), the senseless adding together and crowding stimulant on stimulant must entirely destroy any real sensitiveness; and yet, under these circumstances, the most delicate discrimination is talked of—talked of, that is, in one age to be laughed at in another, as the dinner of Nasidienus would be no luxury to us, and the endlessly varying tastes of different fish in Athenaeus we should not care for. This affectation on the side of luxury is met generally in literature by a corresponding affectation on the other side. There is an essential unreality in both the tones which appear commonly in literature in antagonism with it, which I may call the idyllic and the satirical, in spite of the charm attaching to the former: and people feeling this unreality on the other side are disposed to attribute more reality than they should to the pleasure of luxury. There is a feeble, self-apologetic, tone in the idyllism and a condemnatory tone in the satire, neither of which are warranted. But it is a pity, while the regions of art and possible civilization are unvisited and unexplored to the extent to which they still are, that refinement and thought should be appropriated to subjects unworthy of them, and in which they can only appear under circumstances of what I have called falsehood and affectation: luxury in itself may be considered simply an incident of high civilization, but we cannot but grieve when it takes possession of literature.

It is an element then, generally, of happiness, because it is a natural part of life, to preserve a simple, I will not say coarse, but unluxurious disposition: and this is one point which makes the happiness of the rich and the poor in substance the same.

Is increase of refined sensibility increase of happiness?

If however by simple pleasures we mean pleasures derived from sources at all times at every body's command, it is evident that what is here wanted is the mind and the sensibility. And here the question arises, Is it best that our sensitiveness to enjoyment in general should be keen, or not so? Because of course sensitiveness to pleasure is sensitiveness to pain: refining our nature in any way adds pains to our life, as well as pleasures.

There is no more practical question than this, both as to our own lives, as to education, and as to our estimate of the different conditions of men. We may be sometimes inclined to think that there is no reason why our whole life, with the exception of that, unhappily perhaps, large portion of it which is a season of actual pain, should not be pleasurable; for, saving quite exceptional positions, there is always something which may set in action our imagination or our affections. But then, can we have the imagination and the affections thus alive, without introducing into life as much pain as pleasure, or more? Could we have the labourer alive to the beauty of the sunshine and the scene in which he works, and have him at the same time contented with his wretched cottage, and willing, if necessary, to work in a coal-pit? To put the thing coarsely, can we do without coarseness? Is a life of imaginative sensitiveness or a life with a good deal of roughish insensibility, not to say the more useful—which we are not speaking of now,—but the happier?

It is good as heightening the feeling of life; and joined to the affections is the natural supplement of active life.

For happiness, it seems to me that, beyond that substance of it which concerns life as action, it is of great importance to multiply susceptibilities of pleasure, and that, in spite of the corresponding increase of susceptibility to pain: a man has so much more of *life* as well as of pleasure.

It will be said that cultivated sensibilities and the pleasure arising from them belong to leisure: but in this sense, there is a vast amount of leisure with almost all men and in all classes; that is, there is a very large amount of mere inanity and vacancy. The conscious, uninvolved, happiness of life very much depends upon the fillings up of it. It is here that comes in the obnoxious ἡδονή, voluptuousness, the indulgence of the coarser and lower sensibilities: the higher sensibilities, as of art and literature, are what, it would appear, should work against them, and they much need to do so in all classes. They are also most naturally associated with that other natural filling up of life, the indulgence of the affections.

The recommendation of simple pleasures for happiness, if by this is understood the cultivation of the sensibilities, is in fact recommending cultivation of mind, and quiet pleasures connected with it, as against pleasures of excitement and transport. There is fallacy sometimes about this, and the latter are supposed to have a more manly and active character, while the former are despised. But in this, there is not a true taste for pleasure. There is intellectual mistake or delusion; of which, in regard to pleasure, there is abundance.

The question which was raised before, as to the relation of pleasure to consciousness, will come in also in reference to these simple pleasures. Supposing a man shut up suddenly in solitary confinement, it is doubtful whether he will say to himself, How happy I was when I was free, or whether he will say, What a fool I was not to enjoy the air and society more while I had them: and whichever he said, the meaning would probably be in substance the same, and he would not mean to represent his past feeling as different in the two cases.

"O fortunatos nimium!"
"O knew he but his happiness!"

Difficulty of pronouncing in any particular case whether such pleasures are enjoyed.

Can a man be happy without knowing himself so? Does his knowing himself so and meditating on his happiness, increase his happiness? Or does it spoil it? These are questions which cannot be answered, because, as I have said, we cannot, except in comparatively unimportant cases, look happiness or pleasure in the face.

Freshness of feeling is an undoubted element in happiness.

But though we cannot, in regard of any person, tell whether he really derives pleasure from the sources which are open to all, except to those in pain; because, for all that we know, he *may*, though he gives no sign of it or perhaps, by grumbling, gives sign of the contrary: yet it is important for ourselves to be aware, that in regard of the current pleasure of life, it is here that it is to be got. It has always been a famous rule of morals 'Live this day as if thy last.' It has been given also as a rule of happiness[1]: in which character it is perhaps more questionable. The feeling of the last day in any

[1] Hor. *Epist.* I. 4. 13.

place we are attached to has peculiar elements of sensitiveness, attention, consciousness, tenderness, but is hardly on the whole one of happiness. The real point of happiness is in the 'Grata superveniet quae non sperabitur hora.' The having looked upon yesterday as a last day makes to-day to be looked upon as a first one—as a new beginning of existence. If we really did look upon life each day with fresh eyes, no doubt the sensitiveness, and therefore the pleasure in the look, would be increased tenfold. This would be the real fountain of youth, supposing, of course, there were energy to maintain the perpetual aliveness. As it is, the ordinary sources of enjoyment which I have spoken of only *mark* themselves as sources of enjoyment when circumstances give them novelty and distinct relief. And it is hence that arises the universal fallacy in our judging of the condition of others. We only perceive distinctions. We are fatigued with something which, whether we like it or not, we at least think we have too much of, and whatever we make our escape to, whatever is *different* from this, seems as if it must be all happiness. Hence townsmen's praises of the country and countrymen's of the town. Hence too it is impossible for us to form a single idea of life in the point of view of happiness. Man, as he is known to us, if he were not sometimes unhappy, could never be happy in the sense of *testing* happiness. Supposing, the best we can suppose, life to be a sort of alternation of pleasures setting off each other, as lively pursuit followed by rest or gratification, and so forth; there must be a character of pain in the pursuit to give the necessary alternation to the gratification: this is part of the universal mixture of pleasure and pain, which I have spoken of.

The chief sources of pleasure are open to all.

However, for ourselves, what is needed is to be aware that there are always sources of pleasure at hand, in the main the same for the rich as the poor: and in this consists such truth as there is in the statement which is often made with a good deal of hard-heartedness, that all conditions are alike for happiness. I have observed before, what a ridiculous prospect people's mutual envies must present to any being who could read the hearts of all. The poor man envies the rich, and no doubt with some reason, if we could suppose envy to be right at all. He envies him because of his rich rooms and furniture and his luxurious dinner, whereas it is exceedingly likely that the rich man derives less pleasure from these than he does from a walk in the sunshine, which the poor man might enjoy as well as he; and that he finds his main happiness in some reading, or study, or pursuit, which, by the poor man would be felt to be more irksome than his own most laborious toil.

Maxim, that we should not expect much of life.

One direction which has been given for happiness is that we should not raise our expectations high: and similar in some measure to this is the direction that we should pitch the scale of our living and our enjoyments low; because then any change will be for the better.

It is true that we are not so much to expect, as to accept happiness.

Directions of this kind represent different manners of thought. Sometimes they represent that mild view of things, recommended, but not expected to produce much effect, to which belong also the notions of happiness being in contentment and distraction. Or else they perhaps represent what I will for a moment call Stoico-Epicureanism, I mean Epicureanism developing into a kind of semi-Stoical self-discipline and moderation, which probably *was* rather the character of the early Epicureanism. The view is partly true, partly false, and partly true for some but not for others.

Its truth lies in its being in some respects an exhibition of the undoubted fact, that happiness is not to be sought for, but to be taken. If we are to have it at all, which only very partially depends upon ourselves, it will come to us as we *live:* and by *living* I mean doing our duty in the state to which it shall please God to call us, trying to do what we should do and be what we should be, trying to do our part, large or small, towards advancing the progress of our kind towards its ideal, helping those who are worse off, as to the materials of happiness, than we are, trying to have a clear inward sight and a just and true social feeling. The ground-work or stock of happiness is something which will come of itself so far as we are able thus to live: for the branches or fillings up, our course is, as we can, to cultivate our sensibilities, to increase our interests, or as we frequently speak, our resources. And the absence of thought about happiness, or in this meaning, of expectations of it, is a cardinal rule. Otherwise, whatever our lot in life, we can hardly but be disappointed, and with a self-made disappointment: we are preparing ourselves to be pleased with nothing that comes to us.

But the more we expect of life, independently of thoughts of our own happiness, the better.

But the view is false in so far as it bids us moderate, not only expectations of happiness, because happiness is a thing which we must not thus look at, but expectation in itself. Instead of our saying, Do not expect too much from life, what we should rather say is, Expect what you like and all that you possibly can from it, only do not let your first thought be about your own happiness. It seems very strange that it should ever have been thought happiness would be increased by the damping the great spring of it, hopefulness. Rather say, Expect and still expect: do not be afraid of disappointment. I have taken, as has been seen, as the starting point for happiness the feeling which we see most in youth, that well-feeling which is independent of special pleasures, which is the feeling of *life*, prompting action and pursuit, and accompanied by continually renewed gratification. Of course the energy of youth cannot last: but so far as the substance of that feeling can last, so far there is the substance of happiness: the living so much in an anticipated future is not a weakness to be discarded as we get wiser: it is the proper mental condition of active beings, for all action has regard to the future.

The spur is more needed than the curb.

The view that we should not expect much from life is true for some and not for others, in accordance with the great variety of constitution among men as to their anticipations of the future. There is no harm, as I have just said, even in the utmost amount of hopefulness and imagination: unhopefulness is far less reasonable than any hopefulness; only that, for sober and fruitful action, we want reasonable views. Upon the whole, I think that, for useful action and resulting happiness, the spur is more needed than the curb: the hopefulness, and even capricious arrogance and self-conceit, of youth, is constantly mixed with an unsteadiness and lurking self-distrustfulness which causes the want to be rather of animating and encouraging than of cooling and checking. For some, I am inclined to think for the larger number, the direction for happiness should rather be, Increase your expectations: you will not be really disappointed.

Maxim, to pitch happiness low:

The direction to pitch happiness low, or in other words, not to strain or stretch our resources for it, to leave untouched some things which we possibly might enjoy, to allow room for increase of happiness and addition to it—all these seem to me to be particularizations of the general notion, not to be anxious about it.

If the advice implies any definite rule or theory of life, it is that Stoico-Epicureanism which I spoke of, and it is not easy to draw the limit between this and a sort of moderate asceticism. The not being as happy as we might be, in order that we may really be the happier, is in fact asceticism; though the ascetic might express the purpose differently, as that we should refrain from happiness in order that we may be doing what we should do (however expressed) one result of which will be our being really the happier.

is unmeaning except with a reference to religion.

But in reality, it is impossible properly to speak about this sort of self-denial, which consists in pitching our happiness low, and limiting our expectations as to happiness, without thinking of religion, for it is only in reference to *that* that maxims of this kind can have their full meaning.

Except in view of religion, pitching our happiness low is a kind of trifling with happiness.

APPENDIX ON THE UNHAPPINESS OF HUMAN NATURE[1].

WHEREVER happiness has been made an end, self-discipline and self-control have had to be inculcated, not simply for the purpose of gaining it, but even for the possibility of enjoying it: so that the so-called Epicurean life has often been not far different from the Stoic. Self-discipline and self-control for whatever purpose are good: but how does it answer to facts to consider that in human life they are, or should be, subordinated to the idea of pleasure or happiness? Man's natural view of happiness is of something, not necessarily contrary to, but still independent of, self-control; something which is the better, and the more worthy of the name of happiness, in proportion as it is freer and more spontaneous. And similarly man's natural view of self-discipline and self-control is that, if he is to employ them, which he is perhaps very ready to do, he would rather it was for something different from, and better than, his own happiness. Man's natural view as to life is that there is something to be done in it (whatever it may be) which requires self-control, and of which the result, he hopes, may be his happiness. This is a very different thing from the supposition that his life's task is to be the making himself happy, and that his duty is self-control as the means for this.

Self-discipline is needed for happiness, but human nature grudges it for such an end.

The fact that man is ever unsatisfied in happiness, that he 'never is, but always to be blest,' has been often dwelt upon for the purpose of making it appear that life is not so desirable a thing as some would suppose. This however is in some respects more than the fact bears out. What is made out in this way is, not that happiness is what cannot, or is not likely to exist, but that it can not be fixed by the

Man is never satisfied with happiness.

[1] This and the following Appendix are taken from the MS. marked Series 3. ED.

mind or contemplated, so as to be made itself a particular object of pursuit or end of life. There is a pleasure in effort and in pursuit, which arises from the fact that man is an active being as well as one conscious of pleasure and pain, from volition being as intimate a part of his personality as sentience; just as, corporeally, he has nerves of motion as well as of sensation. Human nature (but in fact every intelligent nature must be the same, so far as we can distinctly conceive it) is in this respect in a continual contradiction, so to call it, with itself. To the state of effort happiness, as looked at, appears to consist in rest: to the state of rest it appears to consist in the pursuit of something, or in effort: in the mean time in each state much of pleasure is actually being enjoyed, except so far as this dissatisfaction or looking after the opposite state prevents it. The only apparent way for happiness and activity of nature to go together, is for man, while more or less in a state of happiness, to have but imperfect power of realizing that it is so, so that there is always something to prevent his resting in the present.

This restlessness is a sign of the imperfection of his nature.

This restlessness of man's nature has often been dwelt upon as a thing sad and pitiable in it. But why is it so? except so far as it shows man's nature to be imperfect: and who thinks it perfect? That man finds pleasure in labour as well as in rest and satisfaction, which is what makes him restless, is the spring of all his improvement. True, it makes him seem to be always hunting shadows: it leaves him in a sort of continual delusion as to his own life: he imaginatively places happiness in a rest and satisfaction, which seems ever denied him, so that according to his own supposition in this respect he should be always unhappy: but in the mean time it is not so: the happiness for which he looked far off, in the gaining of the end, comes to him quietly and unobserved in the pursuit. There is nothing sad in this, and nothing pitiable, except so far as man may not like being thus, as it were, an infant, carried onward in a delusion which his reason may feel ashamed of. But such shame is only felt imperfection: and the feeling and shame of imperfection is in reality the noblest of feelings, for it is the comparison of self with something higher and better; and what is thus thought of may in time be attained.

Epicurean self-restraint is no easier than Stoic.

I have said that human happiness cannot exist without a great deal of self-discipline and self-restraint, not simply for the attainment, but even in the enjoyment of it. And if this self-discipline is to exist, the same expenditure of it might have enabled the mind to be happy under almost any circumstances. Partial self-denial in anything is constantly quite as great an effort as total. There are many circumstances under which the absence of a thing from the thoughts is more for pleasure than the restrained enjoyment of it. Stoic or ascetic self-abnegation is often, as a matter of fact, less painful than Epicurean self-control.

There is a better chance of happiness in adapting ourselves to circumstances, than in changing circumstances to our fancy.

Human nature is capable of such various training, that a man may accustom himself to take pleasure almost in anything. And if he is distinctly to work for his own happiness, it is in this way he will have the most result. Otherwise he has to take the idea of what is for happiness from the opinions of others, and then, when the end is gained, he finds it is no happiness for him. It is not what he can give himself up to: he has not come to a stage of rest: the enjoying and maintaining of it is productive of as much trouble as the first acquisition. After all the pains he has taken, he finds he has still to adapt himself to the supposed happiness. But if he had begun this process before, the same amount of trouble would have enabled him to adapt himself to, and to find happiness in, many other states, involving no such trouble and pain in the acquisition.

Complaints of human misery may proceed either from a querulous disposition: Or from a high ideal of human nature, and a sense of the distance between this and man's actual state.

A complaint has been made from two different quarters as to the unhappiness of human nature.

There is first the voice of querulousness nearly allied to satire and misanthropy and mingled probably with bitterness. Whatever may be said about man's lot on the whole, there is no doubt it is one in which the average amount of endurance has to be considerable. Even to face the fair chances of life requires nerving up the energies: that man is doomed to eat his bread in the sweat of his brow may suffice to provoke the murmurings of weakness.

But the same complaint is echoed by a nobler voice, and in a tone which is not out of harmony with the utterances of religion in such passages as the following:

'Man that is born of a woman hath but a short time to live and is full of misery.'

'The whole creation groaneth and travaileth together in pain until now. And not only they, but we ourselves also, which have the firstfruits of the Spirit, even we ourselves groan within ourselves, waiting for the adoption, to wit, the redemption of our body.'

This is the voice of men who can not only feel the vast amount of the misery which there is, but are able also to picture to themselves a higher and better state, the attainment of which is the object of their keenest longings.

Man's degradation in various ways, the meanness of so many of his occupations and enjoyments, his vice, ill-will and selfishness, press upon such minds more heavily than their own physical privations upon lower natures. Such minds are likely also not only to see through, but to feel a strong revulsion against, much well meant but superficial attempt to describe the world as happy, and determination to see nothing in God, as the governor of it, but a sort of easy and shallow goodness. They will be incapable of being satisfied thus: they will have a complaining within them, not suggested by what they themselves have to bear, not even by what any have to bear (for they can fancy happiness even in enduring), but suggested by something which there appears to be in man's lot contradictory and discordant. Such complaining is in other words a sort of wonder and disappointment that man's reason should be able to do no more to make him happy, and that God should allow so many chances to him of grief and misery.

Religion deepens the sense of human imperfection, but joins with this a confidence in God's loving care.

In some form or other, religion, which has some share in producing the better forms of this state of mind is the only remedy against what is mistaken and wrong in them. What religion aims to produce is a deep feeling of man's wants and imperfection with an equal corresponding feeling of God's friendliness towards men. Those whom we have been mentioning stop short at the former of these: and that partly, as was said, from revulsion at the hasty and superficial manner in which perhaps some, whose minds are little capable of entering into the former, hastily assume and suppose the latter. The latter must be arrived at through the former. It is not merely a good God that is to be supposed, but a God sympathizing with man, and in some way which nothing but revelation can tell us fully about, making man's misery and imperfection the way to something better for him. The too intense and uncorrected feeling of man's misery and imperfection generates what is called *asceticism*, and may very well degenerate into a meaner thing than itself, viz., superstition proper, or the religion which is mainly of fear.

Tendencies to asceticism often betoken a nobler temper than does the disposition to be easily satisfied and thoughtlessly thankful; but they very soon lead wrong, perhaps actually produce another form of degradation of human nature, and in any case distort the view of truth, and estrange man from God, instead of bringing him nearer to Him. It is only when something nobler than they masters them, that they are in their place. The noblest temper of human nature is a real confidence in God, tried by the sight of what the world is, but standing the trial;—confidence in the fact of His goodness, in its persistency, and ultimate triumph, or vindication to mankind and to us. Knowledge of man is enough to tell us, that confidence of this kind is the worthiest bond between those in whom it exists, the most ennobling to the giver, the most delightful to the receiver. Such should be the relation in feeling between man and God. Confidence of this kind, as it arises among men, has its merit and its charm, in its overstepping the point at which, in so many words, it can be justified, and thus venturing beyond actual knowledge in the strength of something which appears to be like a superior kind of knowledge, composed of sympathy, of a generous readiness to risk something, and forget one's own interests, of a going forth of a disposition to love which catches on something answering to it. As felt by man towards God, it involves a higher thankfulness than arises from a mere absence of seeing what there is to sadden us in life. The latter is thankful for man being what he is: the former is thankful not only for this, but for all the promise and hope which there is of man's being something better.

APPENDIX ON THE PROMOTION OF THE HAPPINESS OF OTHERS.

It is a simple rule that we must relieve the wants of others.

So much for notions of our own happiness.

But what is to be said of the happiness of others? Can we not get an idea of *that?* If we cannot, what is benevolence or philanthropy?

We can form a very distinct idea, as to ourselves, of certain materials, or a certain framework which speaking generally is necessary for happiness, though happiness is more than it. This we may call the support or maintenance of life. With some, this is unhappily so difficult for themselves that it is all they can hope for. Happiness with them, is support or life, and is distinct enough in the idea.

The condition of man is such upon earth that there are always many in these circumstances; the support of the race, we may say, is difficult. There is wide scope therefore for philanthropy simply in reference to the support or life of others. If we have no material or corporeal wants for ourselves, requiring our necessary exertion, we have but to raise our eyes, and we see abundance of them around us in others.

Beyond this, it is difficult to know how we are to promote their happiness.

The relieving of the wants of others is thus a notion tolerably distinct. But the making others happy is not so. It is difficult to form the idea of happiness; and *their* idea may very likely be different from *ours.* As soon as we have passed the relieving of want, the distinction of earnest philanthropy from love of power and many other human impulses becomes very difficult. Who shall say what is useful for men, what is for their true happiness? If a man determines from his own feeling and conviction, what is this but claiming a mental dominion over others and assuming himself as superior to them? If he takes theirs against his own, can he believe that he is making them really happy?

while if he takes the feeling which there is common to himself and mankind in general, it is but a vague outline and framework that it will give him.

In respect then of a scheme of happiness on which to found philanthropy we must find out as far as we can what is natural, and for this we must go to physical fact and to history. Nor is it anything but what is very general and widely variable that we can thus gain. We cannot make a scheme of human happiness to act upon. The infliction of such theoretical happiness on others is no real benevolence.

Utility is a mere relative word, and supplies no rule.

The relieving of wants thus remains the main province of philanthropy: it is the *useful*. Usefulness implies, in the idea, a sort of subservience: implies the tone or the purpose coming from without. The *utile*, that which is useful, means what can be used, or what practically serves to effect an end we want. Usefulness is the lending ourselves, so to speak, to the wants of others: and though acting freely and of ourselves, yet having the impulse and suggestion coming from them. It cannot be part of any system, but depends on circumstance.

We cannot lay down a scheme for giving pleasure.

But beyond the relieving of wants, there is the giving pleasure. And what is to be observed about this is, that it, more than all besides, repudiates system and direction. Like everything connected with sympathy it is complicated. The pleasure given is in some respects the greater for the understood intention, and in some respects the less. In the one case the goodwill of the giver is sympathized with by the receiver, in the other the similarity of feeling. On the whole, there is more pleasure given inadvertently, as to the occasion, from general kindness and sympathy of feeling, than there is from special attention and intention.

This latter, unless there is much of mutual understanding is constantly mistaken, and the pleasure which it does give arises only from gratitude for the intention. The helplessness of mere good will is not to be remedied by any scheme or system of what will please others, which we may study and act by. It can only be remedied by the cultivation of sympathy, by habituating ourselves to go out of ourselves so as to be affected by, and interested in, the feelings of others.

We should aim at their real good, but our view of this may be mistaken, or carried out in a wrong spirit.

But again, beyond the giving of pleasure, there is the doing real good. And this can only be according to our idea of what real good is. While therefore we cannot but feel that the relieving of want and the giving of pleasure are of slight importance in comparison with the effecting of this real good, still we must bear in mind that our own view of the way in which such good is to be effected is liable to all the possibilities of mistake which arise from our fallibility, and that it is therefore our duty so to master ourselves as to postpone it in some degree, certainly to the relieving of want, possibly even to the giving of pleasure. There is no doubt but that little of the higher good can be done, as *e.g.* the mind elevated, except more or less *after* the former of them, and *through* the second. If a man, by want of sympathy seems to shew that he has but little care for those whom he is attempting to improve, the conclusion on their part will probably be, that his wish is more connected with a love of power, or a mere desire for action, than with a love of themselves. It is a weakness when desire of pleasing takes place of aim at the real good: but it is a sign of something wrong when it is absent.

Philanthropy then has its first reference to the actual state of man, and its second to the possibility of elevating and improving him. The first tone of our benevolence we must take from wants and things as they are: the second from our idea how we may improve and elevate them.

Indeterminateness of the idea of happiness.

The idea of happiness is thus scarcely to be made more distinct for the race than for the individual; and the idea of usefulness, if it is to be a wide idea, coextensive with happiness, must remain similarly undetermined. It is a strange thing that any should have considered that the idea of utility, thus widely taken, is one upon which men would be agreed, and which could be established on principles of reason which would command the assent of all: and that thus the morality of utility would be something exact, while that of sentiment, conscience, moral sense, would be something vague and arbitrary. If utility means what is conducive to happiness, the one is altogether as vague as the other. Each man's feeling about happiness is at least as individual and arbitrary as his feeling about right and duty. To analyze human sentiment for the purpose of finding out what men consider to be for their happiness is at least as hard as to analyze it in order to find out what they think it right to do. If indeed we limit utility to the things necessary for the support of life, then, no doubt, we shall have more agreement: but in that case we must give up all speaking about happiness; for happiness goes far wider than this.

The real way in which we should speak of human life and of *ευδαιμονία* or happiness in regard of morality, is the following:

The happiness of many is more easily realized than the happiness of one.

We may say that the good of human life is the purpose or end of human action; but we must not interpret this to mean, that the good of his own life is the purpose or end of the action of the individual. Life is lived by men in conjunction: society is a part of human nature. Rational personality makes each individual independent, so far as self-determination and responsibility go; but want and the power of mutual help bind them together: and answering to this objective fact is the subjective fact of sympathy. The general *ευδαιμονία* is in truth a far more realizable idea than that of the individual. The happiness of each one so much depends on others, that it is more easy to imagine a number of individuals making each other and the whole of them happy, than one of them making his particular self so. When therefore we say that human action should be directed to the service of human life, it is this united life which we should mean, and it is to the service of this that, so far as possible, individual action should go: and when we say that happiness should be sought for, we should mean a happiness shared with others.

In common life the happiness of the individual is merged in that of others.

Practically this is the way in which life is lived. Self is a word, as to actual fact, difficult to define and limit. Does it include *family* or not? A good deal of selfishness is what the individual himself neither derives, nor thinks to derive, benefit from: it is for the exaltation *e.g.* of his family by means of labour and endurance on his own part. Selfishness, as it exists, is one of the most imaginative things possible. What the man works for is only associated with his individual being by an imaginative power, which if it took another direction might just as well associate with it almost any other conceivable thing. And so he lives from the first in community, and has in reality no independence in his happiness, which, do what he will, is at the mercy of others. If happiness is to be, it will be by their making him happy and his making them so: this mutuality spreads out, becoming of course fainter and fainter, but so far as it goes, there is what we may call a common life.

Even action aimed at selfish happiness contributes in the main to the happiness of others.

It is human life as thus understood, not human individual life, which should absorb the action of the individual. It will do this more or less consciously. Sometimes all that he can apparently do is to take care of himself: the doing as much as this taxes all his powers. In a civilized community the only way, in general, in which he can do this is by securing a place in the general system of mutual help: he must find something he may do for others in order to get bread for himself. In doing this he is, in the words of the son of Sirach, contributing to maintain the state of the world: but he does this in the main unconsciously, having to think of himself. But supposing a man is not obliged to think so much of his mere support: in that case, what is his superfluous power to go to? Beyond a certain extent, he cannot make it contribute to his own happiness. He may very likely go on working, if we may call it so, for his support upon a larger scale, making a fortune for his family instead of merely providing for them a maintenance: and this with various motives; because it is only a continuance of the process of getting his bread, which he knows is his duty; because others do it; because he must do something; because it increases his importance and that of his family. Whatever may be his motive, what he succeeds in effecting in this course is perhaps gaining happiness for himself and his family; that may be or may not; but anyhow in increasing in one way the materials for happiness of the whole community. It is better to labour for himself, which does them good too, than to cease from labouring. The common life is thus the better for all the self-interested industry and talent which makes the fortune of individuals: the individuals are honourable so far as they have any feeling of the common happiness in what they do, and the public is fortunate so far as self-interest in this manner does not swallow up all the industry and talent. For the common life wants more than what the self-interest of individuals thus exercised will supply it with.

The cultivation of intelligence and mental power in indi-iduals has the same relation to the common life as the ıcrease of individual wealth has. Whatever the motive of , all are the better for it. But in this as in wealth, there every degree of honourableness as to the use which may e made of it. In civilized society there is a vast amount of ealth and power, and a vast amount of want and need over gainst them: and these two sides do not as they should orrespond and fit each other: the happiness of the society is ıeasured by the degree in which they do so. There is on ne side wealth perhaps helplessly possessed and unenjoyed; nd on the other, want which this wealth would relieve, ıereby causing a double happiness. Wisdom and ignorance erhaps stand side by side, the one with no feeling of the ood it might do, the other with no feeling of the benefit hich it might receive. The remedy to all this is more of ublic feeling, of the feeling of the general interdependence, f the feeling that the public happiness is a more real and igher end than the happiness of the individual.

All are the better for the increase of wealth or intelligence in individuals. But society fails in not fitting together the power and the need.

Life is therefore in the first instance *livelihood,* support of fe: in the second, it is this with, added to it, something to ve for, interest in right and truth, self-cultivation, care for thers. As soon as we have come to this, we have got out f the sphere where we have only ourselves to think of, and here individual happiness can be our end. Life then be-omes no longer individual but common. And of life thus nderstood it is the fact, that human life wants all human ower to support it and to make the most of it. The reason civilized society, so far as it is to have a reason, must be ıat, imperfect as it may be, it is the best organization of uman power for this purpose. And the essence of morality onsists to a great extent, in our being able, in such of our ctions as can be free, to take it from ourselves and to give it others.

Reason of civilized society.

There are thus three great forms of duty,

(1) The first, the nearest, homeliest, lowest, but which ust in a manner precede the others, viz. to take care of our-lves.

Four forms of duty.

(2) The second, the definite and plain, but still not xalted one, to do no wrong.

(3) The third, the indefinite and higher one, to do all the good that we can.

Besides these there is a fourth, a secondary one, necessary and subsidiary to the performance of the others, which may be regarded as another form of the first, to take care of our moral selves, to cultivate virtuous dispositions and sympathy.

The first of these, it is to be observed, is not a duty to ourselves (an expression with little meaning, and not desirable to be used) but a duty to others. Care for ourselves to a certain extent is necessary for being able to do anything for others. Want of care for ourselves is simply laying upon others the burden of caring for us. Care for ourselves, or what is apparently so, is often, as we have seen, indirectly, a care and provision for others. But care for ourselves to the prejudice of care for others is selfishness, one great root, as we have seen, of immorality and evil.

Care for family lies between (1) and (2). They are as a part of ourselves, and the not caring for them as such is the doing them wrong.

The idea of *wrong* belongs to law, and wrong is defined for us by an imagined law of which the actual law of our country is a partial representative. We learn this law (and therefore what is wrong) not from a code before us, but from our education, the opinions of the society we live in, and our sympathies. The idea of it within us is our *conscience.*

The idea of doing good to others is suggested to us by the view of the wants of others, and by the feeling of our own wants, sympathetically attributed to them. And so we give them pleasure, or make them happy.

CHAPTER XIV.

ON MORAL ELEVATION.

THE subject which I am going to speak about in this chapter is one which I have two or three times been led to touch, reserving the more full consideration of it for a separate chapter.

Moral elevation is implied in much of the preceding discussion:

I described the first ideal, or that which we should do, as taking two forms according to the degree and the nature of the freedom which we suppose in our action, the forms which I discussed under the names of duty and virtue. Duty is something incumbent upon us, a restraint which presses us down, and keeps us in our place: virtue is, in this respect, the opposite: it is an elevation or expansion.

in the aspiringness of virtue:

Hence virtue is the more really ideal, or, if we like so to express it, it is ideal in a double way, in two degrees: in duty we imagine the restraining law, but then submit ourselves: in virtue we imagine the pattern towards which we work or strive; all is still upwards and outwards; there is no restraint or submission.

the value of actions:

I described also in another chapter, one part, and morally the most important part, of the value of actions, as consisting in what I then called the self-sacrifice involved in them. This value or merit could only have been brought under the head of utility by including under useful actions, not only those productive of, or tending to, good result, and those of a kind generally or often productive of good result, but also those prompted by feelings without the existence of which, independently of any thought of result, much of good result would not be possible.

the estimation of character: I described again, in another chapter[1], the importance of what I there called *self-maintenance*, by which term I expressed care for our moral self as distinguished from care for our interests; care for our character, I said we might call it, but we must mean then by character not estimation, but that to which the estimation is supposed to apply, or which is considered by others to exist in us as the ground of it.

the worthiness of pleasure. Still again, in another chapter, I had occasion to speak of the quality of pleasure, as it is called by some philosophers. By quality is here meant, comparative preferableness of pleasures on some other ground than that of amount or magnitude or quantity of pleasure or pleasingness in them, so far as we can estimate this. A comparative preferability among pleasures other than by reason of quantity, introduces into eudæmonics the first ideal, as I called it, or the notion of something as what should or ought to be in preference to something else: some pleasures are better or worse than others.

All these four different things, or different forms of the same thing, meeting us whichever line of ethical consideration we take,—the aspiringness of virtue, the merit of actions, the estimableness of character, the worthiness of pleasures,—suggest for their expression a metaphor (if we call by the name of 'metaphor' this inevitable practice of language), one which, till this chapter, I have used as little as I could, though it is almost impossible to put two or three sentences on morals together without using it,—the metaphor of *height* or elevation. I purpose

[1] Ch. IX. p. 160.

in this chapter to use it fully, and to explain, so far as I can, the various applications of it just now mentioned, and others which I will mention.

Amongst these others is what I said in a former chapter about the love of excelling or of excellence, how large a contribuent to virtue that was: and in the last chapter on the importance, if we desire happiness, of aiming not at happiness itself, but at that which is good for us, of the attainment of which happiness will be an accompaniment.

Elevation is a metaphor involving three things:

I do not know whether it is possible or likely to be useful to trace thoroughly the meaning and application of such expressions as 'high' in reference to morals. Upwards, away from earth, is the direction leading towards regions in which our imaginations expatiate, but demanding effort in those who would seek to follow it: it is the direction also away from limitation, so that in speaking of measurement to which we suppose an inferior limit or origin, but not a superior limit, we naturally use the terms 'high' and 'low', 'rising' and 'falling'. It is in regard of this last view that we express comparison of any sort by a scale of high and low: it is by the addition to this of the two former views, that we find an expression for *moral* comparison. There are other metaphors for moral comparison, as when we speak of a *great* mind, or a *great* man; but this is the most frequent and significant.

idealism, effort, progress.

It is on account thus of the reference, in morals, to an unseen, on account of the effort of the will against difficulty, and on account of the continued comparison, whether of one moral state in time with another, which is progress or decidence[1], or of one

[1] The word is written 'decadence,' but I have ventured to change this barbarous Gallicism for the true English form, in accordance with the Author's spelling of the same word in another MS. ED.

moral being with another, which is a moral scale of the universe or of creation—it is on these three accounts, in the main, that we may consider men to use the expressions 'high' or 'low', and similar ones, in speaking of morals.

No doubt different schools of morality proceed very differently in their use of these terms—that I will return to: but all use them: and no wonder: for whatever misapplication or abuse may be made of the notions, morality must be ideal, must be an effort, must be a progress; and all these features of it are well expressed, as I have said, by the metaphor before us.

In speaking of the unseen, I do not want to imply, as yet or necessarily, any religious notion: the unseen may be looked upon as matter of belief, which is the way by which morality passes into religion, or it may be looked upon as simply matter of imagination, in which case it is no more than an ideal: on this I say no more now.

It must be supplemented by other considerations.

It must not be forgotten that here, as in each other case, we have before us an abstraction or partial view, which has a pendant to it, and which of itself may be exaggerated into falsehood. The pendant to the notion of the first ideal, or that which should be *done*, as virtue, is the notion of it as duty: in other words, virtue is not simply the aspiration towards an ideal; it is the submission also to something as incumbent on us. Again, the pendant to the notion of virtue as good principle is the notion of it as good impulse: in other words, virtue is not simply effort, struggle, conquest of difficulty; it is feeling also, spontaneous, natural, entirely unconstrained. And so there are various notions which we shall see more fully as we go on, naturally suggesting themselves as pendants to all notions of moral comparison, rivalry, ambition, advance or progress.

In our moral organization 'high' and 'low' may have reference to authority or to worth.

One of the most remarkable applications of the metaphor of 'high' and 'low' has been to the faculties, dispositions, and emotions of the mind, and the consequent arrangement of these, in a scale some above others, as they exist, or may exist, in our moral organization. The notion of height is applicable in different ways to this scale or hierarchy, principally in two ways.

These two different kinds of height or superiority we may call the superiority of authority and the superiority of comparative worthiness, which are not exactly the same thing.

Plato recognizes both kinds of superiority, Butler neglects the latter.

Nobility or aristocracy, and governing or administrative power, do not necessarily go together in politics. We shall probably be right in saying that Plato recognized both kinds of superiority. The inferior mass of desire or impulse had over it two orders; reason or the governing power, and spiritedness, which, while resembling desire in kind, as being itself of the nature of impulse, was understood to differ from it as being superior and nobler. Butler carefully defines the important superiority to be that of *authority* existing in conscience. On the superiority, of a different kind, existing in what he calls the public affections over the private, he says less than he should have done: consequently, on the superiority of conscience to what he calls self-love he gives us no light. This notion of superiority as a simply regulating power converts the notion of a *society* into that of a *system*.

The relation between the superiority of principle and of impulse.

If we are to describe what virtue is by reference to our internal organization, we must describe it as consisting in the double fact, that there exists in vigorous operation, principle, and that there exists a preponderance of higher impulse over lower impulse: and since we must suppose the two portions of this double fact in harmony together, we must consider principle as approving or recommending the higher impulse rather than the lower, and we must consider the higher impulse as restrained and directed, more or less, by principle.

Ancient morality was defective in its view of impulse, and of the results of virtuous action.

Virtue, as presented in the Platonic and Aristotelian systems, has too exclusively the aspect of self-control or self-command. This arises from two things: first, from the separation, by Plato and Aristotle, of the benevolent affections, as modern philosophers call them, from the main consideration of virtue, though they come in for notice subordinately, as in Aristotle's discussion about *φιλία*; and secondly, from their almost entire omission to mention the outward useful results of virtuous action. Hence in Plato, for instance, we have *δικαιοσύνη*, *σωφροσύνη* and *φρόνησις*, all representing, in different views, what I have called principle, and we have *ἀνδρεία* representing an important portion of the higher impulse: while we have *ἐπιθυμία* representing the mass of lower impulse which has only to be subjugated, and has no properly corresponding virtue. Thus not only is the higher impulse imperfectly represented, but of all, impulse and principle alike, we have only the introspective view given, or the relation to oneself: virtue therefore in this view is all self-engrossed or un-self-transcending; it is too much identified with simple self-control; has too much of principle, too little of impulse. It is the same with

Butler is defective in the same way.

Butler: that is, though he, uniting the view of Christian theology with the ancient view, recognizes the *outgoingness* of virtue, and the importance of benevolence or the love of our neighbour, he still keeps to the ancient view in making virtue consist, to a great extent, in a *conscientiousness* whose claim to obedience resides, not in the character of the things which it prescribes, but in its own authority, as a faculty of a superior kind, to prescribe them: and how or why it so happens that the things which conscience prescribes are benevolence and conduct similar to it, rather than selfishness and conduct similar to it, he does not tell us. This is doing what the ancients did; making virtue consist too exclusively in the fact of self-control or a life upon principle; but this is not enough. The view is on all hands incomplete. It does not represent completely the *internal* fact of virtue: still less does it represent what virtue is in our action towards others, for them, in rivalry with them, against them.

Dissatisfaction with this view as not giving sufficient prominence to the utility of virtue:

The impatience, on the part of utilitarians, of a great deal of what is called moral philosophy, has a certain amount of justification, when we consider to what a very great extent such philosophy has occupied itself with balancing and distinguishing our various faculties and feelings, with a view to discover what, in this view, virtuous feeling is: and then, when the question suggests itself, what is it all for? what good does this virtue do in the world? what use does it make of itself? how little attention comparatively has been given to the answering it! Why should we take all these pains with ourselves, they will say, if nothing is to come of it? what does it matter in the universe whether we are virtuous or not, if *this* is all of virtue? It may matter very much in the universe what we *do*, for there is need of a vast deal of useful action in it; but what is the need of spending so much thought on what we *are*, if that is all?

as not bringing out its unselfish generosity.

The utilitarian then may be pardoned some impatience as he looks on at this long and laborious imaginative construction of the moral man, while he is anxious that he should be got into action, and that it should be seen how he performs the work in the world which all this moral nature is wanted for. But, independently of utilitarianism, any one may well have the same feeling in regard of himself. The notion of our living to ourselves alone is not at all a natural notion with us: if we were *sentient* beings only, perhaps it would be: but we are active beings, with powers and faculties: the question, What shall we do with ourselves? is as natural as the question, How shall we be happy? To be told that our work and mission in the world is simply to control and command ourselves, is not altogether satisfactory. We say, I can understand self-control and self-command for a reason or object; but for its own sake I cannot quite: I do not want to be in this way all-important to myself: I am not satisfied with life being an end in itself, its own end: I want to live for something.

Neither this latter view nor that of the utilitarian is altogether a correct one, or at least they are both liable to be exaggerated and misused. I will endeavour to give what seems to me the real truth.

Let us first for a minute or two forget as far as we can that there is any one else in the world except ourself.

The combination of principle and impulse is as important in relation to the virtue, as in relation to the happiness, of the individual.

With respect to our own pleasure, we may be either self-indulgent or self-interested. By which I mean, we may either yield in all cases to the impulses to enjoyment which successively make themselves felt; or we may restrain and manage them, with foresight and prudence, in such a way as to secure to ourselves, so far as we can, a life of what we then call happiness. This latter process is what, when it is considered the whole of moral philosophy, is called Epicureanism. A part of moral philosophy it must be on every system; in utilitarian systems, a large part: for our own happiness and that of others, though very different things to *our* view, yet are the same thing to a *general* or indifferent view; and knowing the one is knowing the other.

With respect to our virtue, we may be either impulsive or conscientious, or we may, as we ought, be both together. In the same way as foresight must not universally preclude indulgence, or there would be no pleasure; so here, we may let some impulses have their way, and others we may variously restrain and manage, so as to convert them, as far as we can, into a life of virtue, virtuous impulses and virtuous habits.

Now what I want to say is this, that the various impulses and the nature of the restraint and government which they should be under, are as worthy and as important an object of study in the point of view of goodness or virtue, as in the point of view of happiness. We are not indeed in either case (as we are looking at the things now) going out of ourselves: we are dealing, so to speak, with two selves, with an enjoying or sentient self, and with a moral self: the ancient self-engrossed views of virtue may be considered as a sort of counter-view or pendant to the ancient Epicureanism: whether or not there is reason to prefer the one to the other, there is no reason to be impatient with the one more than with the other.

In view of thegeneral happiness, the psychology of virtue is as important as the psychology of happiness.

Let us now bring these two views, or imaginative constructions, of our two selves out into life, and suppose existing around us, as it does exist, the world of beings with respect to whom our action is to be.

Then all that portion of moral philosophy which

treats of our own happiness comes to be of importance, as showing us how we may promote the happiness of others as well as our own: but that portion which treats of virtue is not less important, for it is the cultivation of the virtuous disposition in ourselves which is the way to the promotion of the happiness of others: and in the same manner, it is the cultivation of virtuous habits by others (a thing which we may encourage in them), which leads them to the promotion of each other's happiness as well as of their own, however much it may tend to this besides.

The psychology of virtue is thus important in the same way as the psychology of happiness; not merely because virtue is the way to the happiness of the virtuous, supposing it to be so, but because virtue is in itself as important as happiness to each one; and also because, if we consider virtue in its relation to happiness, the way for the mass of men, as sentient beings, to have the greatest amount of happiness, is for them, as individual active beings, to have virtue. The thing wanted in the *active* universe for *general* happiness is not the simple disposition to act for happiness, but the disposition to act for *other's* happiness, which is virtue. Hence we have the two lines of psychologic investigation in moral philosophy: the one that of our feelings of happiness; the other that of those peculiar feelings which lead us to transcend self and care for other's happiness. This latter is virtue.

Still this psychology of virtue must not be taken for the whole of moral philosophy.

The psychology of virtue, that is, the portion of moral philosophy which treats of our internal organization from the point of view of virtue, not from the point of view of pleasure, is not the whole of moral philosophy, for there is besides to be considered the moral world, or life, in which virtue is to be applied.

But it is as practical and at least as important as the utilitarian consideration of our internal organization from the point of view of pleasure: and, unless it is misconceived by being looked upon as the whole of moral philosophy, it is not really self-engrossed and self-regarding only.

The former of these points I have perhaps sufficiently treated both now and previously: the latter, which I have touched upon previously, requires a word still here.

Mistaken view that regard for our own moral character is a kind of selfishness.

There is a kind of unconscious error exceedingly likely to cling to the noblest natures, and almost to them alone, in this matter. We have as it were two selves, our active or moral self, and our sentient, gratifiable, pleasure-capable, self: let us take the word 'self-carefulness' as applicable to both: then it may be considered a moral axiom, that so far from the two kinds of self-carefulness having anything in common, they stand exactly at opposite poles from each other. I do not mean that they are inconsistent with each other and cannot co-exist: quite the reverse: we may care for our moral being and care for our happiness or interest also: but I mean, we must not mistake the doing the one for the other. And when I say that the noblest natures are likely to get into error in this respect, I mean, there is danger of their considering, that all this care for themselves, whether they do right or wrong, is what they themselves are not worth; that whether they, single individuals in an infinite universe, produce or fail to produce some little happiness (the best they can hope), may be a matter of some little consequence, but that whether they do right or wrong can be a matter of no consequence, except to their own particular interest, which, being what in the universe they are, they are quite willing to dismiss the thought of. Why then, they say, all this self-attention? and the unconscious error that I spoke of is, that they think such self-carefulness is akin to self-interest, a sort of higher kind of selfishness.

Antithesis of the two selves, the active and the enjoying.

I mentioned that self-forgetfulness, self-postponement, or self-sacrifice, had a moral value parallel with, but independent of, the value of usefulness in action. But what is to be observed is, that all these feelings, which bear the above names in reference to our *interested* self, would bear, in reference to our *active* self, exactly opposite ones: they are self-remembrance, self-exertion, self-maintenance (as I used the term before). In the one self, we are absorbers of felicific action, in the other, we are outgivers of it: the two are inverse the one to the other: in the one we are sources of good, in the other consumers of it. And to this still is to be added, that there needs self-carefulness, as I used the term, in regard to the one self as in regard of the other, though they are thus mutually polar or antithetic. As regards each self, what stands opposed to self-carefulness is self-indulgence. Self-carefulness in regard of our self of happiness, is self-interestedness or simple prudence: self-carefulness in regard of our other self is that self-maintenance which precludes the acting wrong, the violation of our duty, the betraying of our trust, the sullying of our character, even under the strongest *moral* temptation, if I may so express it. It will be remembered how I mean by character not estimation, but what estimation supposes.

The increase of conscientiousness is the increase of active benevolence.

Of course all general statements such as I have just now made are full of difficulties in the application, some of which I may afterwards treat of: my present concern is with any notion that moral carefulness or conscientiousness is a sort of elevated selfishness, to be postponed to earnest enthusiasm for the results, as to usefulness, of what we do. To which I say, that in this view, we are putting into unnatural opposition to each other, with consequent distortion of both, two things which are most powerful mutual aids, but the better aids in proportion as they are kept genuine and independent. To the extent to which we weaken conscientiousness, by making it appear uncalled for self-engrossment, what we really strengthen is our own self-regard, not the regard for others' interests, so that even in view of results to others, violations of conscientiousness would be wrong.

The terms 'high' and 'low' express the superiority of what is human to what is animal,

It is not then a waste of time to dwell upon our imagined moral being, with its host of feelings standing to each other, in two quite different ways, in the relation of preeminence and subordination; some having their preeminence in virtue of their intellectual and therefore naturally directive character, and forming together what I have called *principle;* others having their preeminence in virtue of their being, as simple feeling or impulse, of a higher quality and nobler character than the rest. This 'higher' and 'nobler' we must a little investigate.

The notions which these terms indicate, (setting aside now whatever of metaphor the terms convey, on which I have spoken,) are compounded of a certain admiration on the part of the persons using them, and a very vaguely recognized quality supposed to deserve the admiration. Setting aside the admiration, we will endeavour to get hold, so far as we can, of the quality: and I will first try to do so by saying, that these higher impulses are the less animal ones.

When the word 'animal' is used in this manner, it is best to take it as implying a rough comparison between man and the inferior animals, and an observation of those parts of his nature which he shares with them.

in respect of imagination; and consequently,

Speaking roughly, they have not imagination. They do not apparently, as man does, combine past perceptions with present ones so as to form general ideas and an internal world of thought, which may influence or direct what they do. They are therefore, more or less, the slaves of the present, of present perception, present feeling, present impulse.

Man on the other hand conceives in his mind something which he *may* be different from what he *is*, something which he may do beyond what this or that felt want immediately suggests to him. This is what I have called forming ideals: and the feelings connected with these are the first which we may assign as standing in preeminence above others, as belonging to *our* height in the scale of creation, not to lower heights.

in respect of affection:

Again, they have not imaginative affections. All affection, as we conceive it, is more or less imaginative, so that we might say they have not affections in our sense of the word at all (this all requires a good deal of qualification): what we mean when we speak of these affections as instinct, is that it is strong even to uncontrollableness, but that it is very particular, that it requires presence, that it is connected with merely corporeal sensations, that it is produced by simple familiarity or custom.

Man's affection is imaginative sympathy engrafted on the simply animal or instinctive feeling: and the vividness of the imagination gives an intenseness to the affection different in kind from the intenseness arising from the simple instinct. And hence it is that human benevolence is a high and worthy feeling.

It is again a part of the same want of imagination

in the animals that, except under peculiar circumstances, (in which, without apparent imagination, the very strongest feelings of self-forgetfulness and self-devotion are closely associated with simply animal feelings, as in the case of affection for offspring) mere self-regard is, we may say, a necessary part of their nature.

Man is capable, by his nature, of entering into the feelings and interests of others as well as of understanding his own: and that same self-forgetfulness, which exists in the animals under the peculiar circumstances which I have mentioned, may exist in man, and is prompted and stirred in him, from the view of the want, not his own, which exists around him, and the imaginative view of the happiness which he may produce. And unselfishness of this nature is one of the kinds of feeling which we think high and worthy.

In the absence of imagination, the capability of pleasure existing in the animals must be but limited. The merely corporeal or nervous pleasure of course they may enjoy, as far as we know, to as great an extent as we do: but remembrance and recombination, thought of the absent and the future, imaginative or ideal construction, multiply our being, and produce an infinite additional amount of susceptibility of pleasure and pain of which the animals can know nothing. Pleasures of this kind, as compared with the coarse or corporeal pleasures which the animals are capable of as well as we, are what we call 'refined' pleasures: and in virtue of this their refinement, we consider them higher and worthier than others. in respect of pleasure:

Lastly, by reason of his imagination, man has a different kind of *will* from that which we may say any animal can have: the mental state which imme- in respect of will:

diately precedes his action is, or may be, of a fulness and complication to which, with them, there can be no parallel. Choice belongs to him, and cannot to unimaginative creatures. And so there belongs to him also that which we might call *wilfulness*, using the term not in the ordinary sense, but meaning by it a concentration of will, a superiority to the changing gusts of momentary impulse, a choice determined by a view extending beyond the immediate and present, and a resolution following on this choice. And thus human will has a special worthiness in that it forms the transition or bond of union between the higher impulse, and principle. It is principle itself in the form of a higher impulse. It is the real union of the intellectual and moral.

in respect of the power of self-improvement.

Connected with this is one consideration, which will come more under our notice in another chapter; that man, owing still to his imagination, has much less fixity of nature than the inferior creatures; what he will be, either as a kind, or as an individual, is much less determined for him by previously existing circumstances; he is, in kind and individually, much more his own master. They, the animals, are many of them, each kind in its peculiar way, specially trainable by man; but, independently of man, each species goes through its necessary and generic course of training, whatever it is, the same for each individual, so that there is no distinctive individuality, no individual progress, and consequently no generic progress. Man is educable, and more than this, self-educative; and consequently *progressive*. And self-education implies imagination and an ideal; the thought of something better, higher, worthier, to which we educate ourselves.

The terms 'high' and 'low' may

So far I have been considering the terms 'higher' and 'lower' in reference to a comparison between ourselves and other animals, the higher impulses are the less animal ones. They may also be considered in another light, as the more spiritual and divine. I will explain how this is so.

also be used in reference to a comparison between man and (supposed) spiritual beings.

In illustrating what I said last, I did not indeed enter into detail as to the difference between the inferior animals and ourselves, but still I did keep rather close to that difference. We may, however, regard the non-animal portion of our nature in somewhat of a different manner. We may look more at ourselves, and less at the animals.

We are not creatures of intellect alone, and morality therefore is not acting simply by reason or on principle. If it was, it would be matter of simpler consideration. It is not perhaps difficult for us to imagine what a being intellectual only, a νουπρακτής, would be: but we are not such.

The non-animal part of man is not exclusively intellectual.

Hence there is no meaning or importance, really, in the saying as the ancients did, that man's specialty or differentia in comparison with other animals is his being rational, and that his special excellence therefore or virtue must consist in the excellence and the predominance of his reason. If, in this, by reason we mean anything definite, as *intellect*, it is not true; if we mean by reason all the higher or non-animal portions of man's nature, it is insignificant, and says nothing.

The non-animal portion of our nature, supposing the expression to have meaning, we may call for convenience the spiritual portion: it consists of our human intellect, or reason, for one part; and, along with this, of a great deal of impulse or emotion of different kinds, of which, from the various things which I have just now said about it, we may to a certain degree see the character. I have dwelt already on the importance, in our constitution, of imagination, and on the various applications of it. Now we ourselves are the highest and worthiest kind of beings that we know of. It may be difficult, if I am asked to say what highest and worthiest means here, to say it: but I think the proposition is one which every one, whatever his views, would allow in some sense: allowed in this way, the proposition is in a manner a definition of what is meant by high and worthy. This is expressing in other words the same thing which I have said already.

One aspect of virtue is that it is an aspiration after a higher than human life.

But although we are the highest kind of being that we know of, we are by no means the highest that we can imagine: and in fact, all morality is, more or less, the imagination of higher. Virtue is the acting in the manner in which, so far as we can conceive, imagined beings higher and worthier than we ordinarily are, would act. It is in this way what we may call a stretching upwards to a higher nature. This ideal of a higher or worthier nature towards which, in whatever way, we aspire, is one which we have not touched upon yet, and it is one which takes many forms; it is itself a form, so to speak, of the first ideal, or what we should do.

This may take the form of religion, or of a belief in progress.

The imagination of, and aspiration towards, a higher nature is what more than anything else gives life and interest to the view of human action, animates human effort, and brings out human character. This is, in fact, the form which the idealizing energy in men mainly takes; for we look with more interest at the combined and concrete, than at the abstract. We may imagine aspiration after a higher nature than our own, roughly speaking, in two manners: we may suppose other natures existing now, independent of ours, but which are or may become known to us, which we may imitate, which may perhaps influence us, towards which we may approximate: or, aware as we are of what I have called the unfixedness and educability of our nature, we may imagine other and superior states of it, or states into which it may change: the first of these is religion, the second is belief in the progress and improvement of the human race.

Virtue is strengthened by the right belief in the existence of beings superior to man whom he may seek to resemble.

We call God 'good,' so far as moral suggestion prompts us to do so, for the simple reason that we conceive, as fixed and realized in His character, the ideal perfection of worthiness of being, which worthiness our own generic superiority to inferior beings, and the comparative superiority of some among us to others, suggests to us. And then, fixing in Him this ideal perfection, we conceive our own worthiness or virtue,—and there is no better or more practical way of conceiving it,—as consisting in our being like Him. But it will be said, in this way we mean by the perfect Divine character no more than an imagination of a perfect human character, which we might as well make without any thought of God. Not so: the supposition, which so naturally suggests itself, of the actual existence of a nature superior to ours, makes the thought more vivid than if what we conceived was only an ideal of what *we* might be: and morality is not the sole, or even the most important suggestive of God to us, as existing, but does *its* part, and fastens *its* character upon what it finds, aiding both itself and the consideration of that which it thus recognizes.

I am not however now going to consider what morality or virtue may have to do with real existence. So far as I deal now with the relation between morality and religion, I mean religious imagination and religious sentiment very widely considered indeed. When Plato condemned the immoral tendency of the popular religion of his times, he condemned it as a falsification and abuse of that which, even as he could understand it, ought to be, and might be, a most powerful moral agent: it is with this general moral bearing of it that I am now concerned.

Such resemblance may be attained in the way of principle or of impulse.

Virtue is thus the acting in a manner superior to ourselves; the doing an act, or feeling a feeling, not belonging to what, in past times perhaps and in lower or worse moments, has been or is our nature, but belonging to a better nature, and brought into ours; now perhaps fully ours, because the result of a moral habit; but still, as ours, belonging to a better or higher part of us, which stands in contrast with a lower or worse part. Such an act may be with effort, or may be without: it may be the result of principle, and be attended with very great effort: it may be the result of the higher impulses, and be quite without effort, apparently merely spontaneons: and in the two cases it may possibly have equal merit of opposite kind. For in any nature morally superior to ours we must suppose higher intelligence than ours, and nobler impulse than ours, to go together: and in our imperfect struggles it may be the one of these, or the other, that we may most be animated by, or most succeed in attaining to.

In attaining it the higher self triumphs over the lower.

The distinction which I made above between our two selves is here to be kept in mind: the most virtuous action, as I have just described it, is that which is least our own; that is, least belonging to our lower, gratifiable, interested self; but just in proportion as it is this, it is most our own, in reference to our higher and active self: it is, more than lower action, our deliberate choice if it is on principle, and, more than lower action, an absorbing and transporting impulse, if it is on impulse.

That admiration which we give to men about us whom we see act worthily, becomes, when we imagine natures superior to ours, the reverence belonging to religion: and we look with something of this feeling of reverence on acts of real nobleness in our fellow-creatures, and still more when we think of them in remembrance, or think of the great ones of our kind who have passed away. In these various ways the imagination of superior natures affects us in ways akin to religion.

The belief in human progress has been, in many cases, a religion, and a most energetic one, with many who have had no other: and to many, who have had much besides, it has been an ennobling belief, confirming their religion, and confirmed by it.

Virtue may also be strengthened by the right belief in progress.

I shall not speak just now about this historically, or about various erroneous views which have been held on the subject. It only belongs to our subject now, and is only ennobling, in so far as it supposes the possibility of man's becoming, by the continued effort of successive generations, in kind a higher and worthier being, a higher animal, if we like so to use the term; and in so far as it combines with this a belief, that man does, as matter of fact, in some respect become such, a hope that he may become so in larger measure in the future, an effort to find out how he may become so, and to aid the progress. It is clear that, where the belief in progress is of this nature, there is formed in the mind an imagination or ideal of what man would be if he were better; in other words, an idea of what being 'better' means. Nor can this ideal well exist in the mind without being, not only a bright dream for the future, but in some degree a guide for action in the present.

CHAPTER XV.

ON THE RELATION OF THE IDEALS TO HIGHER AND LOWER FACT.

The moral ideals are imagina- tions:

IN all that I have written hitherto, I have not been solicitous by what name I should call the mental process, the result of which is the existence in our minds, or presentation before our minds, of the moral ideals which I have described.

I have generally called it 'imagination', as a very vague term: it is at least that, whatever else it is. Imagination, in this use of it, is simply a mental process, similar to sensible perception in so far as it has a supposed object, but different from it in so far as that we do not attribute to the object of imagination the same kind of reality which we attribute to the objects of sensible perception.

to which various degrees of reality and of imperativeness may be ascribed.

For convenience we may assume four degrees of reality or non-reality in the moral ideals; four different processes of mind, we may say, in or by which we may present or represent them to ourselves. They may be looked upon as dreams; or as valuable imaginations; or as beliefs; or as inward perceptions. Similarly we may classify them according to the degree of force which they exert upon our action. We may think of them as something imperative or incumbent upon us; as something fit for us or adapted to our nature; as something desirable or useful; or as something worthy of us and to be aspired after. I have put the ideals here in a different order from before, in order to have them in a sort of scale, which we may call that of incumbency or (taking it the other way) of freedom.

Now when we use the word 'right', we mean to express, as against *lower* fact (by which I mean such fact as is cognizable by means of, or as a result of, the exercise of our sensive powers), an ideal or imagination; but at the same time we mean to express, as against mere vague imagination, visionariness, or dream, a reference to fact of *some* kind. What is the difference between moral philosophy and a simple dreaming about one thing and another as desirable or good?

Moral philosophy has relation both to higher and lower fact.

The difference, or the reference to fact, is double: along with the reference to lower fact, there is a recognition, or suggestion, of *higher* fact of some kind. Both kinds of reference to fact involve the greatest difficulties.

Without the reference to *lower* fact, *i. e.* to the nature and condition of man upon earth, as what is commonly called experience shows it to us, moral philosophy is all in the air, and no useful application can be made of it: which is the same thing as saying it is nothing; for human action and human life are what it is intended to be the art and rationale of. But what is man for this purpose, and what human nature? Is it savage man, or civilized man? man as the subject merely of physical and psychological dissection, or man (as we always find him) with his self-made array of customs, social habits, and elementary jurisprudence? How are we to distinguish between the fact which is to govern our criticism or our ideal, and the fact which is to be the subject of the former, and the contrast, or matter for improvement, to the latter?

Difficulties in regard to both.

Again, without reference to *higher* fact of some

kind, we have really nothing to answer to the man who says to us, Eat, drink, enjoy yourself, the rest is dream; dream, he may continue, which I have myself no objection to indulge in, in so far as it is likely to contribute to that one undoubted reality, my own palpable, tangible, pleasure; but which, beyond this, you must allow me not to trouble myself about, while there is this to be attended to and worked for. But then, assuming that there is such a thing as higher fact, what is its nature, and what assurance are we to get of it? Is it fact *of man's nature*, of *this* kind, that a high and worthy part of this nature is to form ideals for his action, and to care for the happiness of others, which he can only imagine, as well as for his own, which he can feel? Or is it fact of man's nature of *another* kind, viz. that he has thoughts, convictions, beliefs, within him, not suggested by anything which he merely feels as sensation? Or is it fact beyond himself, a perception, or what he thinks so, of a moral world, akin in some degree to that perception which he has, or thinks he has, of the material world in which he physically lives?

I have here, it will be seen, noted the four processes of mind which I described above, the first of which negatives reality, or higher fact, corresponding to the ideals, while the three others suppose it of some kind.

Fact and imagination must be combined for action.

The notion of 'the right', or that which should be done, and other kindred notions, belong to, and imply, a middle region between fact of observation or experience on the one side, and poetry, sentimentalism, the region of beauty and sublimity, on the other side. Is there any such region? what can we, in our minds, make out about it?

It is no use to go on reforming moral philosophy,

as has continually been done, by flying successively, disgusted with the vagueness of *imaginationalism*, to positivism or fact, and then, the next generation, back again, disgusted with the barrenness of fact, to imaginationalism or idealism. Unless we conjoin the two things together, there is no moral philosophy. We must add to our observational knowledge of what *is*, the notion of something as what *should be*. Fact of itself suggests nothing for us to do except the getting rid of actually pressing uneasiness. It is our nature that, along with our sensation of what *is*, we should imagine or conceive what *might be*, and this is what suggests the mass of our action. But this imagination or conception might be altogether wild: we must correct or direct it by itself, *i.e.* by a study of our own and of the general human consciousness, so far as these expressions have meaning and signify something possible: and we must correct or direct it by the actual facts of human nature to which it is, in action, to be applied. If this cannot be done, there is no such thing as moral philosophy. But there *is* such a thing as moral philosophy, because, whether we have a book-science of this name or not, men in life do and must guide their life by views of this kind: they not only look at what is the fact, which would suggest no action, but they think what would be well, or what they want: they not only think what would be well or what they want, which by itself might be vain castle-building, but they consider whether their ideal is reasonable, and, considering actual fact, is practicable. Moral philosophy is the rationale of this: and surely the consideration of the *principle* of that which we *must* do is a reasonable and practical line of thought.

We may look upon the *right* as a sort of half-way house between positive fact and the vaguely ideal:

and again, in another view of the same thing, we may look upon imagination, or the forming of ideals, as a mental process which connects, or brings into relation, two sorts of fact, the lower and the higher, physical or observational, and moral or intuitive.

Feelings of want and of duty are facts indicative of facts beyond them.

Our feelings of want and duty, and our imagining this or that as what we want or what we should do, in accordance with these feelings, are of themselves fact in our nature, and, like all other fact, are indicative of fact beyond them. As I said on a former occasion, our feelings of desire are more or less indicative of the fact of want: our feelings of duty are more or less indicative of the fact of a task or work appropriate to us and belonging to us. To find what is the want we must examine our feelings of desire, which are irregular, shifting, capricious, but in respect of which, by comparison of different times, of corresponding feelings of others, &c., we can approximate to something fixed and stable. To find what is the work or task, we must examine in the same manner our feelings of duty: like the want, they are vague and irregular; but not all chance, not all caprice.

These feelings are recorded in the institutions of society.

The examination of our feelings of want and of duty, and the examination of human nature, or the experience of human nature, are to a certain extent the same thing. Men, as they have come together in society, have expressed their common feelings of want and of duty in the customs which have established themselves, and the earlier and simpler laws which have been formed, previous to the existence of what we might call a legislative consciousness, or a distinct and deliberate thought of the general advantage. When we speak of 'the facts of human nature', we must at least imply all this. By 'man' we must at least mean not savage man, but man in society. How far, by 'man', we should mean what we call highly civilized man, as distinct from man in simpler society, we will see another time.

Imagination transcends lower fact, and presents to us the good and right as what should be, without however losing sight of lower fact: the conception of higher fact controls and fixes imagination, and gives us the notion of the right and fit, as distinguished from the vaguely and generally good.

The disposition to formideals is a fact of human nature, as the superiority of one way of action to another is a fact of universal nature.

We should not have formed ideals for our action at all unless it had been our nature (in this respect differing from the nature of the inferior animals) to do so: and our nature thus is a part of the general nature in virtue of which the ideals present themselves to us as something good and desirable. If all were hap-hazard, neither should we have a nature to think one thing better than another to be done, nor would in fact any one thing be better than another.

Informing moral ideals we put together higher and lower fact.

The formation then of moral ideals, is the putting together observed lower fact with supposed higher fact in some kind of way. The way may be very various. And the fact on each side may be very various also; on the one side there may be scarcely anything, on the other side there may be very much: on this depends the relative amount, in the view taken, of positivism and idealism: but if it is in any way practical, *i.e.* applicable to action and suggestive of it, it must really involve both.

This is done in various proportions by different moral systems.

The state of mind also in regard of the supposed higher fact may be various, in the manner which I have indicated: it may be something which we imagine only (without thinking it therefore to be despised), it may be something which we may believe, it may be something which we think we perceive with the inner eye, an actually objective, though unseen, universe.

This will be best understood by our comparing together the most complete form of positivism, and the most complete form of idealism or anti-positivism, as we know them in actual human thought.

Positivism takes the lower fact and converts that into its ideal.

M. Comte, in calling his system positivism, has evidently intended to exclude, in the most complete manner possible, all consideration of anything as what *might be.* Experience, past and present, shows us what *has been* and *is.* We have now, as to human nature, gone through a tolerably long period of this experience: the sum of it may be expressed thus, that as time advances, man increases his material comforts, enlarges his physical knowledge, and changes his manner of thinking: M. Comte considers that he has himself discovered the law of these changes; and also that he has found that man, in some portions of the earth, has come in substance to the end of the series of change, or to a permanent state. Here then, he says, in this final manner of human thinking, we have given to us, in the first place, a fact of observation (what I have called the lower fact): this is what we *are,* what man is, what takes place, what we do and cannot help doing: it is the actual or positive. And then, in the second place, we can have no other idea of anything as what we *should* be, what man should be, what should take place, what we should do, as beings who direct our own action, not mere natural agents who cannot help doing what they do,—than this idea of what we, the longest-experienced among mankind, *are.* *Consequently,* this which we *are,* is what we should with the greatest urgency *try* to be: we should invest this actual with the characters of the ideal: what we do and must do, think and must think, we should do *as* what we should do, think *as* what we should think: keep the notion of right, but invest the *fact* with it.

Here we have, first, an amplification to the utmost extent possible, of the lower or observational fact, the assumption that 'human nature,' or man in the abstract, is nothing more than the man of our present experience; and, next, a hesitating admission of higher fact to a limited extent, allowing, for instance, that there is a way in which individuals *ought* (for whatever reason) to be educated or to think, or, again, that the course which collective man in his experience *does* take is the course which, for whatever reason, he *ought* to have taken; and then giving back to us civilized human nature, with its supposed positivist manner of thinking, as an ideal to which we should conform ourselves.

Idealism subordinates the lower fact.

Exactly of an opposite nature to this are the various highly developed idealisms, whether they are religious or simply moral.

They may be, as I have said, of imagination, belief, or supposed internal, but actual, perception.

The first of these are the pure, or commonly understood, idealisms; as that of Rousseau, who considered that ever since man had left a primæval savage state he had been, not advancing, but drifting; not developing, but misgrowing; that he ought indeed in the beginning to have formed for himself an ideal of improvement, as we may form one now, but an ideal which should have preserved and developed, instead of destroying, his noble earlier virtues.

In idealist conceptions of progress, the ideal has the form of an imagination.

The man who thinks thus may be said to see, or think he sees, in the lower fact of the observed savage state, higher fact in the form of what he considers possibilities of improvement and tendencies to development. His idealism consists in considering that these are the parts of human nature which *ought* to be cultivated and developed, human nature of itself being very liable to misdevelopment. And with him it is the higher fact, the imagined or half-seen, vague as it is, which is the fact of real importance.

Or, again, there is the idealism of those, who, feeling strongly how little man, civilized and advanced in knowledge as he is, can be taken to represent or be a type of what man ought to be, yet recognize in it an advance on barbarism, and a step, or many steps, towards an ideal, but possible, perfection. This imagined perfection is more or less suggested by what man has done for himself: in so far as there is such suggestion, lower or observed fact is assumed under higher. Between views of this kind and the last, there may be an infinite gradation; and there may be any degree of relation between views of this kind and religious views.

The state of mind which I have last alluded to is that in which, while we are aware that we are only imagining what might be, we still feel that, in doing this, we are not idly dreaming, but that we and others might so act that our imaginations might be realized, and that it would be a glorious thing if they were so.

In regard to duty, the ideal has the form of belief.

The next state of mind is that which I have called 'belief.' It is soberer, but firmer than the preceding, lying nearer to our will and active powers. It is imagination with very little of picture, very little of distinct conception, but with a persuasion and conviction, less animating and stimulating than the other, but more firm and steadily operative.

As an example of what I mean by belief we may take *duty*. Duty is an ideal which we do not imaginatively luxuriate in, as in thoughts of the perfection of human nature, but in which we *believe*. It supposes a fact, but not necessarily an even internally perceivable fact. The feeling of duty, in reference to our action, corresponds to the thought, in reference to our intellect, which makes us really reasonable beings; it is, in a manner, our moral consciousness.

Application of the terms belief and imagination in the intellectual sphere.

I will stop here for a moment, to point out the intellectual reference with which I use the words 'imagination,' 'belief,' and the others.

Two kinds of knowledge, by communication and by thought.

Our knowledge[1] is of two kinds: acquaintance *with* things; and knowledge *about* them, or of their properties. The former arises from the superaddition of consciousness to a communication, of whatever sort, between our frame and the things; this is *cognoscentia, connaissance*. The latter is thought about the things, with the superaddition, whencesoever derived, of the notion that the thought is right: this is *scientia, savoir*.

Manner in which communication produces knowledge.

The fact of the communication between our frame and what we call external nature, the fact, *i.e.* of experience, becomes knowledge in virtue of attention given by us to it; consciousness means the capacity of such attention. For the stone which we touch to touch us in the same sense in which we touch it, there is required in it fibres, sensitive of pleasure and pain in the contact, like our nerves, and a reacting will. For the tree which we see to see the sun, from which it receives the light, in the same way as we, to whom it transmits the light, see *it*, there would be required a high concentration of the (already in some degree existent) expansive and shrinking sensitiveness to internal chemical change produced by light, together with the rudiments of a *will* which might fix attention on it, and also

[1] Cf. ch. v. and *Exploratio*, p. 60.

some relation between the movements produced and the spatial circumstances of the sun. I have just made this passing allusion to indicate roughly the relation between *the fact* of experience as communication, and the *result* of experience with attention to it in our perceptional knowledge.

Concurrently with the communication between our frame and the external world, there is going on *thought* in our spiritual, unspatial, being; time being the link of union between the two. We may follow knowledge, as I have said, along *either* of the paths, only that we cannot blend them. But we do know in the two ways; some things especially in the one way, some in the other.

Belief is originally a moral term transferred to the intellectual sphere.

The word 'believe' is a word transferred in the first instance from a moral to an intellectual application: it signifies to give credit to the word of a person, to yield our judgment to his, or make our judgment follow his. Belief is knowledge, which *as* knowledge, is illegitimate; though it may be accompanied by conviction as strong, and lead to action as vigorous as if it were legitimate.

It denotes incomplete *scientia*, as imagination denotes incomplete *cognoscentia.*

The completeness of the knowledge of experience or perception depends upon the completeness, and more especially upon the variety, of the communication, in order that possible illusion in one manner may be corrected in another. Where the communication is imperfect, it is impossible for us to be certain between perception and imagination. A knowledge in the way of *scientia,* or knowing *about* things, if it be more or less incomplete in a manner analogical to the above, is what I call a belief. So long as the word 'belief' retains any signification separate from that of knowledge, then, though the certainty may be complete, the mind is always more or less in an expectant or prospective position.

We have got in a short, compendious, cross-cut way, knowledge to which properly belonged a different way.

In this chapter the terms are re-applied to moral judgments and conceptions.

As I am using the term 'belief' in the present chapter it is re-applied from intellectual relations to moral ones. I mean it to apply to *judgments* which we are persuaded we make with grounds, and which we act upon, though they are not of a nature to be demonstrated; in the same way as by 'imagination' (in the narrower sense as distinguished from belief) I mean *conceptions* which we are persuaded are not idle and worthless, though they are not matters of our experience. The mass of our conduct which is determined by what I have called 'principle' is based upon such *belief*.

Either kind of knowledge is unsatisfactory by itself.

In reality, our two manners of knowledge each stand in a relation of illegitimacy, or cross-cut way, to the other. Demonstrative proof is the jumping over an infinite mass of possible experience: exhibitory or experimental proof is the supersession of argument by interrogation of nature.

Either involves the other as its own foundation.

In either case, according to the frame of our mind, we are more or less disposed to say for ourselves, Well, I grant it is so, but still, I want to know how it comes to pass that it is so. This we may say equally in regard of our belief of the forty-seventh proposition of Euclid's first book, and in regard of our belief that acids will turn certain liquids red, and alkalies blue. In fact, though we can conceive knowledge in one only of its two manners *at a time*, yet, whichever way we conceive it, the other kind of knowledge lies at the base of that which is present to our minds, as a great co-foundation stone, and a necessary condition; though on the view we then take, insoluble and undevelopable.

If we take the view, *e.g.* that all actual know-

Thus *scientia*, as belief, is involved in *cognoscentia*; *cognoscentia*, as inward sight, in *scientia*.

ledge is experience, *i.e.* that past and existing human knowledge is the sum (variously shortened for convenient expression) of all the noted (or attended-to) communication which has ever taken place between the human organization and the external universe, then the other view of knowledge as *thought*, will lie as a co-foundation at the base of this in the shape of belief in the universe, or a notion of the unity of things, which is what causes the co-ordination of our fragmentary experiences, and what leads, in fact, to the noting of them. If, on the other hand, we take the view that knowledge is correct thought, there lies at the base of it, in a similar manner, what I have called 'inward perception.' Knowledge, as correct thought, is all expressible in propositions: the propositions (*i.e.* their meaning) being the same for all persons, it is transferable from one to another, and might exist in the propositions, as the plant in the seed, during an interval in which all consciousness or knowingness might conceivably cease and be non-existent. In this way of viewing knowledge, the (logical) subject of knowledge is a supposition only, and all the matter of knowledge is the amount of the different things which may be thought about it. But as *experience* in the former case requires *belief* as its co-foundation or condition, so in this case does *thought* require as its co-foundation or condition, what I have called *inward sight*. We do not individually *know* the proposition in question till we have an inward sight of it; just as, in the other case, the particular experience becomes to us knowledge by being accepted as a part of the great universe, in which we believe, and distinguished from the rest of it.

Analogous to these are the be-

All this is intellectual. That which corresponds, in our thought of the moral universe, to

the two above kinds of fundamental consciousness in our thought of the intellectual, is belief or inward sight according to the nature of it. The belief that law or order, as opposed to chaos and randomness, must apply not only to the particulars of things, as we see it does, but to the entire of being, in which case it becomes meaning and reason, as distinguished from insignificance and purposelessness,—this belief seems to me to play the same part in the fragmentary and incohesive mass of circumstance or occasion for action, which we call *life* or the moral universe, as it does in the intellectual universe. No experience could give us this belief, but it seems to me that, intellectually, we could not think for a moment without it: all our actual knowledge might be considered as the development of our one first view, which could not have been what it was unless everything had been what *it* was, the universe on its side and we on ours, and from which, therefore, everything afterwards known was, in its nature, deducible: everything was given in *that*. In the same way, moral consciousness, conscience, or duty, is the imaginative feeling of ourselves as belonging to a moral universe or entirety, with its constitution, reason, and purpose: it is a self-divided feeling of greatness and littleness, the feeling of a contrast between the universe, which we can think of and act as belonging to, and a special individuality and frame which bounds our power. It is imagination, as quite beyond experience: it is belief, as not of itself expatiative, not a separate object of contemplation, but involved in consciousness, and going directly to action. If we endure, or act, as seeing an Invisible Being, then belief passes into what I have called inward sight: if we act upon an abstract law, with a thorough conviction that what we are

lief in the moral law, the inward sight of the Moral Governour.

doing is reasonable, there is nothing of course to see, even inwardly or imaginatively, but that which moves the will under these circumstances is what I mean by belief, as distinguished from the inward vision.

Imagination leads to belief, belief to inward vision.

The application of the unseen, believed in or supposed to be inwardly seen, to the actually seen of life, is morality, often undistinguishable from religion, as in its first entrance into literature in the Hebrew Scriptures, and again, in a more philosophical form, in Plato and the Stoics. I shall at times use the term 'belief' in reference to all the unseen; belief being in this case the more general term, and the inwardly seen being believed in as well. And both the inwardly seen and the believed are imagined as well: we should not be religious without an imagination; but religion is imagination justifying itself and leading on to belief, and belief justifying itself and leading on to inward vision.

Difference among idealists as to the degree in which they have accepted lower fact.

Different idealists, whether philosophers or religious teachers, even under the same nominal system of morals or religion, have differed greatly in the degree in which they have accepted more or less of the actual development of human society, and correspondingly have attempted less or more to apply the unseen or ideal to the correction and elevation of it.

I question whether the different ways in which different teachers and reformers have endeavoured to put together the actual and the ideal (or, which is the same thing, to form the true ideal for action by putting together the observed and the felt or believed) have ever been estimated in fair comparison, or indeed whether they ever can be.

Religious teachers differ from moral philosophers in considering that they have given to them in a special way, viz. by revelation, the particulars of the ideal which is to be the aim, or rule, of action. They thus speak with assumed authority; rightly assumed, in so far as the foundations upon which the religion or revelation rests commend themselves as valid.

Independently of religious authority, the ideal by which moral philosophy must endeavour to direct, correct, improve, elevate, and reform the actual, must be derived from human feeling. This feeling exists to some degree in all; to a great degree in some. The words of the idealist ever are, If all were what some are, what would the world be! And why should they not be? To which the *actualist* ever answers, The moral world, in substance, is *given* by human constitution and circumstance: granted that the good are the aristocracy of the universe, you could not have a world all aristocracy; badness or inferiority on the part of some is a condition of goodness or superiority on the part of others; as the world is, there is unhappily work for the bad in it as well as for the good; or, not to put the matter coarsely and exaggeratedly, the exigencies and temptations of actual life are such that we must be satisfied, morally, with little.

Idealists have not always sufficiently recognized the goodness embodied in the actual state of society.

The history, thus, of moral effort to elevate and improve human life has always presented a mass of noble inconsistency, not unfrequently lending itself as an object to satire and ridicule.

The good feeling has always been more or less at work even in what man, independent of special effort, has done for himself; and constantly this simpler and more general human improvement has justified itself, and with reason, against the more special efforts of moral reformers. Duty has made itself felt in its general character of the notion of restraint of our passion and wilfulness, of a something incumbent upon us to do or to avoid, and in its particular character of the notion of services to be rendered to particular persons concerned in life with us. Societies have been formed with these feelings strongly predominant, tempering, but yet leaving still in vigorous energy, man's natural activity and enterprise, his feeling of want and power, and the impulse to supply the one and to exercise the other. Then comes in the moral idealist, and mourns, as well he may, that there is so little of elevated motive, so much of effort after what is not worth effort, so little thought of what is most worth thinking of. But after all, when we are thinking what men might be in the one direction, it is but fair to think what they might be in the other. The present ordinary condition of civilized human nature represents what, from the point of view of a savage, must be a very lofty ideal. In almost all crises of effort after moral reform, certain portions of good in the actual have had to stand, or try to stand, against certain portions of bad, mistaken for good, in the ideal. And not unfrequently one result of such contests or crises has been to give a momentary glimpse of the possible depths of evil into which man may plunge, when the web he had spun for himself of custom and law has been temporarily broken.

The more influential systems have usually combined value for actual good with enthusiasm for ideal.

In a general way, a moral system, to have really practical influence, must take a great deal both of the lower fact and of the higher to put together, and, as a rule, the more it takes of the one, the more it will attempt to take of the other.

The systems which try to supersede the higher fact, or the ideal, by the lower fact, or experience, are the various forms of what I have called positivism. On these what I shall say now is only this, that they cannot be really true to themselves or to experience. They either misrepresent experience and the real fact, or they unconsciously and unauthorizedly introduce the ideal, while in profession disclaiming it. The former of these is the proceeding of the Epicurean positivism, the latter of the Comtian: though in fact, each of them does both.

The systems which make no account of the lower fact, except to condemn it, in their zeal for the higher, are the various forms of highly idealist, ascetic and mystical morality, involved very frequently in systems of religion. On these also I will say nothing just now.

But in general, as I have said, the more influential systems of morality and religion have sought to unite the proper attention to both kinds of fact. In the Stoic system there was very much of exaggeration and mistake, and so there has been in various developments of the Christian: but the Stoic system in the old times, and the Christian in later, while they gave greater prominence than other systems to the ideal or unseen, did also more than any others to inspire interest in and regard for actual human society. Side by side with the lofty and often exaggerated morality of the Stoic *wise man*, and with the Christian denunciations of the *world*, there were combined, in the one case, reverence for law, respect for active and public life, value for sociality, and in the other case, most detailed and careful recommendation of common duties, without any notion of these being superseded by something higher.

The ideal is the connecting link between lower and higher fact.

I will now proceed to look at the relation between moral imagination and fact from a different point of view, and to explain what I meant some time since by saying, that the moral imagination is a medium to us between the lower and higher fact.

There are three elements of moral consideration: the faciendum or ideal; the lower fact, or human condition and human feeling; and the higher fact, (assuming there to be such) *i.e.* the wider state of things which is the basis of the relation between the first of these elements and the second, or, in other words, which under the circumstances of the second, makes the first what it is, the thing to be done.

The higher fact is a distinct object of speculative ethics, but of practical only in so far as it is involved in the ideal.

In practical moral philosophy the object aimed at is the finding out of the particulars of the first of these from the general notion which we form of it united with an examination of the second. In this general notion is involved to a certain extent the third element, the recognition of the higher fact; but this higher speculation is not what, in practical moral philosophy, we follow out. We look at the ideal in regard of its *application.* And, in connexion with this application, we enter into as detailed an examination as we please of the condition and feelings of man; examine what makes his happiness, what are his natural feelings about virtue or the ideal, how he himself, in his institutions, follows out the notion of ideal duty, and much besides.

How this bears on the division of ethics into theory of sentiments, and criterion of morality.

Moral philosophy has been divided by some into two portions, the theory of moral sentiments, and the criterion of morality: the division is hardly sufficient for the full extent of the subject. The former, or moral psychology, is the examination of an important portion of feeling: the second is one way of expressing what I have called the purpose of practical moral philosophy. We might in any case add to these two a third portion, the theory of moral obligation: this would be really, an examination of the relation of the first of the elements to the third, or more accurately, considering how I described the third element, an examination of that element itself.

In whatever way we put it, we cannot study moral philosophy without having suggested to us not only its practical, but its *speculative* interest, in regard of what I have called the higher fact, *i.e.* the (supposed) moral position of man in reference to the unseen.

Is it because there *is* something which we ought to do that we imagine, believe, or think we see, that there is; and if so, what is there, beyond our own being and experience, which makes it thus proper for us or incumbent upon us? Do we owe it to anybody?

The consideration of this higher fact belongs to speculative philosophy, if we consider it only speculatively; to a sort of transcendental moral philosophy, if we consider it practically; and it constitutes natural religion if, in our practical consideration it brings, or seems to bring us into association with higher moral beings, or one such being.

Different views as to the possibility of knowing the higher fact.

I mentioned the distinction between those who would consider moral imaginations only dreams, and those who would consider them at least valuable imaginations. To the former of course, all that I have called 'higher fact' is simply chimerical. The state of mind of the latter I have described as either imagination (with value), or belief, or supposed perception,—intuition.

Using the word imagination for all these latter states, we may have the following views about the facts imagined: that they indicate a reality, but that this reality is either unseizable, or is very limited, or has mingled with it an element of deceptiveness and misleadingness.

And of this higher fact in relation to the lower fact we may have the following views; that it is less true to us than knowledge of experience; that it is more true to us; that it is equally and similarly true to us; that it is equally and similarly untrue.

Of the three views in the former paragraph I consider the correct one to be a mixture of the first and the second: of the four views in the latter paragraph, a mixture (if we can suppose such a mixture) of the second and the third.

What I mean by this will perhaps appear as I proceed to explain how, as it seems to me, our knowledge of the higher fact is homogeneous with our knowledge of the lower, though it is small in quantity, and very vague. Though such *fact* as is known may have, and must have, a wide margin of imagination; still it is not self-contradictory, and not of such a kind that from the nature of it, we shall be wrong in exercising *any* judgment about it[1].

Philosophical error in regard to the Absolute and Things in themselves.

I am here upon a very different philosophical question, which I shall only just touch, but which I do not like to avoid, as a part of it concerns moral philosophy. I shall put it most simply perhaps by stating what appears to me an error; viz. the supposition that there is any sense or meaning in speaking, or even thinking, of 'things in themselves' which either, owing to the nature of our understanding, appear to us as things other than this, or as to which, what becomes known to us is only their relation with other things, equally unknown also. This is the general philosophical error: the moral case of it is, the supposition that there is any

[1] Compare with what follows, the fuller discussion in the *Exploratio*, pp. 60-67, and generally the chapters on Sir W. Hamilton; also the Appendix on Relativism and Regulativism at the end of this volume. Ed.

meaning in speaking of an absolute morality, for which we men, in virtue of our particular constitution, are obliged to take as morality something other and different.

What I consider to be the error may be put in other words thus: those philosophers, from Kant downwards, who have most strongly taught that we cannot see things in themselves, or know absolute morality, have been at the same time the philosophers who have most strongly given the impression that there is meaning in such an expression as 'things in themselves,' and again that there is, or might be, a so-called absolute to be known. They have given an altogether false force to the notion of our knowledge as *relative*. The consequence is, that they have led to a confusion in the minds of many between the notions of the *absolute* and the *true*. More or less unconsciously, they have taken a pleasure in tantalizing or rebuffing the human intelligence: they have talked so much about the absolute as to fill our minds with the notion that it is something which might be, something which is worth knowing, and then they tell us that we can never know it.

The assertion that we cannot know 'things in themselves' is either nonsensical or untrue:

What appears to me is, that the speaking in this manner of the things in themselves or the absolute, as if they represented the highest truth, the Platonic τὸ ὄντως ὄν, that after which is all the yearning of our intelligence,—is an entire philosophical misconception. To say that we cannot know things in themselves or the absolute, seems to me either false, or else to be like saying that we cannot know something entirely *in alio genere* from knowledge, like the saying we cannot see a sound, or hear a colour. But the feeling of the people who are told that they cannot know the absolute is that the highest knowledge, that which their minds yearn after, is thus denied to them; as if there were something in their nature forbidding them, *in genere*, to attain to the highest and worthiest truth. And so by thorough misapplication, we are told that this is humbling to our nature.

I have here given the impression produced: what the philosophers themselves have thought about it is another thing, for almost every utterance of a philosopher who has tried to pierce deep into things, and give conscientiously all he thinks, has been a text the meaning of which has afterwards to be fought about. Kant, and others after him, may have meant in substance what I have said here; but the effect of Kant's proclamation of the unattainability of transcendental knowledge was to excite an effort after the attainment of it such as there has not perhaps been since Plato. Nobody would have made this effort if they had not understood by what was thus denied to them, not some mere illogical and contradictory notion, but the real view of things, the crowning satisfaction of the thirst of knowledge.

I will very briefly explain the two senses which I said might be given to the assertion that 'things in themselves are unknowable'; in one of which senses I said that the assertion was untrue, in the other that it was nonsensical. I will speak of the latter first.

nonsensical, if the thing in itself is a mere logical entity:

The thing-in-itself may be identified with the logical subject of a proposition: in this case it is merely an unmeaning notion to which we are led by our terms, a metaphysical surd or impossible quantity. If we define or describe knowledge to be knowledge *about* things, of their properties or predicates, as is done in logic, then of course in talking of knowledge *of the things*, as distinguished from knowledge of their properties, we are using terms simply without meaning: in knowing all the properties of things we have exhausted the contents of the notion 'knowledge': there are no things to know further: 'thing' is only a word we use for convenience: thing and property counter-define each other: a thing is what has properties, as a property is what belongs to a thing. We might as well talk of knowing properties in themselves without things, as things in themselves without properties; of predicating without a subject, as of knowing a subject without a predicate.

untrue, if it means the essential nature of the thing.

Our inability to know things in this sense, as contrasted with their properties, is quite distinct from our inability to know things in the second sense to which I alluded, our inability, that is, to know them in their reality, in that which most makes them what they are. The former is a logical deception of view: the latter is the ultimate object of all learning, though it is an object which we can but very imperfectly attain. It is this latter in regard of which I said it was untrue that we could not know things in themselves. This will perhaps appear from the following.

Third-party, or phenomenal, view of knowledge.

There are three elements, or *parties*, if I might venture to call them so, which may enter into our consideration when we are thinking what knowledge is: there is the universe or object of knowledge: there is ourself as knowing, the subject of knowledge: and there is ourself as knowing that we know, or observing the phenomenon of knowledge, of which phenomenon we, the subject, make one constituent part, and the object the other. *We*, in our second or observing self, watch ourselves knowing exactly in the same way as we might, supposing we had power of observing, as to some degree we have, study the chemical properties of the universe which come into communication with our senses. In looking therefore at knowledge as a fact or phenomenon, the best supposition which we can make is that of a third party, or spectator, capable of piercing into all our consciousness, at the same time that he is capable also of piercing into every thing in the object which can possibly come into relation with our consciousness. Knowledge is before his sight or intelligence as a fact or phenomenon, a relation between a subject and an object.

It is only on this view that we can recognize a communication between things on one side, mind on the other.

And what *is* knowledge as such a phenomenon? It is a communication or, more correctly, several concurrent communications between certain things on the one side and certain things on the other: a communication which may possibly be spatial and mechanical, but which we will call chemical, between certain pleasure-and-pain-feeling nerves of our body, and certain properties of what is beyond our body, the result of which communication we call, on our part, taste, smell, perception of colour, &c.: a communication, *measurably* spatial and mechanical, between our will, setting in action certain moving nerves of our body, and certain *other* properties of our body and of what is beyond our body, which properties we describe as resistance, figure, distance, &c.: and finally a communication between *something*, whatever it is, in the object which in *other* particulars communicates with us as above, and our intelligence; the result of which communication is that we talk of the object as a thing, with a unity of its own, in the same way as we are aware of a unity of *our* own, and that knowledge, as a phenomenon, is not a disorderly hotch-potch of tastes, colours, pleasures, pains, efforts, resistances, all wildly jumbled together. To what extent the observer, piercing to the depth of our onsciousness on the one side, and understanding verything which is to be understood about the eality of the *things* on the other side, would be ble to follow, and to pronounce as real, the communication between the fragrant, coloured, figured, istant *thing*, and our *intellect* with its apparatus of ostrils, retina, eye-muscles and limbs, I will not ny further consider just now.

Such is knowledge looked at as a phenomenon y a supposed third party, or by ourselves as such a hird party, scrutinizing our knowing selves.

But things on the one side, mind on the other, elong entirely to this phenomenal or third-party iew: and I think it will be found that all the onfusion about there being, or possibly being, things n themselves which we do not see, arises from our onfusing together in our minds two views which re logically incoherent, that of ourselves as knowing, nd that of ourselves (or a third party) looking at nowledge.

If we remove the supposition of the third party, r of ourselves as a third party, and consider ourelves as single beings, as only knowing, we come to hose two views of knowledge which I have menioned before, of which we may take either, but annot at the same time take both: either of which eaves indeed something insoluble, but of a different ature from that which I am here speaking of.

The highest part of the scale of communication may be considered to constitute the essence of the thing.

In the phenomenal or third-party view, the *thing* s whatever on the objective side communicates with vhat there is on the subjective: we may, if we like t, describe the supposed substance, or nucleus, of he thing as that of which I spoke last, that which ommunicates with the intelligence; what some phiosophers would have called the idea or the form of t; that which, if we had had to make the thing, would have been first and principally in our mind about it; its meaning, reason, purpose, in relation to other things. This we should consider as, in a manner, generative of the other parts of the thing, i.e. of its qualities, in so far as these latter are determined to be what they are by this being what *it* is: at the same time these qualities are of a different nature from that which thus causes them: they communicate with us, we know them, in a different manner. We know them by what the third party could distinctly make out as a special organization, similar in many respects to themselves, adapted to the communication with them, viz. our moveable and sensitive body.

Now this supposed *soul* of the thing, as I will for a moment call it, which we communicate with by our intelligence, this which makes it a thing, or *one*, might very fairly be called the thing in itself, the absolute or real thing, if we like to use that expression: and if we do call it thus, there is much reason in saying that we do not really know it, and with our present intelligence cannot know it; though it is what all our intellectual yearning, all our desire after knowledge, aims at knowing; but our knowledge still stops short of this: we feel and handle by our sensive powers of different kinds the *qualities* of the thing, but the thing itself is only something which our mind leads us to imagine or suppose: we come to know all sorts of *relations* between the thing and other things, and between the thing and ourselves, but we cannot, from comparison of these relations, get at the thing absolutely and singly. [Let it be kept in mind that in all this there are two *we's*, the knowing and the observing self.]

We cannot get a complete

This, I suppose, is the notion of the knowledge of the reality or absolute being of things as a higher knowledge, as the knowledge of the real truth, or that which our minds thirst after. The real *knowledge*, in this view, is the communication of our mind, or pure intelligence, with that in the things with which our mind as such can communicate, viz. the mind embodied in them, their meaning, reason, purpose: to know things, in this view, is to be able, so far as the mind itself is concerned, synthetically to construct them; and in order to this we must begin with what they are for, the scheme, plan, design of them, the old Platonic ἰδέα, which, as the last thing which we get to in analysis, the first which in construction we start with, may fairly be called the thing in itself or the thing absolutely. When man is spoken of as a speculative being, it is constantly forgotten that his speculativeness goes hand in hand with his constructiveness.

Knowledge of this.

This communication of subjective mind with mind objective, or mind in things, which is the real *knowledge*, is something, in Aristotle's phrase, rather εὐκτόν, to be wished for or yearned after, than something which can be attained; but there is nothing in the nature of things to hinder its attainment: it is what we may conceive a continual approximation towards: it is something which the communication between our motive and sensive powers and the qualities of things leads us towards, not something which it diverts us from: nor is there any reason why we should hesitate to admit the suggestions of such communication except where it is misapplied and taken for what it is not.

But we continually approximate towards it by every increase of knowledge about the thing.

CHAPTER XVI.

ACTUAL AND IDEAL HUMAN NATURE.

MORAL philosophy is the exhibiting by human nature to itself of the ideal of what it ought to be and do, with the view of men's raising their own minds towards this, and also of the better among them acting upon the worse.

Practical religion is the exhibiting the above ideal to human nature from some authoritative external source, accompanied by such additional stimulus as may arise from whatever is revealed as to the facts of the moral universe to which we belong.

Man makes his own nature.

In one point of view it might be said, that the nature of man is to have no nature; the same thing might be variously expressed in other words, less pointedly or rudely, by saying, that man makes his own nature, or makes himself what he pleases, or that his nature is to be educable or trainable, and in other ways.

A view of this kind is assumed, to a certain extent, whenever we talk of man, as most philosophers have done, as a moral being; or when, as I have done, we speak in a general way of his forming ideals of what he will be and do, &c.: his doing this would be of no consequence to himself or to any one, unless he was, more or less, master of himself as to what he would be and do, not having his future life and action given him in his nature.

When Aristotle says that man, as man, has a special ἀρετή or excellence, as each animal has his excellence, a horse for instance, swiftness; and then that, man's speciality or differentia being reason, man's special excellence or ἀρετή must consist in the exercise of his reason, he says, in fact, this: for reason as such is of no particular nature. In comparing however, the nature of man with the nature of animals, there is this difference to be observed: the horse confines himself to his special excellence of swiftness, because, being destitute of reason, he has no notion of any other excellence; in fact, the cause of his special excellence is the absence of concentrated consciousness or reason; whereas man has the prerogative or misfortune to be able and to be self-impelled to think and choose what he will be and do. Man, therefore, unlike the animals, has two alternative courses before him in the exercise of his special faculty of reason. He may either, in spite of Aristotle, make himself something quite different from his neighbours, and from the mass of men, and from what his more immediate impulses suggest to him: or, if he chooses to examine himself as an animal living on earth, in order to judge by this examination what he can do well (as a horse, if he had momentary reason, might know by his form that he would *run* well), and then to do this as *his* special excellence,—he will be making what he considers his actual nature his rule and choice in a deliberate manner, peculiar to himself.

Criticism of Aristotle's account of the ἔργον of man.

No doubt with regard to a large part of our action, it is foolish to talk of not acting according to this our actual nature, because as a matter of course we must and do act so. But when we act reflectively and criticize our actions then comes in the doubleness which I have spoken of. We are in the

Our ideal of human nature must be modified by a knowledge of the actual development of man.

position, in regard to our own generic nature, both of the horse and the horse's master at once. We want something, and we use the horse for it. We do not ride and drive the horse in the first instance because it is his nature to gallop and draw, but because we want something, and we mix our thought of this want with a knowledge of his nature, and proceed to the satisfaction of our want by the way of his nature and powers. Let us suppose ourselves in an entirely savage condition, without the slightest knowledge of the actual present development of human nature, but that it was given us to be exceptionally minded, to form (on view of the miseries of our condition) an ideal, utopian but moral and reasonable, of what man might be and how he might live: knowledge then of the manner in which man, as a fact, has developed himself, would be to us like the knowledge of the nature of the horse to its rider: we should still retain our ideal as he would retain his want, but we should modify the ideal, as he would modify his want, by observation of the means of attaining it; the ideal would still be the main incentive to action, the fact would be subordinate or incentive to the manner only. But in us reflective creatures, being and thinking, fact (or *givenness*) and self-formation (or self-improvement), impulse (or disposition) and principle (or self-criticism) are mingled together in a complicated doubleness making it easy for the unthinking to say about human nature anything that they please, and making it difficult, with any amount of thought, to say anything about it satisfactory. And there is added the difficult relation between individual, and what we may call collective thought, or common judgment and custom.

Difficulties arising from the complication of the actual with the ideal.

It may be said that this complication is only because we have not got the key or the clue, and that the moment we have, all will simplify itself; as Newton's thought of gravitation and a central force put an end to the endless confusion of cycle and epicycle, orb in orb in astronomy: and one key after another has been proposed, the latest being the principle of greatest happiness.

Simplicity is not a necessary characteristic of a true theory.

If, instead of the change from the Ptolemaic to the Newtonian system, the illustration had been taken from the change from the Linnæan to the Natural system in botany, this might have suggested that simplicity is not the only consideration which should determine our preference for a theory professing to account for a complicated state of facts. Superior to simplicity, as a presumption in favour of any theory, is its application, without straining, to all the facts, and the absence of any tendency in it to restrict the view, or to cause the eyes to be shut to any of them. Unless it has this element of value, such a theory is merely artificial, and useful as it may be for many purposes, still if considered to represent the entire of knowledge, or the most important knowledge about them, it degenerates into a sort of quackery. In the advance of science of any kind, such theories are not uncommon: and one important part of the advance of science consists often in the return from them to the apparent complication, as has been in a measure the case in regard of the Linnæan system. A third element of value is, that in the true theory, when we come to look at the apparent simplification, we find it rather a shifting of the complication: for nature, which to the animal view consists simply of the things which are to be eaten, drunk and avoided, and, to the thoughtless and uneducated view, of the things which concern employment, pleasures, and pains, becomes ever to the more widely opened eye fuller and more complicated, not morehomogeneous and simple. The *wirrwarr* of the Newtonian or true view of the material universe, without, so far as we know, a single fixed point, everything turning round everything else, and the connexion of this universal motion with chemical, magnetic and other relations ;—all this is a complication probably as fertile in knowledge and in truth, as the most vaunted simplifications are sterile. And much the same complication, it seems to me, must be found in any true theory of human nature: such a system as utilitarianism represents, in my view, a merely artificial simplification, a shutting the eyes to all considerations except one; whereas what man *is* forms only one side of a picture, of which what man thinks he might be, and tries to be, forms the opposite side.

No moral system can be true which fails to exhibit the doubleness of human nature.

Whatever else we consider about man, we must add to this—what constitutes indeed the practical significance of our calling him a rational animal—that he is an ideal-forming animal. Ideal-forming implies a certain amount of dissatisfaction with, or non-acquiescence in, his actual nature: this of course must go with a certain amount of acquiescence in it, or no action could arise: for man to live simply as though he were something which he is not, would be a merely abortive existence.

The actual must be conformed to the ideal as well as the ideal to the actual.

If therefore we are looking at man as moral, if we mean at all to use such expressions as, 'it is better to do this than that,' 'this is what is right,' or 'what should be done,' man is 'progressive,' 'better now than he was,' &c., we must look at the pre-suppositions which he makes, and the ideals which he forms, as quite as important elements on one side of what we are viewing, as the facts of man's actual nature and history are on the other. We must not say, the former are to be conformed to the latter :—

so they are; but not so much as the latter are to be conformed to the former. The conforming of the ideals to the actual state in which they are to be applied is a discipline or restraint of our imagination, to keep it from mere dreaming or castle-building: the conforming of the actual state to the ideal is the very purpose of the practical philosophy or art.

Moral philosophy must help in both ways.

The business of moral philosophy, as distinguished from religion which speaks with authority, is in the first place to grasp with the inward hold, to view with the inward eye, the ideal which we form of something as what we ought to do, or ought to wish for. At this stage of thought what we mean by right, worthy, good is very vague to us, but still the words mean something. The next stage is the passing from this ideal to the *actual;* to the study both of human condition and of human feeling, to see from the former how the ideal may be applied, to see from the latter, how others, like-constituted with ourselves, look upon it. And as, if we want to study a plant, we must examine it when full-grown; so, if we want to study human nature, (so to call human condition and feeling together,) we must look at it developed, that is, in civilized society, with an eye nevertheless to the history of the manner in which it has developed, because misdevelopment is possible, the particular plant which we are studying might be a monster. The consideration of the relations of men, that is, of their simplest inter-relations, as of strength and weakness, previous benefit or previous promise and its consequent indebtedness, and others similar, as well as of those relations which law or custom has instituted, but which we could hardly imagine its failing to institute, as family and property,—this consideration fills up the outline of our ideal duty, and gives us the particulars of it. The consideration also of human *feeling*, the observation of the judgment of men in general as to duty and the comparison of this with our own, fixes and completes our notion of duty in the same manner, as our observation that others see and hear as we do helps to fix our intellectual notion of the true and real. And the work of moral philosophy, as a practical science, is then to aid the improvement of human nature, individual and collective, by the bringing into relief, and encouraging the action of, this which is the good part, or ameliorative element, of that nature. According as we choose to use language, we may say that moral philosophy in some form always exists, or we may say that moral philosophy is only an attempt to think systematically about what man is always thinking of.

The ideal is to a certain extent embodied in the actual state of civilized society.

Whatever stage of human development we take as best representing actual human nature, we cannot be entirely free from difficulty. We have no business to assume that actual human development carries, so to speak, its rightness and justification in itself, even supposing we have a sufficiently marked single development to make our words significant. But what we do is this. We, in view of our moral philosophy, are thinking what human improvement consists in, and how men may live in the best manner: and in this we are doing (*i.e.* thinking) the same which, in the actual course of human development, the intelligent minds which have suggested, animated, forwarded that development, have been doing. For man's growth, as we are now speaking of it, is not the unconscious growth of a plant: it is a continuous self-improvement: and this is produced, with regard to the race, by the action of the more thoughtful and better portion of it.

These minds may have been mistaken, and so may

we be; but when we are thinking out in particular what it is best man should become, we may reasonably, to a certain extent, associate our judgment with theirs, and conclude that, to *this* extent, what man *has* become represents what it was best he should become and what it was in his ideal nature to become.

In looking back thus on the past development of man we see that the ideally good does, to a certain extent, produce itself in the actual or existing. One society is better than another in constitution and laws, and in each society some people are better than others: but there is a kind of general goodness in all societies from which no one society must cast itself quite loose, and there is a general goodness more or less pervading the society, which no individual in it, whatever the height of his aspirations, must despise.

There is a general level of civilized morality:

The world has now lasted for so many years within human remembrance, and a great number of different societies have been formed in it. Looking on these we may perhaps say, that there seems a sort of general level to which man in society attains, and which collective man does not seem to tend to rise above, but which, in some societies and considering what man might be, is a high level. And this general level furnishes a base from which individual virtue may rise up to any extent.

This ordinary type of civilized man is what we commonly call human nature, and what indeed for a great many purposes is human nature to us. If we are led to suppose that there is an absence of tendency to rise above it, this must not be because man has not so risen, (for from what he *has* done we can only very imperfectly judge what he *will* do,) but because the weak and the strong, the bad and the good, elements of it are closely blended together. Many

to which, as to a mean standard, virtue and vice are referred.

of the motives which raise man a certain height seem to have no tendency to raise him higher, but rather to discourage such progress. And many of the motives which will indefinitely raise individual character, are not susceptible of collective application.

This is often undervalued.

Between badness then and distinguished virtue there runs the general level of human society, and the particular level, not materially different from this, of our own particular society: badness is understood as deflexion, in one direction from this : respectability or good character is *it :* any virtuousness which would be mentioned as such is something, it may be little or it may be much, above it. This is the standard of our country and age. Our law, as practically obeyed and in operation, is at the level of it.

There are many reasons why it should be difficult for us to appreciate civilized society, as a moral spectacle. As a rule, I think, we underrate the amount of virtue, self-restraint and self-sacrifice, which goes to it. One reason of our difficulty is the difficulty of morally valuing habit or custom. Another form of the same difficulty is the question of education, on which I hope to speak another time. We may be educated, some will tell us, to anything. Whatever we may think of this and kindred subjects, whatever amount there may be in human society, as there certainly is much, of low feeling and low motive, it appears to me that human civilized society presents in many respects a noble spectacle. The present mean level of human civilized morality, or ordinary respectability, represents a very high standard of moral attainment to the individual who instead of having been subjected to its discipline and education has been subjected to influences all the other way. There is one point especially in regard of which we hardly allow sufficient merit to our present civilization: I mean, not so much in regard of the material results it secures, or in regard of the higher feelings and tastes which it renders possible and encourages in its more educated classes; as in regard of the self-restraint and generous, uncomplaining, straightforwardness with which the mass in humble position set themselves to the work before them, able, with all their imperfections, to see—what it requires some elevation of mind to see—that the benefit of the social existence to them and to all is something of far more importance than its *prima facie* injustice to themselves in particular.

We must have an ideal to estimate it rightly.

In human society, we can both see its goodness, such as it is, and we can see, to some extent, the principles which make it good, which tend to preserve and elevate it. But moral philosophy is more than *sociology*, or the study of human society in any way. For we could not speak with any reason of its being good, or of there being good principles in it, except upon an assumed ideal. It is with the thought of this ideal that moral philosophy begins: we must bring our vague ideal into connexion with the facts of human nature or society: the consideration of the latter, though important, is not the leading line of thought.

What is included in this social virtue.

We might call by the name of *sociality* the general virtuousness, or general character which belongs to or fits civilized society, without rising very greatly above the requirements or standard of it.

The particulars of this sociality will be obedience to the laws, interest in the support and vindication of them, moderate, not revolutionary, effort at the improvement of them; together with a constant feeling how much the best system of law and custom must leave to be done by individual principle; and in this view, watchfulness to supplement laws by respect to claims of all kinds; active benevolence to redress in some measure the inequalities of condition which law could not prevent, even if it aimed at doing so, and which it sometimes even increases; and to meet the vicissitudes, troubles, and difficulties of the less fortunate. The doing these things, more or less, is what is expected by the general feeling from those whom it approves and thinks well of; it constitutes a sort of social law or moral standard. All this is social *virtue*: but to social *character* there goes something besides, which is the first, if not the chief, good element of it, though the manner in which it exists in the individual mind is very various, and sometimes it has features about it not at all those of virtue. This I will roughly describe as *industry*. Morality, as I have said, begins when others are supposed to exist as well as ourselves, whom our action may possibly concern, the simple looking after ourselves having no moral character either way. Acting for happiness, or working for support, is a precondition of virtue, but is not virtue. And much industry may be, so far as the consciousness of the exercise of it is concerned, mere selfishness. Still there can be no common life of men at all, and *a fortiori* no worthy common life, or civilization, without support and, more than support, wealth: and the labour for this is thus the first or underlying social duty: the labourer may be an unconscious, or even vicious, concurrent in a worthy work, but still his work is worthy.

Practical ethics must take it as a starting-point.

It is very important, in all *practical* moral philosophy, that whether it is special virtue on the one side, or wrong-doing on the other, that we are considering, we should take as our starting-point, for proceeding in one direction or the other, this middle ground or level of ordinary human good character.

This is what is due from a man; this is what society has a right to expect from him. For deflexions from this in the *bad* direction, if they are great, it will, in virtue of laws which it has made, (which in fact are so many proclamations of penalty,) punish him: if they are less, it will disapprove, and mark its disapproval. Risings above this will be variously treated. Some will be honoured and admired, some will be not understood, some will be condemned; which latter fact may possibly add to the merit, because to the difficulty of them.

It is a mean between vice and higher virtue, but may not be disregarded by the latter.

This *medium* is not an Aristotelic medium of virtue between two vices, but it is one kind of virtue standing between vice and another kind of virtue: and there are merits of its own belonging to this lower or medium virtue. It is a sort of general expression for a great deal of exceedingly mixed character, which *upon the whole* is virtue: it is virtue in some degree shorn of its individual loftiness and free outgrowth, but in some respects compensated for this by the manner in which the mutual rub and interaction of men draws out one feature and another of it, and keeps in excrescence and exaggeration.

Though, therefore, still cherishing our ideal, and wishing that our civilization should improve into something better, and that there should be as many individuals in it as possible who are more than respectable, who are of distinguished virtue, we maintain our middle point not only against what is below it, but, in one point of view, against what is above it, in so far, that is, as it is *tried*, as it represents something which we understand, and a point at which we may reasonably expect to attend to *all* our duties, not sacrificing the less interesting to the more.

Respect for lower virtue is a precondition for higher.

The good citizen is the man who, in Scriptural language, 'renders their dues to all,' in jural language[1], 'neminem laedit, suum cuique tribuit'; and this, with a wide construction of the dues or the 'suum,' taking in a very large margin of moral dues beyond the legal ones. But still, this is but a medium level; we must recognize an expansive element besides in virtue, as there is in the jural 'honeste vivere,' in the Scriptural 'beyond more definite dues, still hold yourselves bound to love one another.' Only we have got in this middle ground something comparatively firm to stand on. No doubt, it is a ground which is often clung to in an unworthy manner; perhaps more so, where the society is more civilized: but still, the greater part of the practical immorality in literature consists in the neglect of it. Characters with exaggerated virtues brought into relief by exaggerated vices will always have the most of dramatic interest and therefore be tempting in literature. But, with almost all, respect for the ordinary level of virtue is the precondition of higher virtue: our highest mountains will rise from a high table-land, not from a low sea-shore.

Social virtue has much in common with justice.

Justice, when it is described as a virtue, means, like rightness, a variety of things according to the application. Of the notions it involves, what we may have most in view at any given time may be its mutuality or *interhominalism*, its exactness and definiteness, its generality and universality, or its

[1] "Juris praecepta sunt haec: honeste vivere, alterum non laedere, suum cuique tribuere." Ulpian in Dig. I. 1. 10. It would be interesting to know the history of these three primary rules of right, but the tantalizing fragmentary character of the Digest gives them only thus barely. In making "honeste vivere" a part of *jus*, we may conclude that Ulpian and the Roman lawyers considered that law was not to be confined to that part of a man's conduct which had direct relation to others, and that it was competent to do more than simply prohibit doing them a direct wrong.

relation to quantity, measurement, balance. Of these four notions involved in justice, the three first are prominent features of that social virtue which I have spoken of; the last is a feature of it in a way which I shall shew. But mutual, definite, general, regulation of the concerns of a number of men together is the business of the custom and law which make society, and the man whose individual feeling and conduct are in harmony with this, is the man who, in these main particulars, is the *just* man.

His justice will indeed have another employment besides that of falling in with the institutions of the society in which he lives; that namely of judging of them. For justice is fairness; it is concerned, as I said, with quantity, measurement, balance. The units and elements required for this are given in laws; but our feelings of justice judge *of* these as well as according to them; what has *nature*, in the first instance, given or instituted?

It attributes value to general sentiment, but need not weaken individuality.

The man of social virtue is not the mere creature of the society in which he lives. His possession of the social virtue is in fact this, that he makes the society in which he lives give to him, to a certain extent, the ideal of his duty. He more or less believes in it, more or less thinks it good. But men have made its institutions, laws and customs; and in taking his duty partly from them, he does not abdicate his prerogative of judging them by his ideal of what they should be.

Nor is he the creature of opinion: it is not the fact of the approval of what he does by the society in which he lives which makes what he does virtue to him, but it is his *own* approval of it, and his recognizing the reasons of it, which makes it so. He neither despises others' opinion, nor blindly follows it.

Society must be itself corrected in accordance with the ideal which it helps to form.

We have thus, in human society and men's expectations from us according to it, our ideal duty to a certain degree embodied and localized. We have claim and want presenting themselves to us for satisfaction and supply; a common conscience stimulating and keeping alive our individual one. Since the actual thus involves in itself a certain amount of the ideal, we do not degrade the ideal nor distort the actual by associating the two together: while recognizing the actual, or positive, we may also recognize in it the ideal, or that which should be.

It is true indeed that we have duties *towards* the society as well as suggested by it; to judge, it may be, to try to revolutionize it: so far as this is so, we do not recognize it as a result of the ideal human nature, as what should have been; which it certainly is not entirely, perhaps, in the particular case, may not be at all. This belongs to another consideration.

CHAPTER XVII.

ON THE GOODNESS OF CUSTOM.

IN studying the nature of an animal, what we study is, its *anatomy* (in which I include appearance &c.), and what we call its *habits*. These two things are adapted together, so that to a certain extent we may conclude the one from the other; as is done in the case of fossil creatures where the anatomy alone is directly open to observation. And both are fitted to a third thing which again we can only study indirectly, and which I will call an inward nature. Each creature knows and does what is necessary to keep it alive. If a lion had the impulses or instincts of a cow, it would die.

Custom in men corresponds to habit in animals.

As we talk of *habits* of animals, let us talk of *customs* of human nature (I use the word quite generally, not meaning to draw any conclusions from it). Let us divide these customs into three kinds: (1) necessary and universal customs, entirely of the nature of animal habits, as of eating, drinking, sleeping: (2) customs which we may call universal, but of rather a higher kind than the last, or, if we so please to express it, the first kind applied to the wider view and higher instincts of human nature; I mean such customs as speaking the truth, gratitude, being kind to others, &c.: (3) possible or partial customs, about which there is or may be discussion among men, whether they are good or bad, desirable

Three kinds of custom, instinctive, moral, legal.

or undesirable. Laws and institutions (whatever they may be besides) are a definite and exact form of these last customs.

The relation of individuals to the customs in these different cases is as follows. The first set, analogous to the habits of animals, are followed instinctively by all individuals, saving exceptions and particular circumstances, as may be the case with animals: many of them indeed, such as eating and drinking, must in any case be followed, though not necessarily all.

Customs of the second and third kind, individuals may follow or not as they please, subject to whatever consequences their conduct may entail upon them. The second kind however being universal customs, it may be considered that there must be some strong recommendation of them to each individual (saving exceptions), which is the only way in which we can conceive their becoming thus universal.

What I have here called customs, might also be called manners of thought, feeling and action, which are to some extent general, those of the third kind being general in only a limited degree.

Morality is concerned with individual character, with relation of individual to custom, with goodness of custom.

Now morality is concerned with the character of the individual, with the relation of the individual character and feeling to the customs, and with the goodness of the customs. We want morality to tell us, first, independently of any customs, supposing for instance there were no such things as general ways of thinking in the world and no possibility of them, what sort of moral mind the individual, as an individual, should have, and what sort of action he should choose. We want it again to tell us how the individual should stand affected to action by general rules or according to general ways of acting; to what extent he should be independent of them and act upon his own judgment and upon the particular circumstances of each case, or the opposite. And we want it still again to tell us, with regard to general manners of thinking and judgment, whether they are good or bad.

To put the matter in another way, proceeding in a reverse direction, what is morally to be desired in a country is, that the general ways of thinking, judging and acting, the general arrangements, the institutions, all the things which the people, in Herodotus' phrase, *νομίζουσι*, should be good, and not bad: and by a good moral philosophy, in this view, we mean a good rationale of the manner of judging about them. But there might be the best customs conceivable in a country: and yet, if the people were merely slaves or machines acting according to them, doing only what everybody else did; or if, on the other hand, many important individuals stood entirely aloof from the customs and were unaffected by them; then, with good customs, we should yet have a bad state of things. We want the general manners of thought properly to affect the individuals, not too much, or too little: and by moral philosophy in this view we mean a good theory of the action of individual conscience in these respects, and of education. But still again, quite beyond anything which can be general and customary, we want to have feeling of a right kind in individual men: and moral philosophy in this view is the consideration of the moral ideals, the effort to see or form them as distinctly as we can, to compare them, as best we can, with fact, to find out the way of raising our action, our individual and the general action, in the direction which they indicate: this is the leaven, the sap, the life, which sets human nature at work to elevate and improve itself.

Instinctive custom is morally indifferent: there is a general agreement as to moral custom.

Looking at human nature over the globe, and neglecting customs of the first kind as not in themselves morally important, we find a good deal of custom or general feeling of the second kind, which, as I said, is universal. This kind of general feeling, which however at the best is exceedingly vague, has often formed the subject of moral discussion, not so much in the view of testing its goodness, supposing it to exist, as of arguing from its existence that morality is natural to man. It is difficult, in these discussions, to keep in view the exact point at issue. The important fact about the customs is not that men ordinarily do speak the truth and shew gratitude or kindness; for I do not see how we could argue from this as to what individuals should do: a man might say, I do not care to conform to human custom in these respects, nor see why I should. The important fact is, that men, while constantly doing the opposite of these, yet have a custom of approving action of these kinds, of liking the people who do it, of wishing themselves to do it, except for special temptation drawing them the other way. That is to say, alongside of their action they have an ideal: they are two-natured beings, which is the same as saying that they are moral beings: they have conscience or reflexion, a nature judging a nature: they have their nature of fact, and along with it a moral imagination, expanding, elevating and improving it. Of course it is competent for an individual to say that we cannot argue from this any more than from the former, as to what his particular action should be: he may say that he does not choose to admit any 'ought' or 'should'; that granting it to be a human custom, say weakness, to imagine such a call upon us, he thinks it a bad custom. Now without pressing the 'ought' and 'should' (about which, and how far it represents imperativeness or incumbentness, how far a simple ideal or desirableness, I have already spoken), I do not think any man can go so far as to say, that he really sees no reason at all in the nature of things for the custom of men's approving gratitude rather than ingratitude, &c. I do not think it possible that any man could fail to be himself influenced in some degree by the feeling which has generated the custom.

Legal custom is that which causes most difficulty as to the feeling of the individual towards it.

Customs of the second kind being accompanied thus, in some degree, by a feeling recommending it in all individuals, there is not, in regard to it, so much room for the consideration of the relation between individual and customary feeling. In it they are to a certain extent united. It is more in regard to custom of the third kind that I shall have to speak about this, and also about testing the goodness of custom.

Looking again at actual human nature in different parts of the globe, we find an infinite variety as to custom or general feeling of the third kind. And here is one of the great provinces of moral philosophy. Is there any occasion to test these customs morally? May it not be well that one nation should have the institution of slavery, another that of polygamy, another that of a marriage-connexion only during the pleasure of the parties, another that of inheritance by primogeniture, another that of communism, another that of caste, another that of eating meat, another that of strict abstinence from destruction of life, another that of suttee, another that of exposure of infants, and so on: is there any right or wrong, any better or worse, in all these things? or is it only a picturesque variety, like the variety of colour and of language? And if there *is* a good and bad, what is the criterion of it?

Productiveness of happiness is one sign of good custom:

In speaking about happiness, I have said, that right conduct must surely be productive of happiness to the agent; in a great measure, doubtless, visibly; altogether believably, on the supposition that things go in a systematic manner, or that the universe is good. Whether therefore or not productiveness of happiness be the *constituent* of goodness in action, which is what I dispute, I have never disputed its being *a sign* of goodness or rightness in action. But for it to be of any value as a sign to know goodness or rightness by, we must have the ground clear before us for the application of this test of productiveness of happiness: and this is what, for any important inquiry, we never can have. We cannot have a sufficient clearness of view or agreement as to what happiness consists in, nor can we have such as to whose happiness it is that is to be consulted. In saying this I am not disputing the importance of the productiveness of happiness as one test or sign of an action being good.

but not an easy or satisfactory test.

If we are sufficiently agreed beforehand as to what we mean by happiness, and as to whose happiness we want, then *this* mark may be the mark of goodness which is best, because most applicable: but this, I think, will not often be the case. And certainly it will not, in such a degree as to furnish a good argument to utilitarians for the correctness of their system from the readiness, and satisfactoriness, of this test of goodness. Productiveness of happiness might conceivably be the constituent of goodness: in that case, so far as it is capable of application, it would be the proper test of goodness. Again, productiveness of happiness, though only one mark amongst others of goodness, might conceivably, from its nature, be a mark so ready and clear of application that it would be the mark naturally suggesting itself to test goodness by. This last, if it were so, would be an argument for men being *practically* utilitarians: the argument would not indeed prove that utilitarianism was philosophically true, or that productiveness of happiness was the constituent of goodness, though utilitarians doubtless would, as they even now do, use it in that view: but a man might then reasonably say, Well then, I will look no further: I want to know what things are good and right, and if I have a mark of that, I will be satisfied without knowing what *makes* them good and right.

Exemplified in the case of slavery: difficulty of determining *whose* happiness:

I have already disputed productiveness of happiness being the constituent of goodness; I will now examine whether it is a satisfactory mark of it.

Let us take the institution of *slavery*, and see how we can apply the test of productiveness of happiness to judge about that.

You cannot apply the test at all till you have settled that preliminary matter which must be settled before you get to utilitarianism, but in which the whole of moral philosophy is involved, viz. *whose* happiness you mean. Do you mean the happiness of white men or of black? Utilitarianism, you say, teaches that the happiness of all men is to be consulted alike. But in reality, utilitarianism, *as* such, simply teaches that it is happiness that is to be looked to, happiness, not to say of all *men*, but of the whole sentient creation: it says not a word as to *alike*, for it would not venture to apply this 'alike' to each member of the sentient creation, or each creature capable of happiness. The separating men from the rest of the sentient creation, and the saying that the happiness of each *man* is to be consulted alike, belong to something which is not utilitarianism: we will call it *equalitarianism:* it may be right or it may be wrong: anyhow before we can begin to say a word about happiness, we have got to settle this equalitarian business. The Georgian planter will say, I grant you we are to promote the happiness of all the sentient creation, and to distinguish men from the rest of it because there is a natural distinction; but here I leave you: I recognize another natural distinction, viz. between white men and black men; and I apply my *equality* fully to the former, but not to the latter. Here then we have got a question of *nature* to decide before we can settle the equalitarianism; as we have got to settle the latter before we can begin to talk about the happiness. I should differ from the Georgian as much as any utilitarian would; but surely it is plain that here utilitarianism gives us no help to settle the question; we cannot apply the consideration of happiness. The Georgian will say, I am a white-man-utilitarian, and think that we are to use the blacks for our benefit, treating them kindly of course, as you agree we are to use the animals. In an opposite way the Buddhist is a sentient-creation-utilitarian, and thinks that we are to consult the happiness of the animals, as we are that of men, and have no more right to destroy them. Some principle of supposed justice or naturalness is needed to decide between these different forms of utilitarianism, and it is upon this principle that the application of the principle of happiness must rest.

what kind of happiness.

Supposing however, there were no difficulties like these in the way; supposing that these preliminaries had all been settled to the satisfaction of the English utilitarian, and that we were now proceeding to the application of the principle of happiness; still in order that we may hope for any result, the anti-slavery man and the Georgian have got to agree beforehand what is a negro's happiness. If the one says that, with care taken of him, and plenty to eat and drink to the end of his days, he is happier than he would be taking a precarious care of himself, when he would have to work quite as hard with less certainty of support, what is the other to say? I do not say that the question of comparative happiness is not an important one; but I do say, first, that it is not one which will settle the question either way so distinctly as to commend itself for the proper method in virtue of this its distinctness; and second, that the more barely we rest the issue upon this, the more, it seems to me, will the Georgian have to say. It is he who will take his stand upon the genuine Epicureanism or utilitarianism, upon tangible pleasure and quantity of happiness, while his opponent will have to talk in a more shadowy manner about the charm of being one's own master, the worthiness of being a free agent. That is to say, the happiness which the anti-slavery man wants for the negro is complicated with various other considerations, as happiness of any value always is in human life; the happiness which the Georgian thinks it is best the negro should remain in, is happiness of that merely corporeal, semi-animal kind which really can be to a certain extent measured. The anti-slavery man is right just because, as it seems to me, he is the *less* utilitarian of the two. But in any case (what I am concerned with here) it is evident that utilitarianism or the consideration of happiness, as such, brings no valuable help for the distinct settlement of the question.

Whatever important social question, or fundamental institution, we may thus seek to test, the same two difficulties will occur, the one, as to the clearing of the ground for the application of the test, the other, as to the uncertainty of the test itself.

Legal customs divided into those which are, or are not, of moral importance.

The whole mass of custom which comes under this third class, may be divided into that which is of moral importance, and that which is not; and the first thing to be done, if it can be done, is to find some way of making this division. That portion of it is of moral importance in which is concerned, not only men's happiness, but also their elevation of mind either moral or intellectual, their goodness or their intelligence. The whole amount of custom is the fit object of criticism in these respects; but with regard to a good deal of it we should say it cannot be called either good or bad absolutely; it does some good, some harm, not much perhaps of either; this is what I call not of moral importance; and there is no merit or advantage in mere uniformity. But much is of great moral importance.

Men commonly admire their own customs and despise those of others. Philosophic reaction.

It is of course most difficult to judge of human custom from any general point of view; every one has been brought up in his own. The ordinary feeling is, for each man to despise and misappreciate all custom but his own; but this, like all ordinary feeling, creates an opposite feeling in many thinking minds; they see the defects of their own, and rather admire what is not their own; as the noble minds, whose existence testified to the goodness of Athenian custom, were disposed often to admire any other rather than it. Till the world was known as it is now, the remote and the ideal might be to a certain degree blended in thought. Men might imagine in Ethiopians, in Egyptian priests, in Brachmans, in Atlantises, realms of innocence and wisdom, and good feeling, and happiness. We, if we are dissatisfied with the European nineteenth century, and the Times, and Manchester, are obliged (at least since the American contest has begun) to confess that it is human nature and the progress which it has made that we are dissatisfied with; it is perhaps no great vanity or Pharisaism to say that we, the civilized European and American, are the best specimen of it, an improvement on Chinese, Mahometans, and Brahmins.

This fact however makes very much more likely, and not very much less foolish, the ordinary contempt for other custom than our own, which I have spoken of, while it diminishes the likelihood of the balancing feeling of admiration for some, at least supposed, other custom. It by no means follows that because we are foremost of the human race, therefore everything about us is what is best in the human race; and it is quite possible that some of the things which we most pique ourselves upon may be the opposite of this. Our contempt of other custom is no proof that it is contemptible; for we are to the full as much despised as we despise, perhaps rather more. If it were possible for us really to meet in any community of thought with a Brahmin or a Mahometan, he might admit all our superiority in the arts of life, and all our political power and wealth and importance derived from it, and still despise us. If we could prove to him that we were happier than his people were, I think, so far as that went, which is only some way, he would not despise us. But, as I have said all along about happiness, I do not think we could come to any community of thought with him about this, for, beyond a limited range, we can hardly come into community of thought, one with another, even among ourselves. We might tell him that experience, that is, the verdict of competent judges who have made the experiment, witnesses that to live actively, to drink wine, to eat pork, to study science, to have

It is easier to find common ground in regard to morality than in regard to happiness;

only one wife, makes a man happier than to live in *his* way. He might say, It may be so, but so far as I can see, *my* way is the way for happiness. If on the other hand we bring the question to the test of comparative wisdom and goodness, I think that there we shall have more likelihood of finding common ground. It is true we might care as little for the subtilties of Arabian grammar and the flowers of Arabian rhetoric, as he for steam and the electric telegraph, but still I think we might shew him that we were wiser than he, and then he would respect us: and if we could shew him that we were better than he, then I am sure he would. And I think he would understand what was meant by being better. I think the Hindoo, whatever lies he might tell himself, must in his heart acknowledge us as a superior people on seeing our truthfulness and mutual confidence. I think the Mahometan, if we could only make him understand what pains we take in our courts of justice to find out the real right or the real person who has done wrong, and with what integrity we adjudge and punish, would respect us for *that:* it is when we come most to morals and to goodness that we shall have *the most* of mutual understanding.

Thus, though human goodness is in my view a complicated thing and difficult to understand, still I think it is to a certain extent possible to compare the customs of different peoples in reference to it; and that, in so doing, we need not be merely bringing their customs to the standard of our own.

There is a medium between foolish prejudice of this sort and that philosophic indifferentism which is not unlikely to rise against it in minds of less earnestness and more knowledge of variety of custom. The world is large and wide, and nineteenth century civilization is not the only important phase of humanity and human custom which has existed or does exist. We look upon human thought as expanding downwards: more correctly we might look upon it in three divisions; some streams of it have merged into our present thought; some have dried up without doing so; some exist still independent of that, full and abundant, but stagnant.

About any custom then (say the Oriental seclusion of women), what we have first to consider is, whether it is of moral importance; if it is, whether human happiness is affected by it, so far as we can judge of this; and lastly, what is of more importance and in all probability more within our power to judge of, whether the moral and intellectual elevation of individuals and the human race is benefited or injured by it.

The most important thing to know about any custom is whether its tendency is elevating.

But there is something else which in most cases we shall have to consider also. To a certain extent, though not so much with goodness as with happiness, before the test can be applied, or has meaning, there wants a clearing of the ground; and this is in fact, the introducing of the consideration which I will call *naturalness.* Giving it such a name says very little about its meaning. What sort of naturalness is right?

But a prior question is itsnaturalness.

In speaking of morality in general, I have said that it consists of the union of fact with ideal as we can best unite them; that man has a double nature, including, on the one hand, certain things which in a manner exist of themselves, and, on the other, an imagination and an activity which enable him, according to an ideal or principle which suggests itself to him, to make himself in some respects what he pleases. What he thus tries to make himself is his ideal nature. His having this imagination and activity is what makes him a moral being. If we would

This must be determined by sociology.

speak of him as being *one* nature, and give *a single* meaning to the word natural, we must, as I said, unite the fact and the ideal together; we must try to distinguish, in the fact, that part which the ideal takes up, and that which it changes. In the usage about women which I spoke of, what lies at the base is the physical fact, whatever it is, as to the nature of women in relation to men. It is of no use to form an ideal of their active and intellectual companionship with men, if they have not a nature which will admit of such. Are we then to take the seclusion of women in a considerable portion of the world as a mark of their physical inferiority which our ideal about them must recognize, or as a bad portion of fact which our ideal must correct? In the former case the custom is what I have called 'natural.' And to find whether the former *is* the case we must see what women have been and are, in the world and history. An investigation like this is *sociology*, but it differs from M. Comte's in this, that we know what we are looking for. We have got an ideal, and in examining fact we do so in order to modify our ideal, to give it form, and make something practical of it.

What is unnatural must be injurious.

The question really at issue in regard of most of the great customs of men is their *naturalness*, and there is no other way in which we can distinctly put it. We have got hands instead of wings, and though some of us individually might prefer the grand view of nature, which the former might give us, to all our constructive power, yet we cannot change. And it is well we cannot: for the handling and constructive impulse, which goes with our possession of hands, is one of the main constituents of our general understanding, and contributes largely to our separating, distinguishing, and individualizing things as things, or noticing them as particular objects. So it may be with various human customs. Acquisition and associating things with ourselves as our own, may be an impulse of our nature as much as construction is, and if so it is of no more use to form the ideal of a society (other than exceptional) in which no individual property existed, than to wish that we had wings. So far as we could approximate to such a society, it would in that case be only to our loss. To determine what is 'natural', in human customs, is a matter indeed of much observation and difficulty: I offer the term as exhibiting the reality, not as an easy test or method. I have said perhaps enough about ideals to justify myself from too great readiness to acquiesce in fact. But we must study human nature as it exists at its best, as well as think of what we should wish it to be.

It is difficult to determine what has contributed to improvement in the past:

Human nature as a whole cannot judge itself as individual man judges himself, it has not a collective conscience or reflective power: but it can, as a whole, improve, and it is this improvement in which we seem best to see, for collective man, that doubleness of nature which I have mentioned as constituting morality. We must first ascertain, as we can, that the historical course of human nature is upon the whole improvement, and not declension: for by improvement we must mean something different from M. Comte's progress, not, *i.e.* the fact of a course or development the last phase of which, only because it is the last, we are to consider as the best. Then, if we find that there has been real improvement, we must set before ourselves, as well as we can, the features of that improvement; we must see, that is, how the ideal applies itself to human nature. All this is of course difficult. Thus we may find that, in this course of improvement, the condition of women has risen; that the attachment to property has not diminished. The first of these we might at once consider an improvement: it is an advance towards the ideal which suggests itself. On the second, we can conclude no more than that up to the present time men have not seen property to be a mistake and evil: it may be so for all that, only there is a probability, so far as history goes, of its naturalness. We must look at the moral circumstances which in the course of history have attended it; whether it has been associated with things which we recognize as improvements, and seems to have aided them; how it stands with relation to human comfort, and human virtue; and much besides.

and still more difficult to make sure of what will aid improvement in the future.

Difficult as this may be, there is a fresh difficulty added when we come to apply our view of improvement in the past to our action for the future. We have got to judge from the nature of the improvement, whether what is an improvement so far as it has gone will continue to be an improvement carried further. We have got to resist 'la logique des faits', and the notion that what is last is, as such, best: we have got to understand, when we speak of an improvement, why we call it an improvement: and that will, in some degree, guide us in going on.

Real criterion of custom.

Human nature then is moral collectively in virtue of this its continued effort, and more or less success, in self-improvement. Its ideal nature is what it tries to make itself. Its naturalness of mere fact is what men without any ideal effort or thought do: its naturalness, if we try to unite ideal and fact into one notion, is what abides the same for it during its improvement, and this is what we want to find out, for it is no use to try to alter *that*. And therefore a main thing which we want to find out in regard to any human custom is whether it is of this character.

CHAPTER XVIII.

RELATION OF INDIVIDUAL TO CUSTOM.

I WILL now speak about the relation of individual conduct to general feeling or custom.

Close connexion between the ideas of the customary and the right.

To a certain extent, the notion of right or moral conduct which presents itself to the mind is that it is acting as others do, according to general feeling, custom, or opinion. The effort of education is always, to a certain extent, to produce a systematic acting in this way: in an earlier and simpler state of society, it is so especially. In the opinion of many, what such words as the Greek δίκη represent is custom, or recognized usage. However this may be, whether for instance the word δίκη first expressed the 'accustomed,' and then was used to express the 'right', because people really meant by the right no more than the accustomed; or first meant the right, and then was used to express the accustomed, because people concluded that nothing but the right could become the accustomed; in either case it is clear that the words custom and rightness were very closely associated. Hence too, in a great measure, the use of the word 'mores' to express conduct, with its derivatives, 'morals' and 'morality.'

Two views: that custom witnesses to right, that it constitutes right.

There are two notions, similar at first sight but really different, involved in our thinking that the doing the customary is doing the right. The customary is the non-individual, and also it is what most people do. That it is this latter implies a presumption that it is the right: the many, it is presumed, are more likely to be right than the one. Here the independent existence of rightness is recognized: custom is considered a guide to the knowledge of it. But that the customary is the non-individual, in a certain view of rightness, *makes* it the right: rightness has been understood by some, simply as the subjugation of our own particular individuality or self-consideration to a something ruling *it*, as well as other individualities, and making them act similarly. In the former case custom *witnesses* to rightness: in the latter it *constitutes* it. In the former case rightness is judged by fact and human experience, or what is supposed to be such: in the latter case rightness is defined by law; and custom is both a kind of law, and the basis of law, the *νόμος* of Greek, corresponding to the *mos et lex* of Latin. This latter is Hobbism.

Against the first view, individuality denies the validity of its witness:

Individuality may protest against customariness in reference to either of these notions, or both: we may refuse to believe that opinion either makes, or is a valid witness to, rightness. It is in reference to its witness to rightness that, side by side with the grave and sententious teaching of early moralism to do what other people do, there has always existed a counter-feeling of contempt for the ὄχλος, and gnomes like *οἱ πλείους κακοί*: and in a similar manner, in the view of earnest religious systems of morality like the Christian, custom is the world, the witness to the wrong, not to the right.

against the second, it maintains that morality is the non-customary, the free.

At the same time there has always been more or less of opposition to custom (as *constituting* right) on the ground that morality or rightness is just *not* in the customary or commanded, but in the individual and free. Determination from without and self-determination from within are not the same, but opposite. We each make our own rightness: and although, from the similarity of our circumstances and nature, it may be the same in one and another, or common to many, yet this commonness is just what we ought to be suspicious of, and most careful not to be influenced by.

In the former case it is connected with conscience, in the latter with self-respect.

There are thus two sorts of feeling of individuality or of protest against custom, akin in many respects, but still different. The one is the feeling of responsibility for one's self, the other is the assertion of freedom. The former of these we may roughly call (I shall qualify as we go on) the belief in rightness, or in independent rightness; the latter the belief in one's self. This belief in rightness is a kind of conscientiousness, and when it degenerates, it becomes crotchetiness and punctiliousness, an inability to symbolize and associate with others. The belief in one's self is a kind of self-respect, and when it degenerates it becomes mere capriciousness and eccentricity, mixed with more or less of silly or sour vanity.

Education tends to produce customariness: it should aim at increasing conscientiousness and freedom.

All education has necessarily a tendency to produce customariness, or to train the individual to think and act as others do: in fact this is what training means: education must do this, or it does nothing. So certain however is it that it will do this, that in view of almost all who think about education, a main thing to be guarded against is its doing it too much. You are sure to develope a regard to opinion and custom: one thing you want is to make this opinion the genuine wide opinion of the whole society, not that of a particular set, which may be a bad one; but another thing you want is, to develope both the conscience and the independence of the individual under education, and in regard of his conscience, to accustom him to use it not simply for self judgment in association with the opinion of others, but also, with modesty indeed and diffidence, but still really, for judgment and criticism of this opinion of others itself. The developing the independent conscientiousness thus is what education can in a measure do, and what it is specially bound to do, inasmuch as the doing it is the counteracting a possible evil result of itself. The development of the independence of freedom, or trust in one's self, is more difficult for any education or training, if indeed it is possible; the existence of this feeling depends very much upon particular character, and upon circumstances perhaps independent of education.

The conscientious man, while respecting the judgment of others, feelsbound to maintain the independence of his own judgment.

To speak however first of conscientiousness, the belief in rightness or the feeling of individual responsibility; this has nothing of that contempt for custom and the common opinion which often accompanies the feeling of independence. He who is actuated by conscientiousness believes that there is something which he ought to do, and something which other people ought to do also; he believes that *they* want to know it more or less as well as he does; and consequently *their* judgment on the matter, expressed in their general opinion and custom, cannot be indifferent to him, unless he is merely vain and foolish. And, in judging himself, he takes this opinion constantly into account: the imagination how others would judge, if they knew what he does about himself, goes with his moral judgment. But for all that, his reason is his own. This general opinion or judgment, if it is good, has grown so not of itself, if we may so speak, but by the putting together of a number of individually conscientious judgments, each affecting perhaps and affected by the others, but each having its own root. Were opinion of itself the law, there could be, if we may say so again, no opinion: that is to say, opinion would only express the result of some previous accident or fact, and would be no result of human thought. And the person who does not preserve his individuality of thought against it is a traitor to it; his disposition to yield to it should be an argument to him against such yielding, for others have probably had the disposition before, and have yielded to it, and so far as they have yielded, so far there is want of ground for the opinion, or chance that it is wrong.

Systems which make morality a product of education tend to weaken moral individuality.

Moral positivism, that is, any kind of moral teaching which tends to weaken men's belief in independent rightness, or their thought of there being something which should be done, tends to withdraw the foundation upon which individual conscientiousness rests, and though it need not tend to diminish practical conscientiousness, because this may be guarded against, yet it tends to diminish the strength of individual moral character. Justice may be a very good thing, and we may unfeignedly think it so, but if we regard it as only a matter of education, or something which has been taught us; and if moreover we regard education as a comparatively accidental superinduction of something (and it is this view of education, as a superinduction, which is the interest of it in the eyes of positivists), giving no value to the consideration, that no creature, man or other, can be educated in anything except what it is their nature to be educated in;—then undoubtedly the justice does not lie so deep in our mind and character, it will not be so helpful in shaping our moral individuality, as it would be in the case of one who thought differently about it; it may be a good working justice, but there is not so much in it either of interest in the present, or of hope for future progress.

Utilitarianism takes this view of justice, but holds the love of the general happiness to be innate.

Utilitarianism, it is to be observed, is positivist or non-idealist only in certain particulars; and the description of it as a matter of inductive science is profession only, or it would not be moral philosophy at all. The desire of happiness (it being apparently indifferent to us *whose* happiness it is, our own or that of others) is considered by utilitarians a spontaneous and untaught sentiment of our nature, and the one moral sentiment. So far utilitarianism is not positivist; for this happiness is a grand and noble ideal. But any other so-called moral sentiment, as of fairness or justice, is matter of education or association, secondary only, in utilitarian view: it is developed in human society as a result of the institutions which the really innate sentiment, the desire of happiness, produces.

There is no ground for the distinction. One is no more the product of education than the other.

The sentiment of fairness or justice, and the sentiment of the desire of others' happiness certainly deserve to be put into the same class, and both alike be called either spontaneous and natural, or growths of education and society. However, what I am now concerned with is, that the effort of utilitarianism calling itself inductive, is first, as a matter of philosophy, to discourage the thinking of anything besides fact, of any ideal, or anything as what *should* be done; and then when, untrue to its principle, it does become a moral philosophy, to discourage the thinking about some of the moral principles, such as fairness and justice, as other than creations and developments of human education and opinion. To the extent to which men are led to think in this manner, it appears to me that they are led, in regard of some most important portions of morals, to think of human education and opinion more highly than they should, and that they are the less likely to assert their own individual judgment and conscience against this education and opinion. I am not certain that I shall be understood here, for the matter is complex, not I think through my fault, but on account of the exceeding inappropriateness of the assumption of inductivism for anything in its way so idealist as Utilitarianism is. In some points of morals no doubt it maintains the right of individual judgment, but we want it everywhere, and want it intelligent and consistent.

Individuality of freedom. Is it right to hold oneself independent of customary views?

The individuality of freedom is a different thing from that of conscientiousness of which I have spoken. It is indeed a kind of conscientiousness, for conscientiousness and self-presented individuality, if this latter is worth anything, are the same thing. But in the present case the individual asserts his judgment, not in exception or opposition to the general judgment, but independently of it. He says, I will deal with rightness by itself, without the intervention of any general opinion or common notion, I do not discuss or wish to affect the views of others, but simply take my own view.

To what extent is this proper in morality?

Without any disposition to wrong-doing a man may think that all moral philosophy and moral consideration is something importunate and superfluous, a mere result of people's readiness to meddle with others' action and judge about it, whether they have cause or not. Let there be, for the common interest, repression by law of distinct offence which injures others: for the rest, the way in which people in society fall into general manners of judging, the fashion of general approval or disapproval of kinds of action, from which arise such notions as the praiseworthy, the honourable, &c., all this is something superfluous, an undesirable attempt to interfere with the freedom of action: the wise thing is to trouble oneself about it as little as we can, and the desirable thing would be that there should be nothing of it.

Customariness is on the whole a help to morality.

On sober consideration, while some would say that common opinion and judgment *makes* the praiseworthy and the honourable, all, I suppose, would say that without that general interest of all in the acts of each, which is the main source of customariness, the world would fare worse morally. Still, what are the proper limits of that interest, or we may say, supervision? And how far should our free action maintain itself against it? Can we arrive at any principle as to this?

It makes little difference whether there are many contemporaneous standards or one common standard.

In our particular state of society, the disposition to over-meddling in matters of morals is rather taken as characteristic of an inferior level in that society, and the highest society, as we call it, is the freest. And because the tendency of society with us is rather to spread, over the whole of society upwards and downwards, the manner of feeling at present characteristic of the middle portions of it, therefore we seem to observe the spirit of moral meddling, or the restraint on freedom, to be upon the increase in general, and individual freedom to diminish, yielding to general opinion, or as we call it, the tyranny of the majority. What is really taking place is probably that various partial and rival forms of general opinion yield to one overspreading one, and the tyranny of the general majority is substituted for the tyranny of the opinion of our own rank or set. And the reason why at a particular moment, as perhaps the present, the highest society may appear the freest, is merely because the caste or clique opinion has become weakened, while the more general common opinion has not as yet taken its place. The restraints and mannerisms which aristocratical opinion carries with it are very likely to be weakened before the restraints and mannerisms of bourgeois opinion are prepared to take their place. The moral result of this may be good or may be bad. In the last century when something of the kind occurred in France, the result was bad: with us in England at this moment it may be otherwise.

Whether the change from various rival forms of common opinion to one uniform and predominating one is good or bad, depends, in my view, upon the goodness of this latter opinion: for as to the maintenance of individuality as against the opinion, I think the circumstances of it are much the same in the one case as in the other. We are not the more individual for being members, as to opinion, of a small moral society than of a large one. In either case it is well that we should be on our guard against the danger of individuality being swamped in common opinion.

In either case there is need of a proper assertion of independence.

Morally, besides the constant reference of general opinion or custom to our individual conscience, which I have spoken of, we should stand to such opinion and custom in a relation of liberal subordination, as distinguished from servility; if it is on an important matter, because its being the opinion of many is *one* argument, whatever it may weigh, for its being right; if it is unimportant, because then the one should yield to the many. But no doubt, two very different, but constantly concurring, tendencies of human nature, shew themselves in this as in other things. These are servility and the love of domination. And the proper assertion of individual independence is something in opposition to both. If we do a thing because we choose it and there is no reason why we should not do it, we must in reason forbid ourselves the pleasure of meddling and criticizing others in similar things.

Does democracy encourage independence?

Does equalitarianism (the modern *democracy* of M. de Tocqueville and others), by which I mean the feeling antagonistic to aristocracy and privilege, the looking upon men, and their looking upon themselves, as being all in the same position, with its accompaniments of their using the same sort of language, wearing the same dress, &c., bring out individuality, or the opposite?

There is a danger of its leading to simple gregariousness.

On this, which is in substance the same as what I have been speaking of, it seems to me that the same is to be said: equalitarianism acts both ways; you hear a man saying (and there need be no harm in his saying it, that depends on the facts and the view), I am as good a man as that lord or that scholar: and you hear him the next moment say, Now is the day of the masses; now we have done with special interests, special manners of thinking, special privileges; one common way of thinking makes us understand each other and act as one man. This latter is simple *gregariousness:* what made the former state *sociality,* and not gregariousness, was in a great degree the existence of a variety of ways of thinking: these abolished, what must now save us from gregariousness, must be a higher development, leading perhaps to a better sociality; but then greater individuality is required. This *may* be a result of equalitarianism, but so, as we have seen, may gregariousness. I suppose it is the part of a well-wisher to human nature to encourage the former of these tendencies, and discourage the latter.

This may be averted by improved cultivation.

I should think men might be encouraged, when rejoicing in the existence or increase of that equalitarianism, which seems to be the condition of high civilization, to take pleasure—not in the thought, that now superiority to them is destroyed, that all are alike, and that it is a grand thing to be an unit in a force or mass so vast and mighty as a civilized people—but rather in the thought, that now there is nothing to hinder their cultivating and developing their thought and feeling in the way in which their nature seems to lead, and pursuing their ideal, whatever it may be, if only it is reasonable. My saying this will probably excite a smile, when the mass of the hewers of wood and drawers of water in society is considered. But I say it deliberately. I cannot dwell on the subject now, and no one can be more aware than I am of the terrible exigence of mere life in regard of a large portion of society. But self-cultivation and self-development are not in any class, other than exceptionally, the business of life, and as an accompaniment to the business of life, they will associate themselves with the work of the poorer as well as with that of the richer, if there is the mind to make them do so. Leisure, in our active time, is what few wish for, or know what to do with when they have got it, and most rich people are as much occupied as any poor. Let a man be encouraged to be something *as a man* besides what he is as a wheel of the great industrial machine. If the man holding the plough for two shillings a day can become the merchant writing at his desk and earning a hundred pounds a day, let him: in the mean time the energies of both are engrossed, and it requires an effort for either to be anything more than his work: good sense, force of character, imaginative feeling, vigour of mind seem to me quite as possible for the poor man as for the richer, if you can only get him to value them[1].

[1] For a fuller statement of the author's views on this subject, compare a paper entitled 'Thought versus Learning' in *Good Words* for December 1871, and his printed sermons, pp. 126 foll. ED.

What I have just been speaking of has been the merging or sinking of our individual feeling in the general feeling of everybody. What I said before about the assertion of individual freedom, was rather in reference to the interference of the general or common feeling with our individual feeling. The two considerations are cognate: the interference tends to produce the sinking of individuality: if the individuality is not cared for there is no repugnance to the interference.

Is the interference of society desirable in cases which only concern the individual?

But about the interference: is it reasonable and moral in matters as to which, whatever we do, to all appearance, no harm will arise to others; matters which, to all appearance, only concern ourselves?

This, in the *principle* of it, is the question of *moral* philosophy against *social* philosophy: I do not mean that there is any opposition between the two. I have myself rather maintained against the utilitarians that it is not till *sociality*, *i.e.* the reconciliation or putting together of different interests, begins, that the notion of morality begins, whereas *their* view is that rudimental morality is the love of happiness, independently of the consideration *whose* happiness it is: still by moral philosophy we are likely to mean something applying more widely and going more deeply than what we mean by social philosophy. This however, is a matter of language: the terms might be looked on as coextensive, or either might include the other: in the earlier Greek philosophy 'social', if so we translate πολιτικός, was the more extensive, 'moral,' ἠθικός, the less so: in the present day I think we more commonly employ them the other way.

Should 'honeste vivere' be a matter of public cognizance?

The three ancient 'regulæ juris' are, as I have mentioned, 'neminem lædere, suum cuique tradere, honeste vivere:' some will say the last is only an affair of each man's individual consideration.

The question is probably not so much whether the good character of each member of the society is of vital importance to the whole society, for few will deny that it is, but whether the general opinion of the society, or a large portion of it, can be applied with advantage, in the judging of individual character, further than as actions are done which actually affect the interests of others. But it does not seem to me that, in reality, any principle can be maintained on this subject, further than the very general one, that each individual will do well to respect general opinion, but must not be afraid to differ from it, sometimes, because, in the particular instance, he thinks it wrong, sometimes, because he thinks it interfering and importunate. To bring all cases in which he thinks nobody is injured but himself under this last class, seems to me going against the principles upon which we inevitably go in education, and in fact in life altogether. We are each of us properly restraints, to some degree, upon each other, and I think we shall most of us allow that we are the better sometimes for that restraint. I cannot conceive how the line can be drawn, for moral guidance, which this opinion supposes. Between what injures others and what does not, it is hard enough to draw the line even in regard to what is palpable and flagrant, and in the (comparatively) rough way which will do for the legislator and the judge: if we are supposed to be really conscientious, it seems to me impossible. If we want 'neminem lædere' we must 'honeste vivere,' and we must take others' opinion in part-judgment as to what is 'honeste.'

Society is interested in our actions and to a certain extent in our character.

Suppose we draw in the opinion a little, and put it in *this* form, what I *am* (morally) is my own concern only, nothing but what I *do* can be yours—will it stand then? In this form of it we give up from our own exclusive cognizance not only whatever may possibly directly injure others (as we think), but also whatever can possibly be directly known to others, so as to have any effect, for instance, in the way of example. But even in excepting our thoughts, feelings and imaginations, we can hardly do so on the principle that here we arrive at something which cannot affect others: so far as they constitute our present or future character, which determines our action, they may affect them. It is indeed the fact that here we have a knowledge unlike in kind what others can have, and here must be the root of all self-assertion against conventionalism and mere custom: but even here we are not free from moral respects, and in these we are bound to take account of other judgments besides our own.

Are men better alone or in crowds?

Let us now for a moment ask a question which cannot really be answered, but which is useful to think of, and which I will put roughly thus, Are men better in crowds, or by themselves? Is the root of goodness in them more their own feeling, or the common feeling?

It will be judged from what I have said that my opinion is that goodness, and also evil, springs from both and from either, and that it is according to the circumstances whether one or the other of them is the case. Crowds will sometimes do what no individual among them would have been bad enough to do, and individuals will often do what, in a company of others, they would never have thought of proposing. I have been speaking of custom above as a good agent: it is constantly a bad one, people too often make each other worse instead of better. As a general rule we expect to find the more marked good, and evil too, suggested by individuality: the more ordinary, by common opinion.

CHAPTER XIX.

ON CHARACTER, WILL, AND EDUCATION.

Man, unlike animals, has individual, as well as social, customs.

In the last chapter, I spoke of *social* habits or customs, and of individual action or thought only in relation to these. In this chapter I shall treat of the individual and his own custom.

The customs of human nature are the analogue to the habits of animals. Man differs from the animals in the fact that, as compared with them, he makes his own customs or social habits, whereas their habits are generic, or made for them. In their natural state they have one social habit for the race, with but little of individual habit in addition to this. When tamed or domesticated, it is true, they partake, in some slight degree, of men's social circumstances: and individual variety, and individual character, are generated in them beyond what would be possible in a wild state[1].

Moral philosophy is the study of duty and of character combined, though it is from the latter that it has received its name.

[1] Perhaps there is a little exaggeration in the contrast here drawn between wild and tame animals. Of course we have a far better opportunity of observing the latter than the former: but is there any ground for supposing that, if we were able to watch closely a herd of wild horses, say, we should not find among them sluggish and spirited, vicious and gentle, just as we do in our stables? Sir John Lubbock has, I believe, discovered traces of idiosyncrasy in ants; and there is certainly a great difference in the degree of facility with which wild creatures of the same species may be tamed. Ed.

By 'ethics' we mean the science of character, ἦθος, of which χαρακτὴρ denotes the distinguishing feature or characteristic. The Latins, more poorly, spoke only of *mores* or habits. *We* speak vaguely of habits, dispositions, &c.; but we put them all into one whole when we speak of a man's character: in our older language it would have been called his temper, perhaps his complexion.

Character and will in reference to these customs.

It is of this *character* that I have now to speak: habits are the features of it; but character is not only a list, or the sum, of habits; it involves a relation among them, making it one. And it involves another more important relation, which is in many respects analogous to the relation between the action of the individual and the general custom; I mean the relation of the *will* to the habits.

Internal nature of plants:

If we may talk of comparative wonderfulness in the universe, rudimentariness in its application to what I will call, the internal nature, or the generic vital force, seems to me the most wonderful. The seed of a particular kind of plant has, say, a certain definite arrangement of its parts, which we describe as its generic character: but the fact that the seed has this arrangement of parts suggests no reason why the plant should grow up to the particular generic habit of its maturity: along with its arrangement of parts it has its own generic vital force, the source or rudiment of a generic difference which exists throughout every portion of the plant in its future growth; so that there is a vast general difference made up of an infinity of particulars, and the force generative of this infinity is contained in the seed. This I call the internal nature.

of animals:

Animals have more will than plants (if indeed the latter have any, which I do not say they have not), and consequently they have a more marked internal nature. We find in plants a few actions corresponding to the habits of animals, such as might be called semi-instinctive. But animals have in their body a most complicated machine which they must use by effort of will, and which they have got to use in a particular way if they are to keep themselves alive by it. They always do know how to use it: this knowledge, or impulse, or instinct, is a fact in nature as real and as important as the fact of the particular form of the animal. As it has its external nature in a system of organs and limbs, so it has its internal nature in a system of impulses and habits. This moral frame must have parts of different degrees of refinement and importance. The simple impulses to use the particular organizations must be backed by certain natural tempers or habits, or they would fail to support life. If we could conceive a particular carnivorous animal born an exception to the rest of its species, and destitute, we will say, of patience, it could not exist. These tempers or habits give the animal a natural character.

Man has more *will* than the inferior animals; and, corresponding with this, he has an internal nature, which, beginning at first much more poorly than theirs, comes in the result to be infinitely richer. This is on account of the special property of educability in it, which does not exist in them. *of man.*

Animals in a wild state are probably born with scarcely any *individual*, as opposed to *generic* difference of character: this arises from the absence of individual variety in the parents or their circumstances. Human beings are born evidently with a vast amount of rudimentary individual difference, quite independently of anything which education may afterwards add. And the more there is of *Small capacity for education in animals as compared with man* individual difference in the parents, the more will there be of variety in the offspring.

In a wild state, animal education, if there is any, is soon over, and always, it is to be supposed, succeeds. No failure on the parents' part causes birds to grow up without learning to fly. But human character is a most various graft of education and circumstances on the primary individuality by which this may be modified to an extent which we can hardly determine.

Division of the subject.

I shall speak about character upon the following scheme: 1st, on the elements of character; 2nd, on formation of character; 3rd, on the criticism or judgment of character; 4th, on will *in* character; 5th, on will *against* character, or reformative of character; 6th, on will and action entirely independent of character.

Elements of individual character.

Character is general and particular; there is a general character, so to speak, belonging to all men alike, as there is a general conformation of face. The examination of the elements of such general character is general moral psychology, and in that view I shall not treat the subject here. Besides this, each man has a particular or individual character as he has his own features of face: it is this part of general human nature, which is from the beginning different in different individuals, that I shall speak of now.

Individuality is a permanent limitation of the generic nature.

Setting aside exceptional identifications by peculiar marks, and considering as unimportant, in comparison with features of the face, what I may call features of the body, length of legs or arms, &c., we know or identify a man by his face and by the sound of his voice: in each of these there is a portion which we can readily describe, and there is something which goes beyond our description, which is specially individual to the man, which we generally call expression, in the same vague manner in which we talk of instinct. Here the outer passes into the inner nature; or possibly the connexion between the two may be more intimate than this; it may be the inner nature which determines, or there may be inner nature to correspond with, variety of feature beyond that which we generally understand as expressive; and the same with the conformation and size of the brain, and the corresponding shape of the head; these questions of physiognomy and phrenology I do not touch. But the individuality of each, which appears outwardly by feature, and look, and tone of voice, is clearly something more than such feature, look, and voice, and this which it is more is what I call the individual inner nature. Supposing continued life, the outward part will go through change on change; but there will be *something* about it constituting its sameness, which something we may describe in various ways: we may say there is something about the features which will never change, or the man will cease to be the same; we may say that whatever the man becomes, outwardly, at a future time, he becomes by development of, and by a change from what he is now, constituting a line of sequence from this to what he becomes; and there are various other ways in which we might describe the same general fact. Whatever we say thus of the outward nature we may say of the inward. A man's features are one mark of his individuality, and as such they contain in them, to a certain extent, all that he can possibly be to all eternity; they are a prophecy; his individuality is a limitation which he can never get over, and his features are the sign of it.

There are two origins thus for his moral thought,

both independent, and both fixed; the one his ideal of perfection[1], the other his own necessary individuality. The latter of these, if it is rightly dear to him, may be no less dear than the former; it gives him the universe, or fixes his universe; if he *is*, he must be contented to be *himself*, and the moral hope is that each may live so that this may be not only a subject of contentment, but of gladness, and in a measure, of pride. He may be himself, and at the same time he may be what *man should be*, which two united make what *he* should be.

The elements of moral character are predispositions to particular passions.

The elements of moral character are the feelings, emotions, or passions (I use the word quite vaguely): in each of these we suppose a general notion applicable to a large number of minds, though in individual minds it may exhibit special peculiarities beyond what we can at all follow. The features, so to speak, of the native or congenital inward nature are certain predispositions for the existence of these passions, when the occasion shall arise.

It is probable that all such predispositions are in some way marked in the external organization. As examples may be mentioned a tendency, more or less, to animal appetite; more or less of firmness, or on the other hand of softness and yieldingness; more or less of energy and hopefulness. Such predispositions are neither wrong nor right, nor, properly speaking, good or bad. To a certain degree, higher or lower, perhaps better or worse, may be predicated of them: but they are all, without ceasing to exist, so alterable by reason and habit, that what might seem the lowest of them may be made the foundation of the most noble character.

Such predispositions are neither bad nor good in themselves.

[1] That is, I suppose, the objective ideal of the race; the subjective ideal is of course continually changing. Ed.

The nature of men differs from that of animals in this respect, that whatever there may be innate in him, his actual life is sure very greatly to form and modify. Upon the bases of the constitutional tempers, there are formed, by the admixture of will and reason, other tempers, more or less like these, of a more marked and distinct character, and it is these of which the terms virtuous and vicious, good or bad, right or wrong, honourable or disgraceful, may be predicated.

It is impossible to distinguish between what is congenital and the equally natural result of education.

I do not think it is possible to draw any definite line of demarcation between what is congenital and what is result of education. There may be a part of that which is individual to the born human creature which comes from some spiritual source, distinct from the parents: of that I say nothing; in any case we cannot distinguish it. Again, what comes from the parents is undistinguishable from what comes from maternal communication, influence and tenderness, when all is as yet merely plastic and unformed. And so the process goes on: where the congenital individuality ceases, and where education begins, we cannot say. Education is not, in the case of men, a quasi-accident, a thing which might be or might not be: it is to man what that which we call instinct is to each kind of animals, viz. what he has to depend on for being able to live at all: in failure of education of any kind, his individuality would not be the more developed, but the reverse: it would not be brought out at all. Man's having mind or moral nature might almost be said to consist in this, that in his earliest infant life there goes on (except in entirely abnormal cases) an actual education to which there is nothing analogous in animals. As the infant has to be taught, but does learn, intellectual and practical processes which the animals cannot be made to learn, so his feelings become developed by communication with others; in regard of which process, we may consider important either the actual fact that they become so developed, that he is taught, or the fact of his nature that his feelings are such as to be thus developed, that it is his nature to learn. The former is education, the latter nature: how we ought exactly to speak or think on the subject, is hard to say; only this infant education, if it *is* education, is something infinitely more important than any education afterwards. The nature of this importance we shall see more fully soon, when we consider how subsequent education modifies individuality: this earliest education all but makes it.

Predispositions are developed into dispositions, and these into habits and character.

Character consists in the comparative readiness with which one and another of the simple feelings or passions, fear, hope, desire, aversion, love, hatred, anger, gratitude, and others, are drawn out; their comparative intensity and duration; the manner in which they associate themselves with one another and with the intellectual feelings, especially imagination; so that the circumstances of these intellectual feelings become important circumstances of moral character.

The congenital predispositions to the indulgence of one or another of these feelings, being in different measures checked, encouraged, or in other ways modified by the circumstances of early education, are developed into *dispositions:* there is a disposition to indulge fear, hatred, anger, a disposition to be deceitful, or, on the other hand, to be frank, open, perhaps impudent, perhaps bold and violent: this is character in its simpler form. Then again, as time goes on, these dispositions are some of them indulged, some checked, and they become variously complicated together: there are thus formed dispositions very complex and individual, hard to follow in consciousness and observation, and hard to describe, and there are formed besides confirmed habits and regular ways and customs of feeling, thought and action. This is complete and developed character.

Meaning of the term 'habit'.

If we want to form a notion of the state of facts, we must endeavour to present it to ourselves as much as possible independently of the particular words, which are used so variously that without continued definition and re-definition of them, as we employ them, they are worse than useless for thought. The word 'habit' has, we may say, four senses. Properly and etymologically it is a translation of ἕξις, and means a state of mind; being synonymous on the whole with διάθεσις, of which the translation is 'disposition': and this latter, not *habit*, is the term which I mean to employ in this first sense. In the next place the word 'habit' has been loosely used for 'custom' corresponding nearly with ἔθος: I shall not use it thus, but shall have, with some care, to distinguish its moral meaning from this sense. It means, thirdly, 'confirmed disposition'; a state of mind more or less strong, permanent, rooted: this is the sense in which I used it just now, and may probably use it again. It means, finally, a confirmed state of mind as in the last sense, but with this addition, that it is viewed as having some resemblance to a mere custom, secondary and superinduced, and distinguished from states of mind which are supposed to belong to the native, congenital individuality, and are called, in contrast to this habit, 'nature'. I shall generally use 'habit' in this sense; but it is not possible to keep this use quite separate from that just mentioned. When we say 'habit is second nature', we cannot really distinguish whether the word habit is used in this or the previous sense. 'Nature' and 'habit' are both vague.

Growth of character through education.

The character then of each man is his habitual way of thinking, feeling, and acting; and this is generated from the immediate, instinctive, impulsive thinking, feeling, and acting, which life begins with, by the circumstances of the individual social life; in other words, by what in a wide sense might be called his education, of which any deliberate education of him is only a small part.

Education in this wide sense is, for the most part, influence of others in various ways; partly as causing, without any direct action on the will, a custom of acting in some particular manner or indulging a particular sort of feelings; partly in directly commanding some sort of action, which so becomes customary; partly in furnishing example; partly in supplying an object to aim at and a standard to judge by; and partly in other ways. But a portion of it, in some cases large, is direct effort of the individual applied to himself, in what is called self-education, whether intellectual or moral.

The formation of character is the change of feeling into character, or into habit in the wide sense; the change of consciousness and sensibility, as prompters of action, into an immediate and almost involuntary performance of the action without preparatory consciousness: the action gets more and more to do itself, as we might say. This is the process of all practical learning, *i. e.* of all learning the result of which is action, whether action of the mind or of the limbs.

Learning dulls sensibility.

The above consideration is important in various ways. First, in all learning we lose something, though, in all learning which is of value, we gain more. But in all learning *some* sensibility or sensitiveness is extinguished: familiarity blunts. This is the meaning of 'a fresh eye' to things: if it were possible to make learners aware of the bearing of this fact, it would give a new interest to their learning, even though it should in some degree diminish the rapidity of it. We see each thing for the first time in a way in which we shall never see it again: and, if we really valued our own mental processes at their true worth, we should mark our manner of seeing it, and see it with a vividness which would bear fruit in our mind afterwards. If the mature *knower* could add to his knowledge the sensibility of the ignorant, thirsty for knowledge, his knowledge would be more valuable than it is, because fresher, keener, livelier.

Similarly in moral training the impression weakens with the strengthening of the practical habit.

However it is with morals that I am concerned now. Every one's character has its history: it is a tree the shape of whose leaves, and flowers, and fruit depends upon something native, or in the seed, but whose shape in general, as we look at it, the direction and form of whose boughs and branches depend upon a thousand circumstances in the past. As the tree has grown by the conversion of sap and living circumambient bark into strong but comparatively dead wood; as knowledge has grown by the correction of suppositions and imaginations and their fixing into facts and formulas; so character has grown into comparatively unconscious habit by the conversion of ever active feeling and impulse, that is, by a stiffening of our moral being analogous to the stiffening and strengthening of our corporeal frame from childhood to maturity.

What Butler has said in regard to the manner in which impressions become faint as practical habits become strong, is in reality no more than this: it has no special reference to our moral being; and it is of great importance that we should not misconceive and misapply it.

But this is only that a higher sensibility may take the place of the lower.

Though learning, as I have said, is the extinguishing of some sensibility or some consciousness and attention, and the conversion of it into practical aptitude; yet this ought to be always in order to the development of higher sensibility, to an increased consciousness of, and attention to, objects of more consequence with which the existence of the former sensibility and consciousness would be incompatible. The accomplished pianist touches the keys mechanically, in comparison with the beginner who has to think where he shall put each finger, but the former has only learnt this mechanicalness in order to the application of his sensibility and attention to the music with which his imagination is teeming, or the beauties of composition which his higher sensibility tastes. We must become used to some things if we would freshly taste and enjoy others.

Character, like knowledge, is only living while it is growing.

The question of habit, considered as something superinduced, or against *nature*, was the first question about habit which presented itself to us: here we have the question of habit against *sensibility*. What Butler has said has reference also to another question which will shortly arise, that of habit against *will*, or of fixedness of character. If this fixedness arose from increased insensibility, from diminished moral consciousness, it would only be a partial moral advantage. As it is, while the impressions which go to the formation of moral habits wear out, other moral sensibilities develope themselves, and higher ones. Part of the tree is for strength alone, no longer soft and sensible, but it has still besides its fresh and living growth. Character, like knowledge, is only so far truly alive as it is still further growing. Some things are unquestioned, fixed, at once acted upon;

but there is plenty of room still for moral thought and moral feeling. We have not, in virtue of our habit, become a machine or a law.

Of course, while our moral character is forming, we are of more interest, whether to others or to ourselves; but even when formed our moral character ought still to be freshly forming. We must, if we live, grow old corporeally, *perhaps* intellectually, but morally we certainly need not. And we are sent into the world, we may suppose, not only to do right as a result, but to have a moral history in the course of learning it.

We are now however come to the next thing to be considered, which was the criticism or judgment of character.

Criticism of character.

Character, as we have hitherto been speaking of it, should be described as a matter of fact, without praise or blame. There may be described in this manner either the characters of individuals, or certain types of character. Of the latter kind are the descriptions by Aristotle and Theophrastus: of the former, historical descriptions of characters, though it is true that in these praise and blame are often mixed with matter of fact.

Correct observation of character is hindered by over haste to criticize.

In a general way, our perception of the actual facts of character is greatly hindered by our universal tendency to immediate criticism of them, or attribution of praise and blame. This is, indeed, only something which takes place in a great many things besides morals, and something which has its good side as well as its bad. It is a part of that general process of learning, or extinction of sensibility, which I noticed, that, as we advance in generalization and classification and naming, we notice particular facts less: we notice one fact about any thing, according to which we refer it to a name, and then put it aside and have done with it; as if then we know everything worth knowing about it, and the whole use of our senses were to enable us to ticket things and put them on the shelf. So we call a man by a general name, and think we have given his character: if this general name represents a fact, as if we call him desponding or cautious or enterprizing, even so it may smother up a good deal of observation; but if it represents a fact with praise or blame attached, this is far more the case. As the casual observer will pass by the most remarkable Gothic edifice, or the most peculiar vegetable species, provided it has got a tower, or stem and leaves, with, 'Oh, it's only a church,' or 'Oh, it's only a tree,' while some very ordinary thing which he cannot quite make out and give its name to, he will go on spying at; so as soon as we can say, or think we can say, He was a good man, or a bad man, we notice no more, while we go on noticing much meaner and poorer characters, if only this seems doubtful.

In speculating on character, the order we should proceed in is, What did the man do? Of what tempers or habits of mind are these things which he did the sign? Are these tempers or habits to be called good or bad? If we cannot, as we constantly cannot, follow this order, we should yet keep it in our mind, and be aware of the actual course we are taking: instead of which we constantly confuse all together, and are scarcely aware whether at any time we are concluding from facts to character, or from supposed character to probable facts.

Moral Philosophy may be viewed as the rationale of such criticism.

One of the simplest and clearest views which can be taken about moral philosophy in general is, that it is the rationale of criticism, or judgment, about character and action. This criticism we are sure to exercise. A very large part of human thought and conversation is about it. In reality very little pains is taken by people to have any principle in their judgments in this matter, or to make the judgments at all consistently. The epithets used constantly involve the two elements of a description of supposed fact and a judgment about it, of approval or blame: and constantly it is the latter element only which has force in the mind of the user of the epithet. The worst people are quite as fond of using epithets conveying moral blame as the best, though one would have thought that in their mouths they could convey no blame: the blame as connected with the action they show by their own lives they do not mind: it is blame in general, the conveyance of ill opinion, in which the force of the epithet, as they use it, resides.

Surely, if it is worth while having principles upon which to make our judgments in nature and art, it is equally so as to human character. There is an evident analogy, as we have seen already in speaking of the face and form: we talk of features of character, painting character, &c.: and so, in regard to the description of character as in regard to art, there are two kinds of correctness, accuracy as to the facts, rightness as to the ideal or standard of judgment.

The exhibiting moral philosophy as criticism of this kind will doubtless be looked at by some with jealousy. For such criticism seems a human creation, a matter of imagination only. But in reality, this jealousy is applicable, in a measure, to everything which I have said about moral philosophy, and also to that view of it which deals with the τὸ καλόν, the *honestum*, or with moral taste, or with 'high and low.' What I have said is, that moral philosophy is imagination, whatever it is besides; and I think it is a great deal besides. Even if all that could be said was that, as we are sure to judge and talk about character, it is desirable that we should do it, if we can, consistently and reasonably, this would be something: but I think that we exercise our thoughts about character, because there is something really to be known about it, in the same way as we exercise our eyes in looking, because there is something really to be seen; so that, in exercising our minds reasonably about character, we are increasing our knowledge of something real, which I call the moral universe, in the same way as, in using our eyes intelligently, we are increasing our knowledge of the physical universe. For all that we know, everything may be imagination, as I have said a good many times; but we have no more reason to conclude this of the moral universe than of the physical. It is but our own thought which leads us to either, and *it* leads us to both.

The principles of moral criticism are the same as those which determine the value of actions.

The principles of excellence of character must depend upon those of value of action, and in going through them I should simply repeat what I have said before. The two main principles would be utility or serviceableness, and elevation or superiority to selfishness.

The science of character is, as I have said, the true and original *Ethics*, as in Aristotle. It wants, as a foundation for it, the science of action, which I have spoken of under the names of aretaics and deontics[1]; and so far as this science of action has not been brought out, that of ethics is deficient.

Aristotle's Ethics are essentially criticism, for which he fails to give a satisfactory rationale.

The Aristotelian theory of virtue is exactly a theory of criticism of character. It deals with the elements or facts of character, which, as I mentioned, are feelings; the ideal referred to is really an ideal of character, not of action, or of the object of pursuit.

[1] See p. 102.

The virtue of fortitude, for instance, is in this view the amount of self-confidence, in presence of alarming objects, which the ideally virtuous man, or the man whom people consider virtuous, has: more self-confidence than this is rashness, less is cowardice. Unfortunately Aristotle does not tell us, nor without much more upon duty, and the ideal of human action, and the value and purpose of action, could he tell us, on what principle we are to ascertain what amount of self-confidence is desirable. His reference is only to feeling and character and the general estimation shown in actual language.

Viewing the Aristotelian Ethics in this light, we see why they attribute such importance to μετριότης, middleness or moderation. Extraordinary particular virtuousness is difficult to deal with according to any ideal of character. Ideally good character must exclude not only vice, but extravagance of virtue. And the ideal of character being thus more difficult to imagine than the ideal of action or of object, the criticism of character is correspondingly more difficult.

What is meant by 'mixed' and 'inconsistent' character?

There is scarcely any one of the simpler feelings which does not lead to good or to bad action, according to circumstances. Doing good or forbearing from wrong may be the result either of boldness or of cowardice: the feeling of fairness may make a man grateful or revengeful: kindness may lead to falsehood or injustice; all this is familiar. Hence character is spoken of as 'mixed.' The term implies a certain confusion of thought, as if the elements of character were virtues and vices, rather than feelings which according to circumstances may lead to virtue and vice: it is like talking of a face being mixed of beauty and ugliness. There is something of the same confusion in our speaking of a character as being 'inconsistent.'

The phrase is probably used where there is some strong feeling, which in some cases leads to right, in others to wrong, and what we may call *naturally* in both cases: it would, in many respects, be more properly applicable where the feeling, while acting freely towards the right, is controlled and prevented by principle from acting towards the wrong: the inconsistency would then be a merit. As commonly used, it either implies an ideal attained in some particulars, unattained in others (which of course describes all actual character), or it implies a notion formed by us of the character, and some action inconsistent with the notion: the notion is of course so far inadequate.

The extent to which all actual character is mixed sometimes comes out in a very startling manner, and is one of the things which, now and then, most incline people to doubt about morality altogether. It ought not to have any effect of this kind, so far as we think reasonably about it. It gives always a hold upon the bad, and it need not make us distrust the good, though it may fairly make them in some degree distrust themselves. It will come rather into consideration in what I am now going to speak about, the relation of *will* to character.

Will *in* character:

There are three things belonging to character a good deal like each other, but not exactly the same; which I will call strength, individuality, and abundance.

may be seen in strength of character,

Strength of character depends upon the degree in which will is involved in the habits or character. This may be in various ways: the main feature of it is resistance to temptation in virtue of habit combined with more or less of living principle or consciousness. If there were not the habit or usage, it would be simply strength of will: if there were nothing but the usage, it would be a sort of strong stupidity or imperceptiveness; and we must beware lest, in speaking of moral conduct as habitual, we should fall into the error of supposing it to be of this kind.

Individuality of character is *markedness*. It implies a certain degree of strength of character, because the individuality has to be maintained against a good deal which tends to make all characters alike and ordinary. But individuality of thought and feeling may coexist with a character which, from want of energy of will, is ordinary and unmarked. **individuality of character,**

Abundance of character implies the existence of a good deal of perceptiveness or sensibility to start with, and then of something between strength and individuality, or involving both. A character may be strong, but yet poor and uninteresting: by abundance of character I mean that there is a good deal of feature in it, as there may be much expressiveness in a face. **abundance of character.**

The consideration of will *in* character is of most consequence in connexion with the consideration of will *against* character. This latter, as we may readily see, is the same as will employed in the formation of character. For from the first of action, there begins to be something of habit: so far as habits are formed as a result of successive exertions of will, these exertions are efforts against some resistance. When the habits are formed there is the will to action which the habit involves or produces. This will, we will say, is strong according to the strength of the character. Is it all-powerful? Is all our will or power involved in the habits, in the same way as much of our sensibility is extinguished by them, so that our conduct in the future, when character is formed, is rendered in a manner necessary? Or is there room **Will *against* character.**

left still for will, such as that which by its repeated exercise generated the habits in the first instance?

The force of habit is of great moral importance:

There is no question in all moral philosophy more important than this, in various ways.

The quasi-necessity of a man's action according to the habits which he has formed is looked at by Butler as a matter of great moral consequence for encouragement, as affording a pledge that the virtuous will continue virtuous, or be able to stand in his virtue.

but the power of the will to overcome habit is of still more importance.

The circumstances of the vicious are not exactly the same in this respect as those of the virtuous, for there is not likely to be effort on a man's part to make himself vicious, as we may conceive effort to make himself, from vicious, virtuous: but still it is clear that if the habits do become to this extent stiffened and set, and the stiffening means so much, the vicious also is likely to remain vicious. And this consequence Butler contemplates and makes use of also.

But morals would be in a poor position if we did not admit, and that to the very utmost, the possibility of reformation in men. There is much complication in all this, and for different moral purposes, men urge the thing, and with reason, in various ways. We say, By a course of vice you are by degrees producing in yourself vicious habits which will at last be all-powerful in you. But, if we are speaking to any in whom vicious habits are formed, we must not use this language, nor would it be true: we must use the opposite language with all the more vigour because of the tendency in the man himself to believe he cannot change, and because of the tendency of this belief to produce the thing believed. And so if, to believe in the security of the virtuous, we must believe in the hopelessness of the vicious, it will be better for us to give up both beliefs. The cardinal point of morality is the belief in the liberty and the all-powerfulness of the will[1]: if a man really believes in that as to himself, no vicious habit can enslave him.

This power of the will may be denied either on theoretical or practical grounds.

Independent of any moral considerations, the belief that a man acts necessarily according to his character is held in a double way, philosophically and simply practically. The former is when we mean by character the sum of all the circumstances which have hitherto influenced the man, which now, in conjunction with the circumstances of the present occasion, will determine his conduct. This is the moral syllogism[2]. The other is when we believe very strongly in custom, and not strongly in conscience and force of will, which is the case with many: we then say, the man will *wish* perhaps to do so and so, will feel a good deal about the matter, but still, in the result, he will act as he has been accustomed to do.

In both these cases it is supposed that, from a man's past we may predict his future, and only not infallibly, because of course we avow that our knowledge is doubtful and limited.

Some deny the power of either habit or will to overcome the original nature.

As some would predict all a man's future action from his character, so others would predict it all, his character included, from his constitution. And it seems to me that there is the same reason, and the same want of reason, in both these proceedings. We can predict of course in both cases, but very conditionally. A man is never without character, and his character is never fully formed. His constitution, as we call it, is his character to begin with: his character to end with we never see. Habit is a second

[1] That is, of the spiritual principle at work within man. A possible misunderstanding is guarded against in the parallel passage in App. A, p. 462. ED.

[2] Aristotle, *Eth.* VI. 12.

nature to him; as much as a second nature, but no more: and, as it was possible to superinduce a second nature upon the first, so it is possible, in the same way, to superinduce a third nature, more habit, upon the second, and so on. The believers in habit, or character, as indefeasible, may fairly be set against the believers in constitution, or nature, as such. The latter consider that habit, as against nature, is something utterly weak and superficial, against which nature, when occasion arises, will always assert itself, as the cat-nature asserted itself in the princess of the fable, when a mouse came into view. We may fairly conclude, that what admits at all of being so thought of, cannot at any rate be so powerful as to determine all the man's future action, when nature was not powerful enough for this. Will, in fact, holds its ground against both, not of course absolutely: nature determines something, as I said in speaking of a man's inward and outward nature and features: habit goes on and determines more: but they do not determine all.

What is called the mixture of character is a fact favourable to reformation.

The consideration of *mixture* of character, which I spoke of a short time since, comes in most harmoniously with this. When we speak of good and bad habits, we must remember that we are speaking of what I may call realities of the second order: the habits are actually of benevolence, of justice, of revengefulness, of whatever it may be, to which we attach the notions and give the names, and with reason, of good and bad. As when we talk of handsome features; the features are, as a fact, of a particular shape, which shape we call, and ought to have a reason for calling, a handsome shape. Thus each vicious habit, as a fact, has in it various elements which are not vicious. These do not make it not vicious, or not to be condemned as strongly as we please: but they are an argument against our considering it such as to preclude any virtuous action in the matter which it concerns, or any change for the better: for here are the seeds and rudiments of such virtuous action already. Character in each person is, as to the facts of it, something most complicated and individual, with dormant buds, so to speak, all about it, which may shoot out, under favourable circumstances, into directions which we never dream of, good or bad.

Will independent of character.

There remains to be discussed what I called the consideration of will as independent of character. Have I not been saying too much altogether about character or habit? Is it desirable we should be to so great an extent creatures of habit, even moral habit? Is there much significance in the notion of moral education? or much advantage in exercising and disciplining ourselves to virtue?

APPENDIX A.[1]

Feelings, dispositions, character.

Conscientiousness and kindly feeling, the two springs of virtue, act not only to direct particular actions, but also to lay up a stock or store of force for future good action in the fact of good or virtuous *habit*.

It is convenient to make the following distinctions: starting with feelings, as the most transitory, we go on to dispositions (which are more or less permanent feelings, or conditions of the mind in regard of feelings), and finally to character or aggregate of dispositions. Dispositions again may be conveniently distinguished into such as are constitutional; such as unconsciously become habitual; and such as more or less consciously are made so. *Habit* is a word which, in its own proper meaning, signifies state of mind, or way in which the mind *is* or *has itself*, but which, in the use of language, has come very much to signify that unconscious tendency to do things, and facility in doing them, which is brought about in the case of bodily movements by practice and repetition: in this respect it has also come into close resemblance of signification with 'custom' or 'usage'. It is important however, in using the word *habit* for ethical purposes, to keep in mind what, in that application, it must mean, and not to follow too immediately the analogy either of bodily movements or general usage.

Virtuousness is a habitual disposition.

Virtuousness is a disposition made habitual more or less consciously and of purpose. It is this, both because it is, as regards one of its sources, stored up conscientiousness (this latter being in its nature *deliberate*), and also because this storing up itself is one of the things which conscientiousness

[1] The last chapter ends abruptly, merely introducing the discussion of 'will independent of character'. Appendix A, taken from MS. V, seems to give an answer to several questions propounded there. B, C, and D supply further details for the general discussion on habit and character. Ed.

prompts to. The feeling of conscientiousness moves us to take care, not only for our immediate action, but for our prospective action and whole moral life.

The original elements of virtue, principle and feeling, are not extinguished by habit.

I do not think that the view is correct, which considers that it is impulse only that generates, and that all that principle (reason, conscience) has to do is to regulate. I think that conscientiousness or deliberate reason is itself an original source of action. The mixture of these two sources of action belongs to our conception of moral character from the first to the last of it. The notion of the overlaying of them both by habit, and then of the transformation of them both into habit, seems to me a gradual extinction of the moral personality. The reality of this latter consists in the liveliness of the sensibilities and the strength of the conscious principle in conjunction the one with the other: if either of these entirely superseded the other, there would be no longer *human* virtuousness. We might imagine a being acting by deliberate reason alone for the absolute best; *that* would not be a man: we might imagine a being again swayed always, without any self-guidance, by impulse to the best; in such a case, where there was no self-possession or consciousness, we could hardly say there was moral life at all. But the supposition of a being moving only by habit, even infallibly to virtue, would be worse than either of these. Such a being would be little other than a machine. Virtue in him would have no meaning, and no interest.

If we speak of moral habits in general, and in relation to the larger and higher acts of virtue as well as to more frequent and familiar ones, I do not think that the formation of habits is the obliteration or extinction of the sensibility and the consciousness which in the first instance led to them. The virtue which is laid up in the form of habit serves both to determine of itself, without special attention, a large mass of action, and also to furnish a substratum or foundation for larger and higher acts of virtue (the smaller ones thus in a manner taking care of themselves) which are done with as much of deliberate consciousness and lively sensitiveness as if virtue was not an old thing in the mind, but were at this moment fresh and young. The same impressions repeated may get weaker and weaker, but life and action are wide, and there is ever a possibility of fresh ones: with regard to much of action, we may have nothing to do but to follow former precedents of our own conduct; but it is pretty certain that new emergencies will arise, which will call for moral deliberation and resolution, and I think we have no reason to regret that it is so.

On the other hand, feeling and principle must become habitual.

The meaning of describing virtuousness as an habitual disposition is this: A good action may be done, and from good motives, on principle or feeling regarding that action alone, and not at all made what it is by the state of mind of the doer, or even quite in opposition to what that state of mind would lead us to expect. Under certain circumstances, conduct of this kind may be the more virtuous, in the sense of meritorious, from its inconsistency with the general character. But speaking generally, the principle and impulse which are brought to bear upon the question, Is an action to be done or not? are an accumulation, and have been made what they are by previous determination and action. Habits of thought and feeling are always forming, and it is a part of virtuousness that what is thus formed should be virtuous: virtuous feeling or resolve on the spur of each separate occasion, though, so far as it exists, to be acknowledged as true and valuable, yet, considering what man is, is not complete or all that is wanted, because in reality there is a continuousness in man's moral being; he is not simply a machine to produce good results. And in reality the action cannot be good, except by occasional fits and starts, unless the manner of thinking and judging, which mark the habit or state of mind, are so.

Still good action is valuable in itself, not merely as productive of good habit.

Ethical philosophy, however, has not unfrequently treated this question as if the value of good actions consisted in the fact that good habits were formed by doing them, and as if this were the main reason for doing them. The real reason for doing them is first and foremost objective, on their own account, not subjective, on account of any effect they may have on us. No doubt, it is also an important consideration that by the repeated resolution to do them we are making ourselves, in habit or state of mind, better, as by an opposite proceeding we should be making ourselves worse; but in regard of primary reason, the habits are for the sake of the actions, not the actions for the sake of the habits.

Virtuousness then, in its best form or as it should be, is a taught, learnt, practised, habit, never becoming habitual to such an extent as to destroy the principle and impulse which formed the habit, never secure therefore against possibility of much exceptional action, and never secure against a change or unlearning the habit again; but still affording a very strong probability that the action will be according to the habit and that the habit will continue.

Some have held that virtue is an unnatural habit.

The question here suggests itself whether virtue is accepted by the soul as something good and akin to it, or whether it is accepted indeed, it may be, but as something alien and, except for habit, disagreeable. This view of the action of habit, as reconciling us (or doing even more than this) with what is otherwise distasteful, is so far apparent in Aristotle, as that virtue according to him is often a matter of effort and self-restraint, and that whatever of pain there may be in these is by habit diminished or removed. Plato in the first book of the Republic touches on a more important manner in which virtue has been considered distasteful to the soul, that notion, namely, with which the name of Hobbes has been most associated in modern times, that the consulting the interests of others in preference to our own, is a thing so repugnant to human nature that, if men do it, it must be because they are forced to it, and if they do it with any apparent willingness or pleasure, the cause must be that training and habit have reconciled them to what, of itself, they could not like. This, it will be seen, is the exact opposite to the Stoic view that virtue is native to the soul, and what it really likes the best; the view of Aristotle, that it is superinduced, but not as it were by force or as something unpleasant, holding a middle place.

That we do right, if we do it, freely, and yet with a pressure or urgency of it upon us, is the feeling of moral obligation; and that some fact or objective reality corresponds to this latter, is generally a part of the feeling also. It is no wonder that, in the attempt to explain this almost self-contradictory feeling, one side or another of it should be ignored. The view which I have just been alluding to, is to the effect that no virtuous action is really done freely; that it is the result of a force upon us; that whereas a certain part of the ancient ethics taught that no man is willingly, or of choice, evil, the proper teaching would have been that no man is willingly, or of choice, good; that we are *trained* to do good, to a certain degree, and to take a sort of pleasure in it, as many kinds of animals may be trained to do many things most alien from anything which we can call their real nature; that from dread of each other's wickedness, and the probable ill consequences of that to ourselves, we are driven to be in a certain degree virtuous, and to train others to be so; that with the view of enforcing fairly upon all this which all so dislike, we arm, in the law and other 'sanctions' of morality, certain arbitrary powers, which command and, on failure of obedience, punish; that we try also to take off the edge of the dislike itself by habit, and to a certain extent succeed in doing so.

It is really a habit which is essential to the full development of our nature.

The real truth in regard to this is that, though virtue is matter of habit, yet it is not to its habitualness only that is due the pleasure which we take, if we do take such, in it, but to itself also. We are trained to be virtuous, but not by a training similar in kind to that which, with some animals, is able to make them do extraordinary feats and things entirely different from that which they would do in a state of nature, but by an education which the natural state itself requires, in order to bring it out and develope it; an education such as, even with the inferior animals (for whom nature, mindful of the difficulties of education with them, has provided greater facility of learning than for us), is needed to enable them to fly or perform any other natural movement. If it is not our nature to be virtuous, it is our nature to learn virtue; and to learn virtue rather than vice, in the same way in which (though in fact sight itself is a matter of learning just as virtue is) it is our nature to learn to see things rightly, rather than wrongly and different from what they are. I have mentioned before that this is the real point of the question, whether ideas of virtue and of moral obligation come, or do not come, as matters of teaching and education: if they do so come, they come as what, we may say, was meant to be taught, as something which we should not be ourselves, should not be men, without; not as something accidental and superadded, taught us for a purpose, and in regard of which the question might arise, whether it was alien to our nature or not, whether it were well for us to learn it or not. The habits of virtue are needed to complete our nature; they are not something superadded to it.

There is yet another thing to be noticed.

The supposition of formed habits giving a great security against action in opposition to them is no doubt to a considerable extent true. But we must remember that we are not entitled to make any supposition on the side of virtue in this respect, which we are not prepared also to make upon the side of vice. If confirmed virtuous habit is, as habit, omnipotent and unchangeable, there is reason to fear that we should have to consider confirmed vicious habit as irreformable. And rather than do this, it seems to me that it is better that we should consider the security of confirmed virtuousness to reside, not so much in the habitualness resulting from repetition and custom, as in the strength of the principle. The former acts for virtue and vice alike and impartially. It is sure to act on the side of vice; it is our duty to enlist it, for ourselves and others, on the side of virtue. But what is on the side of virtue and cannot act on the side of vice, is conscious principle.

Habit in itself is not more favourable to virtue than to vice.

The more we attend to what we do, the more we are anxious to justify it to ourselves: the less we act from simple habit without such attention, the better it is for virtue, and the worse for vice. And the same in regard of emotions: the mass of emotion, though irregular and untrustworthy, is kindly, and acts on the side of virtue rather than on that of vice. If therefore it were the case that habit, as a source of action, superseded conscious principle and emotional impression to the extent to which some, and I think Butler, consider it does, mankind would not be more virtuous than they are, but less so: in the combat between virtue and vice, habit is neutral: it is other things superadded to habit, which make virtue the stronger. Habit is not therefore a merciful provision of the Creator on the side of virtue: it is simply a condition or quality of human nature, which constantly does serve virtue and always may be made to do so, but which serves against virtue also.

And to me, there is something more grievous in the thought of the bad being irrecoverable than there is pleasing in the thought of the good being secure. The strong feeling of the invincibleness of habit seems to me not to belong to

The belief in the power of the will against habit is

of great moral importance.

the virtuous frame of mind, and not to aid virtue, but the opposite. Anything which weakens our feeling of the force of human free-will (I am not speaking now in a *religious* view, of human free-will in relation to any divine influence) acts, it seems to me, really on the side of vice, not on that of virtue. It is virtue that is the strength, vice that is the weakness, as the very names denote. The more therefore inward spring and force is supposed to maintain itself inextinguishable to the last, against any overpowering influences such as that of habit, the better for virtue. Habit is second nature, and this phrase exactly expresses the Aristotelic notion of habit of which I have been speaking: it is a nature superinduced upon the first: but as it was superinduced upon the first nature, so may another always be upon it: and as, under the first nature, the acts were possible which, being repeated, formed the habit, so, under the habit or second nature, acts are always possible which, repeated, will form a habit different from, perhaps contrary to, the former.

There is no greater aid to vice, in my view, than disbelief in human free-will and moral agency, which in good men leads to despair, to hard and misanthropic contempt in those who are not good. We need not be suspicious about the virtuous, but we may consider the strength of their virtue to consist not merely, perhaps not principally, in its habitualness, but in the goodness of feeling and the enlightenment of principle which produced the virtue first, and which its increase is only likely to have increased. And thinking thus, we may always be hopeful about the vicious. There is always something in them which may be awaked against the bad habit.

As moralists exaggerate the good, so practicalists exaggerate the evil effect of habit.

I am inclined to think that, as moralists have been usually disposed to consider the power of habit in human nature as a fact helpful to virtue, so those who are not moralists, but men of the world and professedly disciples, in practical morality, of experience (a race of men little to be loved), are disposed to consider it as acting the other way, and as rather strengthening vice. Such men do not seem generally to have much confidence in virtuous habit, when they see it, but a very great certainty with regard to vicious habit, when they see *that*, that the man under its influence will never do anything virtuous, and that all attempts to reform him will be in vain. As I have said, I think both the moralists and the men of the world are in error: the moralists are not too confident in the virtue of the virtuous, but rather mistaken in the ground of their confidence: the opposite party should give fair measure to both sides, and, as they distrust virtuous habit, should in all reason put off their heartlessness and cruelty, and *hope* in regard of vicious habit.

APPENDIX B.[1]

Three shells of character, original, made, making.

There are, we may say, three shells of the being, one above another: there is the constitutional framework; there is the actual character of feelings, dispositions, and mental habits which our experience has formed round this; and there is the outer framework still, of practical habits or customary ways of action which are gradually becoming or producing new mental habits with us, modifying the old, and changing our character.

Habit is second nature, as changeable as the first.

Habit is second nature. With animals, where such a second nature is superinduced upon the first, it is an inferior one, because the first is complete in itself, and not meant by nature to be changed and improved upon. But man has given to him, not so much an individual nature itself as the outline and rudiments of one. Hence the second nature which habit superinduces upon him is a superior one to his first. It is not an addition of incongruous habits to a nature not meant for them, but it is adding to the nature something it needed to fill it up and complete it.

The fact that habit is not fixed in the mind as in the body is an argument for the greater longevity of the former.

Habit is second nature, and *as* difficult, but not more difficult, to modify than the first. The life of man, as we see it, is of course divided into one period of growth and another of stability, &c. and it is natural that in the former there should be more of unfixedness and changeableness: but in reality, reason and will are elements of continual youth, growth, and change, and whether we are glad it should be so or not, they must continue so. At a certain period of life the character becomes what we call formed, because the whole organization about that time in a manner settles itself, and the inward man takes something of a permanent shape in analogy with the outer, but in no respect to the same degree, for vast changes of character are made continually afterwards. And that there is this moral youth or con-

[1] Taken from MS. marked II. 1. Ed.

tinuance of growth is one of the things which may help to convince us that we cannot judge of the probable duration of the existence of the mind by the analogy of that of the body.

The limit between the intermediate and the outer shells of moral being is vague and indeterminate in consequence of this continually possible and likely change of character. Mere practical habits are continually passing into new mental habits or dispositions. Ἔθος, custom, is continually becoming ἦθος, character. Actions done for a purpose and as the result of an effort become more and more done for themselves and as the result of a growing disposition.

Habit while still in the making is necessarily awkward.

This uncertainty of the boundary between these two spheres of the moral being is the source of a great deal of moral difficulty and of much immoral opinion also, which can only be met by our facing the fact, that the limits of what is character, and what is not, but element of future character, are thus uncertain. It is impossible but that a man must put on to a certain degree the character which he is aiming at and wishing was his, and contemplating making more and more his; and, so long as this is the case, there will always be people who will treat what is really effort in him, perhaps imperfectly succeeded in, as mere affectation and hypocrisy. A man can only escape charges of hypocrisy of this kind by a conduct really worse and more unworthy than any conduct which can give occasion to them, viz. by an εἰρωνεία and disguise of his efforts after improvement, which is untrue and uncandid. Whatever is in a state of change and improvement is in a state, so far as that goes, of awkwardness and incompleteness: that character should miss of its rotundity and invulnerability for this reason, is no harm to it.

Habit is produced mainly by education and companionship.

Custom, then, or use, practical habit, is the immediate agent in producing change of mental habit or disposition: but there is always reason superadded. Man, unlike the animals, sees always more or less the manner in which his character is changing.

Where there is no attempt at definite education, there goes on in the youthful human being what is in many respects the same thing, by means of his companionship and society. Dispositions are produced by this; and very possibly good ones: at the same time it is likely that in this case the goodness of them will be unconscious and of itself unattended to. The habit of thinking of them as right or otherwise will not exist. For this, and for the producing of several good dispositions, there needs in a general way moral education.

Relation of character to disposition.

In default of our being able to present a portrait of individual character, which should convey a single general effect, giving us the distinctive expression of it, various theories are made as to the relation between character and the particular dispositions.

Ruling passion: besetting sin.

One is, that its unity consists in the strong and almost exclusive prevalence of some one disposition called the ruling passion, not readily perhaps apparent, but traceable by observation, and such that many of what we call separate dispositions are really only varieties of it. Somewhat of the same kind is the notion of the liability of each person to some one particular temptation or besetting sin.

Mixture in character.

Different again from this is the idea of the mixture of elements in individual character, which is often spoken of as a subject of wonder. It is obvious that there is a sort of inaccuracy in speaking of this mixture, for the elements are really of our own mental making, and it is the character that is the unity. The importance of this view consists in our imputing moral qualities to the different elements, and in the manner in which it thus appears that in every individual character there is good and bad together. The study of the manner of their mixture is perhaps the most important part of all practical morality. It is the carrying this latter idea to an extreme, which leads to the supposition that there is hardly such a thing as character at all. The knowledge of a person's character, if it is anything at all, is something which you can more or less predict his action by: there are perhaps some who will say, that human action cannot be even probably predicted.

In our notions of character it is desirable to keep separate the two ideas, of mixture in character of good and evil, and of composition of character out of various qualities and features. The consideration of the second is like the consideration of actual external portraiture. There is charm in individuality, and even in imperfection and defect as contributing to this. We are not however to fall into the error of supposing that it is in the preservation of this given individuality that consists the truth of the character and the best perfection it is capable of. Faces are given us, and are not generally mendable. Character is given us in rudiment and outline, but is eminently mendable and changeable. Between mental and external portrait there is therefore only an analogy: the features of the character are far more fugitive and less distinct than those of the face. Still, it is impossible to draw them at all, if the analysis of them is too immediately associated with separate judgment of them as good and evil. They go together in the character, and what may seem undesirable in one or other of them is tempered perhaps by something in a neighbouring one. The unity is of the whole: the responsibility is unitary: and the judgment must be of the whole.

Variety of circumstance tends to produce variety of character.

It is probable that the rudimentary or constitutional character is to a certain extent more varied in different individuals in circumstances of civilization, owing to the greater development of character in parents. But however this may be, the variety of circumstances of life and companionship into which the infant of civilization is thrown speedily developes character in one direction or another to an infinity of its varieties.

Character is developed by action rather than by thought.

It is true, thought and imagination not connected with action does little as to development of character, and a high state of literature or knowledge is therefore in this respect not important. There is another respect also in which civilization may even diminish variety of character. It generates a great degree of imitation and fashion, which at first sight renders the aspect of civilized society, as to individual character, more unvaried and monotonous than we imagine that of uncivilized to be. This first impression however is superficial in more than one way. It is not so much that variety of character is really lessened in civilization, but that it is rendered less conspicuous than it would otherwise be by the restraint and mannerism which civilization generates in many classes. The idea of civilization also tends to confine our view to what we should consider the more specially civilized classes; in which it often happens that, while thought and

How far is civilization favourable to variety of character?

imagination are developed, there is less familiarity with the actual exigencies and circumstances of life, and it is these which really modify the character. It is not the height to which civilization draws human thought, but the variety of views in which it sets the common and actual relations of life, and the variety of interests in which it invests them, which varies character. Ease, leisure and study, setting the imagination in motion, generate a sort of shadow of variety of it, and what, in a highly developed civilization, is called *society*, gives a certain degree of substance to the shadow: but there needs generally more of actual reality and call upon feeling than goes with these, to produce real character.

However, a certain degree of a kind of uncivilizedness in the midst of civilization is supposed to conduce to the greater variety and interest of individual character. Some consider that there is more variety of character in England than elsewhere; and also more of *humour*.

APPENDIX C.[1]

The habits of the mind are analogous to those of the body, and habit may be called a second nature in both; but there is a considerable difference between the two, according to the nature of that of which they are habits. Habits of the body take their place in a material organization which, so far as it is matter, is out of ourselves and beyond our will; and permanent states or conformations are established, which no power of will can remedy. Habits of the mind are always mixed with a certain degree of estimation, judgment, opinion, which is in its nature alterable, and as such, may lead to alteration of the habits. When therefore habits of the mind are considered to constitute a second nature, it must be considered also, that mental nature can never be counted as immovably and irremediably fixed, but that, reason being always capable of adding fresh knowledge, and feeling being susceptible of fresh impressions, the greatest changes may be produced in the nature and character without destroying the individuality.

Mental habits are more easily changed than bodily.

But quære, though in its nature as mind, or as spiritual, the character may be susceptible thus of change, yet is it not perhaps in its nature for a limited period, in this respect following the analogy of the body: *i.e.* has not the soul or moral character, like the body, a period of flexibility or growth, at the end of which it becomes fixed and limited, with no further power of change than in the way of decline?

Is there any limit to mental change?

This question as to the possible fixation and non-improvability of moral character is, in a practical point of view, the most important question of morals. Almost the greatest service of the many which religion has rendered to the world, is its having reinforced the side which maintains

Religion confirms the hopes of morality in affirming the

[1] Taken from an unmarked MS. written some time ago and apparently forming part of the long series marked I. 1. Ed.

possibility of improvement against habit.

that there is always in the character, however fixed and however educated, a spring and possibility of improvement. This it has done in two ways; both by strongly urging upon us the enduring and immortal nature of the soul, as contrasted with the growing and declining life of the body; and next by protesting in behalf of the individual, and in right of a superior and nobler influence which may be brought to bear upon him, against the absolute and necessary dominion over him of any earthly state and habit, which always *may* be shattered and broken up by the spiritual force within. What religion thus distinctly sets before us, morality had already shadowed forth. There is really more in any of us than the superficial maxims, necessary and valuable for the commerce of life, would recognize; and there is also an inward force of the Spirit deeper and stronger than anything which human agency can breed in us.

Stoic view that virtue, being according to nature, is the condition of stable equilibrium:

It was a remarkable practical application of the theory of the Stoics, (that virtue was according to nature, vice against it,) that they considered a state of attained virtue one of stable equilibrium, *i.e.* one not likely, hardly possible, to be departed from, whereas a state of lapse into vice they considered one of unstable equilibrium, because against nature. It is curious to compare with this some moral theories connected with religion in later times, as that *e.g.* which assumes the opposite to the maxim of the Stoics in regard of human nature, viz. that it is *bad*, and therefore that its state of stable equilibrium, or natural acquiescence, would be in *vice;* a theory nevertheless which, in regard to the permanence of a state of virtue, is to a certain extent in harmony with the Stoic idea, attributing such permanence to perseverance under a special divine influence.

confirmed by Christianity.

On the other hand, the well-known chapter in Ezekiel[1] exhibits the possibility of movement either way, in language looking in some respects as if one way and the other were equally probable: and, as a fact of pre-Christian morality, it will probably be allowed that this view is more in accordance with human experience than the Stoic idea of a state of virtue having an element of stability in it beyond what a state of vice had. At the same time the Gospel, with its doctrine of special divine influence, does introduce a new element on

[1] Ezek. xviii. 26, 27.

the side of virtue, and under it we may rightly suppose that permanence which the Stoic supposed wrongly.

Meaning of the question whether ἀρετή is διδακτόν:

Not to dwell on this longer, I will just discuss for a moment two famous old Greek questions: the one, whether ἀρετή is διδακτόν, *i.e.* whether virtue is matter of teaching; the other, how far it may be said with truth that οὐδεὶς ἑκὼν κακός, no man is willingly or purposely bad.

The former question may mean one of two things: either, is virtue a thing in regard of which teaching is not applicable? or, is it a thing in regard of which teaching is not enough? Or, putting it in another form, and taking the three alternatives, is ἀρετή διδακτόν only (1), ἀσκητόν only (2) to be produced *i.e.* by practice and habit, or is it διδακτὸν and ἀσκητόν together (3), requiring teaching and practice both?

We should generally say now it was the last of these three alternatives, and what I have been saying is simply that it never becomes so absolutely fixed by the ἄσκησις, but that it is possible, at least in the direction of good, to alter it by teaching. In a general way, moral schools the essence of whose teaching is *rationalism* would maintain the first alternative; those the essence of whose teaching is *sentimentalism* would maintain the second.

of the maxim οὐδεὶς ἑκὼν κακός.

The maxim οὐδεὶς ἑκὼν κακός is also susceptible of two meanings: it may either mean 'no one does wrong but by compulsion,' or 'no one does wrong but by mistake.' If it be true that no man does wrong willingly, it must be either that, when he does it, he does the thing which he does unwillingly, or that, though he does it willingly, it is *as* something else, not as what it is.

Wrong being simply mistake involves ἀρετή being simply διδακτόν; and this view in various forms is held, to a certain degree, by several sorts of moralists. The idea of wrong being weakness or yielding, against a better judgment, is one which involves rather the idea of ἀρετή being ἀσκητόν.

Importance of these questions in regard to the treatment of criminals.

The questions are rather dry as philosophical ones, having been thrashed out so much, but as practical ones they are of intense and perfectly fresh interest, not only as regards individual moral conduct, but as regards the proper estimation of offence or crime and the ways of dealing with it. Supposing a wrong or crime done by any one, and we are thinking of the temper of mind in which he did it. Did he justify himself in doing it, do it, that is, not against his conscience? then some will say, he did not do it as wrong, but there is something of the character of error or mistake about it. Did he *not* justify himself in doing it, but do it against his conscience? was it Video meliora proboque, deteriora sequor? if so, then some will associate the *will* with the *probo*, and say, he wanted to do good, but evil was present with him; they will look on him to a certain degree as passive, drifting, acting under compulsion.

Questions about the will frighten practical people through the idea of their abstruseness; but this, of the degree to which people in doing wrong do it with self-justification, is one so important for any moral dealing with wrong-doers that it must be faced. It is most intimately connected with the theory of punishment, for where there is determined self-justification in the mind in regard of what has been done, there any punishment must seem unjust in the mind of the punished, and will produce no moral effect, but an effect only of terror accompanied with a feeling of reaction against the punishment, which will make the man worse. Punishment, as regards the mind of the offender, appeals to the conscience, *i.e.* to the feeling of failure in self-justification, which will have involved an expectation of it, or sense of deserving it.

Punishment implies the negation of the second maxim.

The theory upon which punishment goes then in regard of the mind of the individual is on the *negation* of the maxim οὐδεὶς ἑκὼν κακός, in both its possible senses: *i.e.* it assumes that the man, in doing what he did, knew he was doing wrong, and could have helped doing it. Both these last suppositions are indeed only true in an imperfect degree, but still enough so to make punishment applicable and suitable. The thing done probably presents itself to the criminal in a light very different from that in which it appears to the judge: and the bearing up against the temptation to do it will have been something very different in the criminal's mind from what it may seem in the eyes of the indifferent and untempted. But there has been enough of will in his mind to make him expect punishment and think it natural, and there is a prospect therefore that upon himself as well as on others the effect of it may be good.

Wrong or crime we may suppose in a general way committed in a frame of mind made up more or less of three elements: the first, an effort, often for the moment successful, at self-justification; the second, an effort to banish from the mind all thoughts and considerations which might disturb such self-justification; the third, a feeling of yielding or being overpowered, of the thing being what cannot be helped, of the man's letting himself go, eyes shut perhaps, to do the thing. According to the degree of strength or weakness of nature there will be more perhaps or less of any one of these; but in general I should think something of a mixture of all of them.

Analysis of the state of mind in which the offence is committed.

The consideration of the variety of character is of vast importance in morals. It has been sometimes misused, sometimes neglected, in both cases with the result of error and immorality. It has been misused to the extent of doing away with the reality and absoluteness of moral distinctions altogether, through the consideration of each person having in a manner a distinct duty according to his character, or having a sort of duty to his character, for there are various ways in which we may phrase the thing. The result of the opposite proceeding, neglect of it, has been a good deal of harsh, foolish, and mistaken judgment, and of abortive effort in consequence at improvement and reformation.

Importance of recognizing the variety of character.

The reality of moral distinctions as to action has to be maintained against those who misuse the fact of individuality of character to subvert it, in the same way as it has to be maintained against those who misuse the fact of good being to a good end, and pervert it into the statement, that everything which is to a good end is, as such, good.

How this fact has been misused.

In a general way what is called knowledge of human nature and correct moral thought are considered to be very different things and even not likely to go together. We may arrange and catalogue dispositions and feelings, and we may judge whether they are good or bad according to our moral theory, whatever it is, whether of honourableness, *e.g.*, or utility: but, for valuable action in respect of morals, there is usually needed an experimental and observational element, that is, we must see how these dispositions enter into character or concur to form characters which are the real

Character is the reality, disposition a mere abstraction.

moral units. Virtues, vices, feelings, dispositions, habits, all these are abstractions; men or characters, *i.e.* men as concerns their moral being, are the realities which in ethics we have to do with.

Characters, like all natural realities, are not definable: when they are described by their details or features, there is an effect as to the whole produced by the co-existence of these details which is no more capable of being fixed in description than the expression of a face. No congeries of details, such *e.g.* as the phrenological classification of qualities and accounts of the degrees and amounts of them, can produce any conception of a character as it in fact exists: so far as this can be entered into, it must be by a sort of sympathy, not necessarily of agreement, but at least of understanding. No putting together of parts will make the whole, the conception of which whole, however faint and feeble, must exist in its unity, and the parts must be of the nature of results or developments of it.

Absence of character.

Every one then may be supposed to have a character, as he has a face, more or less distinct and marked. So far as it is not distinct, this is most likely in one of two ways: either the weakness, yieldingness, and tendency to imitation is so great that the individual takes almost entirely the character of those he is with; or else the inconsistency and variability is so great that the dispositions of to-day are not those of to-morrow, and there is no permanence of character. The French when they use the expression 'un homme de *caractère*,' mean in the main the opposite to the former of these, and the poet when he used the line which I never well understood, 'Most women have no character at all,' meant I suppose to express the latter.

Formation of character.

The *formation* of character we commonly speak of as what belongs to youth. In using the word 'formation' we mean it probably in its closer etymological and logical sense, understanding by it a plastic operation upon matter existing. At the first there is no character but only the materials of it waiting to receive their form; the animal, intellectual, and moral being are all, to a certain degree, simultaneously trained and developed.

Man is more

We are always however to remember that the intellectual,

and more especially the moral training of men is distinct from the animal, and that it is a part of the special nature of man to preserve throughout his life, to a certain degree, that flexibility, adaptability, and capacity of change which in animals belong only to the period of their youth. Even as an animal, man is more *convertible*, as we should say if we were speaking of soils, than other animals: as he is fit by his constitution for a greater variety of things, so he can live in a greater variety of climates, and adapt himself; often to a very late period of his life, to alteration of circumstances, &c., and reason and imagination in man, so far as they exist, are really almost a spring of continual youth. There is no need for the stiffening and fixing of them, as the limbs and animal nature stiffen, nor need there be any weakening of the will so that it should not be able to carry out what wider range and altered view would suggest: character therefore as formed in youth is very far from unmodifiable.

capable of modification than other animals.

APPENDIX D.[1]

Character as mixed.

My lecture to-day will be upon human character, as *mixed,* in the same individual.

The first question which arises in regard of this is, What is the meaning of individual character at all? There is no doubt each man has a reputation, good or bad, a character in the eyes of his neighbours: this is an idea or imagination of him with definite form and outline; but what is there in himself which can be considered as corresponding to this? Is he not rather one thing to-day and another to-morrow? If there is individual character, what is its relation to personal responsibility?

Three sorts of moralists: theoretic, didactic, critical.

Before answering this, I will distinguish between three sorts of moralists, theoretical, didactic, and a third class whom I will call critical moralists: they are chiefly the makers of maxims, essays, and remarks. The first set in this triple division might be divided again into two, psychological and ontological, but this does not matter. At present we are chiefly concerned with the difference between the *didactic* and the *critical* moralists.

Critical moralism is analytic and indisposed to recognize unity of character: didactic is synthetic and sympathetic.

As a rule there is a tendency on the part of the critical moralists to think to a certain degree lightly of any uniformity or unity in individual character, whereas didactic moralism must make a great deal of it. This arises from the fact that these critical moralists draw their materials from two sources neither of which are very much fitted to give them a strong idea of individualism of character: these are examination of themselves, and criticism of particular actions in others. Didactic moralism proceeds always more or less on something of a previously formed ideal of what a man ought to be, and might be, and refers the particular actions to this rather than dissects them by themselves. In fact, didactic moralism has always a certain degree of sympathy with the individuals whom it concerns; and this in a way idealizes them, and gives an idea of unity of character. Critical moralism is analytic rather than synthetic, *de-unifies*

[1] Taken from MS. R_3, forming part of series I. 1. Ed.

rather than unifies. Similarly the habit of examination of one's own motives has a tendency to diminish the idea of the real unity of individual character. A man's character is like his writing, which has not usually much individuality to himself, but seems different from day to day, whereas to others it is strongly individual, and marked and recognized. Besides, a man who looks much at his own motives sees so much one way and the other in himself, different from the character he bears with others, that he gets inclined to think individual character a chimera.

You see in the critical moralists many maxims with this tendency. And it appears not in moralists only, but any unsympathizing view of others is likely to produce it, sympathy being the key to perception of character, as distinguished from criticism of actions. In those fits of misanthropy which people at certain times of their lives seem liable to, their fellow-creatures, whom unhappily for them they have got to pass their lives with, are apt to seem to them like a number of sheep similar and undistinguished, without individuality and without interest. The development of any *character* at all in them is somewhat superciliously set down as impossible.

The critical negation of character is immoral, no less than the practicalist assumption of low motives.

The assumption of want of individuality of character among men must be considered to a certain degree an immoral one, not as implying immorality in the maker of it, but as being a view of human nature which it is hard or impossible to adapt to moral relations[1]. The supposition of individuality of character must be considered as a medium between two erroneous suppositions, the one made commonly by practicalists, so to call them, as distinguished from moralists, the other made by critical moralists. The first of them is a sort of vague general assumption of a low tone among men,

[1] So Pope, *Essay on Man:*

"Virtuous and vicious every man must be,
Few in the extreme, but all in the degree.
The rogue and fool by fits is fair and wise;
And even the best, by fits, what they despise."

And Crabbe, *The Borough*, xvii.:

"In man's erroneous kind
Virtues and frailties mingle in the mind."

Rather differently Agamemnon in Soph. *Aj.* 1365:

ἦ πάνθ' ὅμοια πᾶς ἀνὴρ αὑτῷ πονεῖ.

and a rough consequent division of them into certain classes, differently made according to the man who makes them (as for instance that cleverness and wickedness go together, and that every one is knave or fool), but all to a certain degree inconsistent with moral considerations. This is the *practicalist* error; the critical consists in the carrying too far, as all people fond of analysing actions are sure to be tempted to do, the idea of evil being always mixed with good, and good with evil, so as to break down the subjective boundaries of right and wrong altogether. As, on the one hand, the practicalist with a sort of careless contempt sets men down under certain great heads on the supposition of their being only influenced by coarse and palpable motives, so the critical moralists, on the other hand, by their refinements make one part of an action or character neutralize another to such a degree that all colour and shade and distinction is removed; and we cannot say what is right, what wrong, what a man is, and what he is not.

Between these two errors the supposition of individuality of character has to be maintained; men being of different characters, some good, some bad, but these being variously shaded, related and mixed, not capable of being rudely jumbled together in the practicalist manner.

The character of mixed good and evil is sometimes more mischievous than one with less good.

It is a very famous historical observation and one most thoroughly true, that in regard of public injury, as in times of revolution, it is not the vicious character that is most to be feared, but the wrong-headed and narrow-minded virtuous character. Vice, existing in such extent as to constitute in any way the character, is weakness; and hence arises the absolute contradictoriness and inconceivableness of characters supposed indefinitely great, both in viciousness and in strength or wisdom, such as Milton's idea of Satan. The old mediæval association of folly with Satanic viciousness (setting aside the danger of perversion of such an association to the grotesque and ridiculous) was in other respects truer to the real idea of vice and evil than the Miltonic association with it of wisdom and strength[1].

[1] Tacitus says indeed: "In turbas et discordias pessimo cuique plurima vis." *Hist.* iv. 1, but it wants qualification. Corneille is equally strong on the opposite side when he says,

"Pour commettre un grand crime il faut de la vertu."

The consideration of the way in which people whose characters must on the whole be called virtuous, may be the authors of results most evil and wicked, is a proceeding which, though capable of being perverted to immorality, is not in itself necessarily immoral. It is a consideration of great importance with respect to the relation of character to action, and against the supposition that a thing must be right because a man of apparently virtuous character does it, and that the action of such a man must be for good[1].

The mixture of good and evil in character has been much written about, partly for an immoral, and partly for a moral purpose. The discovery and exhibition of the bad which there is in actions apparently or upon the whole good, is what we may call the staple subject of the critical moralists, La Rochefoucauld, &c.; and with them I think it must be considered that the purpose for which it is done is not good; for though this purpose is professedly that of counteracting the pride to which man is liable in what he does, yet what is effected is not so much this, as the depreciation and obscuring of the ideal of good which man is able to form, and which is really the great resource in the inculcating and

The discovery of the evil in good may be done either by way of mockery or to excite to more earnest effort after good.

It results from the different nature of vice and virtue, as being respectively *weakness* and *strength*, independent of goodness and badness, that, while as Ben Jonson says of valour and anger (*New Inn* iv. 3), "Virtue is never aided by a vice," yet *vice*, to produce any bad effects of consequence is aided by virtue, and only produces them when so aided. The simply vicious man is apt to be

"Wicked but in will, of means bereft."

Dryden, *Absalom and Ach.*

But is virtue, as strength, ever rendered more amiable by vice, as weakness?

"Is aught then wanted in a man so wise?
Alas! I think he wants infirmities:
He wants the ties that knit us to our kind."

Similarly

"Nihil peccat, nisi quod nihil peccat." Plin. *Ep.* ix. 26.

[1] The Stoic magniloquence in relation to the importance of particular character over action often tended towards immorality.

"Catoni ebrietas objecta est: facilius efficiet, quisquis objecerit, hoc crimen honestum, quam turpem Catonem."

Seneca, *de Tranquill. An.*

"Envy, to which the ignoble mind's a slave,
Is emulation in the learn'd and brave."

Pope, *Essay on Man.*

seeking improvement. The same thing has been done with a religious view, in order to purify and elevate the ideal and stimulate further effort after it.

The discovery of the good in evil is often done with a bad motive, but is valuable for the reformation of character.

The opposite mixture, of *good* with actions which are apparently or upon the whole *evil*, has, we may say, speaking generally, been pointed out only in one view and for one purpose, and that a wrong one. There is, I suppose, upon the whole, more tendency in human nature to think well of evil, than to think badly of good: and this first tendency has shewn itself strongly in the literature of fiction; so strongly indeed, as almost, one might think, to confound the boundaries of right and wrong in many minds[1].

It is a pity that not more attempts have been made, for a good purpose, to analyse and shew the nature of the good which so constantly enters into combination with evil. It is of course a task requiring very great caution and a very true and sincere mind, so that nothing which is evil shall be set down to the side of good, but only the evil disengaged; and that the good found in combination with the evil should in no respect lessen our dislike for the evil itself, or make us look with less abhorrence upon the mixture. Christians are, we might almost say, to a certain degree committed, as one of their characteristics, to the special notice and recognition, in any who are evil and guilty, of whatever tendencies to good there may be in them. This was one of the most marked features in the character of Him whom we profess to follow, and though we must guard against any possibility in it of immoral connivance or allowance, or the imputation of such, we must no more shrink from the thing because of such possibility, than He did.

The subject is of considerable importance just now, in reference to the possible reformation of criminals.

Character may be bad on principle, or impulse, or habit.

For practical convenience we may distinguish three kinds of badness: a man may be bad on *principle*, or bad through *want of principle* and strength of passions, or bad through *habit*.

I have already mentioned, in regard of Butler's statement

[1] You remember Tacitus' remarkable character of Mucianus, the man "malis bonisque artibus mixtus," which he gives in detail *Hist.* i. 10. Such a character we should certainly set down as on the whole *bad*.

that conscience is, in the nature of things, supreme over passion, that it is in fact reason or the intellectual nature of man, which has this supremacy, but that the supremacy of what thinks and guides over what blindly feels and desires is in no respect the foundation of morals, reason being quite conceivably mistaken and wrong reason, and then morality would be on the side of passion and affection, against it. In point of fact, character is quite as often bad from wrongness and perversion of reason as it is from weakness or insufficient power of it: then the character is what we call one of bad principle.

In all cases of bad principle, we are to remember that the man in fact justifies to himself his crime, and makes out to his own satisfaction that it is right. If it is stealing, he tacitly assumes that the man from whom he takes whatever it is, has no more right to the thing than he himself has, that there is a sort of war between them, and that any ideas of society to the contrary are wrong. And if you say he thinks nothing about all this, just try to put into his mind what *you* think about the matter, *i.e.* the exact contrary of the above, and see how he receives that; you will then find out what he does think. To reform him, you have got to make him see things in a light quite different from that in which he has seen them before.

The first may be met by reforming the principle or by rousing antagonist impulse.

Against character bad on principle, there are therefore two ways of proceeding, both commonly to be pursued in conjunction, the one to improve the principle, or implant a better principle against it, the other to stir up and arm, against the bad principle, any tendency or chance of good which may exist in feeling and affection. So far from its being always desirable that reason, such as it often is in man, should prevail, it is possible that the only chance of reformation of a bad character may consist in the conquering it: where it is impossible to alter it in its own domain, owing to some fixed perverseness, it may be needful to depose it from the actual supremacy which it enjoys. Supposing a man to be firmly persuaded that his own gratification is the only thing he need care for, it may be possible that no argument we could use would give him in this respect higher motives; but we might bring him to the same point by exciting the emotions of affection, pity and sympathy; thus the defeat of the man's reason may be the improvement of his character.

Where the direct attempt to change principle by instruction fails,

Positive bad principle then, or perverted moral judgment, may be either eradicated or conquered; *i.e.* either the reason may be convinced and amended, and the positive bad principle changed for good; or, without a direct attack upon the bad principle, other motives of feeling and action may be awakened instead of it, which may practically supplant and neutralize it. Very commonly it is only the second of these which is possible, and that for two reasons: 1st, because, when once the understanding is occupied by a definite set of ideas or ways of thinking about things, it is very hard, even in matters allowing of clear proof, to change these, the utmost we can do being to supersede them; and 2nd, because many questions of morality about which ideas would have to be changed are not susceptible of this clear proof. Take the right of property or the obligation of truth, matters very easily demonstrable perhaps by me to you, who do not doubt them, and who want no more in regard to the demonstration than the significance and formal correctness of it, but far from easy to demonstrate to one who had been all his life taught to regard nothing as belonging to another in such sense as to preclude the trying to rob him of it, and anything his own which he could without detection lay his hands on, and anything fair to say which would get him out of trouble. It is not altogether easy, as Paley and others have shown, to exhibit clearly the foundations of the right of property and of the obligation of truth, even to those who have no interest in denying them; and against such interest, and habit founded on it, the arms of reason trying to reform the reason of another are very far from powerful.

it may often be met indirectly by arousing affection.

Still of course, direct instruction must be tried, in every way in which it will take hold; where it will not, there we must endeavour to call out any part of the moral nature which still remains unperverted. And no doubt, so far is reason from being more moral than the affections, that they are in a general way less completely pervertible than it, and there is hope from them, where from reason there is none. The transformation of a bad moral view of things, where feeling and affection are awakened; the melting away and dissolving of the false principles and the gradual rise of true principles in their place; the manner in which the most iron resolve of bad reason and will may collapse at the touch of love, and the hardest determination to look at things in one way and no other thaw before the warm wind of sympathy—these are moral phenomena, remarkable indeed, but by no means unfrequent. Nor are we to suppose there is anything wrong in feeling thus conquering reason: it is not true and simple reason which is thus conquered, for such reason is accessible only to reasonable opposition and attack; but it is reason which, not having been convinced while yet reason and convinceable, has now very probably passed beyond the stage of simple reason, the stage of convinceability, has become ingrained into the character and fixed in the habits, and is only accessible to motives acting upon that character in other and different ways.

Where character is bad through impulse, it has to be reformed by strengthening principle and changing impulse.

I will now say a word on bad character arising not from bad principle, but from want or weakness of principle and strength of passion. Here the reason is on the side of good, but has little power. This is a better character than the last, though in one respect we might be inclined to think it worse. Reason is the common referee, talking our first and simplest way of trying to act upon others for their good; and therefore we are inclined perhaps at first to think that where reason is wrong, there is more hope of effecting a change for the better by persuasion and argument; whereas if, when the reason is right, men still do wrong, it is not likely that our talking and convincing them will have much influence. But in truth, reason, in little-thinking and much-acting men, who pass pretty frequently from a youth of utter instability to a maturity of set stiffness, is by no means the ever-living, and therefore ever-open and convinceable thing we seem to think. As I have said, it gets often to be the most immoveable part of a man, and he is young perhaps and flexible in his affections after he has got old and stiff in matter of reason. And therefore to have a man's reason with us is a greater encouragement than discouragement: *discouragement* of course it is, that, his reason having perhaps so often tried to conquer his passions, so little success has been achieved, and we hardly know how to hope now: still sight and approval of the good is some way, and a great way.

With characters of this kind, as with the last, there is a twofold way of proceeding: as in that case we supposed bad reason counteracted by affection or by good reason, so here we have to attack bad affection either by reinforcing the reason or by arousing good affection.

Vows and resolutions.

I have not space to dwell here on the various moral considerations connected with *prævolition*, *i.e.* with resolutions, vows, internal or subjective promises as to future action. Of course the general principle in regard of trying to strengthen our own reason or will or that of others in this way, (I carefully abstain here from any religious reference), is that such resolutions should be wisely formed, by which I mean that they should refer to something not far off and not too difficult, something which there is really a hope of accomplishing. The reasons for this are, first, that every resolution, whatever good effect there may be from it afterwards, has to a certain degree a bad effect, in the first instance; *i.e.* it is a discounting of the action in our conscience; we take and feel some of the conscientious pleasure belonging to the doing it without doing it, a pleasure which of course, so far as it goes, is immoral and wrong: the second is the simple one that a resolution to do a great thing is more likely to be broken than one to do a small thing; and every broken resolution, though not properly bringing us under the guilt of promise-breaking, does us much moral harm, and increases the likelihood of our breaking any future resolution.

I will conclude this lecture by saying a few words upon moral influence.

Moral influence demands sympathy as well as general and individual knowledge.

Influence of this kind is partly involuntary, or what may be so, the effect of character or position: about this I shall not say anything now: it is the Latin *auctoritas* in a moral sense, a most important element of society. The other part of influence is purposed or express, that which rests on knowledge and is exercised in definite action.

The knowledge upon which such influence rests is twofold, partly knowledge of the person under influence, and partly independent objective knowledge. The knowledge of the person is likely to be of his past history and of his mental and physical constitution, with a view to the ascertaining of what hidden springs of action, what tendencies, and probabilities of desire, lie underneath the motives which ordinarily actuate him, in such a manner as to be possibly awakened. The independent moral knowledge is, speaking generally, that of the nature of feelings and actions as mixed, how what is good is weak and vulnerable through mixture of evil, and what is evil is unfixed and improvable through mixture of good. To these two kinds of knowledge must be added sympathy.

The three qualities mix together in the practical drawing of others to good, but are in themselves independent. It is probably because they do not go together more than they do, that so many efforts in this direction are vain. For instance, the moral knowledge is of a nature which is very likely, in the gaining of it, to denude the soul of that sympathy without which the knowledge will, for this purpose, be useless. A good deal of critical or analytical moralism is, as we know, the freezingest of all freezing things, and the rhetoric and psychology of didactic moralism is often not much better. Sympathy of love without this knowledge will do much better than the knowledge without it, because such sympathy carries, by the constitution of human nature, a certain amount of knowledge with it; but yet sympathy without more knowledge added, often defeats its own object. One of the most important purposes of sympathy, besides the fact of the unlikeliness of care and perseverance without it, is as a means and help towards the understanding of the character of the person influenced: without sympathy, this is impossible.

Good mixed with evil may strengthen evil, but at the same time it makes reformation possible.

The moral knowledge necessary for temptation to good (if I may use the phrase) is chiefly of the way in which most evil characters and actions which are *human* have something of good mixed with them, which to a certain degree may weaken the evil, and indicate a breach by which it is assailable. I say *may*, because it is possible that the good may be of such a nature that it practically strengthens the evil; and it may possibly become the duty of those who wish well to good to try to break down the particular good here mixed with the evil, and to raise up instead of it an evil feeling against the other evil. The second evil in this case being on the side of main or absolute good, though subjectively evil, is not evil objectively; evil against evil, like two negatives, being supposed resultant good[1]. A familiar instance is what is popularly called 'honour among thieves,' a good principle mixed with evil, which unhappily it must be the object of justice and of laws as much as possible to break up, because it practically strengthens the evil that it mixes with. Suppose a crime done, and we wish to persuade one whom we believe an accomplice to turn king's evidence; if we could persuade him to do so for the sake of his country and morality, of course the thing would not only be in itself right, but he would be a better man than he was before in doing it. Usually however we have to persuade him by stirring up his cowardice and selfishness, and promising him impunity for himself and perhaps a reward: if we do thus persuade him, though the thing itself which he does is right, we do not in our hearts consider him the better man for it, but in fact the worse, however he may escape and the others be punished.

But in a general way, the good mixed with the evil is that which makes reformation possible, it is that which forms the ground for the hope, and should be the study of, the moral reformer. We want a La Rochefoucauld of a converse kind, who would hunt out, not the root of bitterness in every good action, but of reason and excusableness in every bad; a dangerous and immoral task if done for a bad object, but a task of the noblest morality if for a good.

[1] I think it should have been more distinctly stated that this has reference only to the attainment of some independent good object, *e.g.* the safety of society, not to the reformation of the offender. If we aim at reforming an individual, we may temporarily encourage what we ourselves feel to be inferior motives, provided that, in his view they will be better, or less bad, than those by which he is at present actuated. Thus we might endeavour to replace positive malignity by thoughtless self-indulgence, and this latter by covetousness. In the case supposed of a conspirator turning 'king's evidence,' a father confessor might fairly appeal to prudential motives to deter him from having any more to do with conspiracy, he might urge him to use all his influence with others for the same purpose, and to prevent actual bad consequences by all means in his power; but he could not urge him to get money by informing against others who were not more guilty than himself. To do this would be to destroy the last chance of amendment of character. ED.

CHAPTER XX.

ON DISCUSSION, CONTROVERSY, AND WAR.

I MENTIONED, that the considering utilitarianism to be the whole of moral philosophy, or in other words, the considering utility or productiveness of happiness to be the single 'mot,' key, pass-word, clue, of moral philosophy, seemed to me to imply an insufficient attention to one point, viz. that the *pinch* of morals arises from diversity of interests. If we had no conflicting interests, morality, as we understand it, would not exist at all. I propose then in the present chapter to consider moral philosophy from this point of view, as that which should furnish grounds to us for rightly thinking and judging in reference to the endless dispute which is going on among men. Justice is impartiality between two contending parties, the reconciliation of conflicting interests with a view to peace: virtue consists largely in justice: moral philosophy, as the science of virtue, has thus for its subject all this conflict.

Human quarrelsomeness forms one of the chief fields of moral philosophy.

In one respect however, moral philosophy would seem to be poorly fitted to be a reconciler of conflict, as there has scarcely ever been a subject which has involved more dispute and controversy in itself. I shall try to present the controversy which has existed about moral philosophy, and the conflict of interests which make its main subject, in a single view; in other words, shortly to anatomize the quarrelsomeness of human nature.

It takes the form either of conflict of opinion or of conflict of interest.

History, whether civil, political, military, commercial, or literary, is a 'Journal des Débats,' a record of perpetual conflict. There are two sources of this conflict: it is either conflict of interest, or conflict of opinion; and what stimulates this conflict, in each case, to the excess in which it exists, is a principle of human nature, which, without either of these matters of conflict, would probably of itself produce quarrel and dispute, I mean the feeling of mutual rivalry, or spontaneous opposition and combativeness. This principle is an almost necessary accompaniment of the activity of human nature, quite independently of any ill-will. The conflict of maturity is the stiff and serious form, belonging to that period, of the active playfulness of youth. Action is not action without some resistance to it, just as there could not be physical movement without some resistance. Action is a triumph of our will, and it is in the triumph, and in the amount of success against what is triumphed over, that we are conscious of ourselves, of our liberty and of our power. This is independent of the causes which may give vigour to the conflict, and which are furnished abundantly by the opposition of opinion and interest which I have noticed. Then, from rivalry, it becomes dispute, contest, war.

Good qualities called out by conflict.

Contest once begun, all kinds of heterogeneous elements blend in it, and it derives force from a variety of good motives which it incorporates by the side of its bad ones. Love, friendship, brotherhood, sociality, all are more or less distinctive; and the conversion of this distinction into opposition fuses more strongly together the love or the sociality. Instead of individually conflicting men, we have corporately conflicting parties: we have good and bad elements generated side by side, apparently necessary to each other; until the mind of the spectator shares in the general bewilderment of the scene which he views.

Let us see what can be made out about it.

In all conflict, there is on each side a certain amount of reason, and on each side a certain amount of force. When we bring the reason on one side into contact with the reason on the other, it is what we call discussion. When we introduce violence of any kind, it is what, if the violence is confined to words, we call dispute or controversy; if the violence proceeds to deeds, we call it combat and war.

In conflict of interest, the thing to be desired is its speedy settlement, just if possible.

The moral, general, or public interest in the decision of conflict is of a different nature according as the conflict is of opinion, or of interest. If it is of interest, dispute about it is so much waste of human power, and so much development of human bad feeling—both of them loss—with possibly a certain amount of development of good feeling, which would be so far gain. The moral interest in such a conflict is that it should be decided—so strife will cease—and if possible, justly and properly decided, every possible pains being taken for this purpose. Still, in this case, if the decision of the conflict *properly*, *i.e.* in entire accordance with justice, is impossible—whether because there really is not a right and a wrong in the matter, or because it is impossible to get to the bottom of it, or for whatever reason—then the next best thing is that it should be decided somehow, and strife cease.

In conflict of opinion, the thing to be desired is its just settlement, whether speedy or otherwise.

The moral interest in a conflict of opinion is not exactly the same. There is the same interest that the conflict should be decided properly and satisfactorily, if possible; but, where such satisfactoriness is not possible, there is not the moral interest, as in the other case, that the conflict should be decided somehow, but rather that, with whatever disadvantage, it should remain open till it *can* be decided satisfactorily.

In civilized communities, conflict of interest is settled by judicial decisions.

The conciliation of different interests, or, which is the same thing, the authoritative and forcible decision of conflicts of interest among the members of a community, is one main reason of civil government, and forms the subject of a large portion of law. Authority, power, and reason, are the three things which go to such decision. Authority causes respect to the decision on the part of the well-disposed; power causes obedience on the part of all, however disposed; and reason makes it a decision not only apparently, but really, satisfactory and just. If authority and power are both wanting, their place may be supplied by the previous and subsequent consent of the parties, and the decision is then arbitration; but reason is of the essence of its satisfactoriness.

Discussion, or the conflict of reason, is the operation of the mind putting together various conflicting views with the purpose of ascertaining which of them is the true. All fertile thought is internal discussion, what Plato meant by his διαλεκτική. In the decision of an actual question of conflict of interests, such thought must be in the mind of the judge, each party suggesting the view on his own side. In the law of civilized countries, for such a rough hearing is universally substituted an elaborate argument, by representatives of the parties, collecting and marshalling all the views on the one side and on the other, to furnish the judge's mind for the decision. Judicial decision of this kind is the preventive of what is called 'private war,' and where it is good, is a main element of the 'security of property.'

Were property to remain at the same degree of

simplicity or complication, the better the decisions the fewer they would be; because the law would be clearer, and there would be less hope in the minds of the ill-intentioned of perverting it. But the relations of men in civilization continually increase and become more complicated; and though injustice is less attempted where decisions are trusted, yet this very fact leads to the assertion of rights which might otherwise have lain dormant; so that the need of continual decision does not diminish.

Between two such communities, or in case of conflict of opinion, this is impossible.

Where there is conflict of interest without possibility of judicial decision, or with indisposition in the parties to resort to it, there is combat or war. By war we mean mutual violence which is more or less formal: in our present use indeed the term is limited to a combat between two individuals, with states for individuals.

And war readily ensues.

Combat or war however, whether between states or individuals, does not arise only from conflict of interest; and here is a great matter of difficulty as to the whole of it. It arises also from conflict of opinion. Now there are some cases of private conflicts of interest, in which, with the best law, there is no possibility of judicial decision; and then a party must forego or fight. In conflicts of interest between states, there is never any possibility of judicial decision, except by consent and arbitration: in these cases then, if there is not agreement, there must be either foregoing or war. In conflicts of opinion, whether private or public, there cannot be judicial decision, from the nature of the case. And reference to the decision of a third party, as arbiter, is a different thing in conflicts of opinion from what it is in conflicts of interest. Our interest we are free to resign to the decision of another, or to give it up altogether: we are not free to do this with our conscientious opinion.

Here we are in a dilemma between love of peace and love of justice.

The causes of combat and war, both private and public, have constantly been such as have involved much consideration of truth and justice, quite independently of any interest. To put the decision of these out of our own hands into the hands of a third party, is what men hesitate to do; the truth or justice being of more importance than the settlement. Here arises a doubleness of consideration, which causes one of the great difficulties of human action. In trying to maintain the right by force, why should we suppose we are more likely to succeed than the opposite party, which (supposedly) maintains the wrong? And yet, what is the great purpose of man's action but to maintain the right? In this dilemma men have fallen back upon notions of religion with its suggestions of divine aid on the side of justice.

We cannot broadly assert that war is unlawful, or that all disputes must be submitted to arbitration.

Between peaceableness then on the one side and what we consider truth or justice on the other, it seems to me that there is a very complicated question, which cannot at all be settled by any general principle, such as our saying that war is unlawful, or that international disputes ought always to be settled by arbitration. Those who make the former assertion would have to answer the question, Are we, as individuals, to help an individual whom we see being ill-used, and are we not, as states, to help a state in the same circumstances? In reality, all questions of this kind depend very much on another, which is this, How far are the measures which we take at all likely to secure the end which we have in view?

Quarrel involves dislike as well as active hostility. The latter can only be justified as a means to an end.

Quarrel with another involves two elements, one of which we may roughly call dislike, the other active hostility. The former may exist in any degree from bare disapproval to intense hatred: and I suppose philanthropy requires that it should only exist in something like the former degree, in which, if deserved, it certainly ought to exist. Supposing the latter to be justifiable at all, it is at any rate only justifiable in cases where good result is to be expected from it. This is what is meant by the common saying that the purpose of war is peace. What we call quarrel is very often a mixture of dislike and hostility, the latter simply generated by the former, without there being any definite notion that it can come to any result, or effect any purpose. This is the old notion of war between nations: it is a state existing often between individuals. In the present day war between states is considered to be for a definite reason and purpose; and the question about its lawfulness really becomes the question, How far do nations, by putting themselves into that position with regard to each other which we call a state of war, really effect the purpose which they want? Are nations proper units for a quarrel? Ought they to exist as nations for this purpose? And is there an analogy, in this particular, between them and individuals?

Historical changes in the manner of conducting war.

The notion of war seems to exist in all languages, but it is not, as a notion, very distinct and uniform. It applies to a multiplicity of different states varying from a state of savage, internecine, antipathetic quarrel between all the individuals in one region and all the individuals in another, to a state in which, according to certain rules, a number of people on behalf of those in one region meet a number of people on behalf of those in the other, and combat till one party is taken as defeated. In this latter case the mass of the inhabitants in the two regions are hardly in a state of hostility, they are in a state of mutual ill-opinion; while the actual combatants are to some degree in the position of the advocates in a judicial discussion; they are bound, and pique themselves on doing it, to use their utmost power against each other in certain definite ways; but *outside* these ways they have very strong professional sympathies associating them together, in many respects, far more than they are associated with their own citizens for whom they are fighting.

It is obvious that war at the one end of the above scale and at the other is an entirely different thing.

Historical changes in the grounds of war.

It scarcely seems to me that civilization, as such, has any effect in altering the character of war, except in two particulars: 1st, that in it people are not likely, as in barbarism, to be pleased or satisfied with being in a permanent state of war; they carry on war with a purpose, and in view of an end; 2nd, that as manners in general become milder and less cruel, the usages of war will become so too. But war, as we have just seen, may mean so many things, or have so many forms, that civilization, instead of putting a stop to it, only seems to give it a new character. The course of history, while it advances civilization on the one hand, on the other introduces perpetually new subjects of public quarrel. During the middle ages, in default of caring for commerce and learning, men passed their time in fighting for various chivalric interests, as I will loosely call them. About the time of the revival of letters and the discovery of America these had got out of date, and one might have hoped for peace, when lo, as by a fatality, Western Europe, which had hitherto been of one religion, became on a sudden of two, and the diversity of opinion thus arising was the fruitful source of war for almost two centuries. When, weary of fight, men acquiesced at length in the diversity of religious opinion, other causes arose, balance of power, commercial rivalries &c.: perhaps they are weary of these now, but I fear there is not much reason to hope that we have got to the end of the ever fresh-springing causes of war.

I will make here four observations, with a remark or two on each. First, I do not expect any material diminution of war from international arbitration, unless we expect also, in conjunction with this, a diminution of the independence of nations, and a power which might be oppressive: which I should scarcely wish for.

Question as to the probability of the diminution of war from arbitration (1),

Second, I do not expect, nor wish for, any great diminution of war from men's better knowledge of, and keener look to, their own interest or material advantage.

from better understanding of national interests (2),

Third, I do expect a diminution of war, perhaps a great one, from the increase of what I will call a mutual tolerance among nations; from their acquiescence with much difference of opinion on the part of others; and, in this view, from commerce, mutual intercourse, and advance of knowledge.

from increase of toleration (3),

Fourth, I do expect a diminution of war from people's coming more and more to perceive how little, in many cases, it answers the purposes which they expect of it: how *absurd* it often is (to say in one word what I will shortly explain).

from conviction of its inutility (4).

1. The application of any principles of international law to the main circumstances of war, such as its breaking out, is rendered almost impossible by the perpetual novelty of such circumstances, which seem to defy all foresight or classification: and in connexion with this novelty one great difficulty is, what are the *units* of this international law: it is law between *nations*—what are nations? International law, in this large application, is an attempt to apply the rules of law between individual parties to

Difficulties in the way of arbitration, both as regards the parties,

parties composed of large bodies of men; but upon what principles, and by what power, are we, so to speak, to *incorporate* these parties? The most frequent ground of war is to settle *what are to be* nations; war being commonly the only way in which this can be settled, how are we to apply any international considerations to this?

and the tribunal.

Supposing an arbitrating tribunal, it seems from many considerations such as the above that it can have but little of principle or actual law to go on: it must have therefore a vast discretion. That is to say, it is really no *decision* that it gives; there are not grounds for such; the elements for settlement are the same with it as they are with negotiators of the parties themselves; all that is in its power to do, is to try to satisfy both in the best way it can.

But what is of most consequence is, that with very slight grounds for decision, there is also very slight guarantee of impartiality, supposing real power in the tribunal to enforce its decision.

It seems to me then that from arbitration there is the same hope, and no more, that there is from a better, wiser, and more moderate negotiation and mutual adjustment of relations. The so-called arbitration would be, if not oppression, only another manner of negotiation or amicable settlement.

A stronger sense of the duty of rulers to subjects may tend to check war.

2. There is always likely to be in a country, a good deal of difference of sentiment on the question whether it is chiefly its own interest, or the common interest of nations, help to the oppressed, and its own honour, which should furnish cause for its going to war. A nation is differently circumstanced from an individual in this respect, that it has very definitely and decidedly duties to itself, *i.e.* that the ruling power has duties towards the subjects or individual members of the state. The

interests of a nation therefore are not something which it lies with it, at its choice, to sacrifice and forego, in the same manner in which it lies with an individual; with whom such foregoing is sometimes a duty, almost always a virtue. It might be the duty of the ruling power in a nation to put its honour in its pocket, if I may so say, and to stifle its indignation against oppression, rather than incur the loss and damage to its own subjects which vindication might occasion. With the growth of the feeling that government exists for the good of the governed, this feeling is in some measure likely to grow.

But national sensitiveness increases with the growth of national unity.

At the same time experience seems to show, that it is quite impossible for a number of men to unite at all closely in a society even with a view to economical benefit only, without such society binding them, more or less, in a common feeling and making them, as a society, susceptible of such feelings as honour, sympathy, indignation, resentment, in the same way as an individual is. I do not think therefore that the clearer view of the functions of government and the keener sense of the interest and advantage of the associated, as the one ground of association, will have any tendency to diminish wars, except so far as they may tend to make men really less associated together, and nations less nations. We have not yet done with 'glory.' Nor am I sorry. That is, so long as nations go to war at all, I would rather that they did not go to war only for their own interest, but were susceptible, as there is little doubt they will continue to be, to that various and undefined feeling which is vaguely expressed by the phrase 'love of glory.'

Thus increased feeling of national interest may lead to war.

We come in fact in this again to the large question of utilitarianism in general: if there is any national sympathy among the members of a nation, the feelings which I have above spoken of will be stirred, and the indulgence of them becomes a part of the national happiness; and a most sensible part. Under these circumstances the attempt to persuade them that their happiness is in wealth and in commercial prosperity is equally vain and unreasonable: they know what gives them pleasure; and so far as happiness is to be judged of by experience, they are the judges. And I believe them in this case to be right judges, not simply of happiness, but of that on which it depends, *good*: it is a good thing that men associated together should be accessible to emotion, better than if they could bring themselves to be accessible to commercial interests only.

Association for any purpose often breeds intolerance towards non-associates.

3. Whatever is the occasion of men's associating together, their association speedily binds them (as I have said of specially economical association) in a number of ways quite foreign to that occasion. Nations adopt one manner of civil and religious behaviour, judging others wrong: philosophers, brought together by thought, form themselves into a school, sect, or party, differing speedily from others in many other respects also, and thinking morally ill of those not belonging to them. It is mainly from the fertility of association of any kind in generating these adventitious bonds and repugnances, that the evil principle of intolerance has sprung up by the side of, and as a sort of price for, or shadow of, many good principles. Whatever binds men together is an advantage, because society brings out the individual nature to an extraordinary extent, and man, both as to intellect and feeling, is altogether made for it. It is an advantage also that nations should think alike, except in so far as it makes them intolerant of others, or hinders their thinking what is

true. Similarly sectarianism or intellectual party-spirit of any kind is a form of mental brotherhood: it has brought out many an intelligence, and many a moral nature; but its dark shadow is occasional unwillingness to listen to truth, and almost invariable intolerance.

We are likely, it is possible, to have less war in the world as a part of that process by which we are likely to have less of that unfruitful controversy which is little other than an expression of intolerant hostility.

The growth of mutual respect for each other's convictions, and of carelessness about minor differences, tends to check war.

Some wars have had their *origin* in difference of opinion: all wars, in their carrying on, as felt by people in general, have been much more wars of mutual dislike or antipathetic feeling than of rival interest. We must not consider, as a matter of course, that wars of difference of opinion are ended: such a feeling very mainly contributed to the war at the beginning of the French Revolution; but new differences are continually springing up; and it is by no means the case that, as a matter of course, nations, with advance of civilization, do become more tolerant: such hope as there is arises from this fact, that there is more opportunity for the efforts of those who desire to make them tolerant. Nations will give up the attempt to convert each other by force, whether to religious, philosophical, or political doctrines, not in so far as they cease to value any doctrine themselves, for, in that case, they would only be more inclined to think the conversion of other nations feasible, if they piqued themselves on converting them; but in so far as they hold more conscientiously what they do hold, and understand more what the conscientious holding of it is; because then they will have a truer notion of the difficulty of conversion. No man who truly believes anything himself can believe that belief can be forced.

It is probable that there is a gradual increase of respect for the conscientious convictions of others, and of liberality in judging minor differences of feeling and usage. As this continues we may hope that there will be a corresponding diminution in that chronic ill-will from which, as from a dunghill, springs the rank growth of actual hostility and quarrel.

4. War, or quarrel of any kind, is not only entirely unfit for the maintenance of truth, as we have seen, but it is a very poor method for the maintenance of *right*, though it may sometimes be the only one.

Dispute is more likely to be abolished by justice than by benevolence.

So long as there is wrong done in the world, there must be dispute, nor would it be desirable that moral feeling should keep those accessible to it out of the dispute, while it was not strong enough to influence all, and prevent the wrong being done. As it is, there is a considerable force of motive to make the good quiescent, leaving wrong to its own way. We must put an end to wrong, and then will come an end to dispute.

As the world is constituted, dispute is more likely to be abolished by justice than by benevolence. No doubt deeply felt benevolence or religious love would preclude the causes of dispute, by removing to a considerable degree individual or separate interests; each looking not on his own things, but also on the things of others. Even superficial benevolence may make dispute more unlikely, in so far as it makes people less likely to take offence; and in any case it will make the carrying on of dispute less savage: but where separate interests are strongly looked to, as in the present constitution of the world they are, and are likely to be ever in a greater degree with the advance in civilization and commerce, there nothing can prevent dispute but justice, by which I mean the real application of principle and intellect to the systematizing of such interests, and a readiness on the part of the interested individuals to yield their individual feeling to such common understanding of them.

War is an attempt to enforce justice.

There are two parts of justice, the ascertainment of it and the enforcement of it. With the right-minded the ascertainment of it *is* the enforcement: with the wrong-minded, or in the case where the ascertainment is not admitted, it has to be actually enforced, or force has to be used. This in law is by penalty. A great deal of war (and in fact angry controversy) is the endeavour of each party to enforce upon the other what he regards as ascertained right; each party is, in the view of the opponent, both wrong-minded in the refusal to submit to justice, and mistaken as to what is justice.

So far as it is perceived to fail of this object, so far it is likely to fall into disuse.

War, however, or actual combat of any sort, would hardly exist if it were not for various other elements entering in, chiefly of two kinds; one the activity of human nature, and the consequent constant mutual rivalry; the other the ill-will and intolerant feeling which is more or less the accompaniment, as we have seen, of association. All war and quarrel may thus be said to have the double character of being an outbreak of a more or less constant feeling, and of being an attempt to gain some end. The diminution of the feeling which thus breaks out, is, as we saw just now, one means, or hopeful sign, of the diminution of dispute and war. The other means or hopeful sign is people's more and more seeing how very little, in most cases, any reasonable end of the war or dispute is likely to be gained.

Improvement in the *jus*

In this view, the systematization and perfection of the *jus belli*, or international law as applicable to *belli* is both good in its immediate results and indirectly tends to the abolition of war.

a state of war, is likely to be useful in a double way. Of course it must make war, in the carrying on, better and more humane. This has been looked upon by some as a questionable advantage, because they say it is the abolition of war that is wanted, and it is less likely to be abolished if it is civilized and improved till men see no harm in it. It seems to me, however, that the improvement of international law is likely more and more to impress upon men's minds the absurdity of war, *i.e.* the small degree in which it is likely to effect any good object. The being 'friendlily hostile' is likely more and more to seem to men like the 'cum ratione insanire,' the being reasonably mad, and to make them think that if they are to go so far as this they had better be friendly altogether. War is a barbarism which cannot with any principle and reason be civilized over, and the attempt to do this is likely to help forward the civilizing it away.

The more it is considered the more irrational is war felt to be.

At the same time war and dispute are less evils than the acquiescence in injustice: the maintenance of truth and right is the all-important thing among men, and however evil war may be, it is better that war should exist than that they should go unmaintained. The only question is, what means have we to prevent or redress the injustice, and will our manner of dispute or war have any tendency to do so? Supposing we say we have no means, of course we are in a difficult position. We are inclined to say, I will be in a state of hostility with the offender nevertheless. This may either take the form of non-intercourse, a sort of quarrel not uncommon in private life, or desperation and indignation may even lead to self-injury, and wild readiness for self-sacrifice. But difficult as it may be, still we may keep hold of the principle that action is for a purpose, and that we have no business to enter upon a course of action which will do no good.

Some might say, that a better *jus belli* is no more likely to lead to the abolition of war, than juster laws of property to lead to the abolition of property and of private and separate interests. There is a slight but only a slight analogy between the cases. No doubt it may be said that property and separate interests are a part of the hardness of men's hearts, as well as their quarrelling is; we had better abolish them both instead of trying to regulate them. But the systematic doing harm to another party, which is what the *jus belli* takes as its basis, is of a totally different nature from the simply pursuing individual interest to the comparative neglect of others' interest; more especially when, as is the fact, we cannot in most cases promote our own interest without promoting that of some, perhaps many others. And when this systematic doing harm to another party, the parties being states, is analysed, so many difficulties spring up as may make people less inclined, it is to be hoped, to the thing altogether.

There is an analogy also between the 'jus belli' and the theory of punishment, and several of the difficulties attending the former attend the latter: I will not however dwell any longer on this matter now.

War denotes. moral, as storm denotes atmospheric disturbance.

War is a moral disturbance analogous, in many respects, to the physical disturbances produced by varieties of temperature in the atmosphere. It is war which settles first of all what shall be nations: then where nations differ widely in civilization, there must either be non-intercourse or almost inevitable quarrel, resulting generally in the subjugation, to some extent, of the less civilized: again, there are political and religious sympathies binding some in one nation to some in another, and thus political and religious fermentations produce all sorts of national quarrels: lastly, as nations become more individualized in their relations with other states, the more do they become, like individuals, susceptible as to honour and offence, alive to commercial and separate interests, suspicious of each other, so as to be continually combining together and scheming against anticipated encroachment—and much besides. War will not be got rid of till very much else is got rid of as well.

In civilized countries, private war, or debate of force, is replaced by debate of reason, by which right is ascertained: there exists public force to enforce the right thus ascertained on any refusing to acquiesce in it, but unless the mass acquiesced in it as right, this enforcement would not be possible.

The relation of debate of reason to debate of force in the ancient trial of battle.

The relation to each other of debate of reason and debate of force may be seen well in the ancient practice of settling the truth or falsehood of a charge by single combat. Owing to the imperfect views entertained of evidence, the difficulty of communication, and much besides, it was in many cases almost impossible to settle the matter by reason; so they fought about it, having nothing else to do, without much consideration how far fighting would answer the purpose of maintaining the right, but partly trusting in an over-ruling providence, partly feeling that the right and truth must, where necessary, be maintained by force, and that in default of better ascertainment, it could only be the *asserted* right which must so be maintained.

Truth and right must be maintained, as they are ascertained, by reason.

The maintenance of right and truth by reason, involves the same questions which the ascertainment of them has involved. They are continually re-ascertained and confirmed in the process of maintaining them. We cannot be ready to give a reason for the truth which is in us without knowing the reasons which will commend it to those who do not yet see it to be truth, *i.e.* the reasons by which it is ascertained to be truth; and these must commend themselves to our conscience as valid reasons.

There are many occasions, as the world is now, in which the right, or justice, is to be maintained by force; there may be some few occasions in which the truth is; though then it will generally take the form of right, or justice, as when one people may try to force a change of religion upon another people. But right in a great measure, and truth almost entirely, has to be maintained by the same means by which each was originally ascertained, viz. by reason: the maintenance of them should include continual re-examination: whatever gives itself out as maintainable by reason is ever *questionable.*

Controversy has made the opinion of the present, and is making the opinion of the future.

In the controversy of the past, moral, philosophical, political, religious, we have the debate of reason, the thought of the world, that actual dialectic of human conversation and discussion, which has resulted in present opinion, and upon which whatever is accepted anywhere upon these subjects must be conceived to rest. As discussion, it is going on still, generating the opinion of the next age, confirming or weakening the opinion which prevails now.

Controversy suffers from the ill-feelings which unite themselves with it;

I have already spoken of the extent to which difference of opinion, and the attempt to put different opinions together with a view to progress in truth, has ever been accompanied with other elements not only foreign to the matter in hand, but even destructive of the object aimed at. It might well be laid down as a moral principle, that no person who is intellectually incapable, as many people seem to be, of even conceiving an opinion different from his own, is at liberty to maintain and urge his own; for as he cannot appreciate the grounds upon which other people hold their opinions, he is evidently unable to judge whether they are weak or strong, and whether, in fact, they may not be stronger than his own. Controversy would be likely to have some good result, if a person, as a condition of attacking an opinion, were to be required to give, to an impartial and intelligent auditor, a clear account of it. If this condition were enforced, a good deal of controversy would never be entered on. But, in general, it is a very different audience which is contemplated, and instead of discussion we have attack, *i.e.* more or less of misrepresentation with the introduction of much that is beside the point, as of presumable motives, accompaniments, or consequences: and thus what ought to be a step of the thought of man advancing towards his intellectual goal—the truth, is merely a piece of intellectual force wasted in worthless quarrel, just as life and wealth are wasted in actual war.

and from the unconscientiousness and servility both of disputants and auditors.

The controversialists themselves are probably not more to be blamed for this than kings and conquerors are to be blamed for wars: they are themselves sharers, to a certain extent, in the spirit to which they appeal, in the view of which the truth is secondary to the combat. This is a spirit partly of intellectual unconscientiousness, and partly, if the term does not seem offensive, of intellectual servility, by which I mean a disposition to measure the amount of power by assumption, and the amount of conviction by vehemence. The two spirits very much go together: men have little value in their minds for the truth, and consequently they readily yield themselves to be overborne; while, instead of their thinking, in regard of any controversy, how far the truth is ascertained or maintained by it, it is either looked at as a gladiatorial combat, or one side only is listened to, and any appreciation of the argument is neglected.

Even good feelings may injure controversy as a means of attaining truth.

The fact that this is so, is no doubt one feature of human nature. I have mentioned how much good goes with the evil of actual war, how much evil unites itself with the good in all associations of men. The history of human dialectic thought in controversy is of this mingled character: people are intellectually unconscientious on account of certain developments of their conscientiousness in other directions: they are faithful to their school of thought or their philosophical or religious brotherhood: they care for other things about opinions, (*e. g.* for their moral character) as well as for their truth. I wish all these considerations to be put by the side of what I have said above. What I have said is for the purpose of explaining why controversy is so unsatisfactory as a means of ascertaining or maintaining the truth. Since men at least make profession that this is the result they aim at in controversy, it is a matter which deserves their consideration how they may make it better serve its purpose.

CHAPTER XXI.[1]

IMPORTANCE OF RIGHT BELIEF.

Right belief may be important either as useful or as being in itself a duty.

WHAT is the reason why it is of importance that we should think and believe rightly?

It may be because knowledge or right judgment is necessary in order to our acting in such a manner as to bring about the results we wish.

Or it may be because right judgment has something in it of moral excellence; because, to put the case the other way, wrong belief is in some degree of the nature of a moral or punishable offence.

According to the former view, religious misbelief is a mistake which may have fatal consequences.

The importance of religious belief is viewed, it is probable, in a different light by different people.

We wish to attain heaven or to avoid hell: we must know the way to effect our purpose, and we must take care not to mistake the way, or we shall not effect our purpose. Putting the matter more generally, we wish to do well, and to be happy, to act for the best (understanding 'to do well' and 'the best' here simply of prosperity, without reference to morals): so far as our happiness depends upon ourselves it is only by knowing and thinking the truth about ourselves and the circumstances in which we are placed, that we can hope to attain it.

[1] As far as I can judge, the following was intended to form part of the present treatise, though it contains no distinct reference to what precedes, and though, unlike the other chapters, it bears no special title in the MS. In spite of its fragmentary character, I hope that its intrinsic interest will be felt to justify its insertion here. ED.

Unbelief or misbelief is in this point of view a fearful and fatal mistake.

If we look at things thus, man is responsible for his belief, not in the sense that anybody will call him to account for it, but in the sense that his present believing that to be which is not, or that not to be which is, may hereafter be a subject to him of most bitter regret; his future self will most bitterly reproach his present feeling, if it is wrong.

Such consequences should not be called by the name of punishment.

It would be a great advantage if the notion of *punishment* were confined within the limits which properly belong to it, and applied only where there is moral guilt, in which case only there is real punishment. Where what is intended for punishment is inflicted in consequence of supposed, but not actual, moral guilt, there is not punishment, but (perhaps by mistake and inadvertently) oppression and tyranny: where harm is inflicted without moral offence having gone before, the infliction may be justifiable, and there may be reasons for it, but it should not be described as punishment.

The notion that religion is simply prudence, and that that man attains heaven who is wise enough to find out and to follow the proper road to it, while that man falls into hell who is not wise enough to see in time whither his course of life is carrying him, and to choose a different course—this notion is one more likely to be made use of by defenders of religion than by appliers of it, by apologists than by religious teachers. The reason is, that when men come to look at the whole matter, they cannot be persuaded that their future is so entirely in their power as this would imply, or (as perhaps it might be expressed better) that their future is in their power in this particular way. They are so little able to anticipate, even in the common circumstances

This view, though sanctioned by Butler, really resolves religion into prudence.

of life, what is going to happen, that the saying to them that their whole future, with its terrible possibilities, is left to the hazard of that sort of speculation upon which they are so much obliged to act in life, is almost equivalent to telling them that there is no such thing as religion, no good God or superintending Providence. And yet this is the real meaning of what Butler says, Probability is the guide of life; it will do therefore (as he in effect says) for our guide in religion. The interests which belong simply to this earthly life are not of infinite importance; probability might perhaps do for our guide as to them: but each one of us knows how little his future, even as to this life, is in his own power, how great is the chance of his mistaking, and doing that which, intended to produce his happiness, may cause really his loss and ruin: and is it to be the same with religion? have we really got the fearful chances of an eternal future committed to the speculation on probabilities of beings such as we are?

It is indeed the reverse of religion, and excites opposition on good, as well as on bad, grounds.

The believing that this is so, if any one does believe it, is not religion, but the reverse of religion; the very thought, the very danger, from which religion delivers us. In a future after this life, like this life as our senses present life to us, but of vaster dimensions and with multiplied or intenser sensibilities on our part, whatever might be the alternative possibilities of happiness, the bravest might well prefer shutting his eyes in annihilation rather than run the chance of the possible misery. It is terrible enough to think of all the harm which may come to us in life here, through our mistake either in bringing it upon ourselves or in failing to prevent it: the extension of such a thought to an unknown future, is intolerable.

When the issue is so tremendous, there is no

doubt that the only speculation which can be considered reasonable is that which is *safe*. There is no occasion to put the matter as Butler does, on probabilities: if this issue is what religion deals with, and if there is a *possibility* that religion is true, it is worth while, in view of such a possibility, to do everything in human life which religion directs, and the sceptical rationalist who confines himself to this view will surely think so. In this view the best argument for religion is the most awful portrait of the possible horrors to come. And yet we do not find that men are of necessity religious with this religion of fear. The reasons for this are various, some better, some worse. The better are something of this kind, that they do not really believe it to be religion: the worse are connected with the fact that the present has a greater effect upon them, except now and then, than a prospect apparently so distant.

Various views as to the alarming or consoling influence of religion.

Religion is looked upon by Lucretius as deceitful and alarming; by those who speak or think much about responsibility, like Butler and Newman, as alarming, but true; by those who take, what some would call, a more evangelical view of it, as true, but comforting and gladdening rather than alarming; by the greater number probably of sceptics of our time, as comforting and gladdening, but deceitful, and nothing more than a vain imagination.

That which opens to us the prospect of a world beyond the grave may be either religion, or our imagination independently of religion. If we suppose the former to be the case, then religion, if it is to be other than a curse to man, must open to us a prospect either of moral punishment, or of hope, or of both in conjunction. If what suggests to us life beyond the grave is imagination, not religion,

religion coming in only afterwards to modify our view, then religion, if it is to be a source of comfort to man, must be what will make this prospect one of hope, not of terror.

Lucretius attacked religion as teaching the doctrine of future misery.

When Lucretius considers that he (or Epicurus) is benefiting mankind in showing religion to be false, because he thereby destroys the curse of human life, the dread of future punishment, he forgets the force of the word 'punishment'. His notion of what he was doing might be correct, if what men dreaded after death was simply misery, torment. Even supposing there to be a mere possibility of this, with a counter-possibility of happiness; still a man might think he would rather not run the risk, and that annihilation would be better. Nor, perhaps, would it make much difference, whether the alternative of happiness depended on a man's own action, supposing his wisdom and powers as they are now, or whether it was independent of it. He might think the chance of mistake on his part quite as much to be feared as the chance of misery coming to him independently of his own action.

The objection is weakened if misery is punishment:

But the case is entirely altered supposing that the prospect held out by natural religion is one in which misery or torment enters, as a possibility, only in the way of punishment. None then will suffer but those who have deserved it, and none, we may *in the first instance* say, *need* suffer. And the value of this dread of future punishment in improving human conduct on earth is an ordinary, almost vulgar, consideration, which of course must strike all. All can understand how the removal of religious terrors, in giving freer sway to violence and injustice, would be the reverse of a benefit to human life.

But what is punishment? Is it retribution and

vengeance, or is it corrective discipline, and attempt at reformation? Is it something which only looks back on what is past, or does it look forward also to what is to come? And if it is vengeance, or so far as it has anything of the character of vengeance, what are the principles which govern the proportions of it, according to the offence committed?

provided that we do not identify punishment with vengeance.

If what is dreaded in a future life is punishment as vengeance, inexorable and irreparable, and if there is reason to fear that the amount of it, in proportion to what has provoked it, will be very great and terrible, then since none, however well-intentioned, could be certain of always acting innocently, the risk would be so great that the better among mankind would have cause rather to dread, than to desire the truth of religion. The possibilities of misery in the future would outweigh the advantage of the improvement of human conduct, and therefore of human condition, here, arising from the prospect of such punishment hereafter.

Experience seems to have confirmed what moral considerations of themselves will to some extent teach us, that though the dread of punishment is a very strong motive, it is not one which acts very barely and immediately. Grant it to be the moving spring or weight, it produces its effect in combination with many other motives. We have ceased now, in regard of human punishments, to think that simple terribleness of them is all that is wanted.

Vengeance, as such, is insufficient as a deterrent in prospect;

Punishment then, as vengeance or retribution, is imperfect as a deterrent, in prospect: it is equally imperfect, in act, as a giving back of pain for pain, of suffering for suffering. In fact, of the nature of the suffering of the spirit, as it is in others, or as it may be in general, we can any of us form but little idea. The fountains of pleasure and pain within us are

while, in act, it raises up an antagonism which supports the sufferer against it.

so strangely mingled, that often what we think the one turns out the other, and there are intensities of the one or the other, we perhaps cannot tell which, when for a moment we are able to have full consciousness of them. Man's active and passive nature are two distinct things, and pleasure, if we are to use the word, belongs to one of these as well as the other, and the pleasure, so to call it, of the active nature is something quite different from the *feeling* of pleasure which belongs to the passive or sensible nature, being such, sometimes, as to be awaked rather by the opposite feeling. The most dreadful instances of vengeance have arisen through a vain attempt to conquer the spirit, which they have only stirred up to reaction against them, to firmer self-assertion, to fuller, if frightful, self-consciousness, and, in this respect, to more, and more real, being. Whatever torment the Miltonic Hell may have been to the Miltonic Satan, it *called him out* as no Heaven could have done. Or, to take an instance of an exactly opposite nature, what have most martyrdoms been but a mad and frightful struggle to subdue the human spirit on its strongest ground, the maintenance of the truth; and is there not something in the standing firm, the resistance, the triumph, the energy and fulness of divinely aided self-exertion in them, which puts to shame all mere sensation of pleasure, which leaves no leisure, and no care, for thinking of the pain?

The suggestion of a future life comes not from nature but from religion.

Independently of moral and religious considerations we might believe in a future life, but we have not much ground to do so. Physical analogies suggest rather a presumption against it, while at the same time they suggest also their own insufficiency as analogies. But so far as they do or can suggest to us the likelihood of anything after this life, it is not anything at least which we need dread, no hopeless or irreparable misery.

Their non-suggestion however of anything, or their suggestion of possible annihilation, is that which in respect of *them* is terrible. And it is against this non-suggestion or suggestion in the first instance, that religion comes in the way of comfort. Natural religion first, revealed religion more fully afterwards, brings life and immortality to light.

The phrase 'natural faith' is less ambiguous than 'natural religion.'

For 'natural religion' it might be well in some respects if we used the expression 'natural faith'. The exact force of the word 'natural' in the former expression is somewhat ambiguous: the 'nature' it refers to may be physical nature, which we refer to when we speak of 'natural theology'; or it may be the full nature of man and perhaps of things in general, which is the sense in which the term is used when the old philosophers talked of following nature. *Natural faith* is the persuasion, indistinctly felt, that reality or the universe is, in the whole, good: it is that *trust*, in its application to the present, that *hopefulness*, in its application to the future, without which we could not act at all, at least to any purpose, or even, it might be thought, live a day. It is faith that we *can* know, *can* act; that action, directed by the proper knowledge, will produce the expected effect; that the conclusions, practical or speculative, drawn from one kind of real knowledge will not be at variance with the conclusions drawn from another kind. Were the case otherwise, we could not act at all, or even have any definite thought. It is by faith of this kind that we have the notion, that there *is* really something which we call the truth.

Truth or reality in the world of physical experience is something as to which we have confidence, that, if it is good for one of our powers of sense, it is

Distinction between physically natural, and morally natural (or moral) faith.

good for all of them, so far as they can enter into relation with it, that again, if it is good for the senses and mind of one person, it is good for those of all persons, so far as they are in circumstances to notice and to judge of it. And then again this truth or reality is something as to which we have confidence that it will answer our action; that from experience of the present, we can, to the extent to which our knowledge applies, judge of the absent, and predict the future: it is on this faith that we *act:* without it there could be no rational action.

This is natural faith when by 'natural' we have reference to physical nature: natural faith, when by 'nature' we mean human or moral nature (in which case it might be better to call it 'moral faith'), is something analogous, but higher.

The former is a faith in the order of the physical, as the latter in the order of the moral, universe.

Physically natural faith is belief in the oneness, consistency, uniformity, orderliness, of the physical universe, which is what makes knowledge about it, and action in it, possible for us. The particulars of this uniformity, orderliness, &c., constitute the particulars of our knowledge: of chaos there would be no knowledge. *Morally* natural faith is the same feeling in reference to the moral universe, so to call it. Physically natural faith is confidence in truth or reality, and action according to it is action that is advisable: morally natural, or moral, faith, is confidence in *good,* and action according to it is action that is *right.*

It will be denied by some that there is any meaning in speaking thus of the moral universe, as distinguished from the physical.

The physical universe is that in which action is considered as the operation of *forces* (*natural* forces we call them), and in which sensation is the operation or affection of sensal organs, as of sight, taste, &c.;

the differences of these making its differences, and there being differences corresponding to them in what we call the qualities of objects.

The moral universe is that in which action is considered as the result of *will*, and in which sensation is pleasure or pain.

Each alike is necessary for knowledge and for action.

Morally natural, or moral, faith, is an instinctive or intuitive confidence that our possible pleasures or pains stand in an intelligible relation to each other and to pleasures and pains as they exist in other conscious beings, in such a manner that action is possible, and that knowledge is to be gained upon which we may act with effect.

In reality, the view of the *orderliness* of the physical universe and the view of its goodness (so to speak) or of the goodness of its Creator, are the same thing with us under different names.

Good, which, when looked at from the side of passivity or sensation, is pleasure or happiness, when looked at from the side of activity is 'end' or 'purpose.' The notion of an organization adapted to produce evil or pain is an entire incongruity or impossibility in the conception, serving no other purpose than to bring into relief before us, through contrast, the nature of organization and order.

What we want, in order to be able to act morally in a manner analogous to that in which we act physically, or to put forth our nature in the most important choices and determinations with the same energy with which we constantly put it forth in the less important; and what, in fact, we instinctively and intuitively *have*, or really we could not live—is a faith in the goodness and orderliness of the *moral* world; of there being, if we so choose to express it, moral as well as physical laws; of the *good* which suggests itself, as what we should act for, being homogeneous, harmonious, consistent.

We could not act in the physical universe without consistency of sensations:

If our different senses had no relation to each other, but each told us something about—what would not then indeed be to us a *universe*—but something about something; if again different people's intelligences stood in no relation to each other, and their different views could not be compared, how could we act at all? as it is, our *actional* senses (*i.e.* that part of our sensal organization which gives us knowledge of primary qualities, space, time (perhaps), pressure, &c.) serve as a bond of union between such senses as give us knowledge only of some particular secondary quality; such senses being apparently capable of multiplication to any extent without preventing the putting together of our knowledge into an orderly whole, representing an orderly universe: and in the same manner the inward or higher senses, or *common sense,* serve as a bond of union between different intelligences: and *that* is counted truth, which is alike for all the senses, and for all intelligences: and upon this we know we can act with effect.

nor in the moral universe without consistency of ideals.

But if, in the same manner, the different *goods,* or purposes of action which our intelligence suggests to us, have no relation to each other: how can we act, with any energy or effect, in the moral universe? By action in the physical universe is meant such action as movement, lifting a weight, going a distance, &c.; action in the moral universe is that more important putting forth of will to which this other action is subsidiary, determination to seek this or that object, to go, for whatever reason, to one or another place, &c. We have got to choose whether we will do our own pleasure, or others' pleasure, or God's pleasure, or the praiseworthy, or the rationally just, or the apparently natural, each of which things seem *good* to be done, but seem also to lead us different ways: so far as this is so, there is a moral chaos: there is absence of reason for acting any one way: it is much the same as if we thought at one time reality or truth to be only in *sweetness,* and considered that *that* was the only thing we had to take notice of, at another time thought that *colour* was the only thing to be noticed, and so disputed with one another which was reality, or which was the most real.

Philosophers, in seeking the summum bonum, really sought in all this what was the good, what was to be acted for.

CAMBRIDGE: PRINTED BY C. J. CLAY, M.A. AT THE UNIVERSITY PRESS.

BY THE SAME AUTHOR.

Exploratio Philosophica: Rough Notes on Modern Intellectual Science. Part I. 8vo. 9*s.*

Essays and Reviews: An Examination of some portion of Dr Lushington's Judgment on the Admission of the Articles in the Cases of "The Bishop of Salisbury *v.* Williams," and "Fendall *v.* Wilson"; with Remarks upon the bearing of them on the Clergy. 8vo. 1*s.* 6*d.*

An Examination of the Utilitarian Philosophy. Edited by J. B. Mayor, M.A. late Fellow of St John's College, Cambridge. 8vo. 12*s.*

www.ingramcontent.com/pod-product-compliance
Lightning Source LLC
LaVergne TN
LVHW021241110826
845150LV00002B/381

* 9 7 8 1 4 2 5 5 6 1 2 7 7 *